The Unintended Consequences of Peace

Scholars of international relations generally consider that under conditions of violent conflict and war, smuggling and trans-border crime are likely to thrive. In contrast, this book argues that in fact it is globalization and peaceful borders that have enabled transnational illicit flows conducted by violent non-state actors, including transnational criminal organizations, drug trafficking organizations, and terrorist cells, who exploit the looseness and demilitarization of borderlands. Empirically, the book draws on case studies from the Americas, compared with other regions of the world experiencing similar phenomena, including the European Union and Southeast Europe (the Western Balkans), Southern Africa, and Southeast Asia. To explain the phenomenon in itself, the authors examine the type of peaceful borders and regimes involved in each case; how strong each country is in the governance of their borderlands; their political willingness to control their peaceful borders; and the prevailing socio-economic conditions across the borderlands.

Arie Marcelo Kacowicz is Professor of International Relations and the Chaim Weizmann Chair in International Relations at the Hebrew University of Jerusalem.

Exequiel Lacovsky is a research associate at the Harry S. Truman Research Institute for the Advancement of Peace at the Hebrew University of Jerusalem.

Keren Sasson is a senior consultant for strategic and military affairs in the Israeli Ministry of Defense and holds a PhD in International Relations from the Hebrew University of Jerusalem.

Daniel F. Wajner is a postdoctoral fellow at the SCRIPTS Cluster, Freie Universitat Berlin, and a Lecturer at the Department of International Relations and the European Forum at the Hebrew University of Jerusalem.

T0385009

The Unintended Consequences of Peace

Peaceful Borders and Illicit Transnational Flows

ARIE MARCELO KACOWICZ
Hebrew University of Jerusalem
EXEQUIEL LACOVSKY
Hebrew University of Jerusalem
KEREN SASSON
Hebrew University of Jerusalem
DANIEL F. WAJNER
Hebrew University of Jerusalem

CAMBRIDGE
UNIVERSITY PRESS

Shaftesbury Road, Cambridge CB2 8EA, United Kingdom

One Liberty Plaza, 20th Floor, New York, NY 10006, USA

477 Williamstown Road, Port Melbourne, VIC 3207, Australia

314–321, 3rd Floor, Plot 3, Splendor Forum, Jasola District Centre, New Delhi – 110025, India

103 Penang Road, #05–06/07, Visioncrest Commercial, Singapore 238467

Cambridge University Press is part of Cambridge University Press & Assessment, a department of the University of Cambridge.

We share the University's mission to contribute to society through the pursuit of education, learning and research at the highest international levels of excellence.

www.cambridge.org
Information on this title: www.cambridge.org/9781009009133

DOI: 10.1017/9781009003537

First published 2021
First paperback edition 2024

A catalogue record for this publication is available from the British Library

Library of Congress Cataloging-in-Publication data
Names: Kacowicz, Arie Marcelo, author. | Lacovsky, Exequiel, 1981– author. |
Sasson, Keren, author. | Wajner Adler, Daniel F., author.
Title: The unintended consequences of peace : peaceful borders and illicit
transnational flows / Arie Marcelo Kacowicz, Hebrew University of Jerusalem,
Exequiel Lacovsky, Hebrew University of Jerusalem, Keren Sasson, Hebrew
University of Jerusalem, Daniel F. Wajner Adler, Hebrew University of Jerusalem.
Description: Cambridge, United Kingdom ; New York, NY : Cambridge University
Press, 2021. | Includes index.
Identifiers: LCCN 2021008434 (print) | LCCN 2021008435 (ebook) | ISBN
9781316518823 (hardback) | ISBN 9781009003537 (ebook)
Subjects: LCSH: Border security – Social aspects – Cross-cultural studies. | Peaceful
change (International relations) – Cross-cultural studies. | Transnationalism –
Cross-cultural studies. | BISAC: POLITICAL SCIENCE / International Relations /
General | POLITICAL SCIENCE / International Relations / General
Classification: LCC JV6225 .K32 2021 (print) | LCC JV6225 (ebook) |
DDC 364.1/336–dc23
LC record available at https://lccn.loc.gov/2021008434
LC ebook record available at https://lccn.loc.gov/2021008435

ISBN   978-1-316-51882-3   Hardback
ISBN   978-1-009-00913-3   Paperback

To Orly, Ariela, Dror, and Romi

Contents

Tables

Preface

Writing a book is like taking a long intellectual journey, and this fifth book of mine that I have written and completed in close cooperation with Dr. Exequiel Lacovsky, Dr. Keren Sasson, and Dr. Daniel Wajner is no exception. The journey started about ten years ago. I was invited to contribute a chapter entitled "Regional Peace and Unintended Consequences: The Peculiar Case of the Tri-Border Area of Argentina, Brazil, and Paraguay," for a volume on borders in the Western Hemisphere, edited by Maia Jaskoski, Arturo C. Sotomayor, and Harold A. Trinkunas, *American Crossings: Border Politics in the Western Hemisphere* (Johns Hopkins University Press, 2015). It started as a single case observation regarding the upgrading of peaceful relations between Argentina and Brazil since the 1980s. It also included an interview with the late Special Procurator of Argentina, Dr. Alberto Nissman from the Fiscal Public Ministry in Buenos Aires, Argentina, in September 2012. Dr. Nissman was murdered on January 18, 2015, after having investigated the terrorist attack against *AMIA*, the Jewish Community Center in Buenos Aires in 1994. A particular puzzling question became evident to me: To what extent had the opening of borders and the upgrading of peace among Argentina, Brazil, and Paraguay facilitated the incursion of Hezbollah and Iranian-sponsored terrorists who perpetrated this heinous terrorist attack?

In the past thirty years, I have dedicated my academic life to research and write about different dimensions of peace: peaceful change, regions or zones of peace, peace and security as a normative framework in a regional context, and stable peace. Later on, and mostly in the last decade, I turned to study globalization and the distribution of wealth, motivated by the demands for social justice that were widespread around the world, and not only in Latin America. This intellectual turn enabled me to develop a profound interest in studying globalization and global governance, without neglecting a constant theme I found in my different theoretical quests, regarding the importance of governance and state strength to making sense of international relations, in some cases contributing to the promotion and maintenance of peace, at both the domestic and international levels.

In this book, I chose to bring together all these diverse literatures, while examining the reality of peaceful borders and illicit transnational flows, including drug trafficking, arms trafficking, and human smuggling and trafficking. I do not claim that international peace and globalization cause illicit transnational flows, but rather that they are permissive conditions that enable their occurrence and proliferation. To explain the phenomenon itself, I examine the type of peaceful borders and peaceful borders' regimes; the states' strength or the weakness of the neighboring countries in the governance of their borderlands and their political willingness (or lack of) to control their peaceful borders; and the prevailing socioeconomic conditions across the borderlands. Although these claims are not entirely original, as there have been underlying variegated theoretical arguments regarding these links, the novelty of this book is embedded in how it constitutes the first systematic attempt to evaluate these arguments empirically, in a broad cross-regional testing of their conventional wisdom.

My preliminary idea of writing a book solely about the Americas, a continent of peace, broadened when my former teacher and mentor Professor Uri Bialer convinced me that it would be more interesting to write not only about the Western Hemisphere, but rather engage in a comparative study of different regions of the world. In the same vein, my colleague and friend Professor Norrin M. Ripsman, in the short conversations we had walking along Michigan Avenue in Chicago during the APSA Conference in August 2013, pointed out to me that, at least in terms of international security, there was an unexplored link to be unearthed. In 2015–17, I was very fortunate to get a generous grant from the Israeli Science Foundation and to enroll two of my former PhD students, Exequiel Lacovksy and Daniel Wajner, South Americans like myself (though they are from opposite sides of the Rio de la Plata), to join me in this journey. Keren Sasson, who was completing her dissertation at that time, joined later in this intellectual adventure. Unlike the work of previous research assistants, Exequiel, Keren, and Daniel actually wrote the initial drafts of several chapters of the book dealing with different regions of the world. Hence, they actually became coauthors of this volume. Since the three of them have recent PhDs and are the wave of the future, I think that having them as coauthors was the right decision to take, if we talk about genuine cooperation, and not only in international relations. Having said that, I assume the overall responsibility for any mistakes the reader might find in the following pages.

In this book, we have addressed the relevant linkages between peaceful borders and illicit transnational flows, usually carried out by violent non-state actors, including transnational criminal and terrorist groups. We "divided the world" among us in order to carefully address the analytical and empirical puzzle that we recognized. We started focusing on the Americas (the US–Canadian border, the US–Mexican border, the Northern Triangle's borders of Guatemala–Honduras–El Salvador, the Colombian borders, and the Tri-Border Area (TBA) of Argentina–Brazil–Paraguay), but went far beyond. For the sake of external validity, we extended our research to Europe (the Schengen regime within the EU and Southeast Europe/the Western Balkans), the Middle East (the "triangle of peace" including Israel–Egypt and Israel–Jordan), Southern Africa, and Southeast Asia.

Throughout our journey, many colleagues and friends who have read excerpts and previous versions of this book deserve our deepest gratitude. Galia Press-Banathan read several versions and offered us precious comments on Chapters 1–2, 8–9. The late and genial Carlos Najman Escudé, who read several preliminary drafts, coined the original phrase in Spanish *"No hay bien que por mal no venga"* (positive factors [like peace] might carry negative consequences). Peter Andreas, Efrat Assif, George Gavrillis, Anne Clunan, Andrea Oelsner, and Roberto Domínguez commented on drafts that became Chapters 1, 2, and 3. Rut Diamint and Carolina Sampón commented on Chapters 3 and 4; Isaac Delgado, Marcial Suarez, and Marcos Allan Ferreira also commented on Chapter 4; Tal Dingott-Alkopher suggested insights on Chapter 5; Tamar Arieli, Yaron Schneider, and Alan Dowty read and commented on Chapter 6; Timothy Shaw read and commented on Chapter 7; and Bhubhindar Singh offered comments on Chapter 8. We also benefitted from insights and suggestions from Elena Daniel Baches, Yuval Benziman, Uri Bialer, Tomer Broude, Isabel Clemente, Martín Arias Duval, Gabby Elad, Erik Gartzke, Kristian Gleditsch, Toby Greene, Artur Gruzaczak,

Yoram Haftel, Lior Herman, Piki Ish-Shalom, Maia Jaskoski, Miles Kahler, Andrej Kricovic, Andrés Malamud, David Mares, Dan Miodownik, Mor Mitrani, Carlos Raúl Morales, David Newman, Carlos Rozenkoff, Nicolas Sambanis, George Shambaugh, Miriam Söderberg Kovacs, Ethel Solingen, Arturo Sotomayor, Harold Trinkunas, and Yaacov Vertzberger. We acknowledge the suggestions of the participants of the seminar at the Center for Peace and Security Studies of the University of California San Diego on August 21, 2019, as well as the graduate students in Galia Press-Barnathan's course on "International Security" at the Department of International Relations at the Hebrew University of Jerusalem. The research for this book was generously supported by the Israel Science Foundation during the years 2015–2017 (Grant No. 414/15).

As in my previous books, the reader can follow the example of the intriguing (and more thrilling) book by Julio Cortázar, *Rayuela* (1979), and find four different paths for her reading. You can read the book from Chapter 1 through Chapter 9, in the usual way. Alternatively, those interested in the theoretical and general aspects of the subject can read Chapters 1 and 2, and get quickly to Chapter 9. Students of Latin American issues will probably focus on Chapters 3 and 4 and find there a wealth of empirical material. Finally, those who are interested in a regional perspective and a comparison across different regions of the world can read Chapters 5, 6, 7, 8, and 9.

A few paragraphs that appear in Chapter 8 were taken from chapter 5 of Exequiel Lacovsky's PhD thesis on "Assessing the Emergence of Nuclear Weapons Free Zones: The Latin American Non-Proliferation Experience in Comparative Perspective" (Hebrew University of Jerusalem, 2019). Some excerpts of Chapters 3 and 4 were originally published in a condensed version in an article we authored in the *Latin American Research Review* in 2020 (Vol. 55, No. 4). We are grateful to the journal publishers for allowing us to use the material for this book. In addition, some excerpts from a chapter on the Tri-Border Area are included in Chapter 4 of this volume. These excerpts are taken from Jaskoski, Maiah, Arturo C. Sotomayor, and Harold A. Trinkunas, eds., *American Crossings: Border Politics in the Western Hemisphere* (pp. 93, 95, 96, 97, 101, 102, 103, 104. © 2015 Johns Hopkins University Press). Reprinted with permission of Johns Hopkins University Press.

In the production of this book, we thank two anonymous reviewers for Cambridge University Press who read two different versions of the manuscript, as well as the advise and encouragement of its editor, John Haslam, and his superb editorial team, including Tobias Grinberg, Robert Judkins, Gayathri Tamilsevan as the production manager, and the brilliant copyediting of Ursula Acton. I also thank David Katzowicz for his drawing of *La Triple Frontera*, as an allegoric meeting point between the rays of sun (peaceful borders) and the menacing clouds (transnational crime).

We dedicate this book to our spouses: Orly, Ariela, Dror, and Romi, who have had to bear with us throughout the long process of researching and writing a book for several years. Our love for them is a borderless love. Moreover, in Spanish, the term "spouses" (*esposas*) indicate also handcuffs to secure a suspected criminal taken into custody. This is a very peculiar securitization of marriage. Yet, the term also reminds us of the subject matter of this book.

Arie M. Kacowicz

Abbreviations

ABACC	Argentine-Brazilian Agency for Control and Accounting of Nuclear Material
AEC	ASEAN Economic Community
AFCTA	African Continental Free Trade Agreement
AFTA	ASEAN Free Trade Area Agreement
ALBA	Bolivarian Alliance for the Americas
AMIA	Asociación Mutual Israelita Argentina
ARF	ASEAN Regional Forum
ASEAN	Association of Southeast Asian Nations
AU	African Union
BACRIM	Bandas Criminales
CACM	Central American Common Market
CAFTA-D	Central American Free Trade Area and Dominican Republic
CAN	Community of Andean Nations
CBRN	Chemical Biological Radiological and Nuclear Matters
CBTA	cross-border transport agreement
CELAC	Economic Community of Latin American and Caribbean States
CEPAL	Comisión Económica para América Latina y el Caribe
CICIG	Commission against Impunity in Guatemala
CICTE	Inter-American Committee against Terrorism
CSBM	confidence and security building measure
DRC	Democratic Republic of Congo
DTO	drug trafficking organization
EC	European Community
ECSC	European Coal and Steel Community
EEC	European Economic Community
ELN	Ejército Liberación Nacional
EMCDDA	European Monitoring Centre for Drugs and Drug Addiction

EU	European Union
FARC	Fuerzas Armadas Revolucionarias de Colombia
FMLN	Farabundo Martí National Liberation Front
FRELIMO	Liberation Front of Mozambique
FTA	free trade agreement
GAO	Grupos Armados Organizados (Colombia-Venezuela)
GDP	gross domestic product
GMS	Greater-Mekong Sub-region
ICG	International Crisis Group
IDF	Israeli Defense Forces
IDP	internally displaced persons
ISIS	Islamic State
JI	Jemaah Islamiyah
LAFTA	Latin American Free Trade Area
MENA	Middle East and North Africa
MERCOSUR	Common Market of the South
MFO	Multilateral Peace and Observation Forces
MINUSTAH	UN Stabilization Mission in Haiti
NAFTA	North American Free Trade Area
NATO	North Atlantic Treaty Organization
NPT	Non-Proliferation Treaty
NRA	National Rifle Association
NSA	non-state actor
OAS	Organization of American States
OSCE	Organization for Security and Cooperation in Europe
PCC	First Commando of the Capital of Brazil
PLO	Palestinian Liberation Organization
PMC	private military company
QIZ	Qualifying Industrial Zone
SADC	Southern African Development Community
SADCBRIG	Southern African Development Community Brigade
SADCC	Southern African Development Coordination Conference
SALW	small arms and light weapons
SAPF	South African Police Force
SEANWFZ	Southeast Asian Nuclear Weapons Free Zone
SECI	Southeast European Cooperative Initiative
SEESAC	South Eastern and Eastern Europe Clearinghouse for the Control of Small Arms and Light Weapons

SEM	Single European Market
SICA	Central American Integration Systems
SIS	Schengen Information System
TAC	Treaty of Amity and Cooperation in Southeast Asia
TBA	Tri-Border Area
TCOs	transnational criminal organizations
UN	United Nations
UNASUR	Union of South American Nations
UNDP	United Nations Development Program
UNHCR	United Nations High Commissioner for Refugees
UNODC	United Nations Office on Drugs and Crime
US, USA	United States
USMCA	United States–Mexico–Canada Agreement
VNSAs	violent non-state actors
WCO	World Customs Organization

1 The Reality of Peaceful Borders and Illicit Transnational Flows

Introduction

Scholars and practitioners of international relations have increasingly pointed out significant links between armed conflicts and different types of criminal and terrorist activities in many regions of the world, including the Caucasus, South-West Asia, the Middle East, Western Africa, the Balkans, Central America, and the Andean region in South America (see Andreas, 2011a; and Shelley, 2018). Their underlying logic has been that illicit transnational activities thrive under conditions of war. In historical terms, the occurrence of illicit transnational flows had preceded our current age of globalization, even before the end of the Cold War. As Peter Andreas cogently argues, "the connection between illicit trade and conflict is not a post-Cold War invention. It goes back not just decades but centuries" (Andreas, 2011b: 421). In a similar vein, Louise Shelley has unfolded the sweeping historical trajectory of the "dark commerce," or illicit trade of transnational flows, ranging from ancient times in the Middle East more than four thousand years ago, all the way to the end of the Cold War (Shelley, 2018: 14–60).

In contrast to the *long durée* analyses of Andreas and Shelley, in this book we specifically address the relevant links between the existence of peaceful borders and illicit transnational flows in the post–Cold War period, since the early 1990s. Most of the time, these illicit transnational flows are carried out by transnational criminal and terrorist violent non-state actors (VNSAs), engaged in drug trafficking, human trafficking and smuggling, and arms trafficking. The reality of peaceful borders and transnational crime stands in contrast to most of what has been traditionally argued in sociology, psychology, and international relations about how war and conflict, rather than peace, leads and affects crime within and across countries (see, for instance, Andreas, 2011a and 2011b; and Shelley,

2018). Hence, the major research question we address in the book is: Under which conditions might peaceful borders enable the occurrence and proliferation of transnational illicit flows, usually carried out by violent non-state actors, including transnational criminal groups and terrorists? We answer this question by providing a novel systematic empirical cross-regional analysis of the enabling conditions for the linkages between peaceful borders and illicit transnational flows, including the types of borders, state capacity and political willingness, and the socioeconomic characteristics of the neighboring states.

Across the globe, the terms of the security debate have shifted dramatically over the last thirty years. Since the end of the Cold War, many countries in different regions of the world have confronted new types of security challenges that they have been hard-pressed to tackle effectively. Traditional issues of war and peace have become irrelevant to cope with *intermestic* (international and domestic) problems of national and international security. The end of the Cold War brought with it a more permissive strategic environment that led many states to focus on a different and broader menu of interests and challenges in their foreign policy agendas, such as the global War on Terror or the War on Drugs. It also brought new actors to the forefront of the security environment, including the proliferation of VNSAs. At the same time, this new post–Cold War era exposed the fragility and institutional underdevelopment of many of these states in terms of feeble governance that failed to address issues of human security, crime, and domestic violence (see Felbab-Brown, 2017a: 2; and Shelley, 2014 and 2018).

The conceptualization of security has broadened since the end of the Cold War. An expanded concept of security allows us to include and address the so-called new security threats and risks emerging with the intensification of globalization and regionalization processes. For instance, according to the Managua Declaration of 2006 at the Seventh Conference of the Ministers of Defense of the Americas, "terrorism, drug trafficking, human trafficking, organized crime, money laundering, corruption, and the proliferation of small arms and light weapons all pose significant threats to the security of the American countries" (quoted in Kacowicz and Mares, 2016, 26). All these threats transcend state jurisdictions, so they are transnational by nature, and they are linked to the activities (both licit and mostly illicit) of non-state actors across peaceful borders.

In this book, we delineate and systematically test the links between peaceful borders and the occurrence and proliferation of transnational illicit flows usually carried out by VNSAs. These non-state actors include transnational criminal organizations (TCOs), such as drug trafficking organizations (DTOs), as well as terrorist cells, which exploit the looseness and demilitarization of the borderlands, by taking advantage of the "jurisdictional arbitrage" created by sovereign borders, so they can engage in transnational illicit activities across peaceful borders. By jurisdictional arbitrage, we mean the practice of using and abusing the legal discrepancies, differences, and regulations existing among neighboring countries, in a way similar to financial arbitrage (see Payan, 2014; Shelley, 2014; and Vogeler, 2010).

Borders matter. We argue in this book that there is a significant linkage between the openness, demilitarization, softening, porousness, management, and institutionalization of peaceful borders and the occurrence and proliferation of transnational illicit flows (see Vogeler, 2010). Variation in the permeability of borders, as well as in their management and governance, is an important factor in the empirical cases we analyze. This variation is evident in terms of policing or fortification of the borders (softness or hardness), economic integration, and political integration. In empirical terms, we focus upon the Americas (North America, Central America, and South America), as the Western Hemisphere is characterized by international peace, domestic peace, and regional integration in several of its subregions. There is a stark contrast between the realities of inter-state peace and domestic peace and phenomena of low intensity domestic violence, including a high rate of homicides and transnational crime in Latin America (Briscoe, 2008). In addition, our analysis is a *comparative* one, so we examine cases from other regions of the world experiencing similar phenomena since the end of the Cold War, including the European Union (EU) and Southeast Europe (the Western Balkans), Southern Africa, and Southeast Asia. Although the Americas, without exception, have peaceful borders between neighboring countries, we believe that the linkages and conditions can be traced in other "zones of peace" and bilateral peaceful relations in other regions, beyond the Western Hemisphere.

The Empirical Reality and the Analytical Argument behind It

Since the end of the Cold War, we can identify a distinctive linkage between the existence of peaceful borders and the occurrence of transnational illicit flows, including criminal and terrorist activities. This results in many cases, though not always, from the softening, loosening, liberalization, and demilitarization of borders that become more porous and open.

Moreover, this might be the result of a political decision to weaken the role of the armed forces and their potential threat to democracy, or a by-product of economic and political integration, or geopolitical constraints as in the cases of the Northern Triangle in Central America and the Tri-Border Area (TBA) of the Southern Cone of South America. It might also derive from a lack of interest in the part of the government(s) to address these illicit transnational flows, either because they are corrupt themselves and subject to pressure from criminals, or because their constituencies do not care much about these new security threats. Moreover, there are legitimate, non-criminal actors who seek to obstruct explicit policies against transnational illicit flows, like the National Rifle Association (NRA) in the United States opposing the regulation of the circulation of guns, which is the source of arms trafficking to Mexico and Central America.

In the case of the Schengen borderless regime within Europe, porousness is the result of the EU's opening of the borders of their member-states by choice, as the ultimate form of peace and integration, without becoming a federal state. Moreover, in some cases, porousness of the borderlands might be the result of the weakness, inability, or ineptitude of states to control their borders, regardless of peace or war, as in the case of the Colombian borders (see Idler, 2018). Still, countries might be at peace with their neighbors while having tight control over their borders, like the United States vis-à-vis Mexico and Canada, or Israel vis-à-vis Egypt and Jordan.

The empirical reality that initially motivated our research stems from an initial investigation on the TBA among Argentina, Paraguay, and Brazil. Once these borderlands became peaceful, open, and demilitarized, following the 1979 Agreement on Itaipú, which launched the rapprochement between Argentina and Brazil, and the formation of the Common Market of the South (MERCOSUR) in 1991, there has been an increased incursion of transnational non-state actors, including TCOs and terrorist cells. Thus, the TBA has evolved from including a once militarized border between Argentina and Brazil to becoming a border area that is highly integrated in economic and social terms, though it is overwhelmed by smuggling, trafficking, and transnational crime, and susceptible to transnational terrorism. The TBAs' dangerous combination of ungoverned areas and lack of state capacity, together with poverty, illicit activities, disenfranchised groups, and ill-equipped law-enforcement agencies, have resulted in a dangerous environment conducive to the occurrence and proliferation of illicit transnational activities, ranging from criminals to terrorists (see Kacowicz, 2015).

There is an important variation regarding the effects of violent transnational non-state actors upon the local population in the borderlands, either in beneficial or detrimental directions. In other words, while some VNSAs might serve as pseudo-communitarian agents, providing security, welfare, and other governance functions in the absence of a functioning state, others are predatory in and by nature. For instance, the *Fuerzas Armadas Revolucionarias de Colombia* (FARC) exercised governance functions along the Colombian borders with Ecuador before their dismantling in 2016 (see Idler, 2018; and Jaskoski, 2015). Thus, it is not obvious or evident whether VNSAs in the borderlands fulfill only pernicious functions, when using violence and other illicit mechanisms, or whether they fill positive governance functions when the state is absent (see Clunan, 2010; and Idler, 2018).

Our argument here refers essentially to the prevailing conditions of international peace at the physical land (international) borders, which might coincide or not with a situation of domestic peace within the country, at times following the end of a civil war. For instance, Colombia has a very strong international record of peaceful relations with most of its neighbors, despite significant tensions in the last two decades, particularly in 2008–9 vis-à-vis Venezuela and Ecuador. At the same time, Colombia has not been a peaceful country in domestic terms, to say the least. Even after signing a peace accord with the FARC in November 2016, the Colombian government still confronts the lingering reality of criminal gangs (literally BACRIM, which is the Spanish acronym for criminal bands, *Bandas Criminales*) pursuing transnational criminal activities in Colombia and across its borders (see Ellis and Ortiz, 2017; and Wienand and Tremaria, 2017). Colombian borderlands still sustain the bad reputation of constituting the most lawless and ungoverned of Latin American borders. This relates to the long civil war between the Colombian government and the FARC that raged between 1964 and 2016, as well as the continuing transnational criminal activity across its borders (Briscoe, 2008: 3; see also Gagne, 2015).

Similarly, the end of the civil wars in Nicaragua, El Salvador, and Guatemala about thirty years ago did not bring about a sustainable domestic peace despite the existence of peaceful international borders. This is all the more evident in the Northern Triangle area, involving El Salvador, Honduras, and Guatemala, where we witness the transnational criminal activity of gangs such as the *Maras* MS-13, and Barrio 18, with the highest rate of homicides worldwide. About 150,000 people were killed in the Northern Triangle countries since 2006, an average of more than fifty homicides per 100,000, more than triple the rate in Mexico and more than ten times the US average (see Ellis and Ortiz, 2017).

Although the end of civil wars in Central America generated a renewed environment favorable to international peace in the region, paving the way for a wave of regional integration processes, the optimistic forecast has not yet materialized. This is partly due to the legacy of such long and virulent civil wars that included the militarization and criminalization of societies, vast amount of weaponry, and high levels of corruption and violence against its citizens. In the first two decades of the twenty-first century, the Northern Triangle remains the most violent region of the world, leading thousands of Central Americans to flee and search for refuge and asylum in the United States. VNSAs such as the so-called *Transportistas*, drug cartels, and *Maras* turned the region into a hub of violent transnational criminal activity. The common denominator for this violence relates to drug trafficking, which made the Central American route the main way to pour into the United States. It directly relates to the Mexican DTOs acting at both the US–Mexican border and beyond, in Central America, Colombia, and Venezuela (see Dudley, 2010: 63; Labrador and Renswick, 2018: 5; and UNODC, 2012: 5).

Traditional international norms that regulate border disputes and interstate relations are ill equipped to address the new security threats in the twenty-first century, such as criminal transnational flows (see Simmons, 2019: 5–10). It is precisely the movement toward regional integration and the outbreak of regional peace across borders that makes the traditional military function of borders as an external boundary delimiting territorial sovereignty irrelevant, at least in conventional geopolitical terms. A consequence of the loosening and softening of borders, as a result of their demilitarization and deregulation, is that they become economic meeting places for a variety of actors, both public and private, who engage in significant transnational transactions, both licit and illicit (see Jaskoski et al., 2015a: 1; and Simmons, 2019). These private actors might engage in legal activities, but they might also fulfill illegal and criminal functions.

Paradoxically, most of the illicit transnational flows across the US–Mexican border take place through the open crossing points between the two countries. For instance, about 90 percent of the drugs brought in from abroad into the United States are smuggled via vehicles and vessels entering the country through its legal gates (see Finckenauer and Albanese, 2014; London, 2019; and McKibben, 2015). This makes sense since a greater volume of legal flows provides more opportunities to conceal illicit goods.

We concur with Peter Andreas (2003) that it should not be at all surprising that peaceful borders enable and facilitate transnational crime and terrorism. Still, such possible linkages, despite constituting a conventional wisdom, have yet to be addressed in explicit terms, and systematically tested in the Americas and beyond, as we do in this book. If borders are closed, it is difficult and risky for transnational actors to cross them. Once borders are open, both licit and illicit flows can cross them. After all, most illicit business follows a similar logic to that of licit business; peace is usually good for commerce and trade. The exception might be those specific forms of trade that tend to thrive on armed conflict, such as arms trafficking, embargo bounty, and even stealing humanitarian aid. Conversely, illicit trade uses the same channels and transport mechanisms as licit trade, so it tends to be much more constrained during wartime.[1] Hence, criminals and terrorists might benefit and thrive across peaceful borders. Moreover, whereas illegal markets have been territorially bounded and isolated in the past, nowadays they tend to be interrelated and mutually supportive across borders, as they are embedded in the legal global economy and the

---

[1] We thank Peter Andreas, Asif Efrat, and the anonymous reviewers from Cambridge University Press for their comments on this point.

single market sponsored by processes of economic globalization (see Giraldo and Trinkunas, 2015: 387; Naím, 2005; and Shelley, 2018).

Illicit actors tend to use and abuse peaceful borders; they might prosper when the borders are open and porous. The logical explanation is the following. It is the essential characteristic of international borders, as delimiting lines of international sovereignty and jurisdiction, which attracts the incursion of illicit actors. The borders provide enticing opportunities for those who can navigate through and around them, including illicit actors, taking advantage of the jurisdictional arbitrage.

State agents are usually very reluctant to pursue illicit actors into the sovereign territory of neighboring nations, since that is a flagrant violation of international law. Instead, the United States and the EU have implemented programs such as the Mérida Initiative and the European Neighbourhood Policy in order to cope with illicit transnational flows and illegal activities beyond their immediate borders. They act through the mentioned programs by activating "proxies" like Mexico, the Central American countries, and the West Balkan nations, though they are not very successfully in fighting transnational crime (see Bruns et al., 2016; and Olson, 2017). Hence, differences between states in jurisdictional authority, regulatory structures, level of governance, markets, and socioeconomic conditions drive the activity of illicit transnational non-state actors, which like economic firms, take advantage of this "arbitrage," especially smugglers and transnational criminal organizations (see Andreas, 2003; Idler, 2018; and Simmons, 2019). We now turn to a brief literature review, designed to clarify the basic concepts and ideas we use to understand the linkages between peaceful borders and illicit transnational flows.

Literature Review: Clarifying Major Concepts and Ideas

The reality of peaceful borders and illicit transnational flows can be examined through five different, though related, bodies of literature in the areas of international relations, international security, international political economy, and peace studies, which are not traditionally integrated. These bodies of literature are: (1) the definition of peace, its gradations and transitions; (2) globalization; (3) international borders; (4) governance, the distinction between strong and weak states, and "areas of limited statehood" at the intersection of international relations and comparative politics; and (5) transnational criminal and terrorist activities perpetrated by illicit non-state actors. Whereas we consider peace and globalization as permissive conditions that enable the coexistence of peaceful borders with the occurrence and proliferation of illicit transnational flows, they cannot explain their variance. We explain such variance by explicitly referring to the type of international borders, the degrees of governance, institutional strength, and political willingness, and the prevailing socioeconomic conditions of the neighboring countries.

International Peace

Within the realm of international peace, conceived as the absence of systematic, large-scale collective violence between states, we find a continuum in an ascending order of quality and endurance, from negative or precarious peace, through stable peace, all the way to a pluralistic security community, in both regional and dyadic terms. These gradations of international peace parallel and correspond, in turn, to different types of border regimes, ranging from coexistent, though interdependent, all the way to integrated borderlands.

A dyadic relationship of negative peace (i.e., mere absence of war) is one in which peace is maintained between neighboring countries only on an unstable basis and/or by negative means such as threats, deterrence, or a lack of will or capabilities to engage in violence at a certain time. The possibility of war between the parties remains tangible and real. In this scenario, civil wars, domestic and international conflicts and crises, and even limited military interventions (below the level of international war) are still possible.

A dyadic relationship of stable peace (i.e., no expectations of violence) is one in which peace is maintained on a reciprocal and consensual basis. In this case, the probability of war is so small that it does not really enter into the calculations of any of the parties involved. The essential conditions for the development of a dyadic relationship of stable peace include the following: First, territorial changes are removed from the national agendas, except by mutual agreements and peaceful means. Second, there is a minimum of nonmilitary intervention by each nation in the other nation's internal affairs. Third, in terms of perceptions, the countries sustain an economic, rather than romantic or heroic, attitude toward their national states. Unlike negative peace, stable peace requires a permanent condition of peace both in international relations and within the borders of the states involved. Thus, a dyadic peace becomes stable when the two parties agree to avoid war or threats of war in their mutual relationship, and to use only peaceful diplomatic means to resolve any conflict between them (see Kacowicz and Bar-Siman-Tov, 2000).

Finally, a pluralistic security community of two or more neighboring states, with stable expectations of peaceful change, is one in which the member-states share common norms, values, and political institutions; sustain a common identity; and are deeply interdependent and integrated (see Deutsch et al., 1957; Kacowicz and Bar-Siman-Tov, 2000: 22). The shared expectations of peaceful change are a function of common values, mutual responsiveness and trust, and the abandonment of war as a policy option to resolve conflicts.

In terms of transitions to peace, there is a continuum ranging from war, severe rivalry, lesser rivalry, and the gradations of peace mentioned previously. Accordingly, we identify two significant transitions or movements toward international peace that are relevant as enabling the establishment and consolidation of peaceful borders (1) from war to negative peace; and (2) from negative peace toward stable peace and a pluralistic security community (see Goertz, Diehl, and Balas, 2016: 25–46; and Press-Barnathan, 2009: 11–12). The first transition is easier to identify; it encompasses the public signing of an official peace agreement. The second transition implies a deepening or normalization of the preexisting peaceful relations between the neighboring countries, leading to the stabilization of peace between them (Press-Barnathan, 2009; see also Kacowicz and Bar-Siman-Tov, 2000: 24–25).

Peace and Territory
According to several authors who have written on territoriality and borders (including Atzili, 2012; and Kacowicz, 1994 and 1998), territoriality and borders are an essential part of the modern sovereign state system and of traditional international relations, including issues of war and peace. Throughout history, many, if not most, conflicts and agreements between states involved territories and borders (Atzili, 2012: 10). In terms of territorial peace, and the linkages between borders and peace, the literature has been underdeveloped, with a few exceptions. For instance, Douglas Gibler (2012) has written an intriguing book linking the resolution of territorial issues to peace and

democracy. Gibler's theory suggests that the stabilization of borders in a given region should contribute to democratization, as clusters of peaceful democratic states. In his view, as neighboring countries experience fewer territorial disputes and controversies, they are more likely to enhance their peaceful relations in the first place; and secondly, to become more democratic. In other words, the resolution of territorial disputes leads to peace, and then peace leads to democracy, rather than the other way around, as posited by the democratic peace argument (see Gibler, 2007: 516–517, and 2012: 43).

In a similar vein, Goertz, Diehl, and Balas (2016: 99–150) suggest that stable borders, as prompted by the implementation of the norm of *uti possidetis* (recognition of the formal colonial borders after independence as the legitimate ones), in conjunction with the norm against territorial conquest, bring and enhance international peace. It has become common place since the end of World War II that the norms of border fixity, as derived from *uti possidetis*, the inadmissibility of gaining territory through military conquest, and territorial integrity have become strongly internalized and adopted by the majority of states in the international system (see Zacher, 2001). Thus, significant violent changes in the location of boundaries have become practically obsolete, with several exceptions such as the case of Israel since 1948 (and especially since 1967), the Indian–Pakistani territorial dispute over Kashmir (since 1947), and most recently, the Russian invasion of Crimea in 2014. For instance, in the case of Israel since 1967, Oren Barak (2017) demonstrates convincingly that the failure to establish clear and recognized borders between Israel and its Arab neighbors, including the Palestinians, has been a formidable obstacle to peace. Conversely, Boaz Atzili (2012) developed a counterintuitive argument linking the norm of border fixity to international conflict, war, and instability among and within developing countries.

Globalization

What is globalization? We can conceive it as the intensification of economic, political, social, and cultural relations across borders. Globalization involves more than just the geographical extension of a range of phenomena and issues. It implies not only a significant intensification of global interconnectedness, but also an awareness or consciousness of that intensification, with a concomitant diminution in the significance and relevance of territorial boundaries.

Globalization is pushed by several factors: among others, technological change, economic factors, and policy changes articulated by states and other non-state actors. The principle of territoriality and the logic of "methodological territorialism" contradict the essence of globalization, which involves the de-territorialization of social, economic, and political activity, and the relative denationalization of power. Globalization leads to the integration of states, peoples, and individuals through increasing contact, communications, and trade; thus, creating the possibility for a holistic, single global system. At the same time, globalization is very uneven in both its pace, intensity, and geographical scope, as well as in its different domestic and international dimensions and effects (see Holm and Sorensen, 1995: 1–7; and Kacowicz, 2013).

The end of the Cold War and the disintegration of the Soviet Union shifted the attention of many countries away from traditional security concerns, focusing on non-state actors and TCOs (Simmons, Lloyd, and Stewart, 2018: 253–254). Globalization has transformed international relations, making many of the traditional concerns with international security, such as border disputes, no longer relevant. Alternatively, it has affected and reshaped new security threats according to which states should approach their border security (see Simmons, 2019: 22–28). Among the most relevant subjects for international security in the twenty-first century, we find, in addition to civil wars and terrorism, the phenomenon of transnational crime.

Processes of globalization are usually associated with the vision of a borderless and de-territorialized world, though in reality we still live in a world of international borders. Across borders, we can record movements of people, goods, money, investments, messages, and ideas as "cross-border transactions," many times facilitated by liberalization and relative freedom from state-imposed controls, as "open border transactions" (Scholte, 2004: 520–522). Thus, the withering of the state, insofar as it may be happening, is not necessarily reflected in the fading of international boundaries (see Newman, 2006: 143). At the same time, globalization has a very significant impact upon transnational flows, including the movement of people, goods, and capital, as well as illicit transnational activities, including organized crime enterprises that encompass a significant portion of global economic activity. Thus, we can argue that globalization has created conditions favorable to the occurrence and proliferation of criminal and terrorist activities, due to the intensification of economic, political, social, and cultural relations across borders with the formation of a shared social space by economic and technological forces (see Hall, 2013; Naím, 2005; and Shelley, 2018).

Furthermore, globalization now enables violent non-state actors and TCOs that are not emanating from neighboring states to operate on their borders. They no longer need to be "from the neighborhood," like the terrorist activities of Hezbollah in the TBA of South America, or Colombian drug cartels operating in Europe, the United States, and South Africa (see Shelley, 2018: 1–13).[2] Moreover, many of these activities, whether licit or illicit, take place increasingly delinked from a geography of territorial distances and territorial borders, as a kind of transborder transaction (Scholte, 2004: 525).

A related and relevant question for the *problematique* raised in this book focuses on the potential effects of globalization upon peaceful borders. Reflecting on the development of the EU and other international and regional institutions with some supranational features, some scholars have advanced the argument positing a general de-territorialization of national economies, state sovereignty, and national identity leading to the emergence of a borderless world (see Diener and Hagen, 2010: 4; Zartman, 2010: 15). Geopolitical scholars like Emmanuel Brunet-Jailly have advanced the intriguing idea that nowadays we witness "a-territorial processes," since the border is ultimately embedded upon individuals, goods, and/or information detached, even thousands of kilometers away, from the physical international boundary line (Brunet-Jailly, 2017: 7).

For instance, in dealing with the drug trafficking coming from the Northern Triangle, the United States, in cooperation with Mexico through the Mérida Initiative, has been trying, rather unsuccessfully, to push its security perimeter further south (from Mexico) (see Wayne and Olson, 2017; and Congressional Research Service, 2020). Still, at the same time, and in a dialectic way, globalization might strengthen the relevance of international borders. As Peter Andreas suggests, "Globalization may be about tearing down economic borders, as globalists emphasize, but it has also created more border policing work for

---

[2] We thank Galia Press-Barnathan for her insights on this point.

the state. At the same time as globalization is about mobility and territorial access, states are attempting to selectively reinforce border controls" (Andreas, 2003: 84).

There is a dark side to the effects of globalization processes on the world economy. Economic globalization has increased transportation and it has made communications easier, facilitating trade and investment worldwide. At the same time, non-state actors have also exploited the reduction in transaction costs by engaging in illicit transnational activities, including trafficking of drugs and weapons, stolen and pirated goods, and money laundering (Simmons, Lloyd, and Stewart, 2018: 253; and Shelley, 2014 and 2018). The argument is that globalization has facilitated an exponential growth in transnational organized crime since the early 1990s, and to a lesser extent, it might also encourage transnational terrorism (UN Security Council, 2014: 8).

International Borders in a Globalized World

What is the relevance of physical and political borders in the current age of globalization? What do we mean by international borders? There are about 220,000 kilometers of land borders, involving most of the 193 countries in the world (unless they are islands). Borders might be delimitated by natural barriers, such as rivers, jungles, and mountains, but they are essentially artificial, social, and political constructions, made by human beings to help them organize their lives (see Popescu, 2012: 7; and Simmons, 2019: 11). In the international system, borders are the geographic features, boundaries, hard lines, or markers that demarcate the key political institution of the international society, the nation-state (see Flint, 2005: 6; and Newman, 2005: 321). When referring to international borders, we should consider two important and different dimensions, their functions and their types (see Simmons, 2019).

Functions of Borders

In traditional terms, borders and boundaries have served as international barriers (rather than bridges) between states, by delimiting the contours of national sovereignties from the Westphalia Treaty of 1648 until the present. These functions perform according to the assumption of "methodological territorialism," whereas the materiality of the border stands for the territorial body and sovereignty of the nation-state (Van Schendel, 2005: 43; Wong, 2005: 89; see also Simmons, 2019: 5–10).

We live in a world where globalization has altered the political map, unleashing new communications and transportation technology that facilitates the fast movement of ideas, information, people, and capital. Globalization has made borders more porous, regardless of peace or war. Yet, this is not a borderless world. Borders still reflect power relations and the ability of national governments to determine, superimpose, and perpetuate existing lines of separation, or to remove them according to changing political circumstances (see Newman, 2006: 143, 147). Therefore, borders remain the essential staple and prerequisite for any state-like organization. At the same time, the entire process of state building has been largely about securing a certain overlap between functional and geographical borders (see Simmons, 2019: 22–25; and Zielonka, 2001: 508).

A second function of borders, also related to international security, yet in a different and less traditional sense, is to serve as points of interaction between states and individuals operating across these sovereign territories; that is, as nexus or safe haven for licit and illicit transnational activities. In the former case, borders and borderlands are a no-man's land, becoming what Thomas Risse considers as "areas of limited statehood" (Risse, 2011). This is the result of a combination of open and porous borders, with the proliferation of criminal and terrorist activities, and a limited exercise of sovereignty by the nation-state at the borderlands. Conversely, we define safe havens as geographical spaces where terrorists are able to successfully establish organizational and operational bases that might include fundraising, communications networks, operational space for training, access to weapons, and a logistics network. The necessary conditions for a safe haven are specific geographic features, weak governance, a history of corruption and violence, and poverty and inequality (see Brafman Kitnner, 2007: 308).

Third, turning to issues of international political economy in the age of globalization, we reject the claim that territory does not matter anymore. Rather, international borders have become international political-economic institutions as areas of transactions and economic flows, which bring about both divisible and mutual benefits (see Kahler, 2006: 1–21; and Simmons, 2006: 252, and 2019: 11–14).

Borders become arenas of cooperation and mixed-motive games, rather than zero-sum representations of barriers and tripwires.

Fourth and finally, in addition to the economic dimension, borders might fulfill an important function as shapers (or, alternatively, spoilers) of political identity and the construction of strategic and political cultures at different levels: subnational, national, regional, and transnational. Currently, issues of national identity and ethnicity present challenges to states, as national majorities, indigenous populations, and inhabitants of borderlands debate and contend issues of citizenship, migration, and even the legitimacy of existing borders. Sometimes, the physical erasing of borders, due to economic and political integration, serves to promote a regional, supranational, or transnational identity and to bring about economic and political benefits for the population across the borderlands. Moreover, in many situations, people(s) in the borderlands across neighboring countries might share more common cultural and economic traits, including more frequent relationships among them, than with their fellow citizens from the core of their country, such as the capital city and the hinterland (see Idler, 2018).

To sum up, an essential aspect of international borders is their twofold meaning as lines of separation and contact in space. As Williams cogently puts it, "Borders are confrontational spaces par excellence because they are where the dynamics of globalization, the imperatives of the global space of flows, and the demands of global trade confront the emphasis on national space and the claims of sovereign governments to determine what and who enters or leaves national territory" (Williams, 2010: 44). In other words, international borders both separate and bring into contact different national political, economic, and social systems that coexist, either in situations of conflict and war, or under conditions of peace (see Kacowicz, 1998; Popescu, 2012: 9; and Simmons, 2019: 39–42).

Types of Borders
On the world political map, all boundaries between sovereign states look the same, simple political lines separating one country from another. Yet, borders vary enormously in their types and configurations. For instance, the demilitarized zone that splits North and South Korea is a heavy hard and fortified border, whereas the existing border between Italy and France has been, until recently, a soft and

open border, a kind of stroll-over promenade, where people are allowed to pass through easily with few controls, if any at all (see Lewis, 2011: 1).

Ingolf Vogeler classifies international borders as a function of their physical appearance into three different types: open and soft; controlled; and fortified. In addition, fortified borders come in four subtypes: fenced, fenced and walled, walled, and militarized (Vogeler, 2010: 1). Historically, the majority of the international borders have been open, where no visas, passports, or even inspections were required, as in the Schengen regime of the EU. Regulated or controlled borders might include peaceful borders, as those of the United States (with Canada and parts of the US–Mexican border), where passports and inspections, and sometimes visas are required. Finally, fortified borders include physical barriers, as in one third of the current US–Mexican border, or the Israeli–Egyptian border after 2013 (see Hassner-Wittenberg, 2015; and Payan, 2014: 7).

Border Regimes

The managing of international borders across the world is codified in a variety of border regimes, ranging from closed and alienated borders (such as North Korea–South Korea; Israel–Syria) all the way to open, soft, or nonexistent borders, like in the Schengen regime of the EU. Most international boundaries are located somewhere along this continuum, with varying degrees of openness and closeness across different functional fields (Newman, 2005: 335; see also Zielonka, 2001: 519).

In situations of conflict and war, we expect that the border regime might reflect the alienated end of the continuum. As we move in the direction of conflict management, resolution, and higher degrees of international peace, we assume that the boundary regime will open up to allow for transboundary interactions across the territorial divide to promote, maintain, and consolidate peace (see Newman, 2005: 335). Along the continuum between closed and open borders, we can refer to "coexistent borderlands" (with some form of limited peaceful trans-boundary interaction), "interdependent borderlands" (peaceful, friendly, and cooperative relations), all the way to "integrated borderlands," with unrestricted movement of people and goods across borders (see Martínez, 1994; Newman, 2005: 335; and Popescu, 2012). In this book, we focus upon peaceful border regimes, ranging from coexistent to integrated ones, along the continuum from negative peace all the way to frameworks of integration and pluralistic security communities.

Governance and "Areas of Limited Statehood"

A fourth relevant body of literature refers to the growing concern with issues of governance, at all three possible levels of analysis – national, regional, and global. At the national level, the reference is to the wide-spread distinction between "strong" and "weak" states vis-à-vis their societies, and to "areas of limited statehood" and "ungoverned spaces" (see Clunan and Trinkunas, 2010: 17; Holsti, 1996; and Risse, 2011). Unlike "government," Thomas Risse (2011: 9) defines "governance" as "the various institutionalized modes of social coordination to produce and implement collectively binding rules or to provide collective goods."

Whereas state fragility does appear to exacerbate transnational threats, the relevant gaps in governance refer to political and security variables, including corruption, weak rule of law, and high levels of violence (see Patrick, 2011: 246). At the regional level, the conse-quences of state fragility and porous borders are typically borne by neighboring states, creating the need for some kind of regional govern-ance. Finally, at the global level, transnational crime and terrorism pose significant challenges to the prospects of global governance, by disrupt-ing essential issue-areas where states should cooperate, such as public health and economic stability.

According to Anne Clunan and Harold Trinkunas (2010: 17), "'Ungoverned spaces' are viewed as social, political, and economic arenas where states do not exercise 'effective sovereignty' or where state control is absent, weak, or contested." In a similar vein, Thomas Risse (2011: 4) defines areas of limited statehood as "those parts of a country in which central authorities (governments) lack the ability to implement and enforce rules and decisions, or in which the legitimate monopoly over the means of violence is lacking, at least temporarily." These ungoverned spaces exist when the state has relinquished – volun-tarily or by coercion – its territorial control. In this case, the logic of territorial arbitrage leads non-state actors to take advantage and exploit the asymmetries in the levels of governance across peaceful borders (see Trinkunas and Clunan, 2016: 104; see also Barak and Cohen, 2013: 14, on a similar metaphor on "the Modern Sherwood Forest").

It is evident that gaps in governance are especially prone to facilitate transnational crime. Corruption tends to facilitate illicit transnational activity (see Patrick, 2011: 163). Conversely, it might also be the case that in areas of limited statehood, some of these non-state actors are responsible to provide security when the state is absent, unwilling, or unable to fulfill its basic and vital functions. Moreover, there might be cases where states have the ability, but not the political willingness, to fulfill their territorial sovereignty and exercise their presence at the borderlands. Hence, it is their political decision, rather than their capabilities, which might explain the occurrence and proliferation of illicit transnational flows. For instance, the lax US attitude toward gun control that has allowed arms trafficking across its southern border, along specific political conditions within Mexico itself (see Dube, Dube, and García Ponce, 2013; McDougal et al., 2015: 7; and Simmons, 2019: 18).

There is a considerable variation in the functions of governance when we assess the role of non-state actors through a different lens from that of the official state perspective; for instance, changing the official narrative to that of the local population(s) at the borderlands according to a human security perspective. For instance, in the last two decades, some violent non-state actors, like guerrilla movements and even drug cartels in Colombia and elsewhere, have provided security and fulfilled governance functions for the local population at the borderlands, whereas other VNSAs have remained predatory in nature (see Clunan, 2010; and Idler, 2018).

In this context, one of the trickiest policy questions we should ask is whether local non-state actors' governance structures can be co-opted and enmeshed within official structures of governance, at the municipal and national levels.[3] Several examples from recent Latin American political history seem to offer an affirmative answer in this regard. In Mexico, prior to 2000, the hegemonic regime of the Institutional Revolutionary Party (PRI) co-opted the major DTOs into its corporatist system (McKibben, 2015: 3). Even during the presidency of Felipe Calderón (2006–12), who engaged in a harsh military confrontation against the drug cartels, his former Secretary of Public Security, Genaro García Luna was arrested in the United States for his underground ties with the Sinaloa Cartel. Similarly, in Colombia, three days after his

[3] We thank Anne Clunan for her comments and suggestions in this issue.

election as President in June 1994, Ernesto Samper was accused by
Andrés Pastrana, the opposition leader, of having accepted money
from the Cali drug cartel for his presidential campaign, though he
was impeached (and eventually exonerated) in 1995–6 (see Dugas,
2001: 158; see also Barnes, 2017; and Williams, 2016: 273).

Transnational Crime and Transnational Terrorism

The fifth and final relevant body of literature refers to the twin transnational phenomena of organized crime and terrorism. The two are
interrelated, though they stem out from very different rationales (see
Shelley, 2014). Transnational criminal activity has surged in the last
three decades, since the end of the Cold War, paralleling the dramatic
expansion and proliferation of licit cross-border transactions in our age
of globalization, reflecting a clear economic rationale. Transnational
crime groups and organizations (TCOs) have taken advantage of poor
border control and rampant corruption, which facilitate their transnational incursions across borders. Conversely, transnational terrorism is motivated by political and ideological considerations, not
economic ones. Nowadays, transnational crime and terrorism are considered global problems that seriously challenge international security
and the world order, posing immediate threats to the peace, development, and even the sovereignty of many countries around the world
(see CQ, 2017; NSC, 2013; Shelley, 2014: 1–2; and UNODC, 2010,
2012, and 2014).

Defining Transnational Crime and Transnational Crime
Organizations (TCOs)

There are two general types of misbehavior that transcend the interests
of sovereign countries: international crimes and transnational crimes.
Whereas international crimes are acts prohibited by international criminal law, transnational or cross-border crimes are defined as acts that
violate the laws of more than one country, transcending national
jurisdictions (see Passas, 2003). Thus, a transnational crime is an illegal
activity that occurs, is conceived, or it has effects across national
boundaries. Under the terms of the United Nations Convention against
Transnational Organized Crime signed in Palermo, Italy, in 2000,
a criminal offense is deemed transnational if it meets one of the four
following criteria: "(1) It is committed in more than one state; (2) it is

planned, directed, or controlled in more than one state; (3) it involves an organized criminal group that operates in more than one state; and/ or (4) it has 'substantial effects' on another state" (quoted in Patrick, 2011: 136).

In 1995, the United Nations identified several categories of transnational criminality. Transnational crime was defined as "offences whose inception, prevention, and/or direct or indirect effects involved more than one country" (United Nations, 1995: 4). The list of crimes include: money laundering, terrorist activities, theft of art and cultural objects, theft of intellectual property, illicit arms and trafficking, aircraft hijacking, sea piracy, insurance fraud, computer crime, environmental crime, trafficking in persons and migrant smuggling, trade in human body parts, illicit drug trafficking, fraudulent bankruptcy, infiltration of legal business, corruption, and bribery of public or party officials, counterfeit goods, cigarette smuggling, unrecorded oil sales, illegal timber trade, and traffic in endangered species (see Patrick, 2011: 137; and UNODC, 2010: 1).

For the purposes of this book we focus particularly on drug trafficking, human trafficking and smuggling, and arms trafficking. These activities involve the physical transnational crossing of borders, and they directly affect human security. In contrast, other transnational criminal activities, like money laundering and other cybercrimes are non-territorial, global, and networked in scope, so they take place as transborder transactions, delinked from specific territorial borders (see Scholte, 2004: 525; and Shelley, 2018).

Defining Transnational Terrorism

Popescu (2012: 59) defines transnational terrorism as "politically or ideologically motivated violence that involves the crossing of an interstate border. From a geographical perspective, transnational terrorist organizations display a networked structure that enables them to move through borders from state to state with relative impunity." In particular, in the post-9/11 world, transnational terrorism is considered one of the daunting global security challenges of our century, in spite of the fact that most of the terrorist attacks are not necessarily transnational but rather local, usually carried out by nationals of the targeted state (see Goldman, 2011: 37; Patrick, 2011: 90; and Popescu, 2012: 94).

Possible Nexus between Transnational Crime and Transnational Terrorism

There is a growing convergence between organized crime and terrorism. For instance, in drug trafficking, organized crime groups often run the trafficking organizations whereas terrorist and insurgent groups often control the territory where the drugs are cultivated and transported (see Makarenko, 2004). As UN Under-Secretary General Jeffrey Feltman declared at the United Nations Security Council, "Boko Haram, Al-Qaida, the Taliban, ISIS and their sinister peers make it abundantly clear that the pervasive synergies between terrorism and cross-border crimes foster conflicts, prevent their resolution, and increase the chance of relapse" (United Nations Security Council Resolution 2195, 2014: 1).

This evident symbiosis between crime and terrorism leads to the blurring of goals and modus operandi, confusing the initial assumptions that terrorists are only interested in pursuing political goals, whereas criminals are only interested in economic profits. Nowadays we find criminal groups having an interest in altering the political environment of targeted states, whereas terrorist groups promote an environment prone to the economic success of criminal activities (see Makarenko, 2004; and Shelley, 2014: 11–12). The presence of all these violent non-state actors means that there is an important nexus between international terrorist organizations and criminal networks, leading to a symbiotic relationship in the form of a "terrorist business" (see Novakoff, 2015: 143; and Shelley, 2014a: 17, and 2018: 17). Moreover, some of these VNSAs might experience a metamorphosis from guerrilla and terrorist actions to sheer criminality, such as in the cases of the FARC in Colombia and Hezbollah in Lebanon. There is a financial/economic need for these terrorist and guerrilla groups to find their own resources. In the past, they received these funds from wealthy like-minded states as part of the Cold War proxies; yet, this has dwindled since the end of the Cold War, so they need to find their own means of financing their illicit activities. In sum, transnational terrorism and organized crime have developed a symbiotic relationship where it is not always clear or evident how to differentiate between them.

Preview of the Book

In this introductory chapter, we provided an initial examination of the linkages between peaceful borders and the occurrence and proliferation of illicit transnational flows. In addition, we have clarified several key concepts, stemming from five different bodies of literature: international peace, globalization, international borders, governance and "areas of limited statehood," and the phenomena of transnational criminal organizations and terrorism.

In the next chapter, "A Framework to Explain the Reality of Peaceful Borders and Illicit Transnational Flows," we introduce our theoretical framework, which delineates alternative answers to the research question concerning the conditions under which peaceful borders might enable the occurrence and proliferation of illicit transnational flows. We also discuss the methodology and introduce the case studies that illustrate and test the theoretical argument with its concomitant three hypotheses, underlining the inherent difficulties in gathering reliable data about illicit transnational flows.

In Chapter 3, "The Americas: A General View," we discuss the Western Hemisphere (the Americas) as a continent of peace. Whereas all the international borders in the Americas are peaceful, there is an important variation in terms of the occurrence and proliferation of illicit transnational flows across its borderlands. We assess the thirty-six land borders in the Americas, testing the three hypotheses developed in Chapter 2.

In Chapter 4, "The Americas: From the US–Canadian Border to the Tri-Border Area of South America," we discuss the following case studies: (1) the US–Canadian border since 1994; (2) the US–Mexican border since 1994; (3) The Northern Triangle borders of Guatemala, Honduras, and El Salvador since the end of the civil wars in the early 1990s; (4) the Colombian borders since the early 1990s; and (5) the Tri-Border Area (Argentina, Paraguay, and Brazil) since the signing of MERCOSUR in 1991.

In Chapter 5, "Europe: The Schengen Regime and the Western Balkan Borders," we refer to the European "internal" borders since the establishment of the Schengen Area in 1995, and to the Southeast European (former Yugoslavian/Western Balkans) borders since the end of the war in Bosnia and Herzegovina in 1995.

In Chapter 6, "A Triangle of Peace in the Middle East: The Israeli-Egyptian and Israeli-Jordanian Borders," we examine two cases of peaceful borders in the Middle East. First, we assess the evolution of Israeli–Egyptian relations following the Israel–Egypt Peace Treaty of March 26, 1979, and the Israeli withdrawal from Sinai in 1982, which predates the end of the Cold War. Second, we analyze the Israeli–Jordanian relations and their transition from war to peace with the completion of the Peace Treaty in October 1994 and its aftermath.

In Chapter 7, "The Southern African Borders in the Post-apartheid Era," we assess the Southern African peaceful borders since the end of the regional wars involving South Africa, Angola, and Namibia, as well as the domestic peaceful change in South Africa that ended the apartheid regime in 1994.

In Chapter 8, "ASEAN and the Southeast Asian Borders," we examine the Southeast Asian peaceful borders since the end of the Vietnam–Cambodia War with the signing of the Paris Peace Accords in 1991.

In Chapter 9, "Comparisons, Policy Recommendations, and Conclusions," we draw relevant comparisons across and between the case studies researched, with an emphasis upon relevant theoretical insights. Furthermore, we suggest policy recommendations derived from insights and patterns found across the different cases.

Conclusions

Globalization and regionalization have transformed international relations, mostly by making many of the traditional norms of international law and concerns with territorial border disputes and international security – such as sovereignty, border fixity, and territorial integrity – no longer relevant. Instead, new security threats across borders have been brought to the forefront, including transnational illicit flows of goods and persons, as well as criminal activities. This does not necessarily mean that territory in general, and borders in particular, have lost our attention. Rather, borders now fulfill additional functions, especially against the background of border fixity and the promotion of schemes of regional integration.

With the transformation and evolution of interstate relations from armed conflicts to nonviolent conflicts to international peace, especially since the end of the Cold War, we witness a reality of international peaceful borders coexisting with the occurrence and proliferation of illicit transnational flows. In such reality, peaceful borders that become soft, open, loose, and demilitarized enable the occurrence of transnational illicit flows, usually carried out by violent non-state actors involved in transnational criminal activities and terrorism. In line with these developments, we aim to understand and systematically scrutinize the conditions under which such illicit flows might thrive, and assess what states can and should do about that, in order to better cope with these challenges and threats.

2 | A Framework to Explain the Reality of Peaceful Borders and Illicit Transnational Flows

Introduction

In the previous chapter, we referred to the reality of peaceful borders and transnational illicit flows, as related to the actions of violent non-state actors (VNSAs), including transnational criminal organizations and terrorist groups. These VNSAs are engaged, among other activities, in drug trafficking, human trafficking and smuggling, and arms trafficking across peaceful international borders. The main explanation for this is that VNSAs tend to exploit the peacefulness of the borderlands by taking advantage of the jurisdictional arbitrage created by sovereign borders, to engage in transnational illicit activities across borders.

Yet, this should not be necessarily surprising or counterintuitive. If the borders are closed, it is difficult and risky for non-state actors to penetrate, cross, and thrive along them. Once the borders become peaceful, open, soft, and even porous, non-state actors of many kinds, both licit and illicit, may penetrate these borders, establishing their bases of operations there and crossing them, while thriving at the borderlands. We explain the variation in the occurrence of illicit transnational flows as a function of the conditions under which peaceful borders might enable their proliferation.[1] Therefore, the major research question we posit in this book is, "Under which conditions might peaceful borders enable the occurrence and proliferation of illicit transnational flows, usually carried out by violent non-state actors, including transnational criminal groups and terrorists?"

To answer this question, we assume that international peace and globalization act as permissive conditions that provide the general context for the occurrence and proliferation of illicit transnational flows across peaceful borders as parameters (i.e., these two conditions

---

[1] We thank Assif Efrat for his comments on this point.

are fixed and given). At the same time, we explain the variation in the nature, occurrence, quality, and quantity of these illicit transnational flows according to the following three variables:

(1) *The degree of physical and institutional openness of the peaceful borders*, as a function of the type of borders, resulting from political decisions to make these borders open and soft or controlled and even closed. Whereas the physical openness of the borders refers to the type of borders (i.e., open and soft, controlled, or fortified), the institutional openness refers to the different peaceful border regimes (i.e., coexistent, interdependent, or integrated). Although there is some overlap between border regimes and the physical openness of the borders, they do not always correspond with each other. For instance, whereas the United States and Mexico have interdependent and integrated borders, part of them are fortified.

(2) *The degree of governance, institutional strength, and political willingness of the neighboring states*, with a special focus on border control and the levels of corruption or respect for the rule of law, as a measure for the weakness (or strength) of state institutions. Hence, we assess both the capabilities and the political willingness of states in exercising control over their peaceful borders.

(3) *The prevalent socioeconomic conditions of the neighboring states, with reference to the regional economic characteristics of the borderlands*, which might provide an economic rationale for or against the occurrence and proliferation of transnational criminal activity, as related to an economic logic of supply and demand.

These three variables provide the basis for the formulation of three relevant hypotheses that we test in the empirical chapters, dealing with the reality of the Americas (Chapters 3–4) and beyond the Western Hemisphere (Chapters 5–8).

Explaining the Reality of Peaceful Borders and Illicit Transnational Flows: An Analytical Framework

Permissive Conditions: International Peace and Globalization

We premise the occurrence and proliferation of illicit transnational flows across peaceful borders upon two permissive conditions: the preexistence of international peace and the impact of globalization.

International Peace as a Permissive Condition for Illicit Transnational Flows

The basic assumption that international peace is a permissive condition for the occurrence and proliferation of illicit transnational flows stems from the assessment that violent non-state actors conceive of international borders as too dangerous to cross in times of war and violent conflict. Therefore, criminal and terrorist groups prefer to wait for peace to prevail, when and where they expect to thrive once the border is open. Hence, we assume that these VNSAs actually benefit from peace, like other, legal non-state actors (such as multinational corporations interested in licit businesses), with a similar economic logic and incentive to make as much profit as possible.

The implied logic here is that we expect more illicit transnational activities to take place under conditions of peace than war. We postulate that the existence of international peace is a permissive condition, but it is neither necessary nor sufficient for the occurrence and proliferation of illicit transnational flows.

Why is it the case that international peace, translated into a reality of peaceful borders, might facilitate the occurrence of illicit transnational flows (but without explaining their variance across different cases)? We suggest several answers, as follows:

(1) Under conditions of peace, states often neglect to deploy sufficient numbers of well-trained border guards; thereby, leaving their peaceful borders open and demilitarized;

(2) Under conditions of peace, states are more keen to enable free trade and open communication rather than setting up barriers that might hinder the free movement of goods and peoples. Therefore, peaceful borders might become liberalized (though states still want to effectively monitor the movement of goods);[2]

(3) Under conditions of peace, states no longer fear their neighbors so they neglect the work of intelligence services in their borders; hence, peaceful borders might become soft and porous;

(4) Under conditions of peace, economic and political stability across the borderlands draw large numbers of illicit transnational actors and flows, including the traffic and smuggling of potential (illegal) migrants attracted to the borderlands; hence, peaceful borders

---

[2] We thank Galia Press-Barnathan for her comments on this point.

might become magnets of economic activity.[3] Moreover, a greater volume of legal flows provides more opportunities to conceal illicit goods. Therefore, customs' checks become less effective as the volume of legal trade grows, making it easier to smuggle illicit goods.[4]

Globalization as a Permissive Condition for Illicit Transnational Flows
In addition to international peace, we posit that globalization acts as a permissive condition for the occurrence of illicit transnational flows. Improved mass and interactive communications and the increased mobility of people, goods, and services across national borders have contributed to the proliferation of transnational and terrorist groups, as evident in the cases of networks of transnational crime like drug cartels, and terrorist non-state actors such as al-Qaeda and ISIS. Processes of globalization have multiplied cross-border links, intensifying interconnectedness in the economic, political, and cultural spheres, and leading to the integration of the global economy into a single market. Consequently, criminal and terrorist groups have also become global, as an integral part of the global marketplace (see CQ, 2017: 2; Passas, 2003; Shelley, 2014a and 2018; and UN Security Council, 2014: 1, 8).

Due to the growth in processes of globalization, in terms of scope and pace, transnational criminal and terrorist organizations have become intrinsically networked and linked through the technological features that shrink space and time, in terms of communications and transportation. According to this sinister logic, transnational criminal organizations (TCOs), and particularly drug trafficking organizations (DTOs), become part of a global criminal network that is actually changing the international system and reconfiguring power in international politics and economics (see Naím, 2005: 5; and Shelley, 2018: 1–13).

Until the 1990s, transnational crime was equated with the activities of national and multinational mafias and other criminal organizations. Nowadays, the activities of non-state actors such as TCOs are directly linked to the broader economic logic of globalization. Thus, scholars now use phrases such as "illicit networks," "illicit enterprise and illegal

---

[3] We thank George Gavrillis for his insights and suggestions on this point.
[4] We thank the anonymous reader for Cambridge University Press for his/her comments on this point.

economies," or "dark commerce and illicit economies," in order to better capture the activities of transnational non-state actors in the particular context of the global economy (see Brown and Hermann, 2020; Naím, 2005; Patrick, 2011: 12; and Shelley, 2018).

The increased levels of globalization in trade, finance, goods, and free movement of people have produced an environment prone to transnational violent non-state actors such as TCOs to move illicit profits and illegal goods, provide illicit services, and smuggle people across borders. VNSAs have been successful in exploiting the benefits of globalization in a borderless world, leaving behind the obsolete enforcement agencies that remain within their national boundaries, and taking advantage of the jurisdictional arbitrage across borders. Paradoxically, the globalization of the "legal," "licit," "open" economy has also globalized the underworld, "dark," sinister, and illicit side of it, sometimes blurring the differences between the two (see Galeotti, 2004: 1; Naím, 2005; and Shelley, 2018).

Explaining the Variance in the Proliferation of Illicit Transnational Flows: Type of Borders, Degree of Governance, and Socioeconomic Conditions

In line with these three variables, we explore three working hypotheses as contingent generalizations that focus upon the degree of physical and institutional openness of the borders, the degree of governance, and the prevailing socioeconomic conditions of the neighboring countries.

The Degree of Physical and Institutional Openness of the Peaceful Borders

There seems to be a significant correlation between the configuration of borders in physical terms (openness or closeness), their institutional arrangement (the type of peaceful border regime), and the occurrence and proliferation of illicit transnational flows. In line with this logic, we should expect fortified, militarized, and sealed borders to impede the transnational flows of illicit activities across countries, due to the presence of physical barriers. The goal of these fortified boundaries is not to eliminate the cross-border movement of clandestine transnational actors, but rather to raise the costs of these illicit activities (Hassner and Wittenberg, 2015: 158). Acknowledging the difficulty of eliminating completely the phenomenon of transnational illicit flows, the declared objective is to mitigate them through limiting their scope.

By contrast, we should expect that open and soft borders in the physical sense, alongside institutional border regimes that permit a free movement of citizens of bordering countries in an interdependent, or even integrated bilateral or regional structure (like the Schengen regime in Europe), might facilitate the occurrence and proliferation of illicit transnational activities, usually carried out by transnational VNSAs. In the latter case, the reference is not only to the lack of physical barriers, but also to the lack of institutional controls in an already demilitarized border, such as the lack of police inspection and/ or customs control.

In general, the majority of fortified borders involve countries that do not sustain peaceful relations (probably the best example being the most fortified border of the world, North Korea–South Korea). At the same time, there are fortified borders across countries, which are fenced and guarded, though they constitute peaceful borders between neighboring countries, which are even highly interdependent and integrated. That is the peculiar case of the United States and Mexico, which share a border of about 3,201 kilometers. This long border is already one-third fortified and walled, even before Donald Trump had promised to build a "wall" (that already exists along 930 kilometers of its borderlands!). In the Middle East, Israel has built a fortified fence alongside the Egyptian border, and it is nowadays completing the erection of a fence alongside parts of its border with Jordan, despite peaceful relations among the countries, but with a very low level of economic interactions, so their border regimes are merely coexistent (see Avdan and Gelpi, 2017: 16). Therefore, peaceful borders might also be controlled or even fortified, especially in cases where there is a strong logic of securitization in place. Thus, we formulate our first hypothesis as follows:

H1: The more open, soft, and integrated the peaceful borders between the neighboring states are, the greater the occurrence and proliferation of illicit transnational flows involving violent non-state actors.

Peaceful borders may be hard or soft, as a function of the political choices and decisions of the national governments and the level of governance and institutionalization in the borderlands. Hard borders can be fortified (fenced, fenced and walled, walled, and militarized), and/or controlled. Conversely, soft borders have few controls or none at all, becoming porous and accessible. Moreover, the hard border regime is not an absolute concept; the fuzziness and openness of borders might vary across functional fields. As a matter of fact, the Westphalian model of rigid borders has been a kind of myth, since most of the time states neither could nor wanted to exercise full control over their borders (see Krasner, 1999; and Zielonka, 2001: 519). Furthermore, the logic of building fortified boundaries has been based many times upon socioeconomic and cultural considerations (i.e., rich countries facing poor neighbors; countries divided along religious schisms), rather than mere considerations of national security (see Hassner and Wittenberg, 2015).

There are many cultural and racial (even racist) prejudices and misperceptions regarding the advocacy of hard border regimes, such as the perceived threats of illegal migration and cross-border crime and terrorism that do not correspond to a serious empirical analysis or evidence (see Zielonka, 2001: 519–520). We base the argument for soft and porous borders upon the economic logic of globalization and interdependence, especially at the regional and dyadic levels, deriving from Liberal premises about free trade and peace. Moreover, there are instances where borders are softened by the action of official state policies, through the deliberate creation of free trade zones aimed at facilitating and advancing transnational flows (Williams, 2010: 45). This is the case in border regimes that are interdependent or highly integrated economically and in political terms.

The Degree of Governance, Institutional Strength, and Political Willingness of the Neighboring States in Controlling Their Peaceful Borders

Governance implies institutionalized modes of social coordination to produce and implement collectively binding rules, by state and non-state actors alike (see Risse, 2011: 9). The inherent tensions between agents of disorder and governance play geopolitically at the international borders, which are the meeting points and confrontational spaces between the national claims of sovereign governments and the dynamics of globalization and transnationalism embodied by non-state actors. Whereas the forces of governance are institutionalized at the borders in the form of customs officials, immigration officers, and border guards, the forces of disorder include smugglers, illegal migrants, criminals, and terrorists, in connivance with corrupt officials from the neighboring states (see Williams, 2010: 44). Ideally, we should focus here upon the presence (or absence) of state capacity, and the presence (or absence) of effective authority and governability in the borderlands as an important variable in explaining the variance in the increased level of transnational criminal and terrorist activity.

These encounters between the forces of governance and disorder are dynamic and complex; they become even more complicated when we take into consideration three additional factors. First, there is often an asymmetry in the degrees and forms of governance across neighboring countries. This is as a function of different legal systems and levels of economic development, corruption, institutionalization (or lack thereof) of the rule of law, and political willingness (or lack thereof) in controlling the national borders out of domestic political consider-ations; all this is what we called in the previous chapter jurisdictional arbitrage. Second, the VNSAs can play positive functions of govern-ance, like policing and providing essential social services to communi-ties at the borderlands, within one or more of the neighboring countries, when these functions are neglected by relevant state actors unable or unwilling to perform them (see Cockayne and Lupel, 2011: 3; and Idler, 2018). Third, the official actors that embody the government and should therefore provide governance might be corrupt or criminal, and might collaborate with transnational non-state actors to the extent that it might be difficult at times to differentiate between criminalized state actors and other private, non-state actors, engaged in illicit trans-national activities (see Shelley, 2014a: 12).

In sum, the commitment of sovereign states to control the borders and stop the flow of illicit transnational flows is a combined function of capabilities and political willingness to do so. Thus, control of illicit transnational flows is not only about what happens at the border in physical and institutional terms, or about state capacity. It relates to considerations of policy and politics, the incentives of governments to control the illicit transnational flows or to ignore them, and the polit-ical pressure from various domestic actors within society to enforce or ignore governance of the border.[5] Political willingness is a function of domestic politics calculations, the political power of interest and

---

[5] We thank an anonymous reviewer from Cambridge University Press for his/her comments on this point.

pressure groups, the existence of a corrupt political culture that blurs the distinction between the political elites and criminals, the type of political regime, and in some cases the type of networked relations involving state officials, politicians, and criminals (see Trejo and Ley, 2020).

We can follow here Nicholas Barnes' useful typology and find a continuum in terms of "criminal politics" by establishing a range of possibilities in the complex, hybrid, and at times symbiotic and net-worked relations between state officials, politicians, and non-state criminal actors. The scale ranges from "confrontation" (high competi-tion), "enforcement-evasion" (low competition), "alliance" (low col-laboration), all the way to "integration" (high collaboration), where the state ultimately becomes criminalized, as in the case of Nicolás Maduro's current rule in Venezuela (see Barnes, 2017: 968; and Felbab-Brown, 2017a: 2).

Turning to state institutions, we assess different levels of governance by examining the complex relations between states and their societies, usually in terms of "strong" and "weak" states (see Buzan, 1983; Holsti, 1996; Migdal, 1988; and Nordlinger, 1981). According to Samuel Huntington (1968: 1), the most important political distinction among states refers not only to their form of government (such as democratic or autocratic), but rather to their degree of political insti-tutionalization. In this sense, the weak state/strong state continuum, measured by state autonomy, degree of legitimacy, and institutional-ization, is essential to assess states' capabilities and willingness to control their borderlands.

Strong states have an inherent advantage in keeping their peaceful borders free from the incursion of VNSAs due to their internal capaci-ties and control, low levels of corruption, and high levels of institution-alization and legitimacy. They can also decide the type of borders they want to share (soft or hard, open or controlled). As an important caveat here, we assume that strong states, which have the capabilities to control their peaceful borders, are also willing to do so, based on legitimate rules and a basic respect for the rule of law.

As stated previously, control of the border regarding illicit trans-national flows is subservient to domestic political calculations and manipulations. For instance, in the extraordinary case of the United States, despite its obvious capabilities, it has not shown enough polit-ical willingness to control arms trafficking flowing beyond its southern border and within its own sovereign soil, or drug trafficking flowing north from Mexico and Central America into the heart of its own society. Drug trafficking takes place within a market endowed with supply and demand. In the Americas, the demand comes essentially from the United States. On the one hand, the US market demands narcotics, but on the other hand, the US government forbids its supply. Notwithstanding this prohibition, according to a perverse economic logic, if the production and acquisition of these illicit goods is feasible, a high demand will generate its supply. Thus, although the United States is the strongest state in the world in military and technological terms, it does not implement its proven capabilities to effectively control its border with Mexico, because of its lack of political willingness to seriously address drug trafficking in terms of its demand, and arms trafficking in terms of its supply.

By contrast, weak states, even if willing, lack the capabilities of adequate regulation of social relationships and the appropriation of resources in determined ways. They fail in implementing decisions, partly because of the weakness of their institutional structures (Migdal, 1988: 8, 21–22; see also Centeno, 2002, 10; and Prasad et al., 2007: 464). Moreover, weak states are unable to fulfil the fundamental functions associated with the effective exercise of sovereign statehood, such as preserving a monopoly over the use of force and providing their citizens and residents with minimal protection and security from physical violence (see Patrick, 2011: 8).

In contrast to strong states, weak states tend to show low levels of political institutionalization and governance, and high levels of corruption. They are usually immersed in serious domestic conflicts. They are inherently interested in maintaining the territorial status quo and the formal peace along their national borders, though they do not always control them, due to lack of will, lack of capacity, or both. Moreover, the main consequences of state fragility are typically borne by the neighboring states; hence, we identify a contagion effect of domestic conflicts spilling over into neighboring countries, including flows of weapons, refugees, migrants, and diseases (Patrick, 2011: 43).

Consequently, weak states tend to suffer from a lack of governance and institutionalization at the borderlands in their ability to regulate and control their borders. According to Patrick (2011: 144):

in assessing the capacities of one hundred developing nations, the Secretariat of the World Customs Organization (WCO) identified a slew of crippling performance gaps, including rampant corruption, inadequate legal frameworks, minimal risk analysis and strategic planning, inattention to illicit flows of contraband, low levels of human and financial resources, and inadequate coordination with neighboring countries and the private sector.

Whereas state fragility and weakness do appear to exacerbate transnational threats and the occurrence and proliferation of illicit transnational flows, the relevant gaps in national governance across borders refer mainly to political variables, such as levels of corruption and respect for the rule of law, translated into differential levels of violence (see Patrick, 2011: 246). Thus, gaps in governance across neighboring countries might attract and facilitate transnational crime and terrorism, taking advantage of the jurisdictional arbitrage. Poor regulatory structures impede the efficient control of borders against the occurrence and proliferation of illicit transnational flows, including (but not only) transnational organized crime and terrorist activities. Moreover, high levels of corruption in the police and other law enforcement agencies might hamper anti-criminal and counterterrorist efforts. For these reasons, a state's limited state control of its national borders becomes an important element in our analysis.

In sum, according to our second hypothesis, the linkages between peaceful borders and the occurrence and proliferation of illicit transnational flows are a function of the ability, capability, and political willingness of national governments to control and exercise effective governance in their borderlands. At times, there might be an important variance in the level of national governance across different subregions within the same country (for instance, obvious gaps between the strong core or mainland, and the weak periphery of the borderlands). Therefore, the significant variables here might be the level of state strength or weakness, as evidenced especially in the borderlands, as well as the possible governance gap between the bordering states, in addition to the important distinction between capabilities and political willingness. The problems with an effective border control of illicit transnational flows arise when one of the neighboring countries is incapable or unwilling to control its border. Moreover, these problems exacerbate in exponential terms when *both* (or more) neighboring countries sustain low capacity and political commitment to do so. Accordingly, we can formulate our second hypothesis as following:

H2: *The less committed and able neighboring states are to control their peaceful borders in terms of governance, the greater the occurrence and proliferation of illicit transnational flows involving violent non-state actors.*

The Prevalent Socioeconomic Conditions of the Neighboring States

A third explanatory variable for the occurrence and proliferation of illicit transnational flows across peaceful borders refers to the political economy of the bordering states and their borderlands. There are many instances where states of all sorts of strength might voluntarily absent themselves from establishing border controls (whether physical, or virtual, as in the case of offshore financial markets), for purely economic, cost-benefit reasons, in addition to political considerations. Accordingly, peaceful international borders have become international political-economic arenas of transactions and economic flows that bring about divisible and mutual benefits (see Kahler, 2006; and Simmons, 2006: 252)

There is an evident economic logic of supply and demand underpinning the nexus between peaceful borders and the occurrence of illicit transnational flows. After all, it is not surprising that peaceful borders might enable transnational crime. Most illicit business is like licit business; in other words, peace is good for trade. Illicit trade uses the same channels and transport mechanisms as licit trade, and this is much more constrained in wartime, though wartime itself might create particular demands for certain illicit goods, such as weapons smuggled across the US-Mexican border during the Mexican Revolution of 1910–17, as well as in the case of the Yugoslavian Wars in the 1990s. Yet, it is obviously a lot easier to smuggle weapons and people across the border during peacetime, as we witness nowadays along the same US-Mexican border (see Andreas, 2011b).[6]

There are several political-economic reasons that explain this linkage between peaceful borders and transnational illicit flows. First, the presence and incursion of VNSAs across the borderlands occur simply because of the economic incentives to take advantage of the jurisdictional arbitrage created by sovereign states in terms of socioeconomic disparities and gaps between the neighboring states. In other words, if the VNSAs can find profit in a jurisdiction because it has stricter laws

---

[6] We thank Peter Andreas for his comments and suggestions on this point.

that generate higher prices (for everything from smuggled contraband to illegal drugs), while operating within a jurisdiction with looser or more liberal regulations, then they will seek to exploit it.[7] In this context, cross-border flows are a function of not only supply and demand, but also of currency exchange rates and price differentials across the borderlands. Hence, the borderlands become ideal environments for illegal flows of goods that exploit asymmetries and disparities of value (Williams, 2010: 44–45).

Second, the poor economic situation in weak and fragile states creates a conducive environment for the proliferation of transnational crime. For instance, weak and poor states sustain high rates of unemployment, especially among youth. That creates an enticing economic opportunity for criminal and terrorist organizations to recruit "personnel" who have no alternative source of income and an uncertain future (see Dreschen, 2017: 21). It also creates an incentive for legal and illegal migration from poor countries to neighboring richer ones in the same geographical region, like the flows of illegal migrants to the United States, South Africa, and Thailand.

Third, economic development gaps across borders explain not only licit labor and capital flows, but also illegal flows through illegal migration and transnational crime in the form of human smuggling and trafficking, as people seek to move across borders regardless of what the border regulatory or security apparatus tell them to do (Payan, 2014: 14). Accordingly, we can formulate our third hypothesis as follows:

H3: *The poorer the socioeconomic conditions in the borderlands and/ or the broader the economic disparity across the peaceful borders of the neighboring states, the greater the occurrence and proliferation of illicit transnational flows involving violent non-state actors.*

Conversely, high levels of economic development might balance out the occurrence and proliferation of illicit transnational flows, but only if it holds for all the neighboring countries across their peaceful international borders. According to this logic, following the premises of the Liberal "economic peace," there is a correlation between a high level of socioeconomic development and upgraded levels of peace and integration, all of that within a context of economic interdependence

---

[7] We thank Anne Clunan for her detailed comments on this point.

(see Press-Barnathan, 2006). This usually takes place after a transition from negative peace to higher levels of peace, including stable peace and the emergence and development of a pluralistic security community. We therefore assume that peaceful borderlands characterized by high levels of economic development and integration might provide an environment less conducive for the occurrence and proliferation of illicit transnational flows, even though their borders might become porous, open, and irrelevant (see Press-Barnathan, 2009).

Research Design and Methodology

To answer the research question and empirically test the three hypotheses presented here, we employed two types of methodologies. First, we gathered relevant empirical information concerning illicit transnational flows in the Americas across the twenty-four countries in the Western Hemisphere that share thirty-six land borders, and assessed the different variables in a binary way.[8] Second, we conducted a structured, focused comparison of a number of case studies from the Americas and other regions of the world.

We embed our research design in a relatively simple qualitative model that entails two parameters and three distinct variables. On that basis, we offer useful insights and overall generalizations to explain the variance in the occurrence of illicit transnational flows, though there might be multiple causes, in a typical, fluid, and complex instance of "over-determination" (whereas a single-observed effect, such as illicit transnational flows, is determined by several causes).

Despite the combination of these different methodologies, we decided not to undertake quantitative methods, such as regression probes, due to the inherent difficulties in gathering adequate and reliable data on illicit transnational flows, especially as related to drug trafficking, arms trafficking, and human trafficking. This by definition limits the possibility of establishing causal relations beyond mere correlations. Following Andreas and Greenhill (2010), we are aware that "the illicit nature of certain cross-border flows enables and facilitates a politics of numbers that is defined by speculation, distortion, and sometimes even outright

---

[8] In this book, we do not refer specifically to maritime boundaries, despite their economic and political importance and significance. Hence, we do not address the transnational crime of maritime piracy.

fabrication" (Andreas, 2010: 23). Unlike the documented data on licit flows (such as trade and capital flows), it is much more difficult to gather reliable data on illicit transnational criminal activities, such as the smuggling of drugs, arms, and people. Moreover, the official data on crime in Latin America (and not only in that region) are for the most part unreliable and entail significant questions of validity (see Andreas and Duran-Martinez, 2015: 376 and 387; and Bergman, 2006: 220). The inherent difficulties in embarking in a quantitative study with a big *N* poses methodological obstacles to our research design, so we candidly prefer to be modest in assessing the limitations of causal inference in our research.

Data Collection on the Peaceful Land Borders of the Americas

In the course of our empirical research, we compiled information about the thirty-six land borders in the Americas with reference to the following transnational illicit activities: drug trafficking, human trafficking, arms trafficking, and transborder terrorism, which involve a physical crossing of the international border.[9] We gathered that information from open sources such as the United Nations Office on Drugs and Crime (UNODC), the US State Department, regional organizations from the Americas, and other Latin American sources in English and Spanish for the years 2010–15. On that basis, we decided to record either occurrence or absence of illicit transnational flows, in a binary way. Moreover, we also traced the existence of diplomatic relations and degrees of peace between the neighboring countries based on their historical record (see Kacowicz, 1998), as well as the degree of openness of their peaceful borders, regarding the freedom of movement of people and goods across their borders.

Additionally, we gathered relevant data about the twenty-four relevant countries in the Americas that share land borders for the years 2014 and 2015. The data includes: (1) indicators of governance and state strength

[9] The relevant land borders in the Americas are US-Canada, US-Mexico, Mexico-Belize, Mexico-Guatemala, Belize-Guatemala, Guatemala-Honduras, Guatemala-El Salvador, Salvador-Honduras, Honduras-Nicaragua, Nicaragua-Costa Rica, Costa Rica-Panama, Panama-Colombia, Colombia-Venezuela, Venezuela-Guyana, Guyana-Suriname, Colombia-Brazil, Venezuela-Brazil, Guyana-Brazil, Suriname-Brazil, Colombia-Ecuador, Colombia-Peru, Peru-Ecuador, Peru-Brazil, Peru-Bolivia, Peru-Chile, Bolivia-Brazil, Bolivia-Chile, Argentina-Chile, Bolivia-Paraguay, Paraguay-Brazil, Argentina-Bolivia, Argentina-Paraguay, Argentina-Brazil, Argentina-Uruguay, Uruguay-Brazil, Dominican Republic-Haiti.

or weakness, such as the Corruption Perception Index (for 2015) and the Fragile State Index (for 2015); (2) indicators of political economy, and levels of economic development of the neighboring countries, such as the Human Development Index (HDI) (for 2014), and the gross domestic product per capita (for 2014), as a proxy to measure socioeconomic gaps across the borderlands.[10]

Structured Focused Comparison of Relevant Case Studies

In addition to the compilation of data for the relevant Western Hemisphere countries that share peaceful land borders, we utilized a structured, focused qualitative comparison to examine the three hypotheses presented here (George and Bennett, 2005: 67–72). The analysis of more detailed case studies helps us to focus analysis on variance in the occurrence and proliferation of illicit transnational flows across peaceful borders, taking into consideration international peace and economic globalization as permissive conditions. In addition, we examine other variables as alternative explanations, which are very difficult to quantify, like the legacy of previous conflicts and wars, and the particular geography and geopolitics of the borderlands.

In the context of the Western Hemisphere, the relevant case studies are the following:

- *The North American borders*: We examine the US-Canadian and US-Mexican borders since the establishment of the North American Free Trade Area (NAFTA) in 1994. In both cases, these are peaceful and integrated borders of highly interdependent countries, but with an important variance with respect to the freedom of movement across the US-Canada and the US-Mexico border as well as the volume, nature, and composition of their illicit transnational flows.
- *The Northern Triangle of Central America*: This case involves the borders of Guatemala, Honduras, and El Salvador, since the end of the civil wars and the transition of Central America to an international zone of peace in the early 1990s. The three countries are among the weakest in the Western Hemisphere, and they have

---

[10] The relevant countries are Argentina, Belize, Bolivia, Brazil, Canada, Chile, Colombia, Costa Rica, Dominican Republic, Ecuador, El Salvador, Guatemala, Guyana, Haiti, Honduras, Mexico, Nicaragua, Panama, Paraguay, Peru, Suriname, the United States, Uruguay, and Venezuela.

experienced a high level of domestic violence and transnational illicit activities, especially with respect to drug trafficking, as well as human trafficking and smuggling.

- *The Colombian borders*: We examine the borders of Colombia with Venezuela, Ecuador, and Panama, with an emphasis upon the post–Cold War period (from the early 1990s to 2016). The Colombian borders sustain a reputation of being among the lawless and ungoverned of Latin America, due to the long civil war fought between the FARC and the Colombian government between 1964 and 2016, and the lingering transnational criminal activity across them.

- *The Tri-Border Area (TBA) of the Southern Cone of South America*: The TBA includes the peaceful borders among Argentina, Brazil, and Paraguay, "upgraded" following the establishment of MERCOSUR in 1991. The TBA has evolved from being a once-militarized border between Argentina and Brazil to becoming a peaceful border area that is highly integrated in economic and social terms, though it also harbors smuggling, trafficking, and transnational terrorism.

All the borders in the Americas referred to in these four case studies are by definition peaceful. Yet, there is an important variation across the cases in terms of historical background and trajectories, gradations of peace and integration, transition from negative peace to higher levels of peace, legacies of previous conflicts including civil wars, levels of governance and state strength, and the socioeconomic situation prevailing in the borderlands, including significant socioeconomic gaps between the neighboring countries.

Turning to other regions of the world beyond the Western Hemisphere, we examine the following case studies in Chapters 5–8:

- *The European "internal" and "external" borders since Schengen*: We assess the softening and the complete opening of internal borders among the twenty-six participating countries in the Schengen border regime since its implementation in 1995, in juxtaposition to external border control and the attempts to prevent and fight terrorism and organized crime.[11]

---

[11]   The European countries that participate in the Schengen convention are Austria, Belgium, Czech Republic, Denmark, Estonia, Finland, France, Germany, Greece, Hungary, Iceland, Italy, Latvia, Liechtenstein, Lithuania, Luxembourg, Malta, Netherlands, Norway, Poland, Portugal, Slovakia, Slovenia, Spain, Sweden, and Switzerland.

- Beyond the EU, we examine the *Southeast European (former Yugoslavian) borders* since the Dayton Agreement of 1995, as related to the relevant borders of the Western Balkan countries that emerged from the breakdown of Yugoslavia since its transition to peace.
- *The peaceful borders of the Arab-Israeli conflict*: We assess the peaceful borders in the cases of Israel-Egypt (since 1979) and Israel-Jordan (since 1994), and the variation between these two cases in terms of illicit flows, transnational crime, and terrorism across them.
- *The borders of Southern Africa since the end of the Cold War and the domestic peaceful change in South Africa in 1994*: We examine the occurrence and proliferation of illicit transnational flows once the peaceful borders in Southern Africa were established, following the end of apartheid in South Africa in the mid-1990s.[12]
- *The borders of Southeast Asia since the end of the Cambodia-Vietnamese war in 1991*: We assess the dynamics unfolding in ASEAN peaceful borders since the transition from war to peace (in the case of Cambodia and Vietnam), and their links to the occurrence and proliferation of illicit transnational flows.[13]

The rationale for including these additional case studies beyond the Western Hemisphere is three-fold. First, there is significant variation in the levels of state strength and governance. Second, there are different types of border regimes and levels of economic integration of the borderlands. Third, and finally, there are different levels of threats and challenges posed by illicit transnational flows, ranging from drug trafficking, arms trafficking, human trafficking and smuggling, to terrorism.

---

[12] The relevant Southern African borders are Namibia-Botswana, Namibia-South Africa, Namibia-Angola, Botswana-Zimbabwe, Mozambique-South Africa, South Africa-Lesotho, Swaziland-South Africa, Zimbabwe-Mozambique, South Africa-Botswana, South Africa-Zimbabwe, Zimbabwe-Mozambique, Zambia-Angola, and Zambia-Namibia.

[13] The relevant borders include Vietnam-Cambodia, Laos-Vietnam, Laos-Thailand, Malaysia-Thailand, Singapore-Malaysia, Thailand-Cambodia, Thailand-Myanmar, Myanmar-Laos, and Cambodia-Laos. As in the case of the Americas, we consider only land borders in the Asian continent and across islands, rather than maritime borders in Southeast Asia.

Conclusions

In this chapter we presented a theoretical framework that delineates and scrutinizes the conditions under which peaceful borders might enable the occurrence and proliferation of illicit transnational flows, usually (but not always) carried out by violent non-state actors. These conditions include: (1) the degree of physical and institutional openness of the borders, including the type of border regimes; (2) the degree of governance and institutional strength of the neighboring countries, including their political willingness to control their peaceful borders; and (3) the prevalent socioeconomic situation of the neighboring states.

We embedded these variables in the context of three working hypotheses that suggest alternative explanations for the variance in the occurrence and proliferation of illicit transnational flows across peaceful borders. We operationalize these hypotheses in order to test them empirically in a research design that includes the analysis of the thirty-six relevant land borders in the Americas, as well as the perusal of several case studies across several regions and continents. The American cases include: (1) the North American borders (US-Canada and US-Mexico); (2) the Northern Triangle of Central America; (3) the Colombian borders; and (4) The Tri-Border Area of the Southern Cone of South America. Other cases beyond the Western Hemisphere include: (5) the European internal and external borders since the establishment of the Schengen regime, including a particular discussion of the Western Balkan countries; (6) the peaceful borders in the Arab-Israeli conflict (Israel-Egypt and Israel-Jordan); (7) the Southern African borders; and (8) the South East Asian borders. We assess the empirical evidence for the relevance of the three hypotheses in the next six chapters, with a particular focus upon the post–Cold War period.

3 | The Americas: A General View

Introduction

The relative absence of international wars in the Western Hemisphere since 1881 has affected its border configuration by making it stable and peaceful in terms of the territorial status quo. At the same time, these borders are vulnerable to the occurrence and proliferation of illicit transnational flows and the incursion of violent non-state actors (VNSAs; see Briscoe, 2008; and Kacowicz, 1998). One of the main ironies of the political and socioeconomic reality in Latin America is the startling contrast between the realities of interstate peace, and even domestic peace, in juxtaposition to the twin phenomena of low-intensity domestic violence as epitomized by the highest rate of homicides in any region of the world, and the occurrence and proliferation of transnational crime.

Violence and the dramatic rise in criminality could arguably be considered as the defining problems of Latin America in the early twenty-first century (Bergman, 2006: 213; and Davis, 2006: 178–179). Unlike the violent past punctuated by guerrilla struggles and violent ideological conflicts involving the military, most contemporary violence in the region is domestic and related to crime.[1] It has been caused by multifarious factors such as poverty and inequality, breakdown of social controls, the legacy of civil wars, relative weakness of states and lack of political control, and local-level extortion by urban gangs among widespread corruption. At the same time, Latin American violence is inherently related to the proliferation of illicit trade by transnational organized crime, including drug trafficking, human smuggling and trafficking, and arms trafficking (see Andreas and Duran Martinez, 2015; Mares, 2019; and Williams, 2016).

---

[1] We thank Ruth Diamint for her comments on this point.

In contrast to cases such as Kashmir, Sudan, Kosovo, and the Arab-Israeli conflict, since the end of the nineteenth century there have been almost no interstate wars revolving around the demarcation of national borders in the Americas (see Briscoe, 2008: 1; Jaskoski, Sotomayor, and Trinkunas, 2015: 7; and Williams, 2016: 268). While this has been a blessing in comparison to the bloody history of Europe until 1945 and much of the contemporary Third World since then, it had also slowed the development of Latin American states by damaging their domestic legitimacy and degree of institutionalization, leading to recurrent civil wars and military coups d'état (see Centeno, 2002).

While international borders are mostly peaceful, they have also been characterized by the incursion of transnational VNSAs, including armed criminal networks, transnational criminal organizations (TCOs), and to a lesser extent, guerrilla and terrorist groups engaged in a myriad of illicit transnational activities (see Andreas and Duran Martinez, 2015; Domínguez, 2018; and Williams, 2016: 268). In sum, Latin American borders, while peaceful in traditional security terms, historically have been neglected peripheral borderlands, and they have gradually become epicenters of transnational and domestic violence, with political repercussions and shock waves amplified by the lingering weakness of many Latin American countries (see Chinchilla, 2011: 2; and Idler, 2018).

Once many of the peaceful international borders in the Americas became open, soft, loose, and often times demilitarized and "civilized," transnational crime and occasionally transborder terrorism have gradually proliferated, posing new challenges to Latin America's security landscape and the prospects of cooperation (see Pion-Berlin, 2005: 214 and 216). Some peaceful borders in the Western Hemisphere are particularly prone to the presence of transnational VNSAs due to their relative lack of governance. Those include, among others, Mexico's border with the United States, Colombia's borders, Brazil's Amazon frontiers, the Central American Northern Triangle borders, and the Tri-Border Area (TBA) of Argentina, Paraguay, and Brazil.

To make sense of the linkages between peaceful borders and the occurrence and proliferation of illicit transnational flows in the Americas, we first present a general historical background of the continent, with a particular focus upon Latin America. We then turn to discuss the issue of areas of limited statehood (or ungoverned spaces) that seem to fit the reality of several Latin American borderlands. Next, we shift our focus to transnational crime, referring briefly to drug trafficking, arms trafficking, and human trafficking and smuggling as part of the illicit trade that takes place across the peaceful borders of the Western Hemisphere. In the closing part of the chapter, we introduce the relevant data for the peaceful borders of the continent, as summarized in a series of tables, which allow us to test the three hypotheses presented in Chapter 2.

General Background: Latin America

We briefly present the general background of Latin America through its historical developments in two distinctive geographic areas: the Southern Cone of South America and Central America. In the former, following the end of the military dictatorships in the 1980s, there has been a significant reduction of interstate and intrastate conflicts. Among the most outstanding events in the Southern Cone of South America in the last forty years was the rapprochement between Brazil and Argentina during both transitions to democracy in the 1980s. Since 1985, both countries have established a positive bilateral agenda, mainly through the integration process supported by the successive democratic governments that led to the formation of MERCOSUR in 1991. Another encouraging development in the direction of consolidating peace in South America was the fact that Argentina and Chile's territorial conflict over the Beagle Channel ended after a negotiated settlement in 1984. Both seminal events paved the way for the softening of the political and security environment by the early 1990s (see Kacowicz, 2000; and Oelsner, 2005).

As for Central America, the long South American peace since 1881 finally became a whole "American peace" when the civil wars in the Central American isthmus ended in the early 1990s (see Kacowicz, 1998). Nicaragua, El Salvador, and Guatemala experienced virulent civil wars that raged the region in the 1980s. In Nicaragua in 1979, the Sandinista National Liberation Front overthrew the dictatorship of the infamous Anastasio Somoza. Yet, the Sandinista Revolution found itself facing increasing domestic and international opposition. The United States stepped in and funded an armed an opposition group of ex-Somoza military officers, the so-called *Contras*, whose purpose was to wage a guerrilla counterrevolutionary war against the Sandinistas. The war ultimately reached a death toll of about fifty thousand victims.

Due to the diplomatic intervention of Latin American countries in the political processes of Contadora and Esquipulas in the late 1980s, and the stalemate between the *Contras* and the Sandinista government, free elections convened in 1990 and a peaceful transition eventually took place (see Kacowicz, 2005: 153–160). Ironically, Daniel Ortega, the leader of the Sandinista Revolution of 1979 that ousted Somoza, has become in recent years an autocratic leader himself, not very different in his political practices from the dictator he replaced (see Thaler, 2017).

In 1992, the Chapultepec Peace Accords were concluded in El Salvador after twelve years of war involving the leftist Farabundo Martí Liberation Front and death squads supported by the Salvadorian government, with the backing of the United States. Finally, the civil war also ended in Guatemala in 1996 after decades of bloodshed including the genocide of some 100,000–200,000 among the ethnic Mayan population and massive abuse of human rights, especially during the years of the dictator José Efraín Ríos Montt (see Higonnet, 2009).

A common denominator for all of these Central American peace accords was the reduction of the size and scope of the security apparatus in every single country. Notwithstanding the encouraging fact that there was now civilian control over the military, the record remained a mixed one. On the one hand, former military officers who were disbanded found a livelihood in either illegal activities or private security organizations. On the other hand, the reduction of the state security apparatus left a significant vacuum. In particular, borderlands and peripheral areas far from the populated centers remained uncontrolled by the national governments. VNSAs filled this vacuum, sometimes fulfilling the roles and functions of governance that the state abandoned in these peripheral areas (see Penski, 2018; and Rodgers and Muggah, 2009).

The Latin American Movement toward Regionalism

Since the early 1990s, Latin America experienced a wave of regional building projects along with the emergence of an array of new regional institutions in the economic and security realms. At the hemispheric level, the Organization of American States (OAS) had to reinvent itself after the end of the Cold War, adapting to the new era by adopting new functions such as promoting democracy, preventing terrorism, and opposing transnational crime (see Weiffen, 2012). In parallel, the countries of the Southern Cone promoted their own regional integration mechanisms in the form of establishing MERCOSUR in 1991. Although it was initially designed to consolidate the renewed democracies and to advance the economic development of its member-states, MERCOSUR had important and positive spillovers on security issues, including the stabilization of civil–military relations and coping with new security threats (see Oelsner, 2009).

With the turn of the twenty-first century, new schemes of regional integration developed in the region. In 2000, Brazil hosted the first presidential summit of South American leaders in almost two hundred years of independence. Brazil assumed the leadership role in subsequent years that led to the creation of the Union of South American Nations (UNASUR) in 2004. Afterwards, the Latin American and Caribbean countries established a continental framework in 2010, the Community of Latin American and Caribbean States (CELAC), which includes all of the countries in the hemisphere, except for Canada and the United States. The decline of the Andean Pact favored the formation of the Pacific Alliance in 2011, an economic framework of Peru, Colombia, Chile, and Mexico, aimed at bolstering the ties between the Pacific countries in the region. Conversely, the left-leaning regimes established an alternative regional framework, the ALBA (Bolivarian Alliance for the Americas). Launched in 2004 by Venezuela and Cuba with the goal of establishing an alternative regional and interregional order, it was subsequently joined by Ecuador, Nicaragua, Bolivia, and several Caribbean countries attracted not only by the vision of an old-new America (*Nuestramérica*), but also by the petrodollars of Chavismo in Venezuela that fuelled this regional project (see Wajner and Roniger, 2019).

The Persistence of Traditional Conflicts in the Region

Traditional conflicts have never vanished from the Latin American security landscape. Ecuador and Peru waged a short and last war in 1995 for unsettled border issues, reaching peace after that in 1998. Lately, in 2013, Bolivia sued Chile before the International Court of Justice regarding the former's claim for an access to the sea lost in the

Pacific War back in 1881. In addition, Guatemala sustains a territorial claim over Belize's territory in a long-time dispute that has being discussed at the International Court of Justice (see Domínguez et al., 2003).

The deterioration of bilateral relations between Venezuela and Colombia during the Chávez era (1999–2013) led to several militarized disputes short of war. While volatile rhetoric never translated into actual armed conflict, Venezuela closed its border with Colombia several times, alleging the infiltration of VNSAs aimed at destabilizing the country. At the same time, the Colombian civil war spilled over into Ecuador. In 2008, the Colombian government attacked a FARC camp on the Ecuadorian side of the border, leading to a crisis between Colombia and Venezuela, which was resolved eventually by peaceful means, mediated by UNASUR and the OAS (see Marcella, 2008).

The Role of the United States vis-à-vis Latin America

Since the end of the Cold War, there has been an ongoing discussion regarding the contemporary role of the United States vis-à-vis Latin America. Some scholars argue that the United States has lost its preponderance (see Rigirozzi and Tussie, 2012; and Trinkunass, 2013) whereas others point out that US hegemony in the Americas remains as uncontested as ever (see Mares, 2016; and Russell and Calle, 2009). Notwithstanding these contrasting perspectives, the fact is that the era of direct US military intervention in the region ended in 1989 with the US invasion of Panama, when the United States captured strongman Manuel Noriega, accused of drug trafficking and human rights abuses (see Nanda, 1990).

Since the early 1990s, the United States has been a staunch supporter of a continental free trade agreement embodied in the blueprint of a Free Trade Area of the Americas (FTAA) to continue the wave after establishing NAFTA (the North American Free Trade Area) with Canada and Mexico in 1994. Negotiations progressed by the turn of the twenty-first century but the initiative eventually faded away and was finally buried at the Mar del Plata Summit of the Americas held in 2005. The apparent failure of a continental agreement did not mean a retreat of US status in the region, but rather a reconfiguration of the US relationship with Latin America through bilateral relations in the form of free trade agreements signed with Chile, Peru, Panama, and

Colombia. The United States became a kind of expendable actor, "respectful of desires for Latin American emancipation from a heavily burdened past with America, but willing to strike strong bilateral relationships where these are sought" (Chipman and Lockhart Smith, 2009: 88).

The United States pursued then a sort of "coalition of the willing," embarking on close relations with several Latin American countries, including free trade agreements like the Central American Free Trade Area + Dominican Republic (CAFTA+D), including Costa Rica, El Salvador, Guatemala, Honduras, Nicaragua, and the Dominican Republic, signed in 2005. Due to its less assertive reach, other great powers have increased their presence in the region, first and foremost China, and to a lesser extent, Russia. Thus, even before the Trump Administration, there has been a clear breakdown of the inter-American ideological consensus in the 2000s. This was characterized by heterogeneity in economic policies, a wave of "new left" administrations in several important South American countries that was reversed in the last few years, a relatively low effectiveness of the OAS, and an attempt to balance, at least in ideological terms, the US preponderance in the region by establishing South-South relations with emerging powers. Moreover, the United States has securitized its relations with the Latin American countries, by focusing upon the war on drugs and the war on terrorism, even more so since the 9/11 attacks in 2001. Paradoxically, Latin America's contemporary domestic violence directly relates to the United States, which remains the most important market for illegal drugs from the region, and its main supplier of arms, for both licit and illicit actors (see Andreas and Duran Martinez, 2015: 377; and Mares, 2016).

Security Initiatives of Latin American Countries

During the last forty years, there has been an increasing role for mechanisms of regional security governance in the Americas. The first milestone was the establishment of the bilateral nuclear safeguards regime between Argentina and Brazil, the Argentine-Brazilian Agency for the Control and Accounting of Nuclear Materials (ABACC). It paved the way for Argentina and Brazil to ratify the Latin American agreement that established a Nuclear Free Zone (Tlatelolco Treaty) and to join the Non-Proliferation Treaty (NPT) in the mid-1990s (see Lacovsky, 2021; and Oelsner, 2005). The second milestone was the establishment of the UN Stabilization Mission in Haiti in 2004 (MINUSTAH), the first Latin American peacekeeping mission under the umbrella of the United Nations, which was set under Brazilian leadership and with the participation of both Argentina and Brazil (see Sotomayor, 2014: 127–159). Third, counterterrorism became another field for international security cooperation involving American countries. Argentina became a target of transnational terrorist attacks with the bombings of the Israeli Embassy in Buenos Aires in 1992 and the Jewish Community Center in 1994. These acts paved the way for the establishment in the late 1990s of the Inter-American Committee against Terrorism (CICTE) within the OAS, and the signing of the Inter-American Convention against Terrorism in 2002. This convention followed the events of 9/11 in 2001, which changed the whole US perspective on security issues, including its approach toward the region (see Galicki, 2005). Finally, Brazil sponsored the creation of the South American Defense Council (SDC) in 2009 within UNASUR, aiming at developing a common regional security framework. The SDC followed the successful mediation of UNASUR in managing the Andean diplomatic crisis of 2008, which involved Venezuela, Colombia, and Ecuador (see Medeiros Filho, 2017). In the last few years, many of these regional initiatives declined and lost their relevance, as epitomized by the gradual evanescence of UNASUR and the recent Venezuelan regime crisis of 2019–20.

New Security Threats and the Persistence of Ungoverned Spaces in the Americas

In parallel to the emergence of new security governance mechanisms, the region has confronted a different type of security dilemma, not the traditional one set by the possibility of great power intervention or interstate war. Rather, the reference is to a kind of "insecurity dilemma" set by the existence and persistence of relatively weak states with malfunctioning domestic institutions, as the paradigmatic case of Venezuela nowadays. Broadly speaking, weak states are faced "with uncontrolled borders and confronting criminal groups over the monopoly of force, control of territory, and the heart and minds of people" (Marcella, 2013: 69).

In addition, the traditional concept of security has broadened to include human security, with reference to issues such as unemployment, inequality and poverty, marginality, human rights, environmental degradations, and threats to democratic and to economic development (see Kacowicz and Mares, 2016: 26–27). Ultimately, it seems that international traditional multilateral security in the region has been more successful than its human security.[2]

There seems to be a striking contradiction between the economic growth and progress experienced in the first decade of the twenty-first century and the lack of human and physical security within many Latin American societies, as epitomized by the virulent domestic and to some extent transnational violence in the region. The macroeconomic bonanza of the 2000s that brought economic benefits did not trickle down to generate stability and security for the population as a whole, so levels of domestic violence and persistent situations of political disillusion lingered. This paradox was echoed in Heraldo Muñoz's sharp query about the Latin American reality: How to explain the increase of crime and violence, with more than one hundred thousand homicides per year, concomitant to the largest economic growth experienced in four decades? (Muñoz quoted in Cubel, 2016, 5). Among the possible explanations, Cubel refers to the impunity in the investigation of crimes in the region, failures of the education system, crises of the family as an institution, failure of the judicial system (perhaps with the exceptions of Chile and Uruguay), widespread corruption, socioeconomic inequality, and the proliferation of transnational crime (Cubel, 2016: 15; see also Bergman, 2006).

Back in the late 1990s, Andrew Hurrell (1998: 530) argued that one of the unintended consequences of regionalization and economic integration in Latin America would be that states in the region might become more vulnerable to instability across their borders. Hurrell warned us that these new security threats were directly related to state weaknesses and the failure to provide public goods such as a modicum of minimum order (Hurrell, 1998: 541). At the same time, he avoided the blatant simplification of confronting traditional versus new security threats; instead, we should address the multiplicity and overlapping forms of violence existing in the region (see Hurrell, 1998: 543). In this context, we should refer specifically to the lingering

---

[2] We thank Rut Diamint for her insights on this point.

issue of ungoverned spaces and areas of limited statehood in the Americas.

Ungoverned Spaces in the Americas

Among the security issues that have persisted in Latin America, conspicuous is the issue of areas of limited statehood or ungoverned spaces in the region, which range from urban to thinly populated areas in the borderlands (Trinkunas and Clunan, 2016: 102). These ungoverned spaces are areas where the state's presence is limited, or it lacks the capacity and/or the political willingness to exercise effective control. Consequently, these ungoverned spaces are inhabited by VNSAs that aim at filling the vacuum left by the withering states. Such vacuums are of considerable significance regarding borders and borderlands that are problematic ungoverned spaces in themselves, due to the weak (if not nonexistent) presence of the national governments (Trinkunas and Clunan, 2016: 103). Several examples include the TBA of Argentina, Brazil, and Paraguay; the Northern Triangle of Central America; and many of the Colombian borders (see Chapter 4 for a detailed description of these borderlands).

Criminal groups that hold some territorial control have become an integral part of the Latin American security landscape. There is an array of VNSAs scattered across the continent, including the First Commando of the Capital of Brazil (PCC), the Shining Path of Peru (*Sendero Luminoso*), the FARC (*Fuerzas Armadas Revolucionarias de Colombia*) and the United Self-Defense Forces of Colombia (*Autodefensas Unidas de Colombia*), Paraguay's People's Army, Venezuela's *Cartel de los Soles*, the *Zetas*, the *Maras*, and the Sinaloa Cartel in Mexico and the Northern Triangle. Some of these VNSAs, like the Shining Path in Peru and the FARC in Colombia, sustained radical ideological positions before becoming involved in illicit and illegal activities, mimicking transnational criminal organizations.

All of these non-state actors have been involved, to variegated degrees, in criminal activities such as terrorism, drug trafficking, human trafficking, and mass killings, both within countries and across borders. These VNSAs have undermined Latin American states' legitimacy vis-à-vis their citizens, due to their inability to keep a minimum level of public security, such as a modicum of public order or reducing the scope of homicides. In some cases, these VNSAs became more powerful than the states they confronted, keeping slices of territories under their control. For instance, in the not-so-distant past, the FARC exercised control over wide portions of Colombian territory. Similarly, the *Maras* reigned in Central American urban landscapes; the Paraguay People's Army terrorized farmers and landlords; the PCC was involved in massive outbreaks of violence against public institutions in Sào Paulo, Brazil; and many drug organizations in Mexico still terrorize and undermine local politics in several Mexican states (see Idler, 2018; Penski, 2018; and Williams, 2016). Let us turn now to a more detailed description of the reality of transnational crime in the Americas.

The Reality of Transnational Crime in the Americas

Traditional organized crime in Latin America, both domestic and transnational, conjures up images of menacing drug cartels, violent gangs, arms smugglers, shadowy hacker networks, and traffickers in women and children. Yet, there is a lack of clarity about the phenomena of organized crime and transnational crime (see Muggah and Diniz, 2013: 3; Sampó and Troncoso, 2017; and Williams, 2016).

We refer to transnational organized crime (TOC) with a focus on drug and arms trafficking, as well as human trafficking and smuggling, showing tangible points of origin, transit, and end-use across the region, especially in the Andean region, the Amazon, and the TBA. By contrast, money laundering, cybercrime, fraud, and extortion are conducted extraterritorially, without crossing borders physically in the region, or even outside the region, as a form of international or even "networked global crime" (see Muggah and Diniz, 2013: 10; and Shelley, 2014: 10). For the purpose of this book, we are mostly interested in the former, rather than the latter, though in fact it is difficult to disentangle the physical transnational flows across an international border from the larger, transnational global networks of crime and terrorism.

Transnational organized crime networks have expanded and matured in the Americas, posing a significant threat to the Western Hemisphere as a whole. It is worth quoting the view from the National Security Council of the United States, as follows:

TOC networks – including transnational gangs – have expanded and matured, threatening the security of citizens and the stability of governments throughout the region, with direct security implications for the United States. Central America is a key area of converging threats where illicit trafficking in drugs, people, and weapons – as well as other revenue streams – fuel increased instability. Transnational crime and its accompanying violence are threatening the prosperity of some Central American states and can cost up to eight percent of their gross domestic product, according to the World Bank. The Government of Mexico is waging an historic campaign against transnational criminal organizations, many of which are expanding beyond drug trafficking into human smuggling and trafficking, weapons smuggling, bulk cash smuggling, extortion, and kidnapping for ransom. TOC in Mexico makes the U.S. border more vulnerable because it creates and maintains illicit corridors for border crossings that can be employed by other secondary criminal or terrorist actors or organization. Farther south, Colombia has achieved remarkable success in reducing cocaine production and countering illegal armed groups, such as the FARC, than engage in TOC. Yet, with the decline of these organizations, new groups are emerging such as criminal bands known in Spanish as *Bandas Criminales*, or *BACRIM*. (NSC, 2013: 3)

In sum, TOC poses significant threats to Latin American states and therefore to national and international security in the Americas as a whole. Whereas violence produced by drug trafficking organizations (DTOs) affects local communities within their countries, it is the international and transnational links between supply and demand that provide the main incentives for the occurrence and proliferation of transnational criminal activities, such as drug and human trafficking (see Domínguez, 2018; and Kacowicz, Lacovsky, and Wajner, 2020).

Drug Trafficking
The growth of TOC in scope and scale over the last two decades relates to the expansion of drug trafficking from South America to Central America to Mexico to the United States and to Canada. Among the different types of illicit trade and transnational flows, drug trafficking has a direct impact upon political institutions, by negatively affecting the quality of governance through corruption and violence (see Andreas and Duran Martinez, 2015: 380–382; and Shelley, 2014: 12).

The drug trafficking is not merely across adjoining borders, but it is in fact transnational and global, as part of global networks reaching other illicit markets well beyond North America in Europe, Southern Africa, and East Asia. Latin American drug trafficking includes production in Bolivia, Colombia, and Peru; the widening of transit routes to encompass most coastal countries in Central and South America and the Caribbean (as well as West Africa); and persistent demand from North America, Western Europe, and Brazil. The rise of intermediate and fragmented cartels first in Colombia and then in Mexico, as well as the movement of DTOs to Bolivia, Ecuador, Argentina, and Venezuela, has yielded a contagion effect across Latin America, including Brazil, which is considered the second-largest consumer of cocaine in the world (Muggah and Diniz, 2013: 5; see also Clavel, 2017).

Drug trafficking has posed severe security and political challenges for Latin American countries as it is a phenomenon usually associated with violence and corruption (see Mares, 2019; Shelley, 2014; and Williams, 2016: 257). Among the main drug providers, Paraguay is the major producer of marijuana while the Andean countries such as Colombia, Peru, and Bolivia are the leading cocaine exporters, in addition to the production of other drugs such as heroin and, amphetamines (see UNODC, 2016a: 37).

Drug production in Latin America and the US demand for it are mutually intertwined. Colombia is the central node in the cocaine trade, insofar as it produces about 90 percent of the cocaine trafficked to the United States (Williams, 2016: 269). The Central American-Mexican corridor links Colombia to the United States through the domain of Mexican cartels. As a matter of fact, the US demand for cocaine has never stopped, despite the many attempts made to eradicate the cultivation of the coca and the escalating "war" against drug cartels in Colombia and Mexico. In this regard, the seizures of cocaine in the United States in 2009–14 were around 15 percent of the cocaine's seizure worldwide (UNODC, 2016a: 37).

According to the UNODC report on drugs, heroin and morphine seizures grew from around four tons per year during 1998–2008 to about seven tons per year between 2009 and 2014 (UNODC, 2016a: viii). The same report highlights that the amount of cocaine seized doubled in South America between 1998 and 2014. Moreover, between 2009 and 2014, Colombia accounted for about 56 percent of all the cocaine seizures in South America (more than a third of global cocaine seizures). Colombia was followed by Ecuador (10 percent), Brazil (7 percent), Bolivia (7 percent), Peru (7 percent), and Venezuela (6 percent) (UNODC, 2016a: 37).

Drug trafficking has exacerbated tensions in the already complicated relationships between Latin American countries and the United States (see Andreas and Duran Martinez, 2015: 377; Mares, 2016). While the United States still embraces the criminalization of drugs under the banner of the War on Drugs, some dissenting Latin American voices were raised against the US policy of militarization of the struggle against drugs. In this regard, in 2009, former presidents Fernando Henrique Cardoso (Brazil), César Gaviria (Colombia), and Ernesto Zedillo (Mexico) established the Latin American Commission on Drugs and Democracy as an alternative political initiative. This initiative aimed at overcoming the traditional paradigm that securitized the war against drugs in the form of "prohibitionist policies based on the eradication of production and on the disruption of drug flows as well as on the criminalization of consumption," which have not yielded the expected positive results (Latin American Commission on Drugs and Democracy, 2009: 5).

Uruguay has become the first Latin American country to legalize marijuana in 2013, sustaining a progressive vision according to which drug consumers should not be criminalized (see Walsh and Ramsey, 2016). Similarly, Mexican President López Obrador has initially suggested an alternative path against drug trafficking, insisting on *"abrazos, no balazos"* (hugs, not gunfire), though the results have been far from successful or decisive. He has pledged to alleviate poverty as a way to resolve the Mexican crisis of violence, and he has opened the door to consider legalizing drugs. Mexico had already decriminalized personal possession of small amounts of marijuana during the presidency of Peña Nieto (see Sandin and McCormick, 2019).

Arms Trafficking

Unlike drug trafficking and human smuggling and trafficking, arms trafficking carries immediate security implications, in the traditional sense, by directly contributing to the prevalent violence in the region (see Andreas and Duna Martinez, 2015: 377; Davis, 2006: 178; and Stohl and Tuttle, 2008). In its report on Latin America for the year 2015, the United Nations Office on Drugs and Crime informed that, "Annual seizures of over ten thousand firearms were reported per year by Brazil, Colombia, Iraq, and Mexico" (UNODC, 2015: 18). The largest number of handguns seized was reported in Argentina, Brazil, Colombia, El Salvador, Guatemala, and Mexico (UNODC, 2015: 16).

Mexico accounts for the country with the largest ammunition seizures in the period 2010–13 with about twelve million rounds (UNODC, 2015: 26). In terms of transnational arms trafficking, the flows between the United States and Mexico and among the Northern Triangle countries and other Central American countries are the most salient, as an ominous reminder of the large number of weapons that remained in the region after the end of its civil wars (see Stohl and Tuttle, 2008).

In addition to the US-Mexican border and the Central American region, the illicit small arms trade in Latin America is thriving in areas such as the TBA of Argentina, Brazil, and Paraguay, and across the Colombian borders. Arms trafficking relates to drugs trafficking. Illicit arms trade is a conventional way of paying for the drugs for DTOs as well as gangs. Researchers have identified thirty-seven trafficking routes of small arms from Panama into Colombia, twenty-six from Ecuador, twenty-one from Venezuela, and fourteen from Brazil (see Muggah and Diniz, 2013; Stohl and Tuttle, 2008; and Williams, 2016: 268). Overall, the United States remains the major provider and source of arms trafficking for Mexico and Central America (see Felbab-Brown, 2017b).

Human Trafficking and Human Smuggling
Human trafficking is another major illicit transnational activity that has spread in the Americas, as related to the opportunities created by the global economy (see Shelley, 2010: 38). Human trafficking is defined as

the recruitment, transfer, harboring or receipt of persons, by means of the threat or use of force or other forms of coercion, of abduction, of fraud, of deception, of the abuse of power or a position of vulnerability or of the giving or receiving of payments or benefits to achieve the consent of a person having control over another person, for the purpose of exploitation. (Palermo Protocol 2000, quoted in Simmons, Lloyd, and Stewart, 2018: 251; see also Shelley, 2010: 3)

It is important to differentiate between human trafficking and human smuggling, since these two types of transnational crime are often intertwined. Human trafficking involves exploiting men, women, or children for the purposes of forced labor or commercial sexual exploitation. Conversely, human smuggling involves the provision of a service – typically, transportation and/or fraudulent documents – to persons willing, on a voluntary basis, to gain illegal entry into a foreign country as irregular or illegal migrants (see Shelley, 2010: 8). Yet, in the tragic realities of the Americas, what starts out as human smuggling might degenerate very quickly into human trafficking.

The 2014 UNODC Global Report on Human Trafficking argues that the main cause of cross-border trafficking in Latin America relates to the exponential growth in the level of organized crime, both domestic and transnational. In other words, the more the origin countries are affected by domestic violence and organized crime, the more outwards trafficking there is from those countries toward other destinations. In the Americas, the movement has been essentially from South America and especially from Central America through Mexico to the United States. Central American and Caribbean victims of human trafficking have been identified in the United States, Canada, Japan, South America, and the European Union just to mention a few countries and regions. Moreover, these extra-regional flows are accompanied by a large number of Central American and Caribbean victims within the same region (see UNODC, 2014: 49).

Venezuela and Belize have the worst record in terms of human trafficking. Most recently, we have seen the particular case of millions of Venezuelans leaving their country and looking for refuge and asylum in other countries, becoming objects of human smuggling and victims of human trafficking. In general, trafficking of persons and human smuggling take place from the poorer countries toward richer neighboring countries. For example, Bolivians are trafficked to Argentina, Brazil, and Chile, and Paraguay; Paraguayans and Peruvians are trafficked to Argentina and Chile; and Central Americans via Mexico to the United States (see US State Department, 2019).

Explaining the Reality of Peaceful Borders and Illicit Transnational Flows in the Americas

To assess the three hypotheses presented in Chapter 2, we assembled two tables (Tables 3.1 and 3.2) that summarize the relevant empirical information concerning the presence (or absence) of illicit transnational flows in the Americas with reference to drug trafficking, human trafficking, arms trafficking, and transborder terrorism, across

Table 3.1 *Border dyads and degree of peace, border regimes, and freedom of movement across borders in the Americas*

Border dyad	Diplomatic relations/peace	Fortified borders	Border regime	Freedom of movement?
US-Canada	Stable peace	No	Integrated	Yes
US-Mexico	Stable peace	Partly (about 1/3)	Integrated	No
Mexico-Belize	Stable peace	No	Interdependent	Yes (except the area of Corozal)
Mexico-Guatemala	Stable peace	No	Interdependent	Yes (after 2008)
Belize-Guatemala	Negative peace	No	Coexisting	No
Guatemala-Honduras	Stable peace	No	Integrated	Yes
Guatemala-El Salvador	Stable peace	No	Integrated	Yes
Salvador-Honduras	Stable peace	No	Integrated	Yes
Honduras-Nicaragua	Stable peace	No	Integrated	Yes
Nicaragua-Costa Rica	Negative peace	No	Coexisting	No
Costa Rica-Panama	Stable peace	No	Interdependent	Yes (after 2013)
Panama-Colombia	Stable peace	No	Interdependent	No
Colombia-Venezuela	Negative peace	No	Coexisting	Yes, with sporadic closures
Venezuela-Guyana	Negative peace	No	Coexisting	No
Guyana-Suriname	Negative peace	No	Coexisting	No
Colombia-Brazil	Stable peace	No	Interdependent	Yes

Table 3.1 (*cont.*)

Border dyad	Diplomatic relations/peace	Fortified borders	Border regime	Freedom of movement?
Venezuela-Brazil	Stable peace	No	Integrated	Yes
Guyana-Brazil	Stable peace	No	Interdependent	No
Suriname-Brazil	Stable peace	No	Interdependent	No
Colombia-Ecuador	Negative peace	No	Integrated	Yes
Colombia-Peru	Stable peace	No	Integrated	Yes
Peru-Ecuador	Stable peace (after Peace Treaty of 1998)	No	Integrated	Yes
Peru-Brazil	Stable peace	No	Integrated	Yes
Peru-Bolivia	Stable peace	No	Integrated	Yes
Peru-Chile	Negative peace	No	Interdependent	Yes
Bolivia-Brazil	Stable	No	Integrated	Yes
Bolivia-Chile	Formal rivalry, no diplomatic relations yet	No	Coexisting	Yes
Argentina-Chile	Stable peace	No	Integrated	Yes
Bolivia-Paraguay	Stable peace	No	Integrated	Yes
Paraguay-Brazil	Stable peace	No	Integrated	Yes
Argentina-Bolivia	Stable peace	No	Integrated	Yes
Argentina-Paraguay	Stable peace	No	Integrated	Yes
Argentina-Brazil	Stable peace	No	Integrated	Yes

Table 3.1 (*cont.*)

Border dyad	Diplomatic relations/peace	Fortified borders	Border regime	Freedom of movement?
Argentina-Uruguay	Stable peace	No	Integrated	Yes
Uruguay-Brazil	Stable peace	No	Integrated	Yes
Dominican Republic-Haiti	Negative peace	No	Coexisting	No

their thirty-six land border dyads for the years 2010–15. We gathered information from open sources such as the United Nations Office on Drugs and Crime (UNODC), the US State Department, regional organizations from the Americas, as well as several Latin American sources in English and Spanish.

The data set relevant to the period 2010–15 refers to the following indicators:

(1) The existence of diplomatic relations and degrees of peace, ranging from negative peace to stable peace and pluralistic security communities;
(2) The degree of openness of borders, defined in terms of the regulations pertaining to the freedom of movement of people and goods across the international borders;
(3) The type of border regime, ranging from closed and alienated borders through integrated ones;
(4) The presence (or absence) of transnational illicit activities across the borders in the Americas that includes: (a) drug trafficking; (b) transborder flows of illicit migrants (human smuggling) and human trafficking; (c) arms trafficking; and (d) transborder terrorism and transnational guerrilla activities.

In addition to Tables 3.1 and 3.2, we compiled another table (Table 3.3) that refers to the rankings of all the relevant countries in the Americas: Human Development Index (HDI) (2014); Corruption Perception Index (2015); Gross Domestic Product (2014); Fragile State Index (2015); and

Table 3.2 *Illicit transnational flows across land borders in the Americas*

Border dyad	Drug trafficking[*]	Human smuggling and trafficking[**]	Arms trafficking[***]	Terrorism[****]
US-Canada	Yes	No	No	No
US-Mexico	Yes	Yes	Yes	No
Mexico-Belize	Yes	Yes	No	No
Mexico-Guatemala	Yes	Yes	Yes	No
Belize-Guatemala	No	Yes	No	No
Guatemala-Honduras	Yes	Yes	Yes	No
Guatemala-El Salvador	Yes	Yes	Yes	No
Salvador-Honduras	Yes	Yes	Yes	No
Honduras-Nicaragua	Yes	Yes	Yes	No
Nicaragua-Costa Rica	Yes	Yes	No	No
Costa Rica-Panama	Yes	Yes	No	No
Panama-Colombia	Yes	Yes	Yes	No
Colombia-Venezuela	Yes	Yes	Yes	Yes (until 2016)
Venezuela-Guyana	No	Yes	No	No
Guyana-Suriname	No	Yes	No	No
Colombia-Brazil	Yes	No	Yes	No
Venezuela-Brazil	No	No	Yes	No
Guyana-Brazil	No	Yes	Yes	No
Suriname-Brazil	Yes	Yes	Yes	No
Colombia-Ecuador	Yes	Yes	Yes	Yes (until 2016)
Colombia-Peru	Yes	No	Yes	Yes (until 2016)
Peru-Ecuador	Yes	Yes	Yes	No
Peru-Brazil	Yes	No	Yes	No
Peru-Bolivia	Yes	Yes	No	No
Peru-Chile	Yes	Yes	No	No
Bolivia-Brazil	Yes	Yes	Yes	No
Bolivia-Chile	Yes	Yes	No	No
Argentina-Chile	No	No	No	No
Bolivia-Paraguay	Yes	Yes	No	No
Paraguay-Brazil	Yes	Yes	Yes	Yes

Table 3.2 (*cont.*)

Border dyad	Drug trafficking	Human smuggling and trafficking	Arms trafficking	Terrorism
Argentina-Bolivia	Yes	Yes	No	No
Argentina-Paraguay	Yes	Yes	No	Yes
Argentina-Brazil	No	No	Yes	No
Argentina-Uruguay	No	No	No	No
Uruguay-Brazil	No	No	No	No
Dominican Republic-Haiti	Yes	Yes	Yes	No

[*] Based mainly on *World Drugs Report* 2016a. See also Briscoe 2008; Cuevas and Demombynes 2009; Dudley 2010; Garzón and Olson 2013; and Trejos-Rosero 2015. We include here as transnational drug trafficking flows those borders that are highlighted in at least one of these reports as having a significant level of drug trafficking along the years 2010–15, based on drugs seizures and police estimations.

^{**} Based mainly on *UNODC Global Report on Trafficking in-Persons*, 2015; *US Department of State Trafficking in Persons Report* 2015. See also Garzón and Olson 2013; Kessler 2011. We include here as transnational human trafficking and smuggling flows across borders that are highlighted in at least one of these reports along the years 2005–15, based on captures of victims (including illegal migrants) in the destination country, denunciations at the origin country, and other estimations.

^{***} Based mainly on *UNODC Firearms within Central America Report* 2012; *UNODC Study on Firearms* 2015; *Small Weapons Survey* 2012. See also Briscoe 2008; Garzón and Olson 2013; Milian 2008; and Millet 2007. We include here as arms trafficking transnational flows those borders that are highlighted in at least one of these reports as having a significant level of arms trafficking during the years 2005–15, based on arms seizures, and different police estimations.

^{****} Based mainly on *US State Department Country Report on Terrorism* (reports between 2010 and 2015). See also Bagley 2008; Briscoe 2008; and Mejías 2014. As in most reports, we include guerrilla acts and all related terrorist activities, such as kidnappings, presence of terrorist bases beyond the borders, and fundraising. We particularly identify the Colombian spillover effects of the FARC on neighboring countries, at least until 2016, as well as the spillover effects of groups such as Shining Path in Peru. We also identify parts of the TBA area, among Argentina, Paraguay, and Brazil, for its suspect transnational terrorist activities.

Table 3.3 *Ranking of relevant Western Hemisphere countries (with land borders), with respect to political and socioeconomic indicators*

Country	HDI (2014)[*]	GDP (2014)[**]	Fragile State Index (2015)[***]	Corruption Index (2015)[****]	Freedom House's Annual Report (2015)[*****]
Argentina	40	24	37	107	2
Belize	101	173	62	No data	1.5
Bolivia	119	98	102	99	3
Brazil	75	7	55	76	2
Canada	9	10	10	9	1
Chile	42	42	28	23	1
Colombia	97	32	117	83	3.5
Costa Rica	69	82	36	40	1
Dominican Republic	101	73	74	103	2.5
Ecuador	88	63	93	107	3
El Salvador	116	106	76	72	2.5
Guatemala	128	76	114	123	3.5
Guyana	124	163	71	119	2.5
Haiti	163	142	167	158	5
Honduras	131	110	102	112	4
Mexico	74	15	79	95	3
Nicaragua	125	135	106	130	3.5
Panama	60	88	47	72	2
Paraguay	112	101	75	130	3
Peru	84	52	80	88	2.5
Suriname	103	153	69	88	2
USA.	8	1	20	16	1
Uruguay	52	77	23	21	1
Venezuela	71	31	104	158	5

[*] HDI: Human Development Index ranges from 1 to 188 (1 = the most developed country, in terms of human development).

[**] GDP: Gross domestic product ranges from 1 to 185 (1 = the richest country in the world).

[***] Fragile State Index ranges from 1 to 178. We have reversed the order of the original index, so 1 = the most sustainable country in terms of governance and political development, to fit the comparison with the other indicators in the Table.

[****] Corruption Perception Index ranges from 1 to 167 (1 = the least corrupted country in the world).

[*****] Freedom House's Annual Report: Each country's score is based on two numerical ratings from 1 to 7 regarding political rights and civil liberties; with 1 representing the most free, and 7 the least free.

Freedom House's annual report on political rights and civil liberties (2015). These indicators are reliable proxies to assess the relevance of Hypotheses 2 and 3. Thus, we measure the degree of governance, institutional strength, and political willingness of the neighboring states in controlling their peaceful borders by the relevant indexes dealing with corruption, fragility of states, and political rights and civil liberties. Similarly, we assess the prevalent socioeconomic conditions of the bordering states by referring to their respective human development and economic indicators.

The contiguous land borders in the Americas include the following dyads:[3] (1) US-Canada; (2) US-Mexico; (3) Mexico-Belize; (4) Mexico-Guatemala; (5) Belize-Guatemala; (6) Guatemala-Honduras; (7) Guatemala-El Salvador; (8) Salvador-Honduras; (9) Honduras-Nicaragua; (10) Nicaragua-Costa Rica; (11) Costa Rica-Panama; (12) Panama-Colombia; (13) Colombia-Venezuela; (14) Venezuela-Guyana; (15) Guyana-Suriname; (16) Colombia-Brazil; (17) Venezuela-Brazil; (18) Guyana-Brazil; (19) Suriname-Brazil; (20) Colombia-Ecuador; (21) Colombia-Peru; (22) Peru-Ecuador; (23) Peru-Brazil; (24) Peru-Bolivia; (25) Peru-Chile; (26) Bolivia-Brazil; (27) Bolivia-Chile; (28) Argentina-Chile; (29) Bolivia-Paraguay; (30) Paraguay-Brazil; (31) Argentina-Bolivia; (32) Argentina-Paraguay; (33) Argentina-Brazil; (34) Argentina-Uruguay; (35) Uruguay-Brazil; and (36) Dominican Republic-Haiti.

Table 3.1 summarizes the coding of the relevant thirty-six land borders in the Americas, referring to the degree of peace, the type of border regime, and the freedom of movement across borders. This is usually regulated by regional agreements, such as NAFTA and nowadays USMCA (in North America), SICA (the Central American Integration System), CAN (the Community of Andean Nations), and MERCOSUR (in South America).

Table 3.2 summarizes the illicit transnational flows taking place across these land peaceful borders in the Americas, based on a large data and indicators compiled for the years 2010–15. We assess the presence or absence of the most significant transnational illicit activities, including drug trafficking, human smuggling and trafficking, arms trafficking, and terrorist and guerrilla flows.

In addition to these two tables, we compiled a ranking of the twenty-four relevant Western Hemisphere countries that share land borders.

---

[3] While compiling the Tables, we exclude the Caribbean islands, with the exception of the land border between the Dominican Republic and Haiti.

This was done in terms of (a) socioeconomic indicators (as measured by the HDI and the GDP of each relevant country); and (b) levels of governance and institutionalization (as measured by the fragility of states index, the corruption index, and Freedom House's index on democracy and civil liberties). These are all proxy indicators that help us to refer to the different variables mentioned in the three hypotheses.

From the dataset presented in these three tables, we evaluate and test our three hypotheses, as follows:

Hypothesis 1: The Degree of Physical and Institutional Openness of the Peaceful Borders

Out of the thirty-six land borders, we identify twenty dyads of neighboring states characterized by border integration, as part of a subregional border regime, usually under the umbrella of integration frameworks such as NAFTA (today recalled the United States-Mexico-Canada Agreement or USMCA), SICA in Central America, and CAN and MERCOSUR in South America. In seventeen out of twenty of these cases, we trace illicit transnational flows in several issue areas (the exceptions being the Peruvian-Brazilian border dealing only with drug trafficking, the Argentine-Brazilian border dealing only with arms trafficking, and the US-Canadian border dealing with drug trafficking). Moreover, in all the nine dyads of interdependent border regimes across neighboring countries, we identify instances of illicit transnational flows (but only human trafficking and human smuggling in the cases of Mexico-Belize and Guyana-Brazil).

The incident of transnational terrorism is relatively low in the Americas: of the twenty cases, we trace only five (Colombia-Ecuador, Colombia-Peru, Colombia-Venezuela, Paraguay-Brazil, and Argentina-Paraguay). In the case of the Colombian borders, the instances of transborder terrorism have diminished since 2016 with the dismantlement of the FARC following the Peace Treaty, though the ELN and some FARC renegades are still active at the borderlands (see Sullivan and Beittel, 2016).

Out of the thirty-six land borders in the Americas, the only fortified border belongs to about one-third of the US-Mexican frontier, despite the fact that the two countries sustain a high level of peace (stable peace if not a security community), and that they are economically interdependent. Yet, the fortified border has not deterred the occurrence and proliferation of transnational illicit activities (drugs trafficking, human smuggling, and human trafficking from Mexico to the United States, and arms trafficking from the United States to Mexico). It seems that formidable physical barriers are not an obstacle for illicit transnational flows, provided there is a strong economic incentive for the VNSAs involved in criminal activities to reap high benefits from these flows. Quite the opposite; the closeness of the borders might exponentially increase the economic benefits for transnational criminal groups to penetrate the borderlands, engaging in human smuggling and trafficking, as well as arms trafficking (see Felbab-Brown, 2017b).

As for the freedom of movement of citizens across the borders, we identify that twenty-six of thirty-six of the land borders in the Americas are soft and open in terms of human transit, with the exceptions of US-Mexico (despite of NAFTA/USMCA), Belize-Guatemala, Nicaragua-Costa Rica, Panama-Colombia, Venezuela-Guyana, Guyana-Suriname, Guyana-Brazil, Suriname-Brazil, and Dominican Republic-Haiti. The Colombian-Venezuelan border, though generally open, has been sporadically closed due to the deteriorating relations between the two countries, as well as the recent economic and political implosion of the Venezuelan state, leading to the massive exodus of millions of Venezuelans who search for refuge and asylum in neighboring countries.

As expected, we identify a positive correlation between the freedom of movement of peoples and goods and the parallel incident of illicit transnational flows (twenty-four of twenty-seven), with the glaring exceptions of the borders of US-Canada, Argentina-Chile, and Argentina-Uruguay, since these dyads involve economically developed or relatively developed countries, with no significant economic asymmetries between them. In areas where the border regime is very open and porous, like the Northern Triangle of Central America, we can expect a significant occurrence and proliferation of illicit transnational activities, including drug trafficking, human trafficking, and arms trafficking.[4] Moreover, in the nine cases of restricted movement of persons and goods across borders, we still find illicit transnational flows across all of the borders involving these dyads, with an emphasis upon human trafficking and smuggling, in the cases of Belize-Guatemala, Nicaragua-Costa Rica,

---

[4] Interview with Carlos Raúl Morales, former Guatemalan Foreign Minister, Jerusalem, Israel, November 29, 2016.

Panama-Colombia, Venezuela-Guyana, and Guyana-Brazil. In sum, we corroborate Hypothesis 1 regarding most of the land peaceful borders in the Americas.

Hypothesis 2: The Degree of Governance, Institutional Strength, and Political Willingness

Based on the data drawn from the Fragile State Index of the Fund for Peace (2015) and the Corruption Perceptions Index of Transparency International (2015) recorded in Table 3.3, we compiled a short list of relatively strong states in the Americas: Canada, the United States, Costa Rica, Chile, and Uruguay. In a second category of relatively strong, or functioning, states we find cases with fair rankings in terms of democracy and sustainability, but a high level of corruption, such as Argentina, Brazil, and Panama. Accordingly, the border dyads including strong and relatively strong (or functioning) countries are far apart: US-Canada, Panama-Costa Rica, Argentina-Chile, Argentina-Brazil, Argentina-Uruguay, and Uruguay-Brazil.

From the data presented in Table 3.3, we learn that weak states predominate in most of the Americas, particularly in Central America and the Caribbean: Guatemala, Honduras, El Salvador, Nicaragua, Guyana, Suriname, Paraguay, the Dominican Republic, Haiti, and Belize. In a different category of weak states, we find a number of South American countries with high economic potential and rich in natural resources, but with high levels of corruption: Colombia, Venezuela, Ecuador, Bolivia, Paraguay, and to a lesser extent Peru. A special category by itself is Mexico, a relatively dysfunctional state rather than a weak one. Mexico is a peculiar case since it has relatively strong economic and political institutions, but it is marred in corruption and has significant variance in terms of governance across its large territory and distinct borders with the United States and its Central American neighbors (see Trejo and Ley, 2020).

When we assess the data presented in Tables 3.2 and Tables 3.3, we find that all sixteen dyads involving weak states experience a large number of illicit transnational flows. Therefore, we corroborate Hypothesis 2 in the Americas. In the next chapter, we examine in detail the cases of Mexico (regarding its common border with the United States), the Northern Triangle countries, and Paraguay in its borders' interactions with its stronger neighbors, Argentina and Brazil in the TBA area.

By contrast, by perusing Tables 3.2 and 3.3, we find a significant correlation between dyads involving strong and functioning states and the relative absence of illicit transnational flows. This includes US-Canada (with an incidence of drug trafficking and very low arms trafficking, see details in Chapter 4), Argentina-Chile, Argentina-Brazil, Argentina-Uruguay, and Uruguay-Brazil. In this regard, the Costa Rican-Panamanian border might be the exception to the rule, with clear evidence of drug trafficking and human trafficking.

Hypothesis 3: The Prevalent Socioeconomic Conditions of the Neighboring States

There is a significant correlation between the presence of weak states with poor economic conditions and socioeconomic, as well as political, underdevelopment, and the occurrence and proliferation of illicit transnational flows. Thus, we find that all the dyads involving underdeveloped countries (with low rankings of HDI and of GDP) experienced drug trafficking, human smuggling and trafficking, and arms trafficking. This includes the dyads of Dominican Republic-Haiti, Guatemala-Honduras, Guatemala-El Salvador, Salvador-Honduras, Honduras-Nicaragua, Guyana-Suriname, and Bolivia-Paraguay.

Turning to socioeconomic disparities, we also find a positive correlation between asymmetrical socioeconomic conditions across the borders and the proliferation of illicit transnational flows, as in the cases of US-Mexico, Mexico-Belize, Mexico-Guatemala, Nicaragua-Costa Rica, Venezuela-Guyana, Suriname-Brazil, Bolivia-Brazil, Paraguay-Brazil, Argentina-Bolivia, and Argentina-Paraguay. In cases of socioeconomic disparities across countries, human trafficking proliferates even more than drug trafficking and arms trafficking. In sum, we corroborate Hypothesis 3 by the evidence summarized in Tables 3.2 and 3.3.

By contrast, from the perusal of these two tables we find a very short list of neighboring countries with sustainable and developed socioeconomic conditions: US-Canada, Costa Rica-Panama, Argentina-Chile, Argentina-Uruguay, and Uruguay-Brazil. Not surprisingly, these dyads have experienced less illicit transnational flows across their borders, if any. These bordering countries tend to be relatively strong and developed countries, not only in economic terms but also along political and institutional lines, showing both capabilities and political willingness to control their peaceful borders.

Conclusions

As Maiah Jaskoski, Arturo C. Sotomajor, and Harold A. Trinkunas argued in their excellent collection on border politics in the Western Hemisphere, despite the peaceful relations among the American countries, their borders remain "sites and sources of both tensions and harmonies" (Jaskoski et al., 2015b: 205–206). These borders are affected by the governance of the bordering states, and they shape and are influenced by the population of the borderlands, which might be interdependent across their respective national boundaries.

The existence of peaceful borders is a permissive condition for the occurrence and proliferation of illicit transnational flows, including transnational crime and to a much lesser extent terrorism, though it does not explain the variance in the occurrence of these illicit flows. In other words, the empirical test of the three hypotheses teaches us about the relevance of variables such as the degree of physical and institutional openness of the peaceful borders, the level of governance and institutionalization of the neighboring states, as well as the relevance of political economy indicators in the Americas.

We register three significant transitions from war to peace that took place in the Americas since the end of the Cold War. First, there was the end of the Peruvian-Ecuadorian long territorial conflict, following the war waged in 1995 and the Peace Treaty signed in 1998. Second, the civil wars in Central America that affected Nicaragua, El Salvador, Guatemala, and Honduras all ended in the early 1990s. Third, in December of 2016, the Colombian government and the FARC ratified a peace agreement ending fifty years of civil war. As expected, the softening, demilitarization, and opening of the border between Peru and Ecuador promoted transborder economic contacts between the two countries, and concomitantly, the proliferation of illicit transnational flows as well. As for the end of the civil wars in El Salvador, Guatemala, and Nicaragua, they helped to promote regional integration, but they also left an enduring and tragic legacy of violence, especially domestic, that spilled over across international borders in the form of transnational criminal activities, including arms trafficking and human smuggling and trafficking. Similarly, the demilitarization and dismantling of the FARC left a significant vacuum in the Colombian borders, soon to be replaced by other VNSAs in the form of the BACRIM.

Additionally, open regionalism and increased regional schemes (NAFTA in North America, SICA and CAFTA in Central America, and MERCOSUR and CAN in South America) have increased transnational economic flows, both licit and illicit by opening the already peaceful borders and making them softer, if not irrelevant. As Pion-Berlin (2005: 217) aptly describes, in an irony that echoes the NAFTA case, MERCOSUR's success in breaking down economic barriers among neighboring states and in notably increasing the cross-border flows of people and goods led to the proliferation of illicit transborder activities, alongside the licit ones.

As we learned from the Americas' experience, the terms of the debate as related to international security have changed and expanded beyond traditional conceptions and realities of war and peace, which are no longer relevant to the Western Hemisphere. Hence, to explain the high levels of domestic violence (including the world's worst record of homicide rates in certain countries in Central America, South America, and Mexico), we should refer to drug trafficking, organized crime, insurgency, and the legacy of civil wars. This also includes the incursion of violent transnational non-state actors across borders (see Bagley, Rosen, and Kassab, 2015; and also Mares and Kacowicz, 2016).

As for the theoretical framework suggested in Chapter 2, we corroborate the three hypotheses in the examination of the Americas in general terms, with two major qualifications. First, with respect to the first hypothesis, it is not obvious that fortified borders (the only relevant example in the Americas being that of the US-Mexican border) act always as an effective deterrent against illicit transnational borders. Second, the three hypotheses, which we frame in very general terms, are not specific enough to deal with problems of under- and over-determination regarding other historical and geopolitical particularities with reference to particular peaceful borders in the Western Hemisphere. In other words, alternative explanations, which refer to the specific characteristics of the neighboring countries and their borderlands, could also make sense of the linkages between peaceful borders and the occurrence and proliferation of transnational illicit flows. Hence, it becomes relevant to turn to particular case studies and implement the comparative approach in the next empirical chapter about the Americas.

4 | The Americas: From the US-Canadian Border to the Tri-Border Area of South America

Introduction

In this chapter, we delve into four relevant case studies from North America, Central America, and South America in order to assess the links between peaceful borders and the occurrence and proliferation of illicit transnational flows. All the borders involved are peaceful. Yet, there is an important variation across the cases in terms of historical background and trajectories, gradations of peace and integration, transition from negative peace to higher levels of peace, legacies of previous conflicts including civil wars, levels of governance and state strength, and the socioeconomic conditions of the bordering states. The cases also enhance the validity of a broader concept of security, as they illustrate the variegated nature of threats and challenges posed by violent non-state actors (VNSAs) involved in illicit transnational flows, ranging from drug trafficking to arms trafficking, human trafficking and smuggling, and to a less extent transnational terrorism.

First, we study *the North American borders* (US-Canada and US-Mexico), especially in the period since the establishment of NAFTA in 1994. Second comes *the Northern Triangle of Central America*, which includes the borders of Guatemala, El Salvador, and Honduras since the end of the civil wars in the early 1990s. Third, we turn to *the Colombian borders* with Venezuela, Ecuador, Peru, and Brazil, with a particular focus on the last twenty years that witnessed the tensions between Colombia, Ecuador, and Venezuela, and the long civil war that involved Colombia and the FARC from 1964 until November 2016. Finally, we analyze *the Tri-Border Area (TBA) of the Southern Cone of South America*, which includes the borders of Argentina, Brazil, and Paraguay, especially since the establishment of MERCOSUR in 1991.

The North American Borders

The North American region includes Canada, the United States, and Mexico, all enormous countries sharing long continental borders as well as access to both the Atlantic and Pacific Oceans. In particular, Mexico links South and Central America to both the United States and Canada, which enjoy a high standard of living and income so they are economic magnets for licit and illicit flows from Latin America (see DEA et al., 2006: 1; and Finckenauer and Albanese, 2014: 2).

The borders between Canada and the United States, as well as those between Mexico and the United States are peaceful and integrated, among highly interdependent countries. Yet, these borders vary with respect to the freedom of movement between the United States and its neighbors, as well as different socioeconomic conditions, levels of governance, and the occurrence and proliferation of illicit transnational flows (see Payan, 2014: 8).

In geopolitical terms, the United States has been the primary beneficiary of an exceptionally peaceful regional environment in North America. Thus, neither Canada nor Mexico had been rivals or enemies of the United States for over 150 years, and none of them has posed significant threats to its security (Gibler, 2012: 170). Conversely, the view from the South (from Mexico, as well as from other Central and South American countries) is less benign toward the United States, regarding it as a "difficult neighbor" if not a malign or coercive regional hegemon (Benítez Manaut, 2018: 389).

In 1994, the three countries signed the North America Free Trade Area (NAFTA) agreement, thereby upgrading and deepening their economic integration and interdependence. Later on, the terrorist attacks against the United States on September 11, 2001, further reinforced the preexisting strategic relationship among the three neighbors. Securing their borders became an obvious priority. Shortly after the attacks, the United States signed border partnership agreements with both Canada and Mexico (2001 and 2002, respectively). Following these agreements, cooperation in defense, security, intelligence, police, and border matters intensified. Mexico and the United States signed the Mérida Initiative in 2007, following the Plan Colombia model, in order to cope with drug trafficking, arms trafficking, and transnational criminal organizations originated in Colombia, Central America, and Mexico (see Benítez Manaut, 2018:

397; and Ribando Seelke, 2011). At the same time, Canada and the United States deepened their bilateral cooperation, with increasing legislative and policy convergence taking place between the two countries in the areas of security, with an emphasis upon designing a common border security perimeter (Brunet-Jailly, 2007: 13).

The US-Canadian Border

In historical terms, the US-Canadian border, formally named the *International Boundary*, at 8,891 kilometers, has been characterized as "the longest undefended border in the world" (Salter and Piché, 2001). This definition highlights the openness and porousness of the longest land border worldwide between two contiguous neighbors that enjoy a high level of peace and economic integration. In contrast to the US-Mexican case, ensuring security along the US-Canadian border had been traditionally a low political priority for both countries, at least until 2001. Yet, monitoring and securing the common border is not an easy task, since around four hundred thousand people and over $1.6 billion in goods regularly cross the border every day through more than eighty-five land entry points (see CBS News, 2018).

Despite the shared perceptions of the existence of a peaceful border and the low priority it received in terms of security, a significant policy change took place by the turn of the twenty-first century. Such change was often defined as a partial "Mexicanization of the U.S.-Canada border" (Andreas, 2005), due to the increasing securitization of the border akin to that between Mexico and the United States. The change took place in 1999, when an Algerian-born resident in Canada with a refugee status since the mid-1990s crossed the border with hidden explosives inside his automobile. That episode set an initial alarm in the United States, which was further aggravated by the aftermath of the 9/11 terrorist attacks of September 2001, leading to a further emphasis in the scope of security to be deployed at the US-Canadian border. In addition, the 9/11 Commission recommended the use of passports for those US citizens who want to enter and leave the United States through the Canadian border. This requirement has become legally binding since 2008, as Canada adopted it.

Consequently, that policy led to a change in the status of the border (from soft and open to controlled), since passport control was not required previously for US and Canadian citizens crossing the border. Still, the border is not completely controlled, as we witnessed in 2017 and 2018 regarding the flux of about twenty thousand illegal immigrants in the United States who moved to Canada. This was a clear example of a transnational illicit flow, but without involving any "malign" violent non-state actor (see Craig, 2018; Levitz, 2020; McCullogh, 2018; and US Department of Homeland Security, 2018).

Like in the Mexican case, Canada has a significant asymmetric economic relationship with the United States, being highly dependent on the US markets (Ramos, 2007: 262). Since 1994, NAFTA has increased the bilateral trade between the two countries. As of 2015, Canada was the USA's second-largest trade partner, while the United States was the main market for Canadian exports. According to the Office of the US Trade Representative, US exports were up by 179 percent and exports of services to Canada grew by 237 percent since NAFTA. Conversely, US imports from Canada went up 165 percent, and imports of services grew by 232 percent since 1993.

In the US-Canadian case, we witness an increased process of integration taking place across subregions under the rubric of "cross-border regions" (Brunet-Jailly, 2008). This concept entails that economic interdependence is higher between Canadian provinces and neighboring US states rather than within each country. Thus, economic, ecological, cultural, and even political clusters have been established between Atlantic Canada and the US Northeast Coast, or in the so-called Cascadia region in the Northwest between British Columbia (Canada) and the US states of Washington and Oregon (see Sparke, 2002).

On February 4, 2011, the Prime Minister of Canada, Stephen Harper, and the President of the United States, Barak Obama, agreed on a new long-term strategic partnership, "Beyond the Borders: A Shared Vision for Perimeter Security and Economic Competitiveness," whose core objective was to create a "perimeter approach" to security and economic competitiveness. The initiative aimed at addressing early security threats within, at, and away from borders and cross-border law enforcement, while facilitating economic growth and jobs. This Action Plan furthered the countries' cooperation at the borders and beyond, diminishing the costs of legal cross-border activity, accelerating the legitimate flow of people, goods, and services, and carrying out border functions physically away from the border itself (see Hataley-Leuprecht, 2013: 2; and US Department of Homeland Security 2011).

The US-Mexican Border

The US-Mexican border is an extraordinary example of how changing geopolitical circumstances affect the type of border and shape its transformation from open and soft to controlled and even fortified. The 3,145-kilometer border is the existing longest border between a very rich country (the United States with a GDP per capita of about US$60,000) and a middle-income one (Mexico, with a GDP per capita of about US$8,000). This represents one of the sharpest divides in average income across international borders (see Andreas and Duran Martinez, 2015: 377; Felbab-Brown, 2017b; and Vogeler, 2010: 1).

The open and porous borders between Mexico and the United States were a constant feature of these countries' relations from the beginning of the nineteenth century until the early twentieth century. In the period in which both California and Texas were part of Mexico, these areas were a permanent source of attraction for US settlers and friction with Mexico. In the case of Texas, it ultimately declared its independence and claimed to be incorporated into the United States. The case of California was rather different, as US citizens increasingly settled there, eventually leading to the American-Mexican War of 1846–8. In February 2, 1848, the Treaty of Peace, Friendship, Limits and Settlement between the United States and Mexico (the Guadalupe-Hidalgo Treaty) put an end to the state of war between the two countries, by establishing formal and recognized peaceful borders. The treaty included the forced cession of about 525,000 square miles from Mexico to the United States, including the current US states of California, Nevada, most of Arizona, about half of New Mexico, a quarter of Colorado, and small parts of Utah. After the war ended, the border remained essentially open to the movement of people and goods. There were no border guards, no customs controls, and no checkpoints (see Payan and Vazquez, 2007: 231; and Vogeler, 2010: 1).

The Mexican Revolution (1910–20), which engulfed Mexico in a gruesome civil war for a decade, proved to be a turning point for the management of the common border with the United States. Starting in the late 1910s, the United States began to control its border with Mexico, at least at major highway crossings. Gradually, the United States became actively involved in the Mexican civil war and it even sent troops in punitive missions across the border, including the invasion and occupation of Veracruz in 1914. In 1918, a simple strand-wire fence was erected on the US side of the border in Nogales, creating the first type of fortified border along the US-Mexican borderlands (Vogeler, 2010: 2). Ultimately, the end of the Mexican Revolution in 1920 rendered a drastic change in their bilateral border regime. By the mid-1920s, the United States established customs, immigration controls, and visas for Mexicans, along with the establishment of the Border Patrol (see Payan and Vazquez, 2007: 231). However, such border reform did not mitigate the porosity of the border (see Andreas, 2015). In the 1930s, alcohol smuggling from Mexico was at its peak during the years of alcohol prohibition in the United States. During the rest of the twentieth century, the US approach to its Mexican border became increasingly securitized, in its attempt to cope with increasing illicit transnational flows including the smuggling of goods, people, arms, and drug trafficking at its doorstep (see Andreas, 2015).

In contrast to such securitizing approach, which oftentimes posited the United States and Mexico in antagonistic positions, both countries grew to become significant economic partners and deeply integrated. The evolution of such integration did not take place in a vacuum. In the 1960s, Latin America embraced development ideas and embarked on ambitious infrastructure and industrial projects. Mexico was no exception, launching the *Maquiladora Program* aimed at capturing US investments to be redirected along the Mexican side of the border. Improving living and employment conditions along the border became a main goal for the Mexican government. In exchange, it granted preferential conditions to US firms that were ready to move their manufacturing production south of the border (see Bergin, Feenstra, and Hanson, 2009: 167).

From 1986 until today, the common border has become increasingly enforced, controlled, and militarized, including stronger enforcement measures. These included US patrol officers, stern border control, and the construction of a fence along one-third of the Mexican-US border that started during the Clinton and Bush Administrations and continued under the Obama Administration in 2011 (see Dunn, 1996; and Massey, Durand, and Pren, 2016: 1557). In recent years, the Trump Administration was eager to build a "wall" extending and upgrading the existing barrier (see Felbab-Brown, 2017b).

Following the launching of NAFTA in 1994, the economic ties between the neighboring countries (parallel to that of US-Canadian economic links) deepened and proliferated. NAFTA aimed to liberalize trade and eliminate tariffs among the three countries, leading to economic integration. As regional trade went on the rise as did cross-border investments, Mexico became a paramount exporting country for the United States. According to the Office of the US Trade Representative, US exports to Mexico in 2015 were up 468 percent since 1993, representing 15.7 percent of the total US exports. Conversely, US imports from Mexico grew by 638 percent between 1993 and 2015. According to the US Department of Homeland Security (2015), "Some 1.25 billion dollars in two-way trade and nearly one million people cross our land border each day for legitimate trade and travel." Around 80 percent of Mexican-US trade crosses through their shared land border. Like in the US-Canadian case, NAFTA had also a very positive effect on the integration of the borderlands. For instance, Texas's exports are highly dependent on the Mexican market, while Texas's border communities make their living thanks to their Mexican counterparts. Furthermore, NAFTA has led to an increase in cross-border transportation. For instance, the Texas-Laredo border has experienced an 86.7 percent increase in truck crossing between 1994 and 2004 (see Patrick, 2007: 201). We found a similar pattern regarding pedestrian and car crossings.

Transnational Crime across the North American Borders

In parallel to these licit flows across North American borders, we examine the concomitant occurrence and proliferation of transnational illicit activities, including drug trafficking, human trafficking and smuggling, and arms trafficking. In this context, there is an important variation between the US-Canadian and the US-Mexican borders.

The US-Canadian Border
In contrast to the US-Mexican border, illicit transnational flows and illegal activities have not been very significant. In terms of human migration, the entrance of illegal aliens from Canada to the United States is still very low, in relative terms. At the same time, we have seen, especially in the last few years, a flow of thousands of immigrants (from other countries or non-US citizens) moving legally and illegally from

the United States to Canada, in a human wave that encompasses neither human smuggling nor trafficking (see Levitz, 2020). Regarding the smuggling of weapons and other illicit goods, they exist, though in a very limited scale, as compared to the southern US border.

Drug smuggling has always been one of the financial engines driving organized crime, and a major component of the illicit traffic across the Canadian-US border (see DEA et al, 2006: 1). In the last decade, awareness regarding the US-Canada border security increased, despite the preferred attention given to the US-Mexican border. Beginning in 2010, the US Congress passed the Northern Border Counternarcotic Strategy Act, which mandated the US federal government to establish a National Northern Border Counternarcotics Strategy, published in 2012. The main goal behind the initiative was to reduce the flow of illicit drugs across the US-Canadian border, since Canada is considered a destination, source, and transit country for illicit trade, especially of drug trafficking, with an emphasis on cannabis (see United States Congress, 2016; and United States Office of National Drug Control Policy, 2020).

Additionally, in the 1990s, cigarettes smuggled to Canada from the United States became a profitable industry since the high taxation on tobacco in the former created an economic rationale for that demand. Similar to Mexico (but in much smaller scale), Canada is the final destination for US firearms since handguns are more difficult to obtain and own in Canada than in the United States (see Hataley and Leuprecht, 2013: 8). Yet, the level of violence perpetrated in Canada through US weapons is minor in comparison to Mexico, though there were signs of increasing concern in the last decade, including a surge in gang-style homicides and violence as related to drug trafficking (Cook, Cockier, and Krause, 2009).

In an eloquent criticism of the "Beyond the Border" joint initiative about the establishment of a security perimeter between the two countries, Hataley and Leuprecht (2013) argued that the joint action plan targets human smuggling and trafficking, including refugees and migrants, but not necessarily transnational organized criminals who prefer to move legitimately across different ports of entry. Moreover, whereas the United States prioritizes security concerns over economic goals, Canada prefers to emphasize economic competitiveness. Thus, organized crime might "slip through the cracks and it may profit literally as a result" (Hataley and Leuprecht, 2013: 17). Yet, the amount of illicit flows traced and recorded across the US-Canadian border remains relatively low, as compared to the US-Mexican border.

The US-Mexican Border
Unlike the US-Canadian border, there is a widespread perception that illicit transnational flows thrive across the US-Mexican border, posing four types of perceived threats: (1) terrorism, (2) spillover violence, (3) illegal migrants, and (4) illegal drugs. Yet, the empirical evidence tells us otherwise. As Adam Isacson (2015: 130) illustrates, "in the past decade, the border has seen no incidents of terrorist activity, a remarkable lack of spillover violence, a sharp drop in migration, but a sharp increase in drug seizures." Thus, we record significant incidents of drug trafficking, human smuggling and trafficking, arms trafficking (from the United States to Mexico), and to a lesser extent, other forms of smuggling across the border.

Drug Trafficking

Mexico has long been a conduit and territorial corridor for illegal drugs making their way into the United States, so for decades the borderlands have been the site of drug-related crime, both domestic (within Mexico), and transnational. Mexico has been an indispensable link in the cross-border drug-trafficking route that starts in South America, continues through Central America, and ends in the United States and Canada. About 90 percent of the drugs that enter US territory have made their way through the Mexican border. Although drug-trafficking groups have operated in Mexico for more than a century, the size and scope of their operations, as well as their concomitant violence, have increased dramatically in the last decade (see Dudley, 2010: 63; Finckenauer and Albanese, 2014: 12; and Patrick, 2011: 164).

In the early 1980s, drug trafficking emerged as a contentious bilateral issue for the US-Mexican relations. The first Mexican drug organizations started their illicit activities at that time, when Colombian cartels were still the main actors in drug trafficking worldwide, and the Caribbean Sea was the main cocaine route favored by those cartels to smuggle drugs into the United States. However, US enforcement and success against the Caribbean Route radically changed the geography of trafficking from maritime routes to land routes. Thus, Colombian cartels redirected the cocaine route toward Mexico through the Central American countries, boosting the incipient Mexican drug organizations, such as the Sinaloa

Cartel (see Finckenauer and Albanese, 2014: 11–16). Moreover, the drug trafficking organizations (DTOs) took advantage of the NAFTA agreement, relying primarily on trucks to move about 70 percent of the drugs that come into the United States over its southwestern border through legal ports of entry (see McKibben, 2015: 2; Stephen, 2009: 271; and Williams, 2016: 270).

In domestic terms, many of Mexico's northern states have been home to vicious battles between Mexican criminal groups fighting for control of drug trafficking routes into the United States. Competition and conflict among the diverse DTOs paved the way for an escalation in the level of violence within Mexico since 2000, following the end of the Institutional Revolutionary Party (PRI) monopoly of political power, which used to co-opt the drug criminal organizations (see Astorga and Shirk, 2010: 40; Barnes, 2017: 976; Trejo and Ley, 2020; and Williams, 2016: 297).

In December 2006, Mexican President Felipe Calderón launched a "War on Drugs" by militarizing the battle against drug cartels, mobilizing more than twenty thousand troops, aiming at the drug trafficking complex controlled by the Sinaloa Cartel, the Gulf Cartel, La Familia Michoacana, the Beltran Leyva, and the Zetas. This policy, which continued under the administration of Enrique Peña Nieto in 2012–18 had mixed results. On the one hand, most of the top drug traffickers were jailed, extradited to the United States, or killed. On the other hand, around three hundred thousand people have been murdered and more than twenty-eight thousand reported as disappeared since 2006 (see Lakhani and Tirado, 2016; Trejo and Ley, 2020; and Williams, 2016: 267). Moreover, the dismantling of the large cartels led to the splintering and regrouping of drug dealers and traffickers into smaller and fractioned VNSAs, as it happened also in Central America and in Colombia. Huge quantities of drugs continue to make their way into the United States, including marijuana, cocaine, methamphetamine, and heroin. Drug traffickers in Mexico utilize drug mules, tunnels, boats, vehicles, trains, aircrafts, donkeys, and couriers to get illegal drugs into the United States. At the same time, the drug seizure statistics of the US authorities at the border (except for cocaine) has actually increased since 2005 (see Isacson, 2015: 140–141).

Arms Trafficking

The fact that the transnational criminal flows between Mexico and the United States are a two-way process is evident in the US input to the proliferation of violence in Mexico through the provision of US high-powered guns to Mexico (see Dube, Dube, and Garcia-Ponce, 2013; and Finckenauer and Albanese, 2014: 12). The United States has the most heavily armed civilian population in the world, emanating from its soft regulations and a libertarian political culture that had historical and philosophical roots even before 1776. Despite the fact that US firearms are pouring into Mexico, there are incommensurable hurdles to implement gun regulations within the United States. For instance, powerful interest groups and domestic lobbies oppose any kind of gun limitations, notably the National Rifle Association (NRA). In political terms, the pro-gun groups relate to the US Republican Party, and they tend to fight firearm restrictions. Moreover, trafficking arms from the United States is not considered a federal crime under current US legislation, so that guns' traffickers can feel at ease trafficking weapons across the US-Mexican border (see Vargas and Bhatia, 2019).

The spread of weapons within the United States has an unintended effect in terms of channeling illicit transnational flows; namely, the creation of a large market of illicit arms in Mexico where firearms sales are highly regulated. Thus, about 90 percent of firearms seized in Mexico come from the United States, while 73.5 percent of these firearms confiscated originated from the US borderline states of Arizona, California, and Texas (McDougal et al., 2015: 6). Moreover, the unrestricted movement of weapons from the United States to Mexico has fuelled the ongoing and increasing violence committed there, exacerbated by political instability and competition (see Astorga and Shirk, 2010: 47; Cook, Cukier, and Krause, 2009; Dube, Dube, and Garcia-Ponce, 2013: 399; Felbab Brown, 2017b; Shirk, 2011; and UNODC, 2010: 8).

Human Smuggling and Trafficking

The US-Mexican border encompasses the world's largest migration corridor and includes several million Latin American illegal migrants – mostly from Mexico and the Central American countries – moving to and subsequently residing in the United States. Statistics show that Mexicans are the largest group of illegal residents in the United States, about 6.2 million (56 percent) of the presumed eleven million illegal immigrants.

In the past decade, there has been a sharp decline in the number of Mexicans illegally entering the country. Between 2006 and 2010 the number of Mexican immigrants decreased by two hundred thousand, compared to more than two million who arrived between 2000 and 2005. This has been the result of improvement in the economic growth and development of the Mexican economy, which reached a GDP of $8,000 in 2005, downsizing the migration to the United States (see Runde and Schneider, 2019: 2). In addition, the economic crisis and recession of 2008 and their aftermaths translated into lower labor demand for Mexican immigrants in the United States (see Felbab-Brown, 2017b).

While Mexican migration has slowed down in recent years, Central American migration in transit through Mexico has surged, pulled toward the United States by the lure of family reunification and the hope of better life conditions, fleeing from the looming reality of the Northern Triangle's crime and domestic violence. The Central American migration trend got the attention of the United States public in June–July 2014, in May–June of 2018, and in November 2018. Between October 2013 and September 2014, the US Border Patrol caught close to seventy thousand children, mostly from El Salvador, Guatemala, and Honduras, without their parents (see Isacson, 2015: 143). Following the zero-tolerance policy of the Trump Administration, in April–May 2018, about 2,200 children detained at the US border were separated from their parents, most of them also arriving from Central America. This policy generated furor and a strong emotional response in the United States and overseas, with open criticism to Trump's policy even inside the Republican Party.

Illegal immigration to the United States has been boosted with the assistance of VNSAs such as smugglers and local criminal networks that cross the border (see Olson, 2016). A third of the people annually smuggled into the United States come from Latin America, and most of them cross the US-Mexican border assisted by professional smugglers, the so-called *coyotes*, who tend to abuse them (UNODC, 2010, 4). In this context, VNSAs are involved not only in human smuggling, but also in human trafficking and sexual exploitation.

Explaining the Reality of Peaceful Borders and Illicit Transnational Flows in North America

Hypothesis 1: The Degree of Physical and Institutional Openness of the Peaceful Borders

Mexico, the United States, and Canada have all sustained peaceful relationships for several decades and enjoyed stable peace if not

a pluralistic security community. They have been economically interdependent even before the establishment of NAFTA in 1994. Both the
US-Mexican and the US-Canadian borders fall under the category of
interdependent borders, in spite of the considerable differences
between the two borderlands (Payan, 2014: 8).

Moreover, all economic statistics emphasize the fact that the free
trade area agreement has increased the level of integration and cross-
border exchanges among the three countries. Borderland cities experienced an accelerated process of integration as well; cities across both
the Mexico-US as well as Canada-US border became economically
interdependent. Moreover, millions of people have been carrying on
border crossings on a daily basis and in a massive way.

There is an important variation in the effects of integration upon the
two North American borders. In the US-Canadian case, regional integration has mostly increased licit flows across the borders. Despite
claims of the border's increasing "Mexicanization," transnational
illicit flows have not been significant, except for some increased levels
of drug trafficking. Conversely, the US-Mexican border has witnessed
the occurrence and proliferation of illicit transnational flows before
and after the establishment of NAFTA. Hence, we argue that NAFTA
actually increased drug trafficking across the US-Mexican border
through the opening of the borders. Whether by train, truck, or foot,
the amount of licit traffic crossing the US-Mexican border has
increased exponentially since January 1994. For the sake of comparison, in 2012 the value of US-Mexico trade reached over $390 billion,
up from $97 billion in 1995 (see Barajas et al., 2014). This land traffic
constitutes on average more than 80 percent of yearly US-Mexican
trade. Hence, the amount of illicit traffic (especially of drugs) grew
accordingly. In this sense, NAFTA turned to be a blessing for Mexican
cartels moving drugs across the border through the US legal entry
points (see Andreas, 2009: 58; Hataley and Leuprecht, 2013: 9; and
McKibben, 2015: 4–5).

Historically, both the US-Mexican and the US-Canadian borders
have been open and porous. Yet, the border regime and its physical
and institutional configuration changed over time. The US-Canadian
border has remained open, yet controlled since the early 2000s.
Conversely, the US-Mexican border changed its configuration from
being open and soft to controlled, militarized, and even partly fortified.
In 2006, the United States decided to construct a fence (in some sections

even a "wall") along the Mexican border in order to deter the flock of illicit transnational flows. This fortified border is about one-third of the 3,201 kilometers of borderland, in particular along Texas, New Mexico, Arizona, and California. Donald Trump's main presidential campaign promise back in 2016 was to build a "wall" along the US-Mexican border to curb illegal immigration to the United States, replacing the existing barrier, and despite the lack of a clear budget for that. Yet, the existing barrier has apparently not deterred the proliferation of illicit transnational flows of people, drugs, and weapons. To the contrary, it has apparently increased the role of VNSAs engaging in illicit activities, including drug trafficking and human trafficking from Mexico to the United States, and arms trafficking from the United States to Mexico (see Felbab Brown, 2017b).

In sum, we only partially corroborate Hypothesis 1 with reference to the two North American borders, but for different reasons. The US-Canadian border is highly integrated, and relatively open, though regulated and institutionalized; yet, we do not find enough evidence for significant illicit transnational flows, except for drug trafficking and the limited flow of illegal residents of the United States who are seeking asylum in Canada in the last few years. Conversely, the US-Mexican border has been highly integrated since the establishment of NAFTA in 1994. At the same time, the border has been militarized and even fortified, though transnational crime in the form of drug trafficking, weapons trafficking, and human smuggling and trafficking persists and has even increased (see Ellis and Ortiz, 2017: 1). Therefore, the key for the partial refutation of the first hypothesis refers to the next two alternative explanations.

Hypothesis 2: The Degree of Governance, Institutional Strength, and Political Willingness

Whereas we regard the United States as a relatively strong state, Mexico is a relatively weak state, especially in terms of the corruption of its political system. That weakness is reflected in the existing inequality, poverty, and especially the corruption of some of its political institutions, which have undermined the foundations of the state and the enforcement of the rule of law. Between 1929 and 2000, the semi-authoritarian regime sustained by the PRI used to co-opt criminal organizations in a complex political criminal linkage along the continuum ranging from integration to alliance and to enforcement-evasion. At the same time, we agree with Stewart Patrick that while Mexico might be a relatively weak and dysfunctional state, it is not a completely failed one, as it might sustain some elements of institutional and governance strength. Mexico has been a consolidated democracy since the early 2000s, it does not have major ethnic cleavages or secessionist problems, and some of its institutions are rather robust (see Patrick, 2011: 164).

The policy of co-opting criminal organizations changed abruptly with the transition to democracy by Vicente Fox in 2000 and later on by Felipe Calderón in 2006, leading to an increasing military confrontation between the Mexican state and the criminal organizations. Despite the fact that President Felipe Calderón launched a "war" against the drug cartels in 2006, the results have not been very successful, to say the least. The statistics speak for themselves: over three hundred thousand homicides occurred in Mexico since 2006 (see Cheatham, 2019b). Calderón relied upon military forces that replaced police forces, which were considered either corrupt or ineffective. During his administration, Mexico captured and killed twenty-five of the top thirty-seven drug kingpins. Enrique Peña Nieto (2012–18), who succeeded Calderón, tried to change the approach of the war on drugs by reducing the level of violence against civilians, instead of pursuing drugs barons. While he could reduce violence in the early stages of his administration, later on, homicides reached historical records (see Cheatham, 2019b). At the same time, some of the Mexican officials during the Calderón Administration, like Genaro García Luna, the former Secretary of Public Security, attempted to co-opt the drug cartels by adopting a policy of enforcement-evasion. Eventually, García Luna was arrested in the United States, on December 2019, accused of taking millions of dollars in bribes from "El Chapo" Guzman's Sinaloa Cartel while controlling Mexico's Federal Police force (Woody, 2019).

Popular alienation from the corrupted political class was a key factor in explaining the landslide electoral victory of Andrés Manuel López Obrador (ALMO), who was elected Mexican President in June 2018. In a radical departure, in 2019, ALMO launched a five-year program that includes the legalization of illegal drugs and providing treatment programs for drug addicts. ALMO's strategy focused on drugs as a health issue, rather than a criminal one (Presidencia de México,

2019). In sum, the relative weakness of the Mexican state, in terms of both lack of capabilities and political willingness, has allowed for the continued incursion of VNSAs within its polity and across its borders (see Cheatham, 2019b; and Congressional Research Service, 2020).

As for the United States, despite its obvious capabilities and strength, it has shown a lack of political willingness as related to tackling the domestic sources for illicit transnational flows across its border with Mexico. Reducing drug trafficking is one of the main challenges that faces the United States; yet, it has not succeeded in lowering its demand for drugs. In addition, the United States has failed in the financial aspect of drug trafficking by not seizing the money from drugs cartels (see Felbab-Brown, 2017c; and Wayne, 2017). Moreover, as the United States has not succeeded in imposing gun controls and limitations, it has directly contributed to the legal and illegal transnational flows of weapons from the United States to the rest of Latin America. In sum, we corroborate the second hypothesis with reference to the US-Mexican border. By contrast, the hypothesis seems to be less relevant regarding the US-Canadian peaceful border, due to the higher degrees of governance, institutional strength, and political willingness of the two countries involved.

Hypothesis 3: The Prevalent Socioeconomic Conditions of the Neighboring States

There is significant linkage between the political economy of the borderlands in NAFTA and the occurrence of both licit and illicit transnational flows. In the case of the US-Mexican border, *Maquiladora* industries are scattered south of the US border and they are regarded as having a positive impact in economic terms for Mexico. Across the border, similar positive economic developments stemmed from the increased integration between the two countries; for instance, Texas's economy is highly dependent on its exports to Mexico. In addition, US border cities benefit greatly from Mexican shoppers, who cross the border on a daily basis to buy in retail stores. The same happens in the case of the US-Canadian border, with similarly high levels of integration that also have positive economic effects for both countries (see Barajas et al., 2014; and Sparke, 2002).

At the same time, in the US-Mexican case, any observer of the border dynamics should be aware of the huge socioeconomic gap between the two countries. Whereas the United States is the most highly developed economy in the world, Mexico is still considered a developing economy, despite its middle income (see Payan, 2014: 14). This explains why socioeconomic disparity is a key element in explaining the occurrence of illicit transnational flows across their common border. Thus, different economic environments on either side of the border create economic incentives for the proliferation of transnational illicit flows, based on a logic of supply-and-demand relationships.

In contrast, the highly developed socioeconomic conditions that reign across the Canadian-US border help explain the relative absence of significant illicit transnational flows. In this case, the economic push for illicit transborder transactions along with the licit ones is balanced out by the pull logic represented by the absence of clear arbitrage if the two economies across the border are similar, as in this case where both are rich and developed. Thus, we corroborate Hypothesis 3 in the North American case, but only with reference to the US-Mexican border.

The Northern Triangle of Central America

The so-called "Northern Triangle" is a geographical area in Central America that encompasses El Salvador, Honduras, and Guatemala. For many years, the area has been the focus of a number of initiatives and policies designed to address the severe problems of violence and crime facing these countries. Several actors, including the United States, Mexico, regional and international institutions such as the Central American Integration System (SICA) and the United Nations, have tried several solutions to no avail. In the end, the inability to cope with crime and violence in the Northern Triangle has political and economic causes, including ineffective state institutions, police forces deprived of necessary resources and with low public trust and legitimacy, corrupt judicial systems, and fragile tax collection systems (see Shifter, 2012: 5).

While an integral part of Central America, the Northern Triangle countries share some common characteristics that make them a particular subregion. First, El Salvador, Guatemala, and to a lesser extent Honduras share a violent legacy of civil wars and internal turmoil that took place within their countries and spilled over their borders in the second half of the twentieth century up to the early 1990s. In Guatemala, following a coup d'état instigated by the CIA in

1954, a virulent civil war raged between the government and leftish guerrillas from 1960 to 1996. The death toll reached two hundred thousand victims, hundreds of villages were wiped out, and millions of Guatemalans were displaced. The Guatemalan army carried out genocide against its indigenous population in the early 1980s. In El Salvador, a civil war took place between the military-led government supported by the United States and the leftish guerrilla group, the Farabundo Martí Liberation Front (FMLN) during 1980–92, leaving more than seventy-five thousand people dead. As for Honduras, although it did not experience a direct civil war like its neighbors, it served as the territorial basis for the US-backed right-wing rebel groups of *Contras* that were involved between 1979 and the early 1990s in a civil war against the socialist Sandinista government in Nicaragua. Moreover, Honduras also experienced massive violations of human rights and political violence committed by its military in the 1980s (see Labrador and Renwick, 2018: 4; UNODC, 2010: 238; for a more general background see Berryman, 1985; Child, 1986; and Leiken and Rubin, 1987).

Second, a common socioeconomic pattern that characterizes this region is the high levels of poverty, inequality, and social seclusion and alienation. The Northern Triangle suffers from one of the most unequal distributions of income in the world, comparable only to Southern Africa and to the Andean region (see Cheatham, 2019a).

Third, corruption, institutional weakness, and the lack of effective governance are all pervasive patterns that continue to affect the three countries, particularly with regard to the feeble rule of law. El Salvador, Guatemala, and Honduras have suffered from weak political institutions, and they are bedeviled by high levels of corruption and violence (see Leiken and Rubin, 1987; and Williams, 2016: 274).

Fourth, political violence has mutated into different types of criminal groups, including transnational criminal organizations, many of which are associated with Mexican DTOs; domestic organized-crime groups; transnational gangs such as the *Maras* MS-13 and Barrio 18, as well as *pandillas*, or street gangs. All these VNSAs, both domestic and transnational, have filled the vacuum left by a weak institutional order and have been facilitated by the social exclusion of vast segments of the population. Consequently, the region has the highest murder rate in the world, as well as very high rates of other forms of violent crime (see Cheatham, 2019a; and Labrador and Renwick, 2018: 5).

Fifth, the Northern Triangle states experienced a very peculiar kind of transition to peace after the end of its virulent civil wars in the 1990s. The security establishment and elites of the "old regime" survived the transitions to peace and democracy, acting as informal powerbrokers, leading to a political climate characterized by corruption and impunity, as well as a high circulation of weapons in an environment characterized by urban insecurity (see Barnes, 2017: 971; Cruz, 2011: 7; and Milian, 2008: 7–8).

Sixth, in addition to all these intra-regional dynamics, there is an important geopolitical dimension as related to the geographical location of the Northern Triangle, situated between the main drug production centers in South America (the Andean countries of Colombia, Peru, Ecuador, and Bolivia), next to Mexico, and not far from the largest drug-consuming market of the world, the United States. This adds a pernicious dimension as an ideal transit zone for drug trafficking from south to north, as well as arms trafficking from north to south (see Jácome, 2014: 3; Mesa and Moorhouse, 2008: 7; and Williams, 2016: 270).

Moreover, the violence that characterizes the region relates to the intensification of economic globalization processes, which have allowed for the expansion of illicit activities around the world, providing extraordinary benefits to the mafias and TCOs that act globally. In the particular case of Central America, this is relevant due to its geopolitical position as a transit zone for drugs coming from South America on their way to the United States. Thus, the adverse socioeconomic conditions and political and institutional weaknesses of Guatemala, Honduras, and El Salvador make them particularly vulnerable to these "dark forces" of globalization. These include transnational criminal groups like the *Maras*, originally "made in the USA," which act both within the region and in global networks in other regions of the world (see Mesa and Moorhouse, 2008: 7; and Shelley, 2018).

All these factors together explain why the Northern Triangle is the most violent region of the world, leading hundreds of thousands of Central Americans to flee and search for refuge and asylum in the United States. In sum, the Northern Triangle is a convergence area of not only three countries, but also of three different types of illicit transnational flows: trafficking in drugs, people, and weapons.

During the 1990s, there was a convergence of interrelated positive dynamics leading to a transition from war to peace in Central America.

That included the peace processes of Contadora and Esquipulas that culminated with the end of the civil wars in the late 1980s and early 1990s, a formal process of democratization, and the deepening of regional integration associated with SICA and the signing of a free trade agreement with the United States in 2005. Furthermore, most countries reduced their security sector, allowing significant public resources to be invested in socioeconomic issues and activities. Notwithstanding these positive processes, which led to peace and integration, domestic and international peace had enabled other types of domestic and transnational violence, through the occurrence and proliferation of transnational illicit flows.

Both interstate and civil wars are now relics of the past, yet the violence reigning in the Northern Triangle suggests that the region is a zone of peace only in formal rather than real terms. Although the phenomenon of VNSAs existed previously, the severity and levels of threats increased following the transitions to peace in the region. Moreover, the transitions to peace were carried out without fully dismantling the forces of the old regime and transforming them into positive inputs to the post-war societies. In other words, the demobilization of armed men and women from guerrilla groups, paramilitary forces, and state agencies, meant the availability of an unemployed workforce who found a new living in criminal-related groups.

In the first two decades of the twenty-first century, the Northern Triangle has remained a region marred in drug trafficking, transnational gangs, corruption, and impunity. Political violence has been replaced by that committed by VNSAs, such as the so-called *Transportistas*, drug cartels, and gangs such as the *Maras*, who turned the region into a hub of transnational criminal activity. The common denominator for this violence relates to cocaine trafficking, which thrived and made the Central American route the main way to pour illegal trafficked drugs into the United States. Since the year 2000, the amount of cocaine trafficked through Central America has increased dramatically, especially after Mexico declared its "War on Drugs" in 2006 and militarized its actions against the Mexican drug cartels (see UNODC, 2012a).

According to the United Nations Office on Drugs and Crime, "in response to an increasingly inhospitable environment in Mexico, traffickers have shifted their focus to new routes along the Guatemalan/ Honduran border" (UNODC, 2012a: 5). That led to Mexican cartels, such as the Sinaloa and the Zetas, settling in the Northern Triangle where they found fertile ground for operating in a crime-inducing environment. In sum, Guatemala, Honduras, and El Salvador have become a corridor for illicit movement of drugs, about 40 percent of them coming from Bolivia, Peru, and Colombia, in addition to arms trafficking, as well as human trafficking that includes about seventy-two thousand Cubans and twenty thousand African refugees (see UNODC, 2012a).[1]

The Borders of the Northern Triangle

There are 959.7 kilometers of borders between Mexico and Guatemala; 284 kilometers between Guatemala and Honduras; 266 kilometers between Guatemala and Belize; and 212 kilometers between Guatemala and El Salvador; in addition, Salvador and Honduras share 256 kilometers of borders. All of those borders are open and porous, with the exception of Guatemala and Belize, which share a relatively closed border, as the two countries sustain a long ongoing territorial dispute pending at the International Court of Justice.

The Guatemala-Mexico Border
The Mexican-Guatemalan border is evidently porous since neither Mexico nor Guatemala exercise effective control over their shared border, which includes about eight formal checkpoints and fifty-six informal ones (Dudley, 2010: 81). The shared borderlands are a space of legal and illegal exchanges of goods and persons, characterized by very asymmetric flows. The bulk of these licit and illicit flows go from Central America to Mexico rather than the other way around (Villafuerte Solis, 2007: 318). Due to the porosity of the border, the Sinaloa and Zetas cartels moved to Guatemala in order to manage their drug trafficking and to find a proper safe haven, after the Mexican Government launched its "War on Drugs" in 2006 (Dudley, 2010: 74–75). As an example, Huehuetenango, a Guatemalan province next to the border, suffered from massacres carried out by the Mexican cartels – Sinaloa and Zetas – who have de facto occupied this area. The local authorities and elites had depopulated the province, by selling their land to the drug traffickers, who have fulfilled some governance roles, establishing ties with the local population.

---

[1] Interview with Carlos Raúl Moralez, former Foreign Minister of Guatemala, November 29, 2016, Truman Institute, Hebrew University of Jerusalem, Israel.

Chiapas, in Southern Mexico, borders with Guatemala and is the poorest state within Mexico. This state was the epicenter of the Zapatista uprising in 1995, which broke out because of ethnic and socioeconomic discrimination (Villafuerte Solis, 2007: 319). Tapalucha, a Mexican city located in the southern area of Chiapas, has been known as a safe haven for diverse Central American *Maras*, including Mara Salvatrucha (MS-13), and Barrio 18 (Arana, 2005: 103). Moreover, Guatemalan *Maras* have been trained by the Zetas in the Peten region, next to the Mexican border (Dudley, 2010: 85). Parallel to the presence of these VNSAs, the borderlands between Guatemala and Mexico are economically integrated in specific ways. For instance, Guatemalan workers cross the border daily to work on agricultural plantations on the other side of the border (Villafuerte Solis, 2007: 335).

From the first years of the twenty-first century, Mexico has begun addressing the Northern Triangle threats emanating from its common border with Guatemala. During the Vicente Fox Administration (2000–6), Mexico developed a stick-and-carrot policy. On the one hand, it developed the "Plan South," while on the other hand it implemented the "Plan Puebla-Panama." While the former consisted of police and military surveillance aimed at deterring immigration from Central America through Mexico all the way to the United States, the latter consisted of fostering economic growth in the region. Eventually, both programs were short-lived and replaced by the US-Mexican Mérida Initiative after 2007, focusing on the "War on Drugs" in Mexico (see International Crisis Group, 2018: 1).

In 2013, the Mexican navy created a Southern Border Program by which it took steps to control the border with Guatemala along with the army, police forces, and local and state governments (see International Crisis Group, 2018: 3). Nowadays, tensions between the two neighboring countries have increased as Mexican security forces, in connivance with US officials, attempt to stop the flow of illegal migrants, many of them Hondurans, from crossing the shallow waters of the Suchiate River in an attempt to continue their journey to the United States (Montes, 2020).

Other Guatemalan and Salvadoran Borders

There are three formal border crossings between Guatemala and Honduras and seventy-four informal checkpoints. Guatemala and El Salvador share four formal border crossings and eighty-four informal ones.[2] Furthermore, the uncontrolled, informal crossing posts lack any official enforcement; the legal and formal crossings tend to be neglected by the national governments of the three countries (International Crisis Group, 2014: 1).

Regarding the porous borders in El Salvador, there are more than 300 unmonitored points of entry (Farah, 2012: 11). Salvadoran *Maras* have control over certain border areas, such as the corridor from the Pacific Ocean to the border with Guatemala. In Honduras, as well as in Guatemala and El Salvador, these borders are penetrated easily. For instance, the cocaine that enters into Honduras comes from El Salvador and Nicaragua's border crossings (Bosworth, 2010: 14).

Transnational Crime across the Northern Triangle Borders

Similar to Mexico, organized crime in Central America refers mainly to transnational drug trafficking and the security problems resulting from it – especially the spiral of violence and money laundering, as well as the criminalization of politics and the possible nefarious role of state officials, sometimes allied with crime, who might reinforce or even trigger a spiral of violence. Moreover, the Northern Triangle *problematique* of transnational crime has been exacerbated by the violent legacy of civil wars that destroyed the fabric of society, and above all, by the presence of VNSAs in the form of transnational youth gangs such as the *Maras*, as well as *Transportistas*. We first turn to these non-state actors themselves – *Maras* and *Transportistas*, involved in drug trafficking, and to a lesser extent, in arms trafficking and human trafficking.

Transnational Gangs (*Maras*)

The *Maras*, Central American youth gangs, have become a transnational security problem for the governments of the Northern Triangle, as well as for the United States, in the first two decades of the twenty-first century. These transnational gangs have their origin in the US ghettos of Los Angeles and other US cities crowded with Central American immigrants who escaped from the tragic reality of the Central American civil wars (Arana, 2005: 98). Many of these gang members, raised in the United States, were sent back to their homelands in Central America through deportations of convicted felons in US prisons. The

[2] Ibid.

Northern Triangle has received about 90 percent of the deportees from the United States (Rodgers and Muggah, 2009: 306). These gangs included the infamous MS-13, Barrio 18, as well as an "estimated 63,700 kindred spirits in Guatemala, Honduras, and Nicaragua" (Manwaring, 2007: 13).

The *Maras* have a strong presence, mainly in Guatemala, Honduras, and El Salvador, and have infiltrated Belize in the last decade (see Looft, 2012). Once deported back, these gangs did not integrate back into society, but rather remained as a disenfranchised mass of young people without any visible future. Facing uncertainty and anomie, this dysfunctional youth reproduced the gang-style factionalism "Made in USA." The most dangerous groups, such as Barrio 18 and MS-13 have established transnational cross-border crime networks, posing a significant security threat to the stability of the region and beyond (see Arana, 2005; and Sampó, 2018).

The Guatemalan government has depicted the *Maras* as the main source of crime (Brands, 2010: 236). It is estimated that around 70,000–100,000 gang members are scattered across the Northern Triangle (Rodgers and Muggah, 2009: 303). *Maras* have been involved in assassinations, human and drug trafficking, kidnapping, money laundering, and extortion. They are structured in cells that control urban areas using extreme forms of violence, including warlord infighting and hitman-style mass murders of civilians. Like mafia organizations, they charge protection taxes in the areas that fall under their control (see Cantor, 2014: 17; and Carpenter, 2012: 123).

While *Maras* are considered essentially an urban phenomenon, they also operate in the borderlands of the Northern Triangle as transnational VNSAs. For instance, on both sides of the Guatemalan-Mexican border *Maras* control the routes for drug and human trafficking (Carpenter, 2012: 214). Regarding drug trafficking, *Maras* have received training from Mexican cartels such as the Zetas (Dudley, 2010: 85). In addition, they dominate the *narco menudeo* (Farah, 2012: 14); namely, the distribution of cocaine on a small scale in urban areas. As for human smuggling and trafficking, along the Southern Mexican border with Guatemala, *Maras* turned into an active force behind the *coyotes* who manage the human smuggling and trafficking of Central American illegal migrants in transit to the United States (Arana, 2005: 103). In addition, they maintain their illicit networks across not just the Northern Triangle, but also across and within the US borders, reaching globally and transnationally beyond the region, sometimes in contact with other transnational criminal and terrorist groups, like al-Qaeda (see Manwaring, 2005; and Shelley and Picarelli, 2005: 11).

Transportistas

Transportistas play a key role in the drug supply chain from the Andean countries in South America all the way to the United States. As their Spanish name implies, their function is to *transport* drugs from South America to Mexico. *Transportistas* work on a regional basis receiving, storing, and transporting drugs (Dudley, 2010: 69). These organizations operate mainly in the borderlands and coastal areas and they function as family-run licit businesses.

In El Salvador, *Transportistas* control San Miguel and La Unión, both eastern border provinces (Dudley, 2010: 86). The Perrones family has been the largest *Transportistas* group in El Salvador, responsible for moving cocaine by trucks toward Guatemala and Honduras (Farah, 2012: 16). Based on common economic interests, they have allied with the Sinaloa Cartel and other drug organizations. In Honduras, *Transportistas* such as the Rezascos family have been active on the Nicaraguan side of the border (Bosworth, 2010: 5). The Sinaloa and Gulf cartels along with the Zetas have a strong foothold in Honduras, which plays a key role in the drug trafficking chain that begins in the Andean countries. In addition, drug organizations use Honduran soil for ecstasy production, as a destination for chemical precursors coming from Mexico (Bosworth, 2010: 4).

Arms Trafficking

The increasing violence in Central America has been fuelled by the existing surplus of weapons. Two trends explain the flow of illicit weapons. First, there is a local or regional flow within countries and across the borders within the region, resulting from the surplus and incomplete disarmament following the civil wars in El Salvador, Guatemala, and Nicaragua. Consequently, the post–civil war period allowed for the establishment of a sizable illicit market for firearms.

Second, Colombia and Mexico turned into attractive markets for Central American weapons. In this sense, arms seized in Mexico in the last few years had their origin, for instance, in the Guatemalan military forces, in addition to those provided by the United States. The lack of regulation in the purchase of guns in the southern states of the United

States allows for the smuggling of US weapons to Central America. As expected, the illicit trafficking of weapons relates to the different criminal organizations and networks, including the transnational *Maras*, the local *pandillas* (gangs), and the *Transportistas* (see Salcedo-Albarán and Santos, 2017: 10–15).

Human Smuggling and Trafficking

Human trafficking is the second-largest source of money for organized crime in Central America, after drug trafficking. In addition to Nicaragua, the three countries of the Northern Triangle are the source, transit point, and destination for victims of trafficking, including many cases of sexual slavery. Officials say that Nicaragua, El Salvador, and Honduras are the source of the trafficking, whereas Guatemala (because of its border with Mexico) is the country where most of the victims are enslaved and the ideal place for human trafficking gangs, which are not always associated with the DTOs (see Martínez, 2012: 9–10). There are tens of thousands of human trafficking victims coming from the Northern Triangle. A recent study by the UNODC put the number of sexually exploited victims in Guatemala alone at 48,500, considering that for every official reported case there were thirty hidden victims (UNODC, 2016b).

The Northern Triangle has witnessed the phenomenon of forced displacement caused by criminal groups (see Cantor, 2014). The *Transportistas'* takeover of zones strategic for cross-border smuggling expelled small and medium landowners, who were compelled to sell and relinquish their lands for a ridiculous price (Cantor, 2014: 15). Another example of forced and illegal migration and human smuggling refers to the particular case of minors. About 78 percent of the seventy thousand people who illegally crossed the US border in the last few years were unaccompanied minors coming from the Northern Triangle (Cruz, 2015: 43).

Although there are several reasons that explain this mass child migration, it can be associated with the repressive policies carried out by Guatemala, Honduras, and El Salvador. The so-called *mano dura* against the *Maras* and *pandillas* of poor youth had a lasting impact. These policies were counterproductive since they did not curb violence, but rather increased the institutional violence directed at young people, who desperately turned to illegal migration as the only chance to survive in physical terms (see Cruz, 2015: 7).

In addition, traditional patterns of illegal migration have been very significant, especially with regard to Central American migrants. For instance, in 2016 alone, US Customs and Border Protection intercepted nearly 46,900 unaccompanied children and more than 70,400 family units from El Salvador, Guatemala, and Honduras arriving at the US-Mexican border (Lesser and Batalova, 2017: 1).

Furthermore, on the way to the United States, these prospective migrants have suffered violence perpetrated by VNSAs. The so-called *coyotes* are gangs that charge immigrants significant sums of money in order to smuggle them into the United States (Arana, 2005: 103). A most infamous case took place in 2010 when the Zetas executed seventy-two immigrants, mostly from Central America, in Northern Mexico not far from the border with Texas (see Johnson, 2011). The Zetas have also played an active role in human trafficking in both Mexico and Central America (see Garzón and Olson, 2013: 6–7; and Milian, 2008: 13–14).

In sum, a vicious cycle has evolved when illegal migration turns into human smuggling and human trafficking. Increased border control fuels and feeds human smuggling, promoting transnational criminal organizations that eventually turn it into a thriving industry. Organized criminal groups, ranging from neighborhood gangs to transnational drug traffickers persecute migrants from the Northern Triangle fleeing from poverty and economic deprivation. To make things even worse for these migrants, the Mexican and US governments persecute and prosecute them, while considering them as economic migrants rather than prospective refugees eligible for asylum.

There is enough evidence that organized crime groups from Mexico and Central America – including gangs such as the MS-13 – are engaged with human smuggling and trafficking across the US-Mexican border (Shelley, 2010: 268 and 276). At the same time, TCOs, including drug cartels, are not necessarily the primary culprits of the Northern Triangle human smuggling to the United States, but rather these are ad hoc groups and independent, small illicit operators who directly benefit from human smuggling (see Greenfield et al., 2019; and Martínez, 2012: 8–35).

Explaining the Reality of Peaceful Borders and Illicit Transnational Flows in the Northern Triangle

Hypothesis 1: The Degree of Physical and Institutional Openness of the Peaceful Borders

In the Northern Triangle case, we corroborate the validity of the first hypothesis, according to which there seems to be a direct relationship between institutional openness and porosity of borders and the occurrence and proliferation of illicit transnational flows. Processes of economic integration further contributed to this openness.

Regional integration in Central America dates back to the 1960s, when the Central American Common Market (CACM) was established in 1961. Central America joined the wave of Latin American integration project during that time, along with the Latin American Free Trade Area (LAFTA) in 1960 and the Andean Pact established in 1969. In 1991, the Central American Integration System (SICA in its Spanish acronym) replaced CACM (see Bull, 1999). SICA led to a considerable increase in both intra-regional imports and exports. It also benefited from the liberalization process carried out by several countries. According to the CEPAL statistics, between 2000 and 2010 the overall rate of export increased by 6.1 percent on an annual basis (Fuentes and Pellandra, 2011: 23).

Moreover, the existing porosity in most of the borders of the region (with the exception of Guatemala-Belize) has allowed for the occurrence and proliferation of illicit transnational flows and the free movement of VNSAs. The Mexican cartels' case is paradigmatic here: most of them, the Zetas, Sinaloa, and the Gulf Cartels all have a strong presence in the Northern Triangle. They exert territorial control over parts of the borders, control trafficking routes, and establish formal and informal ties with the local population. Moreover, *Transportistas* and *Maras* are further examples of VNSAs that operate quite freely across the borders of Guatemala, El Salvador, and Honduras.

Hypothesis 2: The Degree of Governance, Institutional Strength, and Political Willingness

During the last decade, both Honduras and Guatemala suffered from several political crises. In Guatemala, in 2006, the United Nations along with the Guatemalan government established the Commission against Impunity in Guatemala (CICIG). This body was aimed at "investigating illegal security groups and clandestine security organizations in Guatemala" (www.un.org/undpa/en/americas/cicig). The CIGIC has been mandated with investigating corruption, which is regarded as an endemic disease in Guatemala. Nonetheless, the CICIG could not prevent the political scandal and crisis of 2015, which led to the resignations of Guatemalan President Otto Perez Molina and his Vice President Roxana Baldetti on charges of corruption (see Labrador and Renwick, 2018: 8). Later on, former President Jimmy Morales tried to expel the Commission from the country after it decided to investigate him and his family for graft allegations. Morales's attempt eventually failed since the Guatemalan Supreme Court eventually blocked his decision (see FIDH, 2019).

In Honduras, in 2009, incumbent President Manuel Zelaya was deposed by an improvised and confusing military takeover of the presidential residence. While Zelaya was replaced by a civil government headed by the speaker of Congress, Roberto Micheletti, the coup caused a lot of political dismay and disarray in Latin America (see Bosworth, 2010: 21). Honduras was suspended from the OAS under the Democratic Charter and many states called back their ambassadors. Eight years later, in December 2017, Honduras was involved again in another political crisis following the contested reelection of President Juan Orlando Hernández.

By contrast, in 2009, El Salvador experienced a different and rather peaceful political transition. The candidate, Mauricio Funes, backed by the leftish party (formerly the guerrilla group) Farabundo Martí National Liberation Front (FMLN) won the first ever election over the rightist party Alianza Republicana Nacionalista (ARENA). The left-wing party consolidated its rule democratically in 2014, when Salvador Sánchez Cerén was elected president as the frontrunner of the FMLN. In contrast to its two other neighbors in the Northern Triangle, El Salvador did not undergo political turbulence in the last decade. Quite the opposite; it illustrated an example of peaceful and civil transfers of political power among parties of different political ideologies. Most recently, on February 3, 2019, Nayib Bukele from the Grand Alliance for National Unity (GANA) won the democratic elections and became a first President who belonged to neither the conservative ARENA nor the leftish FMLN (see Mundt, 2019). Yet, in the last year, against the background of the COVID-19 crisis, he also moved in an authoritarian and illiberal direction.

Data drawn from the Fragile State Index, the Corruption Index, and the Freedom House's Annual Report (as depicted in Table 3.3), all provide evidence that the Northern Triangle is composed of relatively weak states. Thus, institutional weakness and low levels of governance make it difficult for the countries of the region to cooperate facing those transnational threats (see Domínguez, 2018).

The literature about Central America shares a certain consensus regarding the institutional weaknesses of the states in the region –

with the possible exceptions of Costa Rica and to a lesser extent Panama – as a meaningful explanation for the occurrence of illicit transnational flows, especially drug trafficking, human smuggling and trafficking, and arms trafficking. In many cases, security officials are not only overwhelmed in both numbers and capabilities; they actually collaborate with VNSAs in rural and borderland areas, due to high levels of corruption and feeble enforcement of the rule of law. Moreover, the partial demilitarization and reduction in the size of the armed forces in the Northern Triangle states means that large border areas remain porous and unprotected by the central governments. In general, the Northern Triangle states chose policies that partially included alliance or enforcement-evasion in their relations with criminal organizations, punctuated by attempts at confrontation or alternatively, even outright integration with DTOs.

The enactment of national responses by the Northern Triangle governments programs against domestic and transnational crime labeled *mano dura* (zero tolerance, literally "tough hand") had the opposite effect of the one sought. The Honduran President launched Operation *Tolerancia Cero* and Operation *Libertad* in 2002 and 2003, respectively, in order to eradicate gang violence and incarcerate gang members. El Salvador's government followed suit with its *Mano Dura* Plan. Yet, these programs failed to provide security to urban neighborhoods and transformed the prison system into a meeting point for gang networks (Shifter, 2012: 11). Thus, the anti-gang operations and repression methods adopted by the security forces in the Northern Triangle led to organizational changes and adaptation for the *Maras*, who eventually became even more powerful, lethal, and cohesive (Cruz, 2015: 46).

After the failure of *mano dura* policies, the Northern Triangle countries further empowered the military to deal with the *Maras*. In 2010, both the Honduran President and Parliament approved decrees and laws allowing military intervention in domestic violence. In 2011, it was El Salvador's turn to allow military forces to act in the fight against crime, and then Guatemala followed suit. While military forces are usually less corrupt than police forces, the results have not been as expected. High-profile actions such as capturing crime barons and seizing drugs shipments proved to be momentous achievements, though they did not prove to be effective in the long term (Shifter, 2012: 12). Due to the weakness of the state in El Salvador, the virulent violence following the military intervention against criminal groups contributed to the proliferation of paramilitary action, actually increasing the number of homicides committed (see Manz, 2008; and Sampó, 2018).

In sum, Honduras, El Salvador, and Guatemala (in that order), tried repressive policies of confronting gang violence that eventually backfired. Other responses included increasing private security and law enforcement by the state's own citizens, and empowering civil society (see Shifter, 2012: 13). In 2011, the Justice and Public Security Minister of El Salvador, David Munguía Payés, attempted to broker a truce among criminal gangs in order to reduce violence. While this strategy bore some fruit, eventually it was reversed. There are significant political issues blocking the way to reach efficient policies to combat crime and violence, including institutional reform, purge of police forces tainted by corruption, professionalization of police forces, and eliminating impunity (see Rodgers and Baird, 2015; and Savenije and van der Borgh, 2014). Thus, we corroborate Hypothesis 2 in the case of the Northern Triangle.

Hypothesis 3: The Prevalent Socioeconomic Conditions of the Neighboring States

We argue that poor economic conditions in weak and fragile states, as in the Northern Triangle countries, create a favorable environment for the occurrence and proliferation of illicit transnational flows. Espach and Haering's (2012) Report on the causes of regional migration from the region focused on the socioeconomic conditions in the borderlands of the Northern Triangle countries. Most borderland areas are deprived of basic services including transportation, and they suffer from a general lack of infrastructure. Moreover, the Report highlighted the lack of the rule of law alongside the almost nonexistent presence of state security forces at the border. Consequently, poorly serviced and regulated borderlands favor the rise of local non-state actors, who occasionally assume roles of governance and provide services. Among these VNSAs, criminal organizations might compete to fill the vacuum in these ungoverned spaces of areas of limited statehood (see Arias, 2010). For instance, in the Guatemalan case, illicit activities, whether domestic or transnational, had a positive spillover effect on communities that benefitted and profited from the presence of transnational criminal groups, which provide them with health, security, and education services where the state is explicitly absent.

Despite the new economic opportunities for interaction and integration following the signing of the Central American Free Trade Agreement (CAFTA) with the United States in 2005, the economies of the Northern Triangle have remained fragile with high levels of poverty and inequality. While informal employment remains quite common in Latin America, it constitutes a very pervasive feature in Central American economy and society. Whereas in Latin America about 46 percent of the labor force is considered informal, in El Salvador, Honduras, and Guatemala the figures are respectively 65 percent, 72 percent, and 73 percent (International Labor Organization, 2014: 33).

In a similar vein, remittances remain a crucial economic contribution for these Central American countries. The money sent by Northern Triangle immigrants working in the United States to their homelands constitutes one of the most salient sources of income for these backward economies. Today, the population of Central Americans residing in the United States is about 3.5 million, most of them from El Salvador, Guatemala, and Honduras (Lesser and Batalova, 2017: 1). Remittances have reached up to 78 percent of El Salvador exports, contributing about 17 percent of its GDP. The figures for Honduras are equivalent to 93 percent of its exports (about 11 percent of its GDP), and for Guatemala they represent 58 percent of its exports, or about 10 percent of its GDP (see Colburn and Cruz, 2016: 84; and World Bank, 2017).

External actors have been well aware of the pernicious economic logic behind crime and violence in the Northern Triangle, though their motivation is security oriented rather than altruistic. For instance, SICA devoted time and resources to assist Northern Triangle countries in combatting crime. In a meeting in Guatemala in 2011, along with representatives from the United States, Chile, and Mexico, SICA envisioned programs in law enforcement, crime prevention, institutional reform, and prisons. By doing so, they pledged $323 million to implement several programs in the aforementioned areas (see Shifter, 2012: 14).

As for the United States, its efforts to ameliorate the security and economic conditions of the Northern Triangle countries derive from the intrinsic motivation to push the US-Mexican border further south in order to cope with illegal migration and other illicit transnational flows (see Hiemstra, 2019). Thus, in addition to fostering a program of the Central America Regional Security Initiative

(CARSI), the United States has supported several development programs, in particular to assist at-risk youth across the area. In 2015, the Obama Administration, under the Program Alliance for Prosperity Plan, allocated $750 million for Central America. This cooperation program had three main goals: stimulate the private sector, develop economic opportunities, and strengthen public institutions. Similarly, in June 2017, the Trump Administration hosted the Conference on Prosperity and Security in Central America, launching a series of initiatives to advance prosperity, economic growth, and security in the Northern Triangle (see García, 2016; and Hiemstra, 2019). In sum, Hypothesis 3 seems to be very relevant in this case.

The Colombian Borders and the Northern Andean Region

When mentioning the Colombian borders as part of the Northern Andean region we refer not just to the international borders of the current Colombian state, but also to the larger region of "Gran Colombia." This region includes the initial political unit that freed itself under the leadership of Simón Bolívar from Spain in the early nineteenth century, encompassing much of northern South America and part of Central America between 1819 and 1831 when it dissolved. This vast area includes Colombia, Venezuela, Ecuador (the "Bolivarian nations"), Panama, northern Peru, western Guyana, and areas of northwest Brazil.

Colombia is itself a large South American country – fourth in territorial terms after Brazil, Argentina, and Peru – with an area of more than 1,000,000 square kilometers and 6,004 kilometers of land borders with Panama, Venezuela, Brazil, Ecuador, and Peru. In addition, Colombia has 3,208 kilometers of coastline, and maritime borders with Costa Rica, Nicaragua, Honduras, and Jamaica. It is also the third-largest country in Latin America in terms of population, with forty-seven million inhabitants, and fourth in terms of its gross national product (GNP), of about $300 billion for 2017.

After its independence in 1819 and several border disputes that led to brief wars with Peru (in 1828–9) and with Ecuador (1863), in the second half of the nineteenth century, Colombia experienced a series of civil wars, like the Thousand Days War (1899–1902). The fall of the Liberal

Party government that governed the country between 1930 and 1946 was followed by a period popularly known as *La Violencia* between 1948 and 1956, a virulent civil war confronting conservatives and liberals that caused at least three hundred thousand deaths and a significant economic crisis in the vast rural areas. The so-called *Frente Nacional* (National Front), a political pact between liberals and conservatives that was approved in 1957, restored peace and brought formal democracy; yet, it did not address the deep socioeconomic problems that the civil war unfolded.

In 1964 and 1965, following these unresolved political and economic issues, two guerrilla groups were formed: the Fuerzas Armadas Revolucionarias de Colombia – Ejército del Pueblo (FARC-ELP) ("Revolutionary Armed Forces of Colombia-People's Army"), and the Ejército de Liberación Nacional (ELN) ("National Liberation Army"). Both guerrilla groups built on the legacies of La Violencia and the inspiration of the Cuban Revolution of 1959, and on the Algerian FLN's model of armed struggle. While the FARC dismantled and disarmed itself in 2017, following the Peace Treaty of November 2016 and becoming a political party, the ELN guerrilla group continues to be active in 2021, with about two thousand members. The ELN is still involved in violent and terrorist actions, alongside several thousand dissident people from the FARC spreading across the country, with Venezuela becoming a rear-guard area and source of funding for some of these VNSAs (see Venezuela Investigative Unit, 2018: 52–54).

Between 1964 and 2016, Colombia remained in a continuous state of civil war. During these five decades, Colombia faced economic crises, rampant violence, and weak governments. The country remained mired in a morass of drug-related guerrilla, state, and para-military violence, as well as convoluted links among insurgency, counterinsurgency, drug trafficking, and state–criminal relations (see Hristov, 2014). The bloody conflicts led to social and political polarization, poverty and economic inequality, and widespread violence, contributing to the proliferation of transnational criminality, especially drug trafficking (see Holmes, 2002: 217, 225; also Andreas and Duran Martinez, 2015: 383; Barnes, 2017: 971; Dube et al., 2013: 400; and Stone, 2016).

In June 2016, the FARC signed a ceasefire accord with the Colombian government led by Colombian President Juan Manuel Santos in Havana, Cuba. The peace treaty was completed on

August 25, 2016; it was subsequently submitted to a national referendum on October 2, 2016, which rejected it. This led to subsequent negotiations and to a revised and final version of the treaty on November 12, 2016. The Colombian Congress finally approved the revised version of the Peace Treaty on November 30, 2016. More than fifty years of civil war resulted in the tragic toll of more than two hundred thousand victims, mostly civilians, and more than five million Colombian citizens who were forced to leave their homes and became internally displaced persons (IDPs) in their own country (see Piccone, 2019: 1–3).

Many attempts to negotiate peace between the Colombian government and the guerrillas in the 1980s and 1990s led to a continuing deadlock. It also promoted subsequent military plans with the assistance of the United States since 1999, the so-called *Plan Colombia*, as well as joint military exercises with neighboring countries, such as Brazil. By the turn of the twenty-first century, the FARC was at its highest point, with about twenty thousand combatants and about three thousand kidnapped prisoners. During the early 2000s, an important demobilization of right wing paramilitaries also took place; these contingents later became part of criminal gangs or BACRIM (Bandas Criminales in Spanish). The Plan Colombia, reinforced by military counterinsurgency operations since the arrival to power of President Alvaro Uribe in 2002, led the FARC and the ELN to lose ground between 2006 and 2010. The military escalation also led to international crises with neighboring countries, including Venezuela and Ecuador in 2008, whose governments had been supporting the FARC.

The weakening of the guerrillas contributed to the resumption of the peace process after 2012, when former Defense Minister Juan Manuel Santos succeeded Uribe as Colombia's President. The peace process concluded with the Peace Agreement of November 2016. The treaty's main elements included turning the FARC into a political party, establishing mechanisms of transitional justice, disarmament of the FARC combatants and reintegrating them into Colombian society, and increasing the socioeconomic development of rural areas (see text of the Peace Treaty in Colombia Government, 2016; see also Piccone, 2019). Nowadays, the Andean region witnesses a contradictory reality, which includes a difficult demobilization process and peace-building efforts to implement the Peace Treaty in Colombia after five decades of virulent civil war. It juxtaposes the almost total collapse of neighboring

Venezuela, with concomitant implications for the persistence of violence and transnational crime (see Idler, 2018: 71; and Venezuela Investigative Unit, 2018).

Colombia holds a very strong historical record of peaceful relations with its neighbors. With the exception of its militarized dispute with Peru over Leticia in 1932–4, it has not been involved in any international armed conflict since its war with Ecuador in 1863. At the same time, in 2008, a militarized crisis with Venezuela and Ecuador following a Colombian military operation against the FARC in Ecuadorean territory brought the possibility of war, which never materialized due to the mediation efforts of several Latin American and Pan-American organizations, including the OAS and UNASUR.

At the same time, Colombia has not been at peace internally until recently, due to the resilience of the long civil war between 1964 and 2016. There has been a transition from civil war to peace, leading to significant consequences, including the strengthening of alternative VNSAs in the form of the BACRIM. Colombian borders are still a major hub for drug trafficking and other forms of transnational crime. Moreover, we do not know yet how the recent Peace Treaty between the Colombian government and the FARC might ultimately affect the activity of other VNSAs and the occurrence of illicit transnational flows.

The Colombian Borders

Historically, the Colombian state has neglected if not abandoned its country's borderlands. In the absence of state institutions and effective state governance, VNSAs – including guerrillas, right-wing paramilitaries, and transnational criminal groups – have dominated vast portions of Colombia's peripheral areas for decades, often replacing the state and fulfilling alternative governance functions (Idler, 2016: 2 and 2018: 64–69). The Colombian borders have been suffering from both a lack of state authority and the alternative control by illicit groups and VNSAs. These groups included the FARC, itself involved in drug trafficking since the end of the 1970s; and "narco-terrorism" conducted by drug-trafficking cartels. These cartels were internationally infamous, such as Pablo Escobar's Cartel of Medellín and the Cartel of Cali; and most recently the BACRIM (see Idler, 2018; and Stone, 2016).

The convoluted Colombian geography with its tropical jungles and the Andean mountains that isolate and complicate regional communications has turned the Colombian borderlands with Ecuador, Brazil, Venezuela, and Peru into literally *areas sin ley* (lawless areas), truly areas of limited statehood or ungoverned spaces (see Trejos Rosero, 2015: 41–42). Given the enormous extent of Colombian borders, and the almost inexistent presence of the army or border police in areas such the Amazon, these ungoverned spaces fostered illegal practices that include transnational criminal networks (Trejos Rosero, 2015: 47–48). Thus, Colombia's borders have ultimately earned the reputation of being Latin America's most lawless and ungoverned (see Briscoe, 2008: 3–4; and Sanchez Piñeiro, 2012: 1). Let examine in further detail three of these borders: Colombia-Venezuela, Colombia-Ecuador, and Colombia-Panama.

The Colombian-Venezuelan Border

Colombia and Venezuela share 2,219 kilometers of borderlands; this is actually the longest border for both countries. During the long Colombian civil war, the borderlands were used and abused by the FARC and by other drug-trafficking criminals. The borderlands provided a safe haven (or black spot) for non-state actors involved in the cultivation, production, and trafficking of drugs, developing parallel economies. Moreover, the extensive border has served VNSAs involved in a variety of illicit transnational activities, including money laundering, extortion, kidnappings, drug trafficking, and smuggling (see Souza, 2016).

The failure of the Colombian state in controlling its border with Venezuela relates to the lack of effective state presence, geopolitical factors, high levels of corruption, economic underdevelopment, the thriving of an informal economy, and the existence of alternative forms of governance offered by these non-state actors. Moreover, during the Chávez era (1999–2013) and the subsequent Maduro administration (2013 until today), the Venezuelan government developed strong ties with the FARC. In turn, the FARC, itself associated with the Venezuelan Drug "Cartel of the Suns" (Cartel de los Soles), was instrumental in the development of drug trafficking in Venezuela. While the FARC demobilized in 2017 after signing a peace agreement with the government of Colombia, many "FARC dissidents" remained deeply involved in the drug trade with and within Venezuela (see Venezuela Investigative Unit, 2018: 17–18, 48–51).

In the last five years, due to the implosion of the Venezuelan economy and the criminalization of the Venezuelan state under Nicolas Maduro, the country turned into a virulent mafia state. Thus, Venezuela experiences a symbiotic relationship between its government and organized crime, or in Barnes's terms, probably the best nefarious example in Latin America of integration between the state and non-state criminal actors (see Venezuela Investigative Unit, 2018: 3). Criminal elements have pushed across the border back and forth alongside hundreds of thousands of Venezuelan citizens who consider themselves refugees fleeing from their dysfunctional state (see Ellis and Ortiz, 2017: 7; Lozano, 2018; and Venezuela Investigative Unit, 2018: 48–56).

One of the largest contributors to insecurity along the shared border has been the presence of Colombia's neo-paramilitary groups, guerrillas, and criminal groups, including the BACRIM, now designated as the Organized Armed Groups (*Grupos Armados Organizados* – GAOs), the ELN, and FARC dissidents. These groups have expanded into several Venezuelan border provinces, and are reportedly involved in kidnapping, extortion, and drug trafficking (Gagne, 2015: 1; and Venezuela Investigative Unit, 2018: 5, 49–56). Moreover, Colombian drug trafficking organizations have turned Venezuela into a logistical base and one of the principal transit nations for the traffic of Colombian cocaine.

Due to the traditional tension and rivalry between Colombia and Venezuela, the border has been sporadically closed, despite the high level of economic interaction between the countries (Idler, 2016: 2). The implosion of the Venezuelan state has created a new reality of more than two million desperate Venezuelans fleeing into Colombia in 2017–20, leading to the deployment of several thousand Colombian soldiers to keep order at the boundaries. On August 2, 2018, a few days before leaving office, Colombian President Santos granted temporary status to about half a million Venezuelan refugees. The current Colombian President, Iván Duque Márquez, has continued the policy of regularizing their stay in the country (see UNHCR, 2019 and 2020; and Venezuela Investigative Unit, 2018: 10–11).

The Colombian-Ecuadorian Border

Colombia and Ecuador share 586 kilometers of land border. A myriad of VNSAs function along the border between the two countries, some claiming to be guerrillas like the FARC in origin, while others have been following the footsteps of paramilitary groups in the 1990s. All of these groups have been involved in illegal activities, including illicit transnational flows such as drug trafficking (see Chinchilla, 2011: 2).

Over the last decade, Ecuador has emerged as an important piece in the global drug trade, with up to a third of Colombia's cocaine production exported through the country (see Bargent, 2019). In the recent past, the ideological and military tensions between the two countries defined their peaceful relations as a merely negative peace, although there has been a notable improvement in their bilateral interactions in the last few years. The border has remained open, but its control mostly relies on unilateral measures on each side (see Idler, 2016: 2).

As Maiah Jaskoski cogently argues, what is remarkable in the Colombia-Ecuador borderlands is the fact that the FARC in Southern Colombia had physically delineated, kept, and enforced the Colombian borderline with Ecuador. Moving relatively freely across the border between the two countries until the late 2010s, the FARC had controlled border populations by providing governance, order, and economic benefits, given the void and vacuum left by the absence of the Colombian state (see Jaskoski, 2015). Moreover, by substituting the state, the FARC also kept some degree of peace and stability vis-à-vis other drug-trafficking VNSAs in the border area. Thus, once the FARC retreated, withdrew, and eventually demobilized in 2017, there has been an attempt by the two countries to improve their security along their common border confronting new transnational threats, such as those posed by sophisticated and violent international drug cartels and criminal gangs. Ironically, this is another unintended consequence of the Peace Treaty of 2016, as related to the FARC demobilization and dismantling (see Ellis and Ortiz, 2017: 5–7; Sanchez Piñeiro, 2012: 1; and Varela, 2018: 3).

The Colombian-Panamanian Border

Colombia and Panama share a 225-kilometer international boundary, which is also the border between South America and Central America. The border includes the Darien Gap, a 106-kilometer-long swath of underdeveloped swamps and jungle, which had served as a safe haven and black spot for the FARC and other criminal groups. In 2011, Colombia signed a Binational Border Security Plan with Panama, aimed to facilitate cooperation in fighting crime along their shared border, especially in the Darien Gap, which has been a key location for the trafficking of drugs, people, and arms (see Stone, 2011).

Unlike other Colombian borders, the frontier between Colombia and Panama is one of the most closed in Latin America, as people are required to present both passport and tourist cards. In the last decade, the closeness of the border did not manage to stop the continuous smuggling and trafficking of people. In May 2016, Panama closed its borders with Colombia to prevent illegal migrants from Cuba and Africa from entering the country. Yet, the fact that this border is less soft or porous than other Colombian borders has not prevented the occurrence and proliferation of illicit transnational flows, including smuggling, the trafficking of drugs, migrants, and arms, and even transnational terrorist activities in the case of the FARC (see Yagoub, 2014).

Transnational Crime and Terrorism across the Colombian Borders

Similar to the cases of US-Mexico and of the Northern Triangle, the illicit transnational flows across the Colombian borders include drug trafficking, arms trafficking, smuggling, and human trafficking. What is particular about the Colombian case has been the presence of the FARC (until 2016) and the ELN, Colombian guerrillas who metamorphosed over time into transnational criminal groups involved as well in terrorist activities, alongside paramilitary groups that became criminal armed organizations, whether in Colombia or across its borders (see Saab and Taylor, 2008). Despite the almost total disarmament of the FARC in 2017, new criminal gangs, such as the BACRIM, as well as "dissident FARC" guerrillas and the still-active ELN, have taken their role and continue to be engaged in transnational criminality. Moreover, Colombia has also been notorious for its international drug cartels, working across its borders and well beyond. We first assess the roles of the guerrillas and other VNSAs and then turn to the description of these illicit transnational flows.

Guerrillas/Terrorist Groups: FARC and ELN

As mentioned previously, the FARC-ELP and the ELN have historically been the two major Colombian guerrilla groups, also considered terrorist groups or even criminal VNSAs due to their illicit activities, which include kidnapping for ransom, extortion, and random indiscriminate violence (see Saab and Taylor, 2008). These two groups succeeded over time in building a parallel state and a parallel economy – once the Colombian State renounced its role as guarantor of people's security, property rights, and economic well-being – thus becoming providers of governance in certain areas of the country, including some of its remote borderlands (Idler, 2018: 59; and Trejos Rosero, 2015: 43).

FARC's and ELN's territorial control on some of the borderlands with Venezuela and Ecuador allowed decades of stable development of coca cultivation, despite fumigation efforts and militarized efforts to weaken these illegal groups (Briscoe, 2008: 4). The presence of the FARC in these peripheral areas was accompanied by the strengthening of economic activities linked to drug-trafficking business, including illicit cultivation, laboratories for coca processing, and exploitation of border areas (Trejos Rosero, 2015: 50; see also Venezuelan Investigative Unit, 2018: 52–54). Still, since neither the FARC nor the ELN completely controlled the entire cocaine production and distribution chain, they depended on cooperation with drug traffickers and other kinds of brokers and intermediaries to transport the cocaine to the final consumer markets. A similar pattern refers to other economic activities involving the FARC in the past, such as the illegal exploitation of mineral sources, of which the coltan has been the best example in recent years (see Trejos Rosero, 2015: 51–52).

The Colombian guerrillas also succeeded in attaining a certain degree of regional and international legitimacy, with many fluctuations over time. From their beginnings, both the FARC and the ELN built strong ties with Cuba and other left-oriented regimes in the region, as well with some European groups and governments. The rise of Hugo Chávez to power in Venezuela in 1999 and of Rafael Correa in Ecuador in 2007 consolidated the growing support of these two countries for the FARC, raising international tensions and crises that led to the verge of war in 2008 in a confrontation involving Colombia, Venezuela, and Ecuador. At the highest point of the 2008 crisis following a Colombian military attack against a FARC outpost in Ecuador, the Colombian government publicly accused Chávez of sending $300 million to the FARC (Marcella, 2008: 3). Moreover, for some time, Chávez had been campaigning internationally to have the FARC recognized as "belligerents," coordinating diplomatic moves with them, and providing them with money, guns, rocket-propelled grenade launchers, and thousands of rounds of ammunition (Marcella, 2008: 18). Venezuela also facilitated networking between the FARC and armed terrorist groups such as Hezbollah, linked to Iran, allegedly covering money laundering, arms trafficking, drugs, and weapons (see Walser, 2010).

The growing support of *Chavista* governments for the FARC took place at the same time that Plan Colombia and Uribe's military operations during his second term as Colombian president in 2006–10 led to the military weakening of the FARC. Gradually, the Colombian state managed to gain the upper hand over the FARC, leading large number of guerrillas to voluntarily surrender. Yet, as an unintended consequence, the military initiative begun by Uribe and continued by Santos in 2010–14 pushed the FARC out of Colombia's central and more urban regions and into more remote regions and neighboring countries, including Panama, Ecuador, and Venezuela (see Bargent, 2019; and Stone, 2011).

BACRIM

The fragmentation of the traditional drug cartels such as the Cartel de Medellín and the Cartel de Cali has led in the last decade to the appearance of nefarious VNSAs, which have taken on some of the roles formerly performed by the big cartels and by the FARC – the BACRIM (Bandas Criminales, criminal gangs in Spanish). BACRIM were fuelled by the thousands of paramilitary and guerrilla fighters who had demobilized through the 2000s, the rivalries between criminal networks, and the pressure of the Colombian authorities to locate and capture the senior leaders of the drug cartels. Given the exile, arrest, or killings of senior drug traffickers and other criminals, less-experienced or second-rate criminals got local control, with a greater propensity to use indiscriminate violence, assassinations, and massacres on a larger scale against the civilian population. Since 2010, these criminal bands have entered a phase of fragmentation and dispersion (see Garzón and Olson, 2013: 9).

BACRIM proliferated especially in the Colombia-Venezuela border, given the fact that about 350 small drug cartels worked at various stages of the cocaine production and transit process, linked to diverse transnational cartels, including the Mexican ones (see Garzón and Olson, 2013: 5). The relevant nodes and networks are not only transnational and regional; they are occasionally global. For instance, alliances between Colombian BACRIM and Russian criminal organizations provide access to illicit international markets to national criminal groups including money laundering facilities and sources of illegal weapons. The BACRIM have also been able to expand and generate new sources of income, such as smuggling of hydrocarbons, nonformal gold mining, and smuggling of consumer products. In this way, they have achieved expansion and diversification of their networks, making some tactical adjustments, such as refraining from cultivating coca so as not to attract the attention of the Colombian authorities; mobilizing part of their operational structure into licit avenues; and limiting (albeit not completely renouncing) their violent actions (Garzón and Olson, 2013: 15). As Naím (2005) suggested, the modus operandi of these organizations is very similar to that of the licit ones, like multinational corporations.

Nowadays, the BACRIM embody the third generation of Colombian drug trafficking organizations, after the dismantling of the Medellín and Cali Cartels (first generation), into federations of "baby" cartels, which amalgamated with the paramilitary forces of the AUC until their co-optation and demobilization in the early 2000s by the Uribe Administration (second generation). Nowadays, the BACRIM cooperate and compete with Mexican DTOs operating in Colombia and across its borders (see McDermott, 2014; and Venezuelan Investigative Unit, 2018: 56).

Drug Trafficking
Three of the key drug borders of Latin America include several Colombian borders: with Venezuela (Arauca; Apure); with Ecuador (Department of Putumayo and Narino; the Provinces of Esmeraldas, Carchi, and Sucumbios); and with Peru (the areas of Leticia, Trapecio Amazónico, Tabatainga, and the city of Caballococha) (see Venezuelan Investigative Unit, 2018; also Bargent, 2019). In addition, Colombian criminal groups have also cooperated (and eventually clashed) with Brazilian organized crime regarding the control of the so-called Route of Solimões, as one of the main links for the cocaine traffic to Europe, Asia, and West Africa (see Ferreira and Framento, 2019). Since the early 1980s, Colombia has become a central node in the cocaine trade, even though initially coca cultivation was far more intensive in Peru and Bolivia (Williams, 2016: 269). As we have described, all these borderlands constitute geopolitical corridors for the global cocaine industry and are sites of supply and operation for the major VNSAs involved in Colombia's decades-long armed internal conflict, attracting

guerrillas, paramilitaries, and criminal organizations alike (see Idler, 2014 and 2018).

Whereas the traditional management of drug trafficking has been attributed to the large drug cartels, guerrillas and paramilitaries played a significant role in it as well. Based on intelligence sources, a report of the International Crisis Group (ICG, 2008) estimated that about 50 percent of the coca production in 2008 took place in territories controlled by the FARC. In other words, it was the interaction and interdependence among insurgency, counterinsurgency, and drug cartels that played a critical role in reconfiguring the economics of the borderlands and shaping its cross-border ramifications. Several studies estimated that by the end of the 2000s, Colombia's cocaine export capacity encompassed, alongside with other drugs such as heroin and marijuana, about $13,780 million. If we deduct the production costs of about 20 percent, this left a net income of $11,120 million, quite a lucrative business (see Kessler, 2011: 6). Likewise, the UNODC 2012 annual report disclosed that the total area, globally, devoted to illegal crops associated with cocaine was around 153.7 thousand hectares in 2011, out of which 64 thousand were located just in Colombia (Bartolome, 2002: 53).

In the last decade, the relative importance of Colombia in the transnational drug trafficking industry has declined. Although Colombia remains the main source of cocaine found in the United States and Europe, direct shipments from Peru and Bolivia have become more and more common (Mejía, 2014: 94). Moreover, one of the effects of the US-funded fumigation policy through Plan Colombia had been the transfer of coca crops to remote areas along the border with Ecuador, the Amazon region, and the northeast border with Venezuela (see Briscoe, 2008: 4).

Arms Trafficking

Although there seems to be less awareness of this illicit transnational activity, arms trafficking is in fact the other side of the coin of the drug market, and the two are very much interrelated. In contrast to drug trafficking, there is insufficient data regarding illegal arms trafficking, given that it is based on estimations derived from seizures, and that there is a lack of transparency about public stockpiles, legal owners, and arms transfers between countries (see Kessler, 2011: 11).

The Colombia-Brazil border deserves particular attention, due to the concern of the Brazilian authorities operating in the Amazonian region regarding this trafficking as a significant security threat. Central America represents the single largest source of illegal weapons to Colombia, with five countries – El Salvador, Honduras, Nicaragua, Panama, and Costa Rica – accounting for more than a third of all arms trafficked into the country. The land arms trafficking takes place through the Darien Gap along the Colombian-Panamanian border. Moreover, Colombia's immediate neighbors all act as both sources and transit routes for small arms trafficking (see Cragin and Hoffmann, 2003: xvii–xviii).

Human Trafficking: Transnational and Domestic
More than fifty years of civil war have ravaged Colombia leaving hundreds of thousands of people dead, millions displaced, and countless others who have suffered violations of their human rights, including human trafficking. Moreover, impunity and illicit governance structures in Colombia's borderlands have facilitated cross-border illegal migrant flows, becoming a significant incentive for human trafficking (Idler, 2018: 71). While it is difficult to assess the exact number of victims, there have been estimates of about fifty thousand to seventy thousand Colombians trafficked each year, the majority of them women and children. These figures refer both to transnational and especially to domestic trafficking of persons (see Wells, 2013: 1).

One of the tragic human consequences of the multiple conflicts involving the military, paramilitaries, guerrillas, drug cartels, and BACRIM in the Colombian borderlands has been the massive forced displacement of the civilian population, including illegal migration across borders. By 2005, between 250,000 and 500,000 Colombians were forced to leave their homes and move to Europe, while another 500,000 were living in Venezuela at that time (see Briscoe, 2008: 4). Several thousands of Colombian immigrants suffered from human trafficking, especially in Ecuador and Peru.

In the Colombian case – and due to the enormous number of internally displaced persons, estimated at about 5.7 million people – the problem of internal human trafficking was much worse than the transnational one. Both criminal gangs and, in the past, the FARC forcibly recruited children. Women in poor rural areas, indigenous people, and relatives of members of criminal organizations had been particularly vulnerable to being trafficked within the country, especially to urban areas (see Wells, 2013: 2–3; also Parkinson, 2013).

In the most recent reversal of fortune across the Venezuelan-Colombian border, the massive exodus of Venezuelans to Colombia has led to the proliferation of sex workers. Venezuelan migrant women and men selling sex in Colombia are at high risk of trafficking into forced prostitution, and we know little about this recent and largely invisible problem (see Moloney, 2017: 1–5).

Explaining the Reality of Colombian Peaceful Borders and Illicit Transnational Flows

Hypothesis 1: The Degree of Physical and Institutional Openness of the Peaceful Borders

Due to the combination of their territorial length and their convoluted geography and topography, the Colombian borders are very difficult to control, especially in the Andean and Amazonian areas. Consequently, as these borders tend to be open and porous, so they are prone to the occurrence and proliferation of illicit transnational flows. The evident physical and institutional limitations to controlling 6,000 kilometers of border weaken the manifestation of effective sovereignty, so this border porosity is a catalyst for the presence of VNSAs.

US aid since the early 2000s in the form of Plan Colombia, together with growing military counterinsurgency offensives against the FARC and the drugs cartels have contributed to reinforcement of border control. However, in absolute terms, the border regime has remained open and porous, even in parts of the Colombia-Panama border, which is the most closed among the Colombian borders. In some Amazonian border departments of Colombia, the presence of its national army, air force, or another form of state authority is still virtually nonexistent (see Trejos Rosero, 2015: 47–48). Land borders remain soft not only in terms of drug trafficking and arms trafficking, but also in terms of human trafficking and smuggling.

In the last decade, we detect an increasing perception of the security threats in Brazil, Venezuela, and Ecuador with respect to their common borders with Colombia that led to a stronger control of the borderlands on their part. This threat perception has recently become irrelevant and even superseded by the economic and political implosion of Venezuela in the last few years, which has escalated into the worst refugee crisis in the Western Hemisphere ever, with the exodus of about four million Venezuelans to neighboring countries, mainly to Colombia, Brazil, and

Ecuador (see UNHCR, 2019 and 2020). Therefore, we corroborate the first hypothesis in most of the Colombian borders, except for the peculiar case of the Colombian-Panamanian border.

Hypothesis 2: The Degree of Governance, Institutional Strength, and Political Willingness

Most of the relevant countries in the North Andean region belong to a special category of relatively weak South American states with high economic potential and rich in natural resources, although they rank very high in terms of corruption; namely, Colombia, Venezuela, Ecuador, and Peru.

Considering the Fragile State Index, the Corruption Index, and the Freedom House Index as shown in Table 3.3, the Colombian borders cover an area that we should consider as very fragile in terms of level of governance. Thus, Colombia and Venezuela are among the most fragile states in Latin America, with a score of 117 and 104, respectively, and thus considered in an "alert" situation. They are also "highly corrupted," especially Venezuela and Ecuador, which rank 158 and 107. Moreover, the trends of the last decade show that Venezuela is one of the few countries where scores changed drastically for the worse, so it is experiencing a tragic process of imploding, being officially absent from the borderlands (or alternatively, openly collaborating with criminal groups like the Cartel de los Soles).

Hence, we validate the second hypothesis in the case of the Colombian borders. The incursion of VNSAs initially from Colombia has spilled over and spread over to neighboring countries, in the form of guerrilla and transnational terrorist activity, as well as drug trafficking, human trafficking, and arms trafficking. There has been a constant process of weakening of the Colombian state over its borderlands in far-away areas, and that process had a contagion effect upon its neighbors (see Briscoe, 2008: 4). Moreover, in the last few years, we have seen an improvement in the ranking of Colombia in terms of governance, whereas both Venezuela and Ecuador have deteriorated to the bottom of the indexes of corruption and political ineptitude in the Americas.

The relative lack of control and governance over the Colombian borders relates to the lack of capabilities of the Colombian state. It refers to an endemic political problem regarding its meager political willingness and lack of collective action in enforcing its presence in this vast country, beyond the major cities where the political and economic elites reside (see Idler, 2014 and 2018). Violence, ineffective government, and impunity have been a common thread in Colombia's long political history, For instance, we can mention the attempted impeachment of President Ernesto Samper for his alleged links to the Cali drug cartel in the mid-1990s (see Dube et al., 2013: 400; Dugas, 2001; and Holmes, 2002: 217). At different political levels – local, regional, and national – and similar to the case of the PRI in Mexico between 1929 and 2000, there have been symbiotic relationships between organized crime and political elites in Colombia that explain the relative lack of governance in many parts of the country (see Stone, 2016). Perhaps the encouraging news is that the third generation of criminal organizations (the BACRIM), has weaker ties to the political elites than their predecessors, moving away from alliance or enforcement-evasion in the direction of confrontation (see Barnes, 2017: 968; and Stone, 2016).

Hypothesis 3: The Prevalent Socioeconomic Conditions of the Neighboring States

It is difficult to discern the relevance of the political economy of the Colombian borderlands, built on the data on the HDI and the GDP as reported in Table 3.3. In terms of the Human Development Index, Colombia ranks 97, Ecuador 88, Peru 84, Brazil 75, and Venezuela 71. In terms of the GDP, Brazil is an overwhelming economic power compared to its neighbors, although its richness is territorially uneven; hence, Amazonia does not seem to contribute substantially to its national wealth or to attract its neighbors as a magnet for economically motivated migration. Moreover, Colombia and Venezuela were ranked in similar terms (before the most recent implosion of the Venezuelan economy), ahead of Peru, Ecuador, and Panama. Thus, we cannot record here striking socioeconomic gaps among the neighboring countries that justify the occurrence and proliferation of illicit transnational flows.

Having said that, it is clear that socioeconomic gaps between the borderlands of Colombia and its political and economic core promote a political-economy rationale for the thriving of parallel, informal, and illicit economies. Moreover, unlike the previous cases discussed in this chapter, Colombia's borderlands have been both sites of production and the supply points for drug trafficking networks, setting the ideal conditions for the thriving of a great and dense illicit market. For instance, the Colombian-Venezuelan border has been traditionally a focus of smuggling, drug trafficking, oil stealing, and many other networks of extortion (see Venezuelan Investigative Unit, 2018). Nowadays, it is the dramatic scenario for millions of Venezuelans seeking refuge and asylum in Colombia itself.

In the not so distant past, the Colombian borderlands have been a meeting point where the ideological divisions between the FARC and former paramilitaries, or even the political differences between neighboring countries just disappeared due to the vast shared economic opportunities open for illicit entrepreneurs. As Briscoe suggests, "within the context of a kind of free market, transnational criminal organizations can buy the rights of transit for drugs from smaller groups, like commercial rights" (Briscoe, 2008: 6). In sum, we validate the relevance of the third hypothesis for the Colombian borders.

The Tri-Border Area (TBA) of the Southern Cone of South America

The Triple Frontier (or Tri-Border Area, TBA) comprises about 2,500 square kilometers at the meeting point of three MERCOSUR countries – Argentina, Brazil, and Paraguay – in the east-central part of South America's Southern Cone. The population is concentrated in three border cities: Ciudad del Este in Paraguay (about four hundred thousand inhabitants), Foz do Iguaçú in Brazil (about three hundred thousand inhabitants), and Puerto Iguazú in Argentina (about eighty-two thousand inhabitants). Foz do Iguaçú and Ciudad del Este are linked by the Puente de la Amistad ("Friendship Bridge"), completed in 1965, over the Paraná River; Puerto Iguazú and Foz do Iguaçú are linked by the Puente Tancredo Neves ("Fraternity Bridge"), completed in 1985, over the Iguazú River. Daily, about forty thousand people cross the Puente de la Amistad, and about four thousand people cross the Puente Tancredo Neves (see Guerrero, 2006: 13–14). There are about two million tourists a year (especially visiting the spectacular Iguazú Falls), and about fifty thousand daily workers, who usually cross the border between Paraguay and Brazil. Many of those crossing the borders are *Transportistas* ("transporters") – couriers, runners, and smugglers, and in Portuguese they are called *sacoleiros* (see Aguiar, 2015). They carry goods like electronics, subsidized agricultural products, and toys from Ciudad del Este, the largest commercial center in Latin America, with an annual trade movement of $5 billion (see Folch, 2012).

The "prehistory" of the TBA refers to the territorial dispute between Argentina and Brazil over the territory of Misiones, which was peacefully settled in 1895. The relations between the two regional powers of South America remained tense until the turning point in 1979, when they signed a tripartite agreement, alongside Paraguay, to share the hydroelectric power generated by Itaipú, the giant dam built by Brazil and Paraguay across the Paraná River. Economically, the region developed and prospered following the establishment of the MERCOSUR trade agreement in 1991 (see Jimenez Aguilar and Thoene, 2019).

Between 1895 and 1979, Brazil and Argentina competed over regional hegemony in South America. This rivalry was exacerbated by geopolitical doctrines that amplified frustration in Argentina and the desire for power in Brazil, the latter of which developed in economic terms vis-à-vis its neighbors throughout the twentieth century. In the late 1970s, Brazil initiated a policy of Latin-Americanization toward its Spanish-speaking neighbors with the goal of building better relations with the rest of South America. The converging motivations of Argentina and Brazil, together with Paraguay's interest in new sources of energy and economic development, led to the resolution of a thirteen-year dispute over the hydropower generation of energy along the Paraná River in 1979 with the building of the Itaipú Dam on the border between Brazil and Paraguay (see Gardini, 2006).

The most important outcome of the tripartite agreement was to put in motion a process of rapprochement that included economic and military cooperation, especially regarding the nuclear issue. In 1980, Argentina and Brazil further expanded and improved their bilateral relations by exchanging presidential visits and signing a package of ten cooperation agreements, including joint arms production and nuclear cooperation. After democratization took root in both countries in the mid-1980s, Argentina and Brazil launched a bilateral integration program (ABEIP) in 1986, which upgraded bilateral relations in the direction of establishing stable peace. The convergence of national interests between the two countries in 1985–90 led to their integration in the economic sphere, first at the bilateral level (1986–9), and later through the addition of the two small buffer states of Paraguay and Uruguay and the establishment of MERCOSUR in 1991 (see Gardini, 2006; and Kacowicz, 2000: 204–207).

With the signing of the Tripartite Agreement over Itaipú in October 1979, Argentina and Brazil moved along the continuum from a relationship of negative peace through the stage of stabilization and rapprochement in their bilateral relations (1979–90), toward consolidation of their stable peace (1991–9) and the emergence of a loose pluralistic security community (see Kacowicz, 2000; also Hurrell, 1998). The "upgrading" of peace enabled the occurrence and proliferation of illicit transnational flows, the thriving of terrorism, and transnational criminal activities such as money laundering that pose new challenges to the region's security (see Pion-Berlin, 2005: 214–246).

Unlike border flows in the case of North America and the establishment of NAFTA, border movements across the TBA have been relatively recent. The TBA first began to develop as an important economic region in the early 1970s, especially with the agreement to build the Itaipú Dam between Paraguay and Brazil in 1973. This brought an economic boom to the area. The population of Foz do Iguaçú grew from 30,000 in 1970 to 150,000 in 1985, when Argentina and Brazil also built an international bridge. Moreover, the importance of the TBA as a trading and integrated region drastically increased with the signing of MERCOSUR in 1991. MERCOSUR significantly contributed to the promotion of regional trade, taking advantage of the energy produced at Itaipú, the world's largest hydroelectric plant, and the tourist potential of the Iguazú Falls (see Umaña, 2012: 3). The importance of Itaipú is paramount in both Paraguay and Brazil: it provides about 90 percent of the electricity of Paraguay, and about 30 percent of that of Brazil (Guerrero, 2006: 26).

The Open Borders of the TBA

The TBA has evolved from a once-contested area including a militarized border between Argentina and Brazil to a border area that is highly integrated economically and socially, though it records smuggling, trafficking, transnational crime, and possibly terrorism. Once the borderlands became peaceful and demilitarized, following the 1979 Tripartite Agreement of Itaipú, the rapprochement between Argentina and Brazil, the transition from negative peace to stable peace, and the formation of MERCOSUR in 1991, there has been a proliferation of illicit transnational flows, carried out by transnational non-state actors, including TCOs and terrorist cells.

The TBA's bleak combination of ungoverned areas, together with poverty, illicit activities, disenfranchised groups, ill-equipped law-enforcement agencies and militaries, and fragile democracies, has resulted in a dangerous environment for the occurrence of transnational illicit flows, ranging from criminals to terrorists (see Shelley and Picarelli, 2005: 61–65). At the same time, and despite the fact that the TBA constitutes an epicenter of a variety of flourishing illicit trade activities, in comparison to the borders of Mexico, Colombia, and the Northern Triangle, it has remained far less violent than the other American borderlands described in this chapter (see Andreas and Duran Martinez, 2015: 383). This is related to the type and volume of illicit activities – more involvement with money laundering and smuggling of goods, rather than drug and arms trafficking (see Mares, 2019).

Nowadays the borders among the three countries are open, porous, and practically nonexistent, while airspace is free, without radar supervision. The weak monitoring of border controls, especially between Brazil and Paraguay, makes the TBA an ideal place for illicit activities. Furthermore, the interconnectedness through two international bridges further blurs the physical borders that separate the three countries. Thus the whole region – with a particular emphasis upon Ciudad del Este, Paraguay – has become a dizzying black void (or black spot) of billions of dollars in contraband, drug trafficking, arms trafficking, money laundering, car theft, piracy, and corruption of public officials (see Hudson, 2003; and Sverdlick, 2005).

Transnational Crime and Terrorism in the TBA

Compared to the previous three cases, the TBA is peculiar for its vast array of criminal activities, with a special focus on merchandise smuggling, contraband, and money laundering rather than drug and arms trafficking. In addition, the area is probably a hub for transnational terrorism. Hence, it is a convergence point between transnational criminal flows and global crime, with a focus upon financial crime. Moreover, the TBA illustrates the potential links between terrorist financing and illicit flows of money derived from the international criminal economy (see Shelley and Picarelli, 2005: 61).

Criminal Activity in the TBA

All types of black market and other criminal activities take place in the TBA, especially in Ciudad del Este, Paraguay. They include, among others, identification and document fraud, counterfeiting and smuggling of consumer products, intellectual property theft, drug trafficking, arms trafficking human trafficking and sexual exploitation, money laundering, and terrorist financing. The amount of criminal activity has ranked Ciudad del Este third worldwide, behind Hong Kong and Miami, in the volume of cash transactions. The TBA generates over $6 billion annually in illicit finance, and other reports estimate that the amount of money laundered in the TBA averages $12 billion annually (see Umaña, 2012: 3; and Shelley, 2010: 44).

Transnational criminal organizations, mafias, and other criminal groups engaged in transnational illicit activities and flows conduct business transactions in the TBA. These TCOs include the Yakuza from Japan, Nigerians con artists, and a variety of criminal groups from Brazil, China, Colombia, Ivory Coast, Ghana, France (from Corsica), Lebanon, Peru, Russia (from Chechnya), and Ukraine (Umaña, 2012: 9). Thus, the TBA provides a haven that is geographically, socially, economically, and politically permissive for local, regional, transnational, and global organized crime.

Terrorist Activity in the TBA

In several occasions, there have been accusations and sustained arguments about the existence of Islamic fundamentalist terrorist organizations in the TBA. These accusations are based on the existence of a considerable and prosperous Muslim and Arab community in the region (between thirty thousand and fifty thousand people), consisting of a Shi'a majority who arrived in the late 1970s and early 1980s, a Sunni minority, and a small population of Christians. They emigrated from Lebanon, Syria, Egypt, and the Palestinian territories. Most of the Arab immigrants are involved in commerce in Ciudad del Este, though they mainly live across the bridge between Paraguay and Brazil in Foz do Iguaçú, on the Brazilian side of the Iguazú River. Foz do Iguaçú has the second largest Arab community in Brazil, after Sao Paulo (see Abbott, 2004). As a hub for illegal traffic and money laundering, the

TBA provides funds and logistical support for terrorist organizations such as Hezbollah (in Lebanon), Gamaa Al-Islamya (in Egypt), Hamas (in Gaza), and al-Qaeda (see Guerrero, 2006: 47). Hezbollah operatives and supporters have been especially present in Ciudad del Este, as related to criminal activities such as drug smuggling, piracy, and especially money laundering.

The criminal–terrorist nexus is a very controversial topic for the TBA countries, which until recently formally denied the presence of terrorist cells in the region. For instance, only in July and August 2019, respectively, did Argentina and Paraguay finally agree to define Hezbollah as a terrorist organization. Still, international organizations such as Interpol have specifically linked organized crime groups and the thriving black market in the TBA to terrorist groups. In 2007, for instance, the United States formally declared that tens of millions of dollars were laundered in the TBA and disbursed to terrorist organizations. Moreover, a 2005 Paraguayan intelligence report corroborated that about $20 million were collected every year to finance the activities of Hezbollah and Hamas (see Ferreira 2016; Gleiss and Berti, 2012: 70–74; and Umaña, 2012: 10).

More than two decades ago, with the terrorist attacks perpetrated in Argentina in 1992 and 1994, the operational origin of these attacks was traced to Ciudad del Este, Paraguay. The city was and still is a major hub for drug trafficking, black market commerce, and, with a large Arab population, even a safe haven for terrorist groups such as Hezbollah, held responsible (together with Iran) for the terrorist attacks in Buenos Aires.

The TBA is rather unique in comparison to the other American cases in that it is a convergent point between transnational crime and terrorism that physically crosses borders (rivers in this case), in juxtaposition to international crime that is global, virtual, and unrelated to physical borders (such as cybercrime or some forms of financial crime). In this sense, it is a striking example of the "dark side" of globalization in a context of regional integration, whereas the long list of TCOs that prosper in Ciudad del Este, involved in both licit and illicit business, seem to embody the conglomerate of "International Criminals Inc."

In the case of the TBA, we conclude that the necessary conditions for creating a safe haven and a black spot of transnational crime and terrorism are all in place. First, the particular geography of the borderlands makes them very difficult to monitor. Second, the required resources to enforce central authority and coordinate activities to adequately govern and protect the relevant countries and populations are very limited, especially in the case of Paraguay. Third, all three bordering countries rank at the top of the Corruption Perception Index of Transparency International (2015), with their high levels of corruption. Lax immigration controls and corrupt officials at the borders have also facilitated the relatively free movement of transnational criminal organizations. Finally, poverty is a widespread phenomenon across the borderlands of the three countries (especially regarding Paraguay), despite the vast wealth of countries endowed with huge natural resources like Argentina and Brazil (see Brafman Kittner, 2007: 315–318; and Pion-Berlin, 2005: 211–227).

Explaining the Reality of Peaceful Borders and Illicit Transnational Flows in the TBA

Hypothesis 1: The Degree of Physical and Institutional Openness of the Peaceful Borders

The cross-border flow of goods and people in the TBA has increased substantially following regional integration since the mid-1980s and the early 1990s, which deepened with the signing of MERCOSUR in 1991. For instance, in 2002, the MERCOSUR countries signed an agreement making it easier for their citizens to travel and obtain resident visas. The agreement also allowed inspection-free transportation of commercial containers. Nowadays, there is a very high volume of traffic within the TBA, especially across the border between Brazil and Paraguay. Every day about forty thousand people go unchecked as they cross the bridge between Ciudad del Este and Foz do Iguaçú, along with more than two thousand vehicles, including many trucks laden with freight containers (see Kacowicz, 2015: 99). Thus, the establishment of MERCOSUR and the expansion of transnational economic exchanges have led to concomitant increases in both licit trade and illicit trafficking.

The presence and increase in criminal and terrorist activity has become possible in the TBA due to the effects of the MERCOSUR agreement on the open nature and type of states' borders. Open borders create enticing economic opportunities for criminals and terrorists, turning an already difficult law-enforcement situation into a much worst scenario (see Birch, 2014; and European Commission, 2010: 33–37).

The peaceful borders in the TBA have become open and loose, demilitarized and "civilized," and falling under police control, partly from an ideological and political decision to wrest control from the military and transfer spheres of authority to civilians. For domestic political reasons, the governments of the TBA prefer to address the new security challenges and threats posed by the proliferation of illicit transnational flows by framing them in nonmilitary terms (see Pion-Berlin, 2005: 219–220). This position starkly contrasts with the obvious preference of the United States to lead the global "war against terrorism" by militarizing criminal issues in the Americas, such as drug trafficking, under the rubric of "narcoterrorism" (see Kacowicz, 2015: 102; and Guerrero, 2006: 66, 69).

The constitutions of several Latin American countries prohibit the use of military forces for internal security (Sotomayor, 2015: 51–52). Furthermore, memories of the harsh military dictatorships of the 1970s and early 1980s further inhibit the civilian governments from expanding the military's role in coping with security problems that are framed as internal (only criminal), rather than international security (see Pion-Berlin, 2017). Thus, there is a political reluctance to securitize the borders of the TBA. This means that, in the context of the Tri-Border Area, responsibilities for security have fallen into the hands of the ministers of interior and justice, rather than those of defense or war. Rather than the armed forces, it is the police, border patrols, immigration officials, civilian courts, and intelligence agencies under their jurisdiction that play a paramount role. Hence, we corroborate Hypothesis 1 in the TBA case.

Hypothesis 2: The Degree of Governance, Institutional Strength, and Political Willingness

The political responses and reactions of the three national governments in the TBA are important to explaining variance in the occurrence and proliferation of illicit transnational flows in the region. Thus, it is relevant to consider the historical and political realities and political cultures of Brazil, Argentina, and Paraguay in order to understand their rather ambiguous positions regarding criminal and terrorist activities in the TBA region.

The paradigmatic example is that of Paraguay, a quintessential weak state. In Paraguay, under General Stroessner's thirty-four year's dictatorship that ended only in 1989, money laundering and counterfeiting were actually encouraged by the political regime, so it promoted a policy of enforcement evasion and alliance, if not wholesome integration with criminal non-state actors. Furthermore, as mentioned previously, all three countries, not only Paraguay, suffer from a high level of corruption. According to the Corruption Index of 2015, Brazil is in 76th place, Argentina in 107th, and Paraguay in 130th.

Paraguay's lenient laws corroborate the claim that Ciudad del Este, as the TBA criminal hotspot, is relatively devoid of government control. Specifically, Paraguay has weak regulations of its financial sector, and tax laws are easily ignored in Ciudad del Este. Apart from a debilitated financial sector, Paraguay maintains a poor regulation system on illicit markets. At the same time, Paraguay has implemented some procedures to enhance its counterterrorist apparatus. Yet, Paraguay's level of corruption hampered those efforts, leaving its porous borders in place. In 2009, it revised its penal code to bolster penalties against trafficking crimes and reintroduced its customs office at the bridge connecting to Brazil (Umaña, 2012: 15).

The region has remained largely ungoverned due to the prevalence of weak, inadequate, or ignored laws. Thus, the TBA's role in harboring transnational criminals and terrorists has been exacerbated by the inability of the Paraguayan, Brazilian, and Argentine governments to effectively enforce the rule of law in the region and govern in a transparent and decent way, due to widespread corruption. This is particularly evident in the case of money laundering, which allows for other criminal and terrorist activities (see Golding, 2002: 4).

In contrast to Paraguay, which fits squarely into the category of a typical (or even stereotypical) weak and corrupt state, Brazil and Argentina can be considered relatively strong or functioning states, with good rankings in terms of democracy and sustainability, but poor records in terms of corruption, which leads Argentina and Brazil not to control their borders properly. In the case of the TBA, the evidence is that the bulk of transnational criminal and terrorist flows have taken place between Paraguay and Brazil (crime) or between Paraguay and Argentina (terrorism), more than directly between Argentina and Brazil. At the same time, the relatively high levels of corruption in Brazil and especially in Argentina create a political environment conducive to the commission of transnational crimes, especially those of the financial type (for instance, tax evasion is the predicate crime in the majority of Argentine money-laundering investigations) (see Kacowicz, 2015: 102). Despite a seemingly indifferent approach toward transnational crime and terrorism, in the last decade the TBA countries have undertaken several measures to combat the rise of illegal activities in the area, including several high-profile operations in cooperation with Interpol and the World Customs Organization (Umaña, 2012: 11). Hence, we validate Hypothesis 2 in the case of the TBA borders.

Hypothesis 3: The Prevalent Socioeconomic Conditions of the Neighboring States

The criminal/terrorist problem in the TBA follows an economic logic. While Brazil is the largest Latin American economy and the seventh in the global ranking, Paraguay, at the other extreme, is one of Latin America's most corrupt and poorest countries (Shelley and Picarelli, 2005: 61). Political and economic instability have made Paraguay reluctant to change the reality of criminality in the TBA, since it heavily relies upon the informal economy in Ciudad del Este. Since the creation of MERCOSUR in 1991, Paraguay, as a relatively poor and landlocked country, has opened itself to the opportunities of foreign markets, leading to significant economic growth in the last fifteen years.

Huge disparities in income and prices within and among the three economies have contributed to the creation of a smuggling and money laundering paradise. The economic disparities exist both across the countries (especially between Paraguay and its two larger neighbors, Argentina and Brazil). Moreover, there are huge socioeconomic disparities between the TBA borderlands and the metropolitan areas of Buenos Aires, Argentina, and Sào Paulo, Brazil. In other words, the TBA is a transnational economic space, where the movements of people and goods actually reflect the economic asymmetries within and among the three countries (see Gimenez Beliveau and Montenegro, 2010: 15). Thus, we corroborate the validity of the third hypothesis.

Conclusions

In this chapter, we examined in detail four American cases that display an important variation in terms of types of transnational illicit flows and VNSAs who evolve, act, and thrive under different conditions. A common American parameter for almost all of the Western Hemisphere countries has been the existence and persistence of peaceful international borders. At the same time, we traced two different transitions of peace. First, there have been transitions from civil war to peace in the cases of the Northern Triangle of Central America in the 1990s and the end of the Colombian civil war in 2016. Second, we identify transitions to higher levels of peace and integration (higher integration with preexisting stable peace in North America with NAFTA in 1994; and transition from negative peace to stable peace and integration in the Southern Cone with MERCOSUR in 1991, with reference to the TBA).

These different transitions to peace facilitate the occurrence of illicit transnational flows in different ways. For instance, the legacy of the civil wars in Central America is an important factor in explaining arms trafficking and human smuggling and trafficking. Similarly, in the case of the Colombian borders, the relative vanishing of the FARC left a vacuum that was filled by other VNSAs such as the BACRIM, the new generation of criminal gangs, in connivance with the close integration of crime and politics in neighboring Venezuela.

Moreover, we recorded significant variations in terms of the type and occurrence of illicit transnational flows, sometimes related to geopolitical reasons (the location of the Northern Triangle, or the length and location of the Colombian borders). In other instances, detailed perusal of the four case studies has demonstrated the relevance of alternative explanations to the occurrence of illicit transnational flows. For instance, different degrees of levels of governance, as evidenced in different capabilities and political willingness, are very relevant to the linkages between peaceful borders and illicit transnational flows. Moreover, the political economy of the borderlands, with an emphasis upon the socioeconomic gaps between the bordering states, is another important variable to consider.

In the opposite direction to that which Columbus took in 1492, we should leave now the Western Hemisphere to embark in the next four chapters in an intellectual voyage that will take us to other continents and regions, including Europe, the Middle East, Southern Africa, and Southeast Asia to further explore these links.

5 | *Europe: The Schengen Regime and the Western Balkan Borders*

Introduction

In this chapter, we examine the links between the European peaceful borders and the occurrence and proliferation of illicit transnational flows. We refer to the European internal borders since the implementation of the Schengen Agreement in 1995, the Southeastern European borders (regarding the Western Balkans/former Yugoslavia) since the end of the Bosnian War in 1995 with the signing of the Dayton Agreements, and the borders between the EU and its Western Balkan neighbors. We assess the softening and the complete opening of the internal borders among the twenty-six European participating countries in the Schengen agreement in contrast to the external border control, as related to the occurrence and proliferation of illicit transnational flows. The two major European concerns in the last two decades are related to illegal migration and to transnational crime, including drug trafficking, human trafficking and smuggling, arms trafficking, and terrorism. The last few years have registered an enormous turbulence at Europe's external borders, caused by the massive inflow of illegal migrants and asylum seekers from the Middle East, Afghanistan, and Africa, providing an economic boom for individual and organized human smuggling (see Farrah and Muggah, 2018).

All the current European international borders are formally peaceful, with the exception of the Ukraine-Russian border. Yet, there is a significant variation across the different parts of the European continent in terms of gradations of peace and integration. Moreover, there is a variance among the European countries in terms of different levels of governance and state strength, as well as in their socioeconomic conditions.

The Evolution of the European Borders, 1914–2020

The Italian historian Enzo Traverso (2016) aptly characterized the violence experienced in Europe between 1914 and 1945 as a "European

133

Civil War." During this period, Europe witnessed overlapping violent conflicts across the continent: "classic wars between states; civil wars; wars of national liberation; genocides; violent confrontations arising from cleavages of class, nation, religion, politics, and ideology" (Traverso, 2016: 23). Moreover, the European borders were reshaped many times. With the end of World War I in 1918, the breakup of the Austro-Hungarian and Russian Empires led to the creation of new independent states such as Yugoslavia, Poland, Lithuania, Latvia, Hungary, and Czechoslovakia. After the end of World War II in 1945, borders changed again. The Baltic republics were absorbed by the Soviet Union, Germany was divided between West and East, and Poland's borders were modified. Most Eastern European republics were restored after the war, though they remained under occupation by the Soviet Red Army until the late 1980s (see Joll, 1976; and Thomson, 1966).

The end of the "European Civil War" (1914–45) did not completely stop the cycle of violence in the continent. Soon after the end of World War II, Europe faced many new conflicts: the civil war in Greece, border disputes and demarcations, population transfers, and the Communist takeover of Eastern Europe. According to the historian Tony Judt (2005: 5), "the history of the two halves of post-war Europe cannot be told in isolation from one another." The most important event that took place in post–World War II Europe was indeed the territorial and ideological division of the continent between two spheres of influence in 1945–89: Western Europe and Eastern Europe, politically attached to the United States and to the Soviet Union respectively. The two European halves formally kept the precarious or negative peace until the end of the Cold War that reunified the continent, although tensions rose and crises broke out from time to time, like over the status of Berlin in 1949 and again in 1961 (see Gaddis, 2005; Joll, 1976; and Thomson, 1966).

In Western Europe, interstate peace consolidated in the 1950s with the first steps toward the European integration and the emergence of a pluralistic security community. In 1951, Belgium, France, Germany, Italy, Luxembourg, and the Netherlands established the European Coal and Steel Community (ECSC). A leap forward was taken in 1957, when the Treaty of Rome created the European Economic Community (EEC). Later in the 1970s, Spain, Portugal, and Greece initiated their transition to democracy that allowed them to join the European integration in the 1980s (see Lodge, 1993; and Moravcsik, 1998).

Conversely, Eastern and Southeastern Europe remained in a state of internal strife. In the Soviet-controlled areas of Eastern Europe, the Communist takeover of countries such as Czechoslovakia, Poland, Hungary, Romania, and Bulgaria was rapidly followed by purges and massive repression. In some cases, the Soviet Union intervened militarily in Hungary and Czechoslovakia in 1956 and 1968. In multiethnic Yugoslavia, domestic stability was maintained thanks to the dominant figure of Marshal Josip Broz Tito, though this stability remained short-lived after his death in 1980 (see Buzan and Waever, 2003: 377–396; and Miller, 2007: 256–305).

The end of the Cold War in 1989–91 brought about the democratization of Eastern Europe and the rapprochement between both European halves. Borders were redefined again with the peaceful reunification of Germany in 1990, the relatively peaceful dissolution of the Soviet Union in 1991, and the violent breakup of Yugoslavia in the early 1990s. The Baltic States regained independence from the USSR, Czechoslovakia peacefully disintegrated into the Czech Republic and Slovakia, and the Russian military presence ended in Eastern Europe.

In contrast to Eastern Europe where the post-communist transition was relatively peaceful, the Western Balkans followed a virulent pattern of violence, as related to the implosion of Yugoslavia (perhaps with the exception of the relatively peaceful Slovenian secession in 1991). Yugoslavia, which until the early 1990s encompassed today's Serbia, Macedonia, Bosnia-Herzegovina, Croatia, Slovenia, Kosovo, and Montenegro, broke up into several new states. The disintegration of Yugoslavia caused bloody wars in the early 1990s in Croatia and Bosnia-Herzegovina (see Miller, 2007: 256–306). The Dayton Accords, signed in December 1995, put an end to the Yugoslavian/Balkan wars and established the post–Cold War order in Southeast Europe.

In an ironic turn, European violence only ended in the last year of the twentieth century in the Western Balkans, regarding the conflict between Serbia and the seceding province of Kosovo. The atrocities and human rights violations carried out by the Serbian regime of Slobodan Milosevic vis-à-vis the Moslem population in Kosovo in the late 1990s met strong international condemnation and eventually brought about an armed intervention by NATO in 1999.

Since the end of the Cold War, Europe has seen a massive loosening and softening of borders; first, the Iron Curtain disappeared, then the

Schengen regime allowed for control-free movement across most
European Union (EU) state borders (see Lewis, 2011: 1). The collapse
of Communism in Eastern Europe in 1989–91 and the dismantling of
the former Cold War frontier (the Iron Curtain) between East and West
contributed to the increased movement and permeability of European
borders. Moreover, the signing of the Schengen Agreement in 1985 by
five of the ten members of the then–European Community (EC) member-states and the completion of the Single European Market (SEM) in
1992 became landmark political events even before the formation of
the European Union on November 1, 1993. They helped reduce the
relative importance of internal borders to mere symbolic demarcation
lines among the EU current and future member-states (see Andreev,
2004: 382; and Lewis, 2011: 1).

The reunification of the continent in the 1990s led to the enlargement and expansion of the EU membership toward the east. The first
wave occurred in 2004 with the inclusion of Cyprus, the Czech
Republic, Estonia, Hungary, Latvia, Lithuania, Malta, Poland,
Slovakia, and Slovenia. Romania and Bulgaria joined the EU in
2007, and Croatia followed suit in 2013. The Western Balkans,
including Albania, Bosnia-Herzegovina, Macedonia, Montenegro,
Serbia, and Kosovo are still not part of the EU, despite the promise
of the EU at the Thessaloniki Summit back in 2003 to recognize the
Western Balkan countries as potential new members. Yet, seventeen
years after, with the exception of Croatia and Slovenia, the rest of the
countries are still a long way from achieving full EU membership
(Kmezić, 2020: 1).

The European Union embodies the ultimate example of a zone of
peace as a highly integrated pluralistic security community, where
stable peace is the norm within a system of interdependent member-
states (see Kacowicz, 1998: 18–19). The economic integration of the
EU is nearly total nowadays: free flow of goods and persons, the
adoption of the euro as a common currency for most of its members,
and high levels of intraregional trade. Yet, the EU integration has not
been uniform or homogeneous.

The integration of the European continent went through several
stages. In the 1950s, the original group of Western European countries
launched the integration process; in the 1980s, Portugal, Spain, and
Greece joined it; and in the 2000s, the rest of Eastern Europe became
part of the EU. Consequently, there are different degrees of integration

of the borderlands, much deeper in Western Europe than in Eastern Europe. For instance, we observe these differences in the case of the Visegrád Group that comprises the Czech Republic, Hungary, Poland, and Slovakia. This grouping quite often presents dissenting views vis-à-vis Brussels at the European Parliament, in particular regarding its controversial policy on illegal migrants and refugees (see López-Dóriga, 2018).

The Schengen System (1995–2020): European Internal Borders and Common External Borders

A central element of the European integration is the free flow of persons, in addition to the free flow of goods, as embedded in the Schengen agreement. This agreement dates back to 1985 when Belgium, France, Luxembourg, the Netherlands, and West Germany decided to deepen their integration and abolish their internal borders while regulating common controls at their external borders. This has included a common visa regime; common regulations for procedures at land and coastal borders and airports by Frontex, the European Border and Coast Guard Agency, and extensive police cooperation that includes the Schengen Information System (SIS) database (see Grabbe, 2000: 525).

The Schengen Agreement became effective on March 26, 1995. Since 1995, it has gradually grown and today it encompasses almost all the EU members and a few associated non-EU countries. Currently, the Schengen area includes twenty-six European countries, within which citizens, including many non-EU nationals, business people, and tourists can freely circulate without border checks (see European Commission, 2014).

According to the Schengen *acquis* (legal base and body of law comprising it), two categories of borders are established: "internal" and "external" (see Schwell, 2009). The former are the borders within the EU, whereas the latter consists of the borders with nonmember European states outside of the Schengen perimeter.[1] The internal

---

[1] The European countries that participate in the Schengen system are Austria, Belgium, Czech Republic, Denmark, Estonia, Finland, France, Germany, Greece, Hungary, Iceland, Italy, Latvia, Liechtenstein, Lithuania, Luxembourg, Malta, Netherlands, Norway, Poland, Portugal, Slovakia, Slovenia, Spain, Sweden, and Switzerland.

borders of the EU are soft borders because they enable a free flow of goods and people without any passport controls, and the "lack of stationary border controls in favor of mobile controls" (Schwell, 2009: 246). Conversely, the external common borders of the EU have remained hard and they have even tightened and sharpened, in order to ensure the security of those living or traveling within the EU. Thus, extending the EU and the Schengen border regime eastwards implied a political trade-off: freer movement westwards at the price of not allowing free movement from East and Southeast Europe (see Bigo, 2010: 14; European Commission, 2014; Grabbe, 2000: 527; Hokovský, 2016: 75; and Zielonka, 2001: 517).

The Schengen system allows for the reintroduction of border controls under a certain set of conditions due to security considerations, for a limited period of time. In particular, the refugee crisis of the last few years, especially in 2015 and 2016, which brought about two million "irregular migrants" across the European borders, has put enormous pressure on the Schengen countries. This led to the introduction of internal controls and checks to deter the flow of illegal migrants, igniting an intense securitization of the issue (see Eurostat, 2015). For instance, Hungary and Slovenia hardened their borders along the external Schengen border, quickly followed suit by Austria, Germany, Denmark, and the Netherlands, which erected also internal borders. Moreover, some of these countries reimposed controls and military presence along their borders with other member-states within the Schengen area. Thus, they tacitly acknowledged that they could not or did not want to properly cope with the flow of thousands of illegal migrants and asylum seekers who arrived each day to their territory (see Dingott Alkopher and Blanc, 2017; Gruzaczak, 2017; and Traynor, 2016). In a similar way, during 2020, the COVID-19 pandemic has led to the resurgence of makeshift national borders in the form of fences, barriers, and walls between EU countries, despite the formal abolishing of internal border controls according to the Schengen regime (see Pallini, 2020).

There is a substantial division of labor, if not contradiction, between two major EU projects, one being about enlargement and extension to the East and South, and the other about the functioning of the Schengen regime, which established hard external borders with non-EU members. Whereas enlargement is about inclusion, the hard border regime is about exclusion (see Smith, 2005: 757; and Zielonka, 2001: 254). Due to security motivations and circumstances, the Schengen system of internal soft borders created another sort of stratification within Europe. That is, between those states that are not close to the external Schengen borders (most of them are the Western EU members), and those who are located right on the external border, such as Spain, Italy, Greece, and many of the new Eastern and Southeastern European members. In other words, the burden of European borders' security is nowadays on the shoulders of some of the new EU members of Eastern Europe, as the EU border has moved eastwards. This reality has posed a significant challenge for the EU because of the relatively weak foundations of some of its new members, lagging behind in terms of state capabilities, governance, and economic development.

The inclusion of new eastern and southern peripheries to the EU, such as the Western Balkans, has brought new security threats, including the occurrence and proliferation of illicit transnational flows in the form of human, drug, and arms trafficking, in addition to the refugee crisis, which includes many instances of human smuggling. In this regard, the inclusion of new EU members has motivated the EU to design a policy strategy of governance promotion and integration vis-à-vis its weaker (non-EU) neighbors. This strategy was based on programs such as the Stability Pact of 1999 (vis-à-vis the Western Balkans/Southeast Europe) and the European Neighbourhood Policy (ENP) of 2004, which aimed at linking the EU periphery, including the Mediterranean countries in the South and the Near East (Middle East), and the former Soviet republics in the East (Delcour, 2010: 536).

The Western Balkan/Southeast European Region: Geopolitics and Borders

Southeast Europe represents a particular geopolitical area whose stability and security directly affects Europe's political and security infrastructure due to its geographical linkage to three different regions. First, the Balkan region is located on the border between Western Europe and the Southern Mediterranean region. Second, it straddles the geographic intersection among Europe, Asia, and the Middle East. Third, it links to the Black Sea area, which at the same time connects to the Caucasus and the Caspian regions. Moreover, the proximity of the EU makes the Western Balkans a suitable route for the illicit flows of drugs, small weapons, and human trafficking coming from the aforementioned areas (see Moustakis, 2004).

Since the end of the Cold War, new risks and threats have increasingly affected European security stemming from regions immediately adjoining Western Europe, such as the Western Balkans (Moustakis, 2004: 141). These security threats include illegal migration or undocumented migration, in addition to terrorism, small arms, drugs, and human trafficking, and the overall spread of organized crime (see Giatizdis, 2007; and The Global Initiative against Transnational Organized Crime, 2019).

The Yugoslavian Wars of the early 1990s created the background conditions for illicit transnational flows through the proliferation of criminal groups, with public officials who profited from the relative lack of governance, institutional capabilities, and political willingness to enforce the rule of law. Furthermore, borders have become porous due to corruption, geography, and lack of technical and human capabilities to exercise effective border control (see Bacon, 2007: 91).

In this context, Girard Stoudmann, Director of the OSCE Office for Democratic Institutions and Human Rights identified three major challenges involving the EU in relation to the Western Balkan states: first, extending and implementing the Schengen regime; second, preventing and combating human and drug trafficking, as well as fighting organized crime and corruption in Southeast Europe; and third, integrating multicultural values across the EU and Southeast Europe (Moustakis, 2004: 144–145). To cope with these challenges, after the Kosovo War of 1999, the EU took the initiative of establishing the so-called *Stability Pact for South Eastern Europe*, as an international compact aimed at strengthening peace, democracy, human rights, and economic development for the countries of Southeast Europe, including Albania, Bosnia-Herzegovina, Bulgaria, Croatia, Macedonia, Moldova, Montenegro, Romania, and Serbia. The "Stability Pact" emphasized the need for better relations within the Balkan region, as a move toward regionalization by the Southeastern European countries that regard themselves as candidates to join the EU (see Tamminen, 2004: 400). We turn now to a general assessment of transnational crime and terrorism in the European continent.

Transnational Crime and Terrorism in Contemporary Europe

Drug Trafficking

Organized crime groups make considerable profits from trafficking illegal drugs: around 230 billion euros per year (see European Commission,

2018a: 2). Drug consumption within the EU remains very high, with about a quarter of the EU's adults (about eighty million) having used illicit drugs, and as much as 1.5 million law offences registered in Europe in 2017 (European Commission, 2014: 9; and EMCDDA, 2019: 37). In parallel, the demand for drugs is also rising in countries neighboring the EU, including the Southeastern European states (see van der Laan, 2017: 3).

According to UN and EU data, the Western Balkan countries have played an increasing role in drug trafficking. Although relatively marginal and underdeveloped in terms of the formal global and European political economy, the Western Balkans have become an important hub in terms of illegal trading networks. Drug trafficking was already known to be on the increase in the late 1980s and early 1990s, particularly the importation of heroin from the Far East through the Balkans and Turkey (see Lindstrom, 2004: 46; and The Global Initiative against Transnational Organized Crime, 2019). Once a transit territory for criminal groups, Southeast Europe has become a launching pad for illicit transnational flows, where the traffickers of human beings, drugs, stolen vehicles, and cultural and historic valuables are located (US Department of State, 2013, quoted in Krasniqi, 2016: 211).

The market for cannabis is by far the largest and most popular in Europe, with an increase in its use by young people (EMCDDA, 2019: 16). According to the *European Drugs Report* 2018, 70 percent of the cannabis seized entered the continent from Morocco, with Spain as the main entry point into the EU. Moreover, the Western Balkan countries have been also an important source of cannabis trafficking (EMCDDA, 2018: 20, and 2019: 11; and The Global Initiative, 2019: 4–5).

Cocaine is produced in Latin America and is trafficked mainly to Spain, which has traditionally been its main entry port, along with cannabis. However, this trend began to change in recent years. In 2016, Belgium became the country that registered the main volume of cocaine seized after Spain. The number of seizures and the volume of cocaine seized are at their highest historical level. This is a result of the organization of the supply chain, in which new smaller and fragmented DTOs have come into the illicit markets (EMCDDA, 2019: 14).

As for heroin, it is possible to see a decline in its use and in treatment demand. The EMCDDA Report praised European policies of pragmatic harms reduction and treatment measures that contributed to that decline. However, the quantity of heroin seized has gone up, showing that the supply is still growing. Moreover, the Eastern European treatment and harm reduction policies are still less available than in the Western part of the continent (EMCDDA, 2019: 11). Heroin enters Europe from four main trafficking routes (EMCDDA, 2018: 24). The two most important are the "Balkan route" and the "Southern route." Southeast Europe is still a major transit route for heroin destined for Western Europe (see Moustakis, 2004: 149; and UNODC, 2008: 5). The Balkan route links Afghanistan, the main heroin supplier of the world (about 90 percent) with Europe, its principal consumer market (see Alexandra-Arbatova, 2004: 373; and Krasniqi, 2016: 207). This route flows through Turkey and continues through the Western Balkan countries to the rest of the European continent. Alternative routes include Africa, the Caucasus, and the Black Sea.

Arms Trafficking

It is difficult to estimate the exact scale of illegal arms trafficking into the EU. Until 2013, the reports of Europol, the EU Agency for Law Enforcement and Cooperation, suggested that the market was relatively small, as compared to other regions of the world. Yet, the possession of arms by criminal organizations poses a certain security threat to European countries. As of 2020, arms trafficking has remained high on the European agenda due to its obvious link to terrorism. Moreover, there has been growing concern that criminal networks acquire more heavy weapons provided from Southeastern European sources (see Duquet and Goris, 2018: 73; and van der Laan, 2017: 7).

A recent European report on arms trafficking confirms that illicit markets in the EU rely on two main sources (see Duquet and Goris, 2018). These are cross-border smuggling from outside the EU, especially from the Western Balkans, and intra-EU arms trafficking. The two main routes for smuggling firearms from the Western Balkans to Western Europe are the southern route, via Italy or Austria; and the northern route, via Hungary. The main supply countries are those of former Yugoslavia: Serbia, Montenegro, Bosnia and Herzegovina, Croatia, and Kosovo, in addition to Albania. The main destination countries for firearms trafficked from the Balkans include France, Germany, Greece, Ireland, Italy, the Netherlands, Spain, the United

Kingdom, Norway, Sweden, Denmark, and Finland (see Savona and Mancuso, 2017: 56–57).

Following the end of the Yugoslavian Wars in 1995, a large number of weapons has remained in the hands of civilian and criminal groups, similar to the case of the Northern Triangle in Central America. Governments in the Western Balkans still do not have the capacity nor the political willingness to prevent the export of small weapons to other regions, especially to Western Europe. In this regard, there is a nexus between the recent terrorist attacks in Europe and arms trafficking (see Europol, 2018: 9).

With reference to the Western Balkans, the Stability Pact for South Eastern Europe Regional Implementation Plan in 2006 presented one of the first plans of action toward "Combating the Proliferation and Impact of Small Arms and Light Weapons (SALW)" in the Balkans. Yet, the plan has not been fully implemented. As of 2012, most of the illegal firearms in Western Europe had their origins in the Balkans, through the same smuggling routes used by drug traffickers. Firearms trafficked from, to, and within the Western Balkans remain one of the main security threats in the continent. It is estimated that 2.3 million weapons in the hands of civilians in the region are registered, and another 3.9 million are unregistered (European Commission, 2019: 6; see also Duquet and Goris, 2018: 107–108).

In late 2014, in order to address the problem of arms trafficking from Southeast Europe into Western Europe, the EU and the Western Balkan countries issued a joint action plan to address the illicit trafficking of firearms for the period of 2015–19 (European Commission, 2019: 2). Yet, many of the steps envisioned in the cooperative scheme were not taken: the establishment of firearms focal points was not fully advanced, no harmonized data collection for firearms seizures was effected, and no standardized reporting format for the exchange of information took place.

Human Smuggling and Trafficking

There has been a rapid increase of human trafficking in Europe since the end of the Cold War, due to the opening of borders in the continent after the fall of the Soviet Union, the spread of free markets, and an unparalleled level of interconnectedness and information exchange (see Marinova and James, 2012: 231–247).

In the EU alone, several hundred thousand victims are trafficked each year for a variety of purposes (though the official recorded figures of "registered victims" are about 20,000 per year), including sexual exploitation, forced labor, forced begging, domestic servitude, and removal of organs, generating a gross annual income of 3 billion dollars for their exploiters (see European Commission, 2018c). Women are trafficked from Eastern Europe, Nigeria, Latin America, and Asia, usually by criminal organizations collaborating with their European counterparts. In this regard, the Schengen regime of open borders has been an important facilitator of human trafficking (Shelley, 2010: 31; see also European Commission, 2014: 8; Kligman and Limoncelli, 2005: 3; Shelley, 2014b; and UNODC, 2010: 1).

According to the Eurostat Working Group on Crime Statistics (2015), most of human trafficking victims are women (67 percent), whereas the majority of registered victims suffered from sexual exploitation (69 percent), or labor exploitation (19 percent). The same report points out that the majority of registered victims (65 percent) come from EU member-states, mainly from Romania, Bulgaria, the Netherlands, Hungary, and Poland. In particular, citizens of Hungary, Slovakia, and Lithuania have been trafficked across borders. In a similar vein, 69 percent of the traffickers are European citizens (Eurostat, 2015: 21).

As for human smuggling, the number of irregular crossings of the EU's external borders has increased dramatically since 2014, due to crises and dire conditions in countries like Syria, Afghanistan, and Iraq reaching a number larger than a million in 2015 (van der Laan, 2017: 4). In a joint report, Europol and Interpol concluded that about 90 percent of irregular or illegal migrants use the services of facilitators involved in human smuggling. Although human smuggling and human trafficking are two different types of crimes, migrants who have been smuggled over the EU borders are a large vulnerable group that are susceptible to exploitation (van der Laan, 2017: 5–6). According to Europol, the Schengen area is a comfortable operations area for human traffickers (Europol, 2013, quoted in van der Laan, 2017: 7). Still, the main illegal movement of people in Europe involves human smuggling rather than human trafficking (see von Lampe, 2014).

EU responses to human trafficking have been carried out through several initiatives, instruments, and formal documents, to put in motion a concerted common policy. Most European countries legislate in favor of criminalizing trafficking in human beings, according to the requirements of the UN Trafficking in Persons Protocol of 2003 and Article 5 of the Charter of Fundamental Rights of the European Union. However, only in the early 2010s did the EU start dealing with human trafficking in a more systematic and concerted way. In 2011, the EU approved Directive 2011/36/EU aimed at preventing human trafficking, by focusing on human rights and gender-specific victims.

In 2012, the EU promulgated its overall "Strategy towards the Eradication of Trafficking in Human Beings for 2012–2016." According to the Commission to the European Parliament and the Council (2017 and 2018), that evaluated the 2011 Directive and the 2012 Strategy, there were some positive outcomes. Cross-border cooperation seemed to have increased through Europol and Eurojust (the European Union Agency for Criminal Justice Cooperation). As a result, a large number of joint investigation teams were set. Improvements have also been reported after carrying out financial investigations and developing national and transnational referral mechanisms. Still, the EU found hurdles on the road since the overall levels of prosecutions and convictions were far lower than expected. Sometimes prosecutors failed to find sufficient evidence to advance investigations and bring cases to court. Eventually, offenders ended up being accused of other crimes such as money laundering or prostitution-related offences. Thus, despite all the efforts and resources given to Europol, Eurojust, and Frontex, human trafficking flows continue to grow (see Commission to the European Parliament, 2017 and 2018; Grundell, 2015; and Shelley, 2014b).

In the particular case of the Western Balkans, human trafficking has been a pressing security issue due to its large scope (see Fosson, 2011). Being an area of transit, the former Yugoslavian countries produce two categories of trafficked humans: women used for sex trafficking, and illegal migrants (see Kligman and Limoncelli, 2005; Lindstrom, 2004; and Corrin, 2005). However, according to the UNODC Global Report on Trafficking in Persons (2016b), victims from the Western Balkans have not been detected in significant numbers in Western Europe, as compared to those from Romania and Bulgaria (which joined the EU in 2007). These two countries have been the main source of trafficking in Europe (UNODC, 2016b: 75).

This report shows that the majority (65 percent) of the victims of trafficking detected in Europe had as their original point of departure the subregions of Central and Southeast Europe (UNODC, 2016b: 58; see also UNODC, 2018a: 53). Moreover, about 75 percent of the victims detected in Central and Southeast Europe during the period 2012–14 were women (UNODC, 2016b: 78). Albania, Romania, and Bulgaria are major sources for human trafficking, whereas Bosnia-Herzegovina, Croatia, Macedonia, Serbia, Montenegro, and Kosovo are transit and destination countries (Surtees, 2008: 41). In a more positive note, the UNODC Report points out that "the detection of these flows has declined markedly compared to 2012 and 2014." Yet, the Southeastern European countries have failed to stop human trafficking originating within their boundaries (UNODC, 2018a: 53).

Over recent years, Southeast Europe has become a critical entry point for refugees and migrants from conflict zones in South Asia, North Africa, and the Middle East whose goal has been to enter the EU searching for a better life. Hence, this refugee problem has proved to be a fertile ground for local criminal groups to engage in human trafficking and smuggling. The refugee crisis poses a grave danger for the Western Balkans due to the lack of available resources for many regional countries to carry out proper vetting and control of the enormous flux of refugees passing though their borders (see Cocco, 2017).

Terrorism

Terrorism has been a longstanding problem in Europe. Since 2001, more than 2,400 people have died in terrorist attacks conducted in Europe. Yet, in most of the cases, local European-born terrorists perpetrated those actions, which in many cases were unrelated to Islamic religious sources, but rather derived from other ideological motivations, such as separatism and extreme right-wing ideas. Moreover, a 2016 Europol report indicated that the number of people arrested for terrorist activities quintupled between 2011 and 2015 (see Berthelet, 2017).

Western Europe has experienced a significant increase of jihadist terrorism in the last few years. There are two main sources of Islamic terrorism. The first source refers to individuals who went through a radicalization process that brought them to Syria or Iraq, or were recruited by ISIS to act on European soil. At least 104 Islamist extremists entered the EU's external borders using long-haul irregular migration methods between 2014 and 2018. The second source refers to the phenomenon of lone wolf terrorists, individuals who do not formally belong to terrorist organizations and act in their own countries. Terrorist attacks were carried out in London, Barcelona, Manchester, Paris, and Berlin. Yet, most of the terrorists were Europeans, or have lived most of their lives there. Hence, most of the European terrorist attacks have been local with global resonance, rather than transnational (see Voortman, 2015).

According to the *EU Terrorism Situation and Trend Report* (Europol, 2018: 23), in 2017 there were 205 failed, foiled, or completed terrorist attacks in the EU; ethno-nationalist and separatist groups carried out 67 percent of them, whereas jihadist groups only 16 percent. Yet, fundamentalist terrorism has been the bloodiest in terms of victims: of the thirty-three attacks, ten of them accounted for a total of sixty-two people killed. For their part, separatist groups carried out 137 terrorist attacks: forty-two in France, seven in Spain and eighty-eight in Northern Ireland.

Against the backdrop of the September 11, 2001, terrorist attacks, the EU took several steps to address the terrorist threat. In 2002, the EU approved the Europe Arrest Warrant, though it only became operational in 2007. The EU also issued many legal documents and policy strategies to cope with terrorism. Among them were the European Security Strategy (2003), the EU Counter-Terrorism Strategy (2005), the European Agenda on Security (2015), and the Directive on Combating Terrorism of 2017. A milestone in the struggle against terrorism occurred in 2015, after the Charlie Hebdo attack in Paris. The EU established the European Counter-Terrorism Centre (ECTC) within the Europol framework, in order to deal more efficiently with the terrorist threat (see European Commission, 2018b).

Southeast Europe has not suffered terrorist attacks of the magnitude that hit other regions or countries in the European continent, such as Spain, the United Kingdom, France, or Russia. In comparative terms, terrorism is neither a daunting issue nor a looming threat. Bosnia is probably an exception, since it is considered a haven for some elements of radical Islam. In this regard, the possibility of al-Qaeda infiltration in Bosnia, as well as other radical elements from the Middle East, has been raised (see Alexandrova-Arbatova, 2004; Gibas-Krzak, 2013; and Tziampiris, 2009). By contrast, in countries such as Kosovo, Serbia, and Montenegro, the activities of fundamentalist groups have been limited to propaganda distribution (see Europol, 2018: 34).

Southeast Europe has also witnessed the phenomena of local populations that underwent a radicalization process that brought them to participate in the Syrian and Iraqi civil wars. The US State Department Country Reports on Terrorism (2016) indicates that a significant number of Bosnians traveled to Syria and to Iraq, joining terrorist groups there. To a lesser extent, Albanians and Macedonians also travelled to Syria. In Kosovo, around three hundred terrorists travelled to Syria and Iraq and joined terrorist organizations such as the Islamic State or al-Nusrah Front. In 2016, sixteen persons were arrested for plotting an attack against the Israeli football team during the World Cup preliminary competition in Albania. In 2015, Macedonia experienced a terrorist incident in which ethnic Albanians (many from neighboring Kosovo) clashed with authorities in a city near the Serbian-Kosovan border. In addition, two terrorist incidents that occurred in Bosnia in 2015 involved so-called lone wolves (see Europol, 2018: 34).

Explaining the Reality of Peaceful Borders and Illicit Transnational Flows in the European Continent

Hypothesis 1: *The Degree of Physical and Institutional Openness of the Peaceful Borders*

The softening and increasing dismantling of borders in Europe after the Cold War has enabled the occurrence and proliferation of illicit transnational flows. Thus, the physical dismantling of hard and fortified borders has allowed more crime and terrorism to proliferate across the European borders (see Grabbe, 2000: 520–522; and Holmes, 2009: 283).

As established by the Schengen Agreement, the right to free movement has created significant security challenges and opportunities. On the one hand, the mobility of goods, people and services has enormously increased the amount of economic cooperation. On the other hand, that same mobility might enhance the occurrence and proliferation of illicit transnational flows, facilitating the incursion of transnational crime and terrorism that disrupts the internal security of the European Union. The Schengen Agreement has led not only to the erasing of physical borders, but also to the blurring of virtual boundaries regarding crime, terrorism, and illicit flows of migrants. At the same time, it is not necessarily the case that the Schengen regime has increased transnational crime since the logic of jurisdictional arbitrage does not work in this case within the Schengen perimeter, but only between the EU and its eastern and southeastern neighbors (see Killias, 1993).

We argue that there is a significant linkage between the high degree of border integration, especially in Western Europe, and the occurrence of illicit transnational flows in the form of drug trafficking, human trafficking, arms trafficking, and terrorism. Trafficked cannabis and cocaine first stops in Europe via Spain and lately via Belgium. From there drugs are distributed to many other countries in the continent. As for jihadist terrorism, though it is mostly local and relates to the poor integration of Muslim communities within their own countries, it also benefits from the unrestricted flow of weapons within the European integrated borders.

Moreover, the enlargement of the EU contributed to the incursion of violent non-state actors, many of which operate from weaker EU states such as Romania, Bulgaria, and Hungary. As mentioned, Romania and Bulgaria are the main sources of human trafficking in Europe. In this regard, human trafficking, heroin trafficking, and arms smuggling made their way from Eastern Europe to the western part of the continent due to the integration achieved.

Thus, we confirm the relevance of the first hypothesis, especially with reference to human smuggling and trafficking, and to terrorism. The open, soft, unregulated and uncontrolled borders within the Schengen perimeter have allowed the illicit transnational flows of drugs, weapons, and human trafficking from several post-communist states, which are nowadays EU members. Terrorism and illegal migration flows might take advantage of the lack of internal borders within the EU. At the same time, due to a common European policy regarding police and legal rules, VNSAs involved in transnational crime activities cannot take advantage of the jurisdictional arbitrage, which does not exist within the EU, in contrast to the Americas and other regions of the world.

Moreover, a significant amount of drugs, weapons, and human trafficking comes to the EU from the Western Balkans. The borders between the EU and the former Yugoslavia are hard and controlled, since the Western Balkan countries are still not members of the EU, with the exception of Slovenia and Croatia. Unlike the rest of Europe, the borders among the countries in the region and between them and the EU still matter, since they are hard rather than soft, and exclusionary rather than inclusionary (Andreev, 2004: 382). Yet, the borders among the Western Balkan countries are also porous, due to their geography and topography. Moreover, there has been a transition from closed borders during the Communist regime to a de facto situation of more open borders existing among the post-Yugoslavia republics.

As borders became more open and porous, human trafficking and smuggling increased in scope and reach, along with the flux of drug trafficking (see Kligman and Limoncelli, 2005). In the last few years, the lack of physical borders has exacerbated the movement of illegal migrants and refugees without any kind of visa documentation. As mentioned, the illegal activities nurtured in the former Yugoslavia come across Hungary, Bulgaria, and Romania to make their way to Western Europe.

Hypothesis 2: The Degree of Governance, Institutional Strength, and Political Willingness

The enlargement of the EU brought into the fold countries from the east and southeast of the continent that are weaker than the western countries. At the same time, the external borders of the EU moved further toward the east and the south. In the specific case of the Western Balkans, the Yugoslavian Wars of the 1990s left a gloomy legacy and a plethora of problems, including weak states, corruption, organized crime, lack of rule enforcement, pervasive nationalism, human trafficking, spread of light weapons, and porous interstate borders.

The growth of organized crime in the Western Balkans has been related to the political, economic, and social instability generated by the simultaneous impact of the political transition from totalitarian rule to democracy with the end of Communism, in conjunction with the legacy of the virulent wars of secession that disintegrated Yugoslavia in the early 1990s (UNODC, 2008: 11). As we know from other cases like the Northern Triangle in Central America, post-conflict situations are often associated with rising crime rates and a common practice of engaging in illicit transnational flows due to the remaining stocks of weapons and the lingering malpractices from the violent times of civil and international wars.

The existence of relatively weak states might create grey zones of terrorism, crime, and instability prompting low levels of governance, institutional capacity, and political willingness to effectively address the problems posed by these illicit transnational flows (see Alexandrova-Arbatova, 2004; and Andreas, 2011a: 41). Countries like Bosnia-Herzegovina (divided along ethnic lines), Albania, and Montenegro are nicknamed as "stabilocracies"; that is, weak democracies headed by autocratically minded leaders, who govern through informal, patronage networks, claiming to provide pro-Western stability in the region (The Global Initiative, 2019: 3).

According to the Fragile State Index as published by the Fund for Peace (2015), Southeastern European countries occupy a middle category regarding their state strength; there is a significant national variance across the region. Bosnia-Herzegovina and Serbia rank as the weakest states in places 91 and 81, followed by Macedonia (68), Albania (55), Montenegro (48), Bulgaria (47), and Croatia (43). The outlier in the region is by far Slovenia (19) ranked as a very stable country, a relatively strong state with a ranking similar to that of Western European countries.

Many of the Western Balkan states lack significant governing capabilities to cope effectively with transnational crime across their borders, despite the progress made since the end of the Yugoslavian Wars. For instance, they face several domestic political problems concerning the provision of public goods and services to their populations. This task is even more daunting due to a shared pattern of public corruption, lack of rule of law, weak political democratic culture, frailty of the civil society, institutional mechanisms devoid of accountability and transparency, and the lack of a working and functional bureaucracy. All these states' weaknesses leave the space open for the thriving of criminal organizations that act to co-opt and subvert the state's structures (see UNODC, 2008; also Giatzidis, 2007).

Unlike some states in Latin America where criminal groups act like parasites living off the hosting state (Venezuela, Honduras), the relationship between state structures and criminal groups in some countries of the Western Balkans is as a kind of joint venture, ranging from integration to alliance in terms of criminal politics. Thus, political power is allocated based on political clientelism, giving material goods or benefits in return for political support. Local politicians establish close links with the ruling party and/or criminal groups, so there is an ecosystem that permeates the region, including cozy relationships between the political, business, and criminal elites (The Global Initiative, 2019: 30–33). Accordingly, many former Yugoslavia and some Eastern European countries have become key points for trafficking drugs, weapons, and people to Western Europe. Hence, we mostly validate the second hypothesis in the case of the Western Balkans, with the possible exception of the Slovenian borders. In this context, we should keep in mind that Slovenia has been a member of the EU since 2004.

As for the EU countries, we can neither clearly corroborate nor completely discard the relevance of this second hypothesis, at least with reference to Western Europe where states are strong in comparative terms. According to the Fund for Peace (2015), most Western European countries rank at the top of the index as strong states with high degrees of governance and institutionalization. This fact does not completely prevent the occurrence and proliferation of transnational illicit flows across borders within the Schengen perimeter. For instance, in the last few years, most jihadist terrorist attacks were carried out in Western European countries such as France, Belgium, and Spain, although the perpetrators were nationals from their own countries, disenfranchised populations that became radicalized rather than transnational terrorists (see Ranstorp, 2010). Yet, they could move freely across borderless Europe.

In the case of drug trafficking, the main European entrance ports for cocaine and cannabis have been Spain and Belgium, which are relatively strong states. At the same time, the high degree of governance and institutionalization allows for effective cooperation and a common and comprehensive response to cope with cross-border crime and terrorism. Yet, since the EU is not a political federation but rather a conglomerate of distinctive sovereign national policies, the common efforts do not always translate into firm collective action that fulfills a consensual political willingness to address the different types of transnational crime. Hence, there has been a relative failure in suppressing drug trafficking, human trafficking, and arms trafficking in the continent (see European Commission, 2018a and 2018c; and van der Laan, 2017).

Hypothesis 3: The Prevalent Socioeconomic Conditions of the Neighboring States

We validate this hypothesis based on the socioeconomic stratification of the European continent, which has created a supply/demand relationship. There are significant differences in economic terms between the eastern and the western parts of Europe, between the Western Balkans and the EU, and within the Western Balkan region itself (see Lindstrom, 2004: 50; and Zielonka, 2001: 512).

On the supply side, we find the poorest countries in Europe. In the case of the Western Balkans, the Yugoslavian Wars of the 1990s caused the destruction of national infrastructures and economies, constraining the development of the region. Most of the states in the region have witnessed depletion in their infrastructure and capabilities, leading to significant social problems and the proliferation of crime. In addition, several states in the region suffered from economic blockades during the early 1990s. The economic sanctions established the conditions for the emergence of an informal economy, planting the seeds for the black market and the proliferation of illegal activities and illicit non-state actors. Moreover, the sanctions pushed states into the hands of transnational criminal networks, leading to criminal-political links of alliance if not integration. Thus, illicit transnational flows through ports, cities, and border crossings in the Western Balkans are enabled by a political economy of crime that is embedded in many countries in the region (The Global Initiative, 2019: 1; see also Giatzidis, 2007: 334).

In some countries, the scope of the informal economy reached its highest levels during the first years of the twenty-first century. Statistics show that the informal sector in Bosnia was about half of the GDP, in Serbia it reached about 35 percent of the GDP, whereas in Albania it accounted for 28 percent of the GDP (UNODC, 2008: 26). Overall, these unfavorable social and economic conditions affected and enabled the continued existence of transnational crime across the former Yugoslavian countries. The consequence of millions of people with no economic horizon and hope is that this region "exports" people who have to flee to find better opportunities elsewhere. That produces an illegal movement of workers to Western Europe and even worse, a thriving human trafficking business. Thus, the more prosperous and developed Western European countries attract the trafficking of people for sexual exploitation and cheap labor (see Moustakis, 2004: 149).

Because of the combination of these multiple factors, there is a perverse economic logic regarding the activities of transnational criminal organization groups in the former Yugoslavia. States that undertook the transition from closed to market economic systems have been particularly vulnerable to organized crime. The new governments were encouraged by the West to adopt rapid market-led reforms, including the privatization of state-controlled enterprises and the convertibility of their currencies. Yet this opened new opportunities for economic exploitation by criminal actors. According to this economic logic, the profitability of illicit transnational flows for political elites, border police, smugglers, and people living around the borders relates to the ability of these criminal groups to replace state institutions. This leads to the institutionalization of criminality and the privatization of criminalization, facilitated by the breakdown of law and order and the prevalent corruption of the political elites, in a scenario similar to what we learned about the Americas in the previous two chapters (see CQ, 2017: 1).

It is useful to contrast the Western Balkan countries, which are not part of the EU, to the privileged two that joined the European Union and are the richest countries in Southeast Europe: Slovenia and Croatia. Slovenia was ranked 25th in the HDI ranking in 2017 and had a GNP per capita of $31,400 (in 2017). Similarly, Croatia was ranked 46th in the HDI ranking in 2017 and had a GNP per capita of $15,219 (in 2017). Both countries show lower levels of illicit transnational flows and a reduced non-state actor presence, as compared to Serbia, Montenegro, Bulgaria, and Albania. Not by chance are sustainable and better socioeconomic conditions key factors in the strategy of EU enlargement toward Southeast Europe. Economic performance is thus regarded as an essential step in which potential candidates for inclusion in the EU have to demonstrate their advances in terms of economic development.

Conclusions

The European zone of peace is a fascinating laboratory to examine the possible links between peaceful borders and the occurrence of illicit transnational flows. We have disaggregated the analysis of Europe into the Schengen area and the former Yugoslavian countries in the Western Balkans as well as examined their mutual relations. The assessment of the three hypotheses has led to contradictory results and conclusions.

First, the large-scale softening of borders between Western and Eastern Europe with the end of the Cold War, in addition to the erasing of physical borders according to the Schengen regime, has contributed to the occurrence and proliferation of illicit transnational flows, including drug trafficking and human trafficking. Second, and conversely, the harmonization of internal border controls among the Schengen countries has abolished the logic of jurisdictional arbitrage. In this regard, the logic of Schengen seems to be similar to that of a federal state rather than to an array of distinct and contrasting sovereignties, thus disabling rather than enabling transnational criminal groups to take advantage of different national jurisdictions. Third, peaceful borders that are "hard" between the EU and its Southern and Eastern neighbors remain more controlled, though that it is not necessarily a formidable obstacle for the occurrence of illicit transnational flows between the Western Balkans and Western Europe. Fourth, terrorism is a problem that exists in Europe – unlike the Americas – though it has mostly local and national roots and manifestations. Yet, the terrorists' ideology might be transnational, stemming from the Middle East and North African (MENA) region and influenced by ISIS and al-Qaeda, and, in logistical terms, it might use and abuse the illicit transnational proliferation of weapons. Fifth, the particular configuration of Europe as a "pooling of sovereignties" creates better functional conditions for regional cooperation in coping with the challenges of transnational crime and terrorism in Europe and beyond. At the same time, since the EU is not (yet?) the "United States of Europe," these better functional capabilities and high degrees of governance in terms of capabilities do not always translate into effective policies due to the lack of a consensual political willingness to implement the adequate instruments, as a problem of collective action.

6 | A Triangle of Peace in the Middle East: The Israeli–Egyptian and Israeli–Jordanian Borders

Introduction

In this chapter, we examine what we call the triangle of peace in the Middle East, with reference to the peaceful international borders established upon the completion of peace treaties between Egypt and Israel on March 26, 1979, and between Israel and Jordan on October 26, 1994. These two peace treaties ended, respectively, the state of war that prevailed since 1948 between the State of Israel and its two neighboring Arab countries, formalizing a transition from war to negative peace. As in previous cases, we examine in this chapter the links between the existence of peaceful borders and the occurrence and proliferation of illicit transnational flows, in the form of drug trafficking, human and arms smuggling and trafficking, and terrorism. Unlike the European case analyzed in the previous chapter, the analysis is dyadic rather than regional, resembling the analysis of the American cases from Chapter 4.

The formal peace established between Israel and its two Arab neighbors manifests cases of negative or "cold" peace. Still, forty-two years of formal peace between Israel and Egypt, as well as twenty-seven years of peace between Israel and Jordan separate these two peaceful dyads from the other inconclusive and complicated dyads in the Arab-Israeli conflict, with reference to Lebanon, Syria, and especially the protracted and complicated Israeli-Palestinian conflict (see Kacowicz, 1996).

In geopolitical terms, the Middle East, especially with reference to the Fertile Crescent and the Israeli-Egyptian border, is a continental hub that connects Asia, Africa, and Europe (Mann, 2013: 84). As such, it constitutes a strategic location for the occurrence and proliferation of illicit transnational flows, including the trafficking of persons and transnational terrorism. There is an important variation between the two peaceful dyads regarding the occurrence of transnational criminal activity, including terrorism. This is partly a function of different geopolitical contexts: the Sinai Peninsula is a natural buffer between Israel and Egypt, whereas Jordan is itself a buffer state located between Israel, the Palestinian Authority in the West Bank, Syria, Saudi Arabia, and Iraq (Sharp, 2018: 6).

Following the peace agreements signed between Egypt and Israel in 1979, and between Israel and Jordan in 1994, their interstate relations experienced a formal transition from war to peace. Yet, the degree of peace remains negative in both cases, though there is an important variation regarding their initial expectations about the quality of the peace. From a formal point of view, on the one hand, the borders of Israel with both Egypt and Jordan are peaceful borders, opened to the free but controlled transit of their respective citizens and goods. On the other hand, there is a recognition that the degree of peace has remained "cold" (from the Jordanian standpoint), or even "frozen" (from the Egyptian standpoint). The public opinion and general attitudes of most of the Israeli, Egyptian, and Jordanian populations, including the opinion of practitioners and experts, corroborate that assessment (see Bar-Siman-Tov, 2000). Thus, the potential economic, social, cultural, and political benefits from a state of peace, the so-called peace dividends, have not yet materialized (see Press-Barnathan, 2009: 3–34; 57–59). At the same time, none of the neighboring countries anticipate a serious military threat from the other, even though they have not reached a stage of stable or "warm" peace (see Eisenberg and Caplan, 2010: 125). Thus, in both cases, we have examples of bilateral peace deprived of meaningful integration, so the regime borders merely coexist.

The Evolution of the Triangle of Peace in the Context of the Arab-Israeli Conflict

The peaceful international borders between Israel and Egypt and between Israel and Jordan are actually the former colonial borders demarcated at the beginning of the twentieth century. The border between Israel and Egypt is the same international border demarcated in 1906 between the United Kingdom and the Ottoman Empire, confirmed in the Rhodes Armistice of 1949, and finally ratified in the March 26, 1979, Peace Treaty between the two countries (see Kliot, 1995). The final demarcation of the border was completed by an international arbitration in 1988 that ruled in favor of Egypt regarding the small coastal resort of Taba.

Similarly, the border between Israel and Jordan is the former administrative colonial border unilaterally created by the former British Secretary of State for the Colonies, Winston Churchill, in 1921, as defined in the 1922 British Transjordan memorandum, which divided the Mandate over Palestine (the historical "Land of Israel") into two parts. The Eastern part became a British protectorate, an autonomous emirate (becoming later the Hashemite Kingdom of Transjordan in 1946, renamed Jordan after 1949). The Western section of the British Mandate of Palestine (1922–47), became the State of Israel after May 14, 1948. It includes also the West Bank (annexed by Jordan between 1949 and 1967 and occupied by Israel since 1967, partly under the administration of the Palestinian Authority), and the tiny Gaza Strip (occupied by Egypt between 1949 and 1967 and by Israel between 1967 and 2005, currently under the control of Hamas) (see Eisenberg and Caplan, 2010: 3–13, 125–127).

Between 1948 and 1967, the Arab-Israeli conflict remained absolute and intractable, since the formal goal of most of the Arab countries was the ultimate liquidation ("politicide") of the State of Israel (see Harkabi, 1972). To describe the initial conflict confronting Israel and its Arab neighbors, including Egypt and Jordan, as merely territorial would be misleading, since their goal consisted of undoing Israel rather than only redrawing its territorial boundaries[1] (see Harkabi, 1977). In the attempt of fulfilling such maximalist goal, the Arab states proved incapable of forcing Israel to its knees by military means. Israel emerged triumphant from the 1948 to 1949 war, from the 1956 Sinai campaign against Egypt, from the 1967 Six-Day War, and even from the difficult Yom Kippur War of October 1973. Yet, military victory did not render political triumph, since the Arab states continued to deny Israel's right to exist. Thus, as Israel found itself unable to translate its military victories into political gains, peace could not be established with its Arab neighbors (see Kacowicz, 1994: 120–121).

The First Arab-Israeli War of 1948–9 was a direct consequence of the Arab and Palestinian decisions to oppose the establishment of a Jewish state in any part of the territory of the British Mandate of (Western)

---

[1] Still, in the specific context of Jordan and Egypt, Israel had secret and informal ties with them, without any public recognition. Attempts were made before 1967 to engage in negotiations toward a political and territorial settlement. These patterns consolidated after Israel's standing in the subsequent wars, so the "politicide" goal remained mostly rhetorical (see Podeh, 2015).

Palestine. The war began in November 1947 as a civil war precipitated by the Arab rejection of the UN Plan for the Partition of Palestine into two states, Jewish and Arab. The declaration of Israeli independence on May 14, 1948, did not deter an Arab invasion. On the contrary, on May 15, 1948, Israel was invaded simultaneously by the Egyptian Army from the south, the Transjordan Arab Legion from the east, and the armed forces of Syria, Lebanon, and Iraq from the north and the northeast (see Dowty, 2012: 89–93; Podeh, 2015: 36–46; and Sela, 1998).

The First Arab-Israeli War concluded with a clear Israeli military victory and the Rhodes Armistices of 1949 that did not bring a permanent state of peace between Israel and its Arab neighbors. Still, the Rhodes Armistices eventually determined the current legal boundaries of the State of Israel, the so-called 1949–67 borders that lasted until the Six-Day War of 1967, though they are still considered the standard reference point for any potential two-state solution. The significant territorial changes caused by the 1967 war gave Israel and its Arab neighbors a unique opportunity to strike a political bargain, whereas the terms for a political settlement were outlined in Resolution 242 of the UN Security Council, which established, on November 22, 1967, the equation of "territories in exchange for peace."

Following its victory at the 1967 war, Israel conquered the Gaza Strip and the Sinai Peninsula from Egypt, the West Bank (including East Jerusalem) previously annexed by Jordan in 1949, and the Golan Heights from Syria. The Israeli-Egyptian diplomatic and political process started in the aftermath of the Yom Kippur War of October 1973 with gradual interim agreements in 1974 and 1975 designed to manage their conflict. The dramatic visit of Egyptian President Sadat to Jerusalem in November 1977 formally opened a peace process between the two countries from late 1977 to March 1979. By contrast, the formal peace process between Israel and Jordan came to fruition only following the signing of the Declaration of Principles (the so-called Oslo Accords) between Israel and the PLO on September 13, 1993. Let us examine in more detail the evolution of the relations between the neighboring countries, from war to peace.[2]

---

[2] For an overview of historical patterns in the Arab-Israeli conflict, see Eisenberg and Caplan, 2010, 15–29. See also Podeh, 2015; and Dowty, 2012.

The Egyptian-Israeli Relationship: From War to Peace

The Egyptian-Israeli peace process of 1977–9 marked a successful attempt to end the state of war that characterized the relations between the two countries throughout three decades (see Eisenberg and Caplan, 2010: 35; 45–51). Egyptian President Anwar Sadat's dramatic visit to Jerusalem on November 19 and 20, 1977, opened the way for political negotiations, followed by the Camp David summit of September 5–17, 1978, mediated by US President Jimmy Carter, and culminating with the Peace Treaty concluded on March 26, 1979. The Camp David Agreements of September 17, 1978, transformed the "existential" Egyptian-Israeli conflict into a "normal" territorial dispute that could be resolved through peaceful means based on the Israeli withdrawal of territories conquered in 1967 and the formal recognition of Israel by Egypt, leading to peace and diplomatic relations (see Kacowicz, 1994: 119–149).

In the case of the Egyptian-Israeli relationship, the peace process of 1977–9 aimed at ending the state of war that characterized the interaction between the two countries throughout three decades, rather than establishing a path of future economic cooperation, integration, and higher degrees of peace (see Eisenberg and Caplan, 2010: 33, 45–51). Whereas Israel regarded "normalization" as the natural result of the peace treaty, Egypt remained reticent about deepening peace, making it dependent upon a significant political process involving Israel and the Palestinians. Some scholars even argue that from the beginning, Egyptian President Anwar Sadat did not think about peace with Israel in terms of "normal" or "warm" peace, but rather as a formal end to belligerence and war, which had led to a frozen type of peace. Among the reasons for this cold peace we can mention Israel's actions against other Arab states and particularly vis-à-vis the Palestinians; the fact that the Israeli-Egyptian peace remained a separated peace; the lack of resolution of the Palestinian problem; and the lack of ideological legitimation and reconciliation with Israel on Egypt's part (see Bar-Siman-Tov, 2000: 226–229; and Press-Barnathan, 2009: 33–34).

The bilateral part of the Camp David accords, dealing with the Israeli-Egyptian negotiations, as well as the subsequent peace accord, were based on the formula of UN Resolution 242. Israel agreed to withdraw completely from the Sinai Peninsula back to the 1906 and 1949 borders, in return for a contractual peace that formally normalized relations between the two countries (Rabinovich, 2004: 277). Moreover, the Egyptian-Israeli Peace Treaty established a security regime in Sinai, leading to its partial demilitarization, including stern limits to the deployment of Egyptian troops and weaponry in the Sinai Peninsula, next to the Israeli border. The security regime included the deployment of a multinational peacekeeping force that was regarded as a necessary confidence and security-building measure to monitor the security provisions of the treaty, as related to the artificial buffer zone created between the two countries (see Watanabe and Nunsind, 2015). The private (non-UN) multinational force and observers (MFO) deployed to Sinai in 1982 consisted of 1,156 soldiers by December 2019, including personnel from Australia, Canada, Colombia, the Czech Republic, Fiji, France, Italy, Japan, New Zealand, Norway, the United Kingdom, the United States, and Uruguay (MFO, 2019).

The 1979 Egyptian–Israeli Peace Treaty did not envisage a situation in which violent non-state actors in Sinai would threaten their respective security. The Israeli and Egyptian decision makers who established the semi-demilitarization of Sinai considered it necessary to consolidate peace. They did not foresee that the area would become a haven for arms smuggling, terror infrastructure, and drugs and human trafficking by the early 2000s. Under the agreement, the Sinai Peninsula was divided into several zones of relative demilitarization, whereas in Zone C, close to the Israeli border, no significant Egyptian military presence was permitted. Despite these restrictions, the treaty allowed for mechanisms for ad hoc changes in the deployment of Egyptian forces in Sinai, pending Israeli approval. That actually happened in the last few years, with increased security cooperation between the two countries. Since 2014, the Israeli authorities furthered their cooperation with Egyptian security forces in Sinai, far beyond the limitations of the demilitarized zone established in the peace agreement. Israel has agreed to increase the level of forces that the Egyptian army could deploy in Sinai in order to cope with the terrorist threats emanating from Sinai (see Baker, 2012; Gold, 2015: 36; and Watanale and Nunlist, 2015: 4).

Since the signing of the peace agreement in 1979, and particularly since 1982, when the final stage of the Israeli withdrawal from the Sinai Peninsula took place, the Israeli-Egyptian peace has never been in danger of a collapse or a major crisis, which might escalate into a war. Nevertheless, the bilateral relations never transcended a minimal security and political cooperation that was required to maintain peace (Bar-Siman-Tov, 2000: 220). The peace agreement has been under constant criticism and objection from Egyptian public opinion, as well as some governmental and military officials. Although it has never been broken or jeopardized, it has been extremely unpopular at both the grassroots and intelligentsia levels in Egypt to these days. At the same time, since 2013, there has been strong and increasing intelligence and security cooperation between Israel and Egypt stemming from the common threat posed by terrorists affiliated with the Islamic State and other jihadist elements within Sinai. In addition, the two countries increased the number of possible issue areas of further cooperation in economic and civilian affairs, including the recent agreement about the supply of natural gas from Israel to Egypt (see Hassanein, 2018).

A complicating factor in terms of the common boundary between Israel and Egypt is the 12-kilometer border between Egypt and the Gaza Strip (out of the 245-km length from Rafah to Eilat). In 2005, Israel evacuated its remaining military forces and civilian population from the Gaza Strip. In 2007, Hamas took control over the Gaza Strip after a successful coup against the Palestinian National Authority. Israel and Hamas have been in a continuous state of armed conflict, punctuated by actual wars and military campaigns in 2008–9, 2012, and 2014. Moreover, the Egyptian-Gaza border has become a site for transnational illicit flows including arms smuggling and terrorism (see Ronen, 2014; and Siboni and Ben-Barak, 2014). As a reaction to that, Egypt did erect a massive steel barricade in its border with the Gaza strip, a "wall" designed to stop the smuggling of contraband into Egypt, and the trafficking of weapons, explosives, and other goods to the Palestinians (Flores, 2017: 11).

The Israeli-Jordanian Relationship: From War to Peace

With the end of World War I, the British established the Mandate of (Western) Palestine and the Emirate of Transjordan (later on the Hashemite Kingdom of Jordan) in 1919–22. Since then, both the physical and the imaginary border between Western Palestine (later Israel) and Eastern Palestine (later Jordan) have occupied key ideological, political, and strategic roles in the design and convoluted regional dynamics of the Fertile Crescent/Levant. While wedged between Syria, Iraq, and Saudi Arabia, the Hashemites saw the whole territory as part of a common *Sham* area (Levant), under their direct political domain. This left open the possibility of political cooperation with the political leadership of the Jewish community in Palestine at the expense of the Palestinian Arab population and its leadership (see Kashgari, 2011; Sela, 1998; and Shlaim, 1988).

The Jewish Zionists also initially saw the Eastern territory of the Mandate of Palestine as part of a common political unit. Yet, since the establishment of the Hashemite Kingdom of Transjordan in 1946, the Zionist mainstream leadership increasingly considered Jordan as a potential buffer between a future Jewish state in Western Palestine and the Arab countries to the East (see Sharp, 2018: 6; and Shlaim, 1988). Such a position stood in contrast to that of the Revisionist Zionists, who have traditionally regarded Jordan as an integral part of the original Mandate of Palestine, including the Balfour Declaration of 1917, guaranteeing a national home for the Jewish people in Palestine. Thus, the scope and depth of Zionist-Transjordan and Israeli-Jordan contacts from the 1920s to the present have been remarkable. As Eisenberg and Caplan (2010, 73) cogently suggest, "Israel and Jordan are, after all, the Solomonic baby who survived" (see also Bar-Joseph, 1987; and Shlaim, 1988).

The controversy regarding the extent of the Israeli-Jordanian cooperation experienced a first significant territorial change following the 1948–9 First Arab–Israeli War and the Rhodes Armistices. Following the war, the Hashemite Kingdom of Transjordan occupied and subsequently annexed a land area of 5,640 square kilometers that was supposed to be part of the Arab State in Palestine that was never established. The area is generally called the West Bank (or "Cisjordan," in contrast to Transjordan), Judea and Samaria (by Israeli Jews), or an integral part of Palestine (by the Palestinians). Meanwhile, the "Jordanian option" among Israelis was formulated, referring to Jordan as the original Palestinian state where the rights of the Palestinians could and should be fulfilled.

The discussions surrounding this Jordanian option only intensified following a second significant territorial change, after the 1967 Six-Day War, when Israel militarily occupied the West Bank, remaining undecided until today regarding what to do with the conquered territories and its vast Palestinian population. Up to the outbreak of the Palestinian first intifada in the Gaza Strip and the West Bank in December 1987, Israel considered the possibility of reaching a territorial compromise with

Jordan over the West Bank, thereby bypassing the Palestinians and divid-
ing the disputed land between the two countries. Yet, the legitimacy
vicissitudes of these negotiations and the first intifada terminated the
Jordanian option (see Wajner, 2020: 92). On July 31, 1988, King
Hussein officially declared Jordan's political disengagement from the
West Bank, explicitly stating that the territory was an integral part of
Palestine and it should belong to the Palestinians (King Hussein, quoted in
Laqueur and Rubin, 2008: 338–341). Yet, several political circles in Israel
still support an agreement with the Arab countries bypassing the
Palestinians, reaffirming the feasibility of a Jordanian option[3] (see
Eisenberg and Caplan, 2010: 73–91; and Podeh, 2015: 47–57, 184–195).

From 1967 to 1994, Israel and Jordan shared a de facto peace or an
"adversarial partnership" with common interests and concerns, including a long border, a common animadversion toward the Palestinians,
and the same US patron (Eisenberg and Caplan, 2010: 76). Jordan's
security and stability have always been a core interest to Israel due to its
geographical proximity, Palestinian demographic and political concerns, and its geopolitical importance as a buffer between Israel and
the former Eastern Front of Syria and Iraq. Examples of that concern
date back to 1970 when, despite the absence of formal relations, Israel
assisted King Hussein to repel the threat of a Syrian invasion following
a gruesome civil war confronting the PLO and the Jordanian monarchy. This conflict ultimately led to the massive killings of Palestinians
in the Black September events and the subsequent deportation of the
PLO leadership from Jordan to Lebanon (see Ryan, 2015 and 2018).

Despite the failure of the London Agreement of April 1987, con-
cluded between Israeli Foreign Minister Shimon Peres and Jordanian
King Hussein, the two countries continued their informal contacts and
their de facto peace. The negotiations since the Madrid Conference of
October 1991, the Washington Talks of 1991–2, and especially the
Oslo Accords of September 13, 1993, signed between Israel and the
PLO, were the turning point to begin formal peace negotiations

---

[3] The "Jordanian option" has been an option only for Israel, since it was never an
option for Jordan. Jordanians and the Hashemite kings have consistently refuted
the notion of constituting a Palestinian state and have refrained from even
addressing this option. The fact that, in 1988, King Hussein declared his
disengagement from the West Bank does not mean that he ever conceived of his
country as a Palestinian state. This has always been a very sensitive issue in
Jordan, which refrains from discussing the extent of its Palestinian population
publicly.

between Israel and Jordan, leading to the conclusion of the Peace Treaty on October 26, 1994 (see Wajner, 2020).

In security terms, unlike the Israeli-Egyptian border regime, and due to the high level of initial trust existing between the political leaderships of both countries at that time, the Israeli-Jordanian Peace Treaty did not mention any special bilateral security arrangements such as demilitarization or any foreign supervision by international peacekeeping forces. Instead, the agreement explicitly referred to Jordan's preoccupation with the specter of a Palestinian massive expulsion from the West Bank by Israel, as well as Israel's interest in preserving Jordan as a stable buffer state between Israel and the Eastern Front (Iraq and beyond) (see Susser, 1999: 20–22; and Article 2 of the Israeli-Jordanian Peace Treaty).

Regarding the border demarcation, the two countries agreed that the international boundary would be delimited according to the British Mandate. The agreement included special territorial regimes under Jordanian sovereignty with reference to the Naharayim/ Baqura (about 0.83 square kilometers) and the Zofar/al-Ghamr (1.3 square kilometers), to be leased to Israel for agricultural purposes, for a period of twenty-five years.[4] Israel and Jordan share a 240-kilometer border, in addition to a 95-kilometer border in the Jordan Valley, within the West Bank, currently occupied by Israel. As part of the peace agreement, Israel returned to Jordan about three hundred square kilometers taken over in the late 1960s, and there were also some minor land exchanges of about thirty square kilometers in the Arava/Wadi'Araba long border (see Susser, 1999: 20–21).

In contrast to the 1977–9 Israeli-Egyptian peace process, the Israel-Jordan Peace Treaty (Wadi Araba Treaty) that Israeli Prime Minister Yitzhak Rabin signed with Jordan's King Hussein did generate high mutual expectations of a warm peace due to the leaders' close personal relations. In searching for a mutually accommodating and encompassing agreement, the peace treaty not only concluded the formal state of war and established peace and diplomatic relations between the two countries; it also emphasized a future path of economic cooperation,

[4] In October 2019, these two borderlands returned to Jordan, after being leased for twenty-five years.

downgrading the relevance of security clauses, emphasized in the Egyptian-Israeli compact.

Indeed, the 1994 peace agreement proposed several concrete steps for cooperating in a myriad of economic and social issue areas. It promoted several concrete steps for cooperating in many socioeconomic issue areas, including tourism, cultural and scientific exchanges, trade, transportation and communications, aviation, health, agriculture, environment, energy, and joint development of the Red Sea cities of Eilat and Akaba. It also referred to actions to jointly combat terrorism, crime, and drugs (see Ariel, 2016; Ariel and Cohen, 2013; Eisenberg and Caplan, 2010: 125; Press-Barnathan, 2009: 57–58; see also Article 12 of the Israel-Jordan Peace Treaty).

Eventually, both the formal and informal intentions of the treaty signatories regarding further normalization did not translate into higher levels of peace. One of the main obstacles that stood in the way of a warmer peace between the neighboring countries stemmed from the lack of legitimacy among many sectors of the Jordanian society regarding high-profile cooperative initiatives with the State of Israel. This Jordanian reticence will remain in place until Israel concludes (if it concludes) a final agreement with the Palestinians leading to the establishment of an independent Palestinian State in the West Bank and the Gaza Strip. Thus, despite the fact that Jordan has been officially at peace with Israel for the last twenty-seven years, it remains, as in the Israeli-Egyptian case, a cold peace between governments rather than a genuine peace between societies. Like in the relations with Egypt, Israel recently upgraded its economic cooperation with Jordan by the provision of natural gas (see Arieli and Cohen, 2013: 248–29; and MEMO, 2019).

Transnational Crime and Terrorism across the Borders of the Triangle of Peace

In this section, we briefly examine the occurrence and proliferation of illicit transnational flows across the borders of the Middle Eastern triangle of peace. First, we focus upon Sinai and the Egyptian-Israeli border, regarding drug trafficking, human smuggling and trafficking, and sporadic terrorist attacks, emanating from Sinai to the Gaza Strip and to Israel. Second, we examine the Israeli-Jordanian border, focusing mostly on drug trafficking and potential terrorist threats.

The Sinai Peninsula and the Egyptian-Israeli Border

The Sinai Peninsula is a territory in the shape of an isosceles triangle covering an area of about 61,000 square kilometers – about three times the size of the State of Israel. Northern Sinai is located on the Mediterranean littoral, west of which lie Egypt and Libya, with Israel and the Gaza Strip to the east. The local population constitutes about half a million inhabitants, most of them Bedouins. Since the signing of the Egyptian-Israeli peace treaty in 1979 and Israel's withdrawal in 1982, the two countries considered this borderland as an important buffer zone. It aimed to provide Israel with the necessary strategic depth, whereas Egypt mostly neglected Sinai, alienating its Bedouin population and allowing for a security and military vacuum in this vast territory (see Ronen, 2014).

Since the Israeli withdrawal of 1982, Egypt exercised only partial sovereignty over the territory, allowing for its continuing marginalization and institutional chaos (see Laub, 2013). Gradually, Sinai has become a hub of transnational illicit activities, including trade in drugs, weapons, and the trafficking of goods and people in and out of the area, posing new security challenges to both Egypt and Israel (see Baker, 2012; Dyer and Kessler, 2014: 12–13; and Ronen, 2014).

Black markets and transnational crime have flourished in the Sinai Peninsula since the late 1990s. A decade later, the Sinai landscape changed following the increased incursion of Jihadist ideology and terrorist modus operandi in the early 2000s, intensified by Israel's 2005 pullout from the Gaza Strip, Hamas' coup in the Gaza Strip against the Palestinian National Authority in 2007, and the subsequent blockade imposed by Israel and Egypt on that Palestinian enclave. Thus, Sinai has been transformed into a logistical, strategic, and military hinterland for the planning, training, and execution of terrorist attacks; storage and smuggling of arms, drugs, and contraband; and human trafficking and smuggling of infiltrators and African refugees from Eritrea and Sudan seeking for asylum.

As for the activity of smuggling from Sinai into the Gaza Strip, including weapons, the Egyptian state turned a blind eye, and, according to some evidence, official representatives of the Egyptian regime, including security officers, have even cooperated with non-state actors such as Bedouin smugglers, for their own benefit (see Ashour, 2016; and Schneider, 2020). Different Sinai Bedouin *chamulot* (clans), mainly the Tarabin and the Tiaha, have played a major role in the thriving human, drug, and arms trafficking trade. At the same time, some of their people have engaged with jihadist groups, which around 2012 counted more than twelve thousand members (see Gold, 2014; Ronen, 2014; Shay, 2014; and Watanabe and Nunlist, 2015: 2–3).

Drug Trafficking from Sinai into Israel

There have been some official reports of drug trafficking from Sinai into Israel in the last decade, mostly before 2013. The main channels for smuggling drugs have been the official land border crossings, involving Israeli Palestinians (Arab Israelis) in smuggling drugs, benefitting from some degree of corruption along both sides of the border. About one hundred tons of marijuana have entered Israel mainly through the Egyptian border. In 2012 alone, the Israeli National Police and the Israel Customs confiscated approximately 2,400 kilograms of marijuana, which entered Israel mainly through the Egyptian border (see Israeli Anti-Drug Authority, 2011; and *The Times of Israel*, 2018).

Arms Trafficking from Sinai into the Gaza Strip

Following the Arab Spring uprisings in Libya and Egypt, there have been reports of arms trafficking from Libya into Sinai, and from Sinai into the Gaza Strip. Due to growing regional instability, vast stockpiles of weapons have found their way to the black market and to the illicit economy. Stemming from Libya's security breakdown, large amounts of Libyan arms have been smuggled into Sinai, including light to heavier arms, landmines, RPGs, and Grad rockets. Thus, violent non-state actors in the Gaza Strip and the Sinai Peninsula have been arming themselves through smuggling networks operating in North-East Africa and the Middle East (see Zohar, 2015; also Dyer and Kessler, 2014: 17–18).

A smuggling industry has proliferated in Sinai for decades, channeling an abundance of sophisticated weaponry and arms into Sinai – both as a destination in itself and in transit to the Gaza Strip. Before the 2011 Egyptian revolution, a major route of weapons smuggling via Sinai started in Iran, continued to Sudan, from there into Sinai, and from Sinai into the Gaza Strip, posing a significant security threat to Israel. According to foreign reports, Israel took several steps to thwart this weapons trafficking, including attacks within Sudan (see IDF, 2014: 10).

Human Smuggling and Trafficking from Sinai into Israel

Trafficking in human beings in Sinai has been an extremely profitable business for organized crime. According to the UNHCR, complex trafficking networks have been set up involving people smugglers; kidnappers, such as groups of Rashada tribesmen in Eritrea and Northeast Sudan; intermediaries inside refugee camps; bribed military, police, and border control staff; and criminal elements within the Egyptian Bedouin communities in Sinai (see van Reisen, Estefanos, and Rijken, 2012). Growing numbers of asylum seekers, mostly from Eritrea and Sudan, started crossing Israel's borders with Egypt in 2006 (see Paz, 2011). According to the Israeli official figures, about 26,635 people crossed the border by July 2010, and over 55,000 by January 2012.

The Israeli policy regarding human smuggling has been a confrontational one, denying asylum petitions, incarcerating some asylum seekers, and attempting to deport them to their countries of origin, or to neighboring African countries. While 10,445 citizens of various African countries entered Israel by illegal means in 2012, only 43 did the same in 2013, after the completion of the main section of an electronic barrier erected along the Israeli-Egyptian border. After the entire fence was completed, the number of illegal migrants crossing the border had dropped to only sixteen in 2016 and none in 2017 (see Bar-Tuvia, 2018; and Ziegler, 2015).

Terrorism in and from Sinai

The Sinai Peninsula has also seen a string of terrorist attacks against foreign tourists – in 2004 in Taba and Nuweiba, in 2005 in Sharm el-Sheikh, and in 2006 in Dahab – that collectively killed at least 123 people. Since then, contact of local terrorist cells with al-Qaeda, Muslim Brotherhood and Hamas leaders, as well as the joint training of their fighters and shared arms production, has been strengthened (see Dyer and Kessler, 2014: 14–15, 18; Gold, 2014; and Ronen, 2014).

Since the Egyptian revolution of 2011 and the military coup of 2013 staged by then General and now President Abdel Fattah el-Sisi, there has been an unprecedented growth in the volume of terrorist groups operating from Sinai. These insurgencies have taken advantage of the chaotic situation that ensued in the peninsula, further taking advantage of the marginalized Bedouin population, and drawing them closer to terrorism. The Sinai insurgency included mostly local Bedouin tribesmen, who exploited the disruptive situation in the rest of Egypt and weakened central authority to launch a series of attacks on government forces in Sinai. Leaders of certain Sinai armed groups have links to ISIS, and reportedly, unspecified leaders of al-Qaeda in the Islamic Maghreb. There are also strong indicators of a foreign fighter presence in Sinai including contingents from the Gaza Strip and Yemen, as well as Saudi Arabia, Syria, and North Africa (see Dyer and Kessler, 2014).

Strengthening of terror cells followed the 2011 fall of Egyptian police stations throughout Sinai and the subsequent crises in Libya, Syria, and Yemen. After the massacre of more than three hundred Muslim worshippers by allegedly Jihadist militants in November 2017, President el-Sisi launched a military campaign, "Comprehensive Operation-Sinai 2018," with the aim of putting an end to terrorism and restoring security in the Sinai Peninsula. The results have been at best inconclusive, due to the relative weakness and lack of political willingness on the part of the Egyptian authorities (see Dentice, 2018).

Since 2014, the ultimate affiliation of some of the jihadist groups like Ansar Beit-al-Maqdis to ISIS posed a potential terrorist threat against Israel across the international border (see Gold, 2015; Watanabe and Nunsind, 2015; and Zohar, 2015). By 2014, Israel was targeted at least nineteen times by acts of sabotage and terrorism originating in Sinai, mostly bombings and shootings (Dyer and Kessler, 2014). For these reasons, the Israeli authorities contemplated better security cooperation with Egyptian security forces far beyond the security limitations embedded in the Peace Treaty, regularly allowing the introduction of Egyptian ground and aerial forces exceeding the limits agreed upon regarding their shared buffer zones of demilitarization. Moreover, the militarization and fortification of the Israeli-Egyptian border, completed through the erection of a formidable barrier after 2013, have substantially reduced both terrorist attacks across the border, as well as drugs and arms trafficking. Yet, the security threats posed to both countries are far from eradicated (see Baker, 2012; Dyer and Kessler, 2014: 3–5, 12–13, 20; Gold, 2015; Shay, 2014; and Siboni and Ben-Barak, 2014).

The Israeli-Jordanian Border

According to the Israel-Jordan Peace Treaty of October 26, 1994, the parties agreed to combat crime and drugs. Article 12 stipulated: "The parties will cooperate in combating crime, with an emphasis on smuggling, and will take all necessary measures to combat and prevent such activities as the production of, as well as the trafficking in illicit drugs, and will bring to trial perpetrators of such acts." Similarly, Israel and Jordan agreed in Article 4 to cooperate in combating terrorism of all kinds, including preventing and combatting cross-boundary infiltrations. Indeed, the occurrence and proliferation of transnational illicit flows across the Israeli-Jordanian border is relatively small, in comparison to the Israeli-Egyptian case. Jordan faces larger security threats stemming from its other borders, especially with Syria and Iraq, as spillovers of violence, terror, and foreign fighters from the Syrian civil war (including ISIS operatives) and the implosion of Iraq after 2003 (see Ryan, 2012, 2015, and 2018; also Idris, 2019a: 1–4). While there is a limited amount of drug trafficking from Jordan and Israel, there is no clear record of human smuggling and trafficking across the borders, and only potential terrorist transnational threats.

Drug Trafficking from Jordan to Israel
Israel is not a major narcotics producing or trafficking country, but it has a significant domestic market for illegal drugs, facing an increasing demand for cocaine, hashish, and marijuana, as well as heroin, LSD, and ecstasy. By contrast, Jordan remains primarily a transit country for illicit drugs because of its geographical location between drug-producing countries to the north and drug-consuming countries to the south and west. Jordan continues to be a transit country for drugs, and it remains vulnerable to illicit drug smuggling through its vast desert borders (see Idris, 2019a: 4). Since the end of the Second Lebanon War in August 2006, the Jordanian border has become a gate for drug entry into Israel, in particular for heroin, cannabis, cocaine, and hashish (see Council of the European Union, 2014: 1–4; and *The Jordan Times*, 2018).

Terrorist Threat from Jordan to Israel
There is no evidence for transnational terrorist activity reported from Jordan across its border with Israel in recent years. At the same time, there is the fear of potential terrorist incursions from Jordan, since Salafi-jihadi terrorism remains a long-term concern for countries bordering Syria and Iraq, notably Turkey, Jordan, and Lebanon. This has been further emphasized as a security concern after ISIS fighters have

referred to Jordan's porous borders as a potential destination through which they could move forward to other targets in the Middle East, including Israel (Marteu, 2018: 85). Due to the vicissitudes of the Syrian civil war, in 2017, pro-ISIS jihadists acquired a stronghold in the triangular region bordering Israel and Jordan, posing a potential threat to the Israeli border.[5] The ISIS terrorist threat has been one of the major motivations behind the Israeli decision to build a massive fence along the border with Jordan, in order to prevent ISIS operatives from spreading into the Jordan Valley in the West Bank (see Avdan and Gelpi, 2017: 16).

Explaining the Reality of Peaceful Borders and Illicit Transnational Flows in the Middle Eastern Triangle of Peace

Hypothesis 1: The Degree of Physical and Institutional Openness of the Peaceful Borders

There are important differences in the geopolitical dimensions of the borders between Egypt and Israel, in comparison to those between Israel and Jordan. The main distinction resides in the physical proximity of part of the Israeli-Jordanian border to the capital cities of both countries (Amman in Jordan and Jerusalem in Israel), in contrast to the remoteness of the Israeli-Egyptian border along Sinai to any major city in either country. In fact, the Egyptian-Israeli border has been relatively neglected and less controlled than the Israeli-Jordanian one. From the Egyptian standpoint, and with a few exceptions after 2013, the Sinai Peninsula remains an area of limited statehood.

Since the establishment of peaceful borders among the neighboring countries, there has been an important physical change in their configuration, in the form of the construction of a fortified border in both cases. Israel erected and completed an electrified computerized border fence along its entire border with Egypt in 2013, turning it from a relatively soft to a hard and fortified border. Israel also upgraded the already fortified border with Jordan in 2017, with the erection of

---

[5] For instance, many ISIS foreign fighters conceive of Jordan as the potential "nest Jihad arena"; namely, they recognize its vulnerability in terms of its porous borders with Syria and Iraq, its geographical proximity to their location, and its potential as a network of operations. This might jeopardize Jordan's security and stability, and indirectly, it might threaten its secured regime border with Israel.

a thirty-kilometer fence in the proximity of the Red Sea resort of Eilat and the new international airport at Timna. Thus, in terms of the linkage between the degree of the physical and institutional openness of borders and its possible impact upon illicit transnational flows, we corroborate the validity of our first hypothesis in the Israeli-Egyptian case until the completion of the barrier by Israel in 2013. As for the Israeli-Jordanian border, we prove the logic of the hypothesis in a reversed way, pointing out the effectiveness of a militarized and fortified border in reducing transnational terrorism (see Avdan and Gelpin, 2017).

The Egyptian-Israeli Border

Regarding the Egyptian-Israeli border, we emphasize the peculiar geographical characteristics of the Sinai Peninsula as a buffer region that bridges North Africa and the Levant, remote from both the Egyptian hinterland (the Nile Valley), and from the Israeli population centers. Until the early 2000s, the Sinai Peninsula in general and the Egyptian-Israeli border in particular remained relatively soft and open, exposed to the illicit transnational flows of drugs, weapons, human trafficking, and terrorism, carried out by non-state actors including Bedouin clans and jihadist groups.

Following the counterrevolution (military coup) in Egypt in July 2013, the Egyptian army engaged in harsh repression measures and counterinsurgency to cope with the security threats emanating from Sinai. In parallel, during the same year, Israel completed an electrified, computerized fence along the entire length of its border with Egypt, which led to a complete stop of human trafficking and smuggling and a significant reduction of drug and arms trafficking. Thus, since 2013 there has been a drastic decrease of terrorist and criminal activity along the border (see IDF, 2014: 26).

Moreover, increased military cooperation between the two countries to restore order and security in Sinai, in addition to the completed Israeli-Egyptian border fence, have reduced both the volume of terrorist attacks and the arms trafficking while completely stopping the human smuggling and trafficking from Sinai to Israel. Since there has not been any economic integration across the neighboring countries, the fortification of the common border has been much more effective in neutralizing illicit transnational flows than in other cases, like the US-Mexican fortified border. At the same time, the security threats have changed in the direction of terrorist attacks by "remote control," using rocket launches toward Eilat that literally bypass the physical border between the two countries (see IDF, 2014: 23).

The Israeli-Jordanian Border

Unlike the Egyptian-Israeli border, which was relatively soft and porous until 2013, the peaceful borders between Israel and Jordan since 1994 have remained hard and controlled, due to the common political and security interests of the neighboring countries. Since 1967, Israel has attempted to physically impede the illegal infiltration of Palestinian refugees residing in Jordan (the East Bank of the Jordan River), to the militarily controlled West Bank. Conversely, Jordan still fears a demographic debacle in the form of a massive Palestinian expulsion from the West Bank to its sovereign territory, fulfilling the nightmare scenario of "Jordan is Palestine" (see Tal, 1993: 54). Thus, the two countries share a common interest in having a peaceful but regulated and controlled border, hermetically closing the possibility of illegal transnational flows, including human smuggling and terrorism. That partially explains the absence of significant illicit transnational flows, perhaps with the exception of drug trafficking.

Unlike the absence of any type of economic relations along the Egyptian-Israeli border, there have been some initial moves in terms of economic relations between Jordan and Israel. Trade and tourism grew to a very limited extent between the neighboring countries, propelled by the Qualifying Industrial Zone (QIZ) signed in 1997 (see Press-Barnathan, 2009: 58–59). Moreover, there has been a particular case of constructive cooperation across borders in the form of municipal committees of the Aqaba-Eilat area, which includes eight cooperative subcommittees that have been active since 2005 to discuss shared regional problems and suggest operational solutions to local needs (Arieli and Cohen, 2013: 247). Yet, the Jordanian-Israeli border remains far from integrated along the lines of the other European or American cases assessed in this book.

The Israeli decision to fortify the Israeli-Jordanian border next to the Southern city of Eilat refers to the potential threat of transnational flows of Jihadist terrorist attacks from Jordanian territory, as related to the chaotic geopolitical situation created by the Syrian civil war and the (former) rise of ISIS. In addition, this security move was adopted in response to other potential illicit transnational flows such as drug, weapons, and human trafficking, once the illicit routes from Sinai had been effectively curbed by the new and effective barrier erected in 2013 along the Israeli-Egyptian border (see Amidror and Lerman, 2015).

Hypothesis 2: The Degree of Governance, Institutional Strength, and Political Willingness

To analyze the relevance of the second hypothesis, we consider Israel as a relatively strong state regarding its level of governance and institutionalization, in comparison to its Arab neighbors. At the same time, there is an important variance in terms of institutional strength, governance capabilities, and political willingness, when we compare the Egyptian-Israeli and the Israeli-Jordanian borders with respect to the respective Jordanian and Egyptian capabilities and political willingness. Thus, we claim that Hypothesis 2 is mostly relevant for the analysis of the Israeli-Egyptian dyad. In a reversed logic, we argue that the hypothesis is also helpful to explain the Israeli-Jordanian case.

The Egyptian-Israeli Case

Contrary to Jordan, Egypt was historically supposed to enjoy stronger institutional and governance capabilities, given both its national history and its ethno-national, homogeneous composition and distinctive national identity (see Karawan, 2002: 155–156). Yet, since mid-2011, Egypt descended into bloody domestic strife following the Muslim Brotherhood Revolution (in 2011) and the military coup and counter-revolution (2013), with violent repercussions in Sinai. Moreover, Egypt never exercised a high level of stateness with regard to Sinai. Large parts of the Sinai borderland have lacked any effective government security policies or forms of domestic security governance since Israel's withdrawal in 1982 (see Ronen, 2014; and Schneider, 2020).

Until 2013, the Egyptian central government had failed in exercising effective control over the vast territory of the Sinai Peninsula (see Ronen, 2014; and Zohar, 2015). Violent non-state actors such as jihadist organizations in Sinai exploited the failure of Egyptian governance and the subsequent security and military vacuum in Sinai to strengthen their position as central players on the local stage. The growth of a security vacuum on the peninsula has transformed Egypt's backwater into a stronghold of terrorism and other transnational illicit flows (see Watanabe and Nunlist, 2015).

By contrast, in the last few years, the Egyptian regime of President el-Sissi has increased its security control over the Sinai Peninsula. This has led both to the strengthening of security cooperation mechanisms with Israel, as well as to the increasing militarization of the Sinai Peninsula, drawing large military forces to enforce sovereignty along the border-lands. In terms of the complex relationships between state and criminal (and terrorist) non-state actors, we argue that Egypt has chosen a series of options in the continuum ranging from alliance (essentially at the local and regional level), enforcement evasion, all the way recently to confrontation, whereas the Israeli policy has been more coherent along the lines of confrontation. Thus, we corroborate the second hypothesis.

The Israeli-Jordanian Case

The complex and heterogeneous ethno-national distribution of (Trans-)Jordan, since its foundation as an emirate by colonial Britain in 1921, made it historically a candidate for instability and institutional weakness (see Tal, 1993: 46). This is the case when we look at its social and demographic composition (with a clear Palestinian majority in its popu-lation), as well as its geopolitical location vis-à-vis its neighbors, includ-ing Syria, Iraq, and Saudi Arabia (Ryan, 2015: 42).

And yet, it was perhaps the shadow of the "Jordanian option" of Jordan becoming Palestine that contributed to the strengthening of the Hashemite regime over time, and its political survival, resilience, and relative strength in terms of governance and institutional performance. In this respect, its Arab heritage and the illustrious Islamic lineage of its Hashemite royal family also explain its relative success in terms of legitimation strategies (see Ryan, 2018: 111–112). Moreover, the pro-Hashemite, pro-monarchist security apparatus has generally been a key pillar of support and has improved its effectiveness over time following periods of state formation, coup attempts, and civil wars (see Sharp, 2018: 1; also El-Anis, 2018). Furthermore, the Hashemite Kingdom of Jordan has managed to confront the complexity of war in neighboring Syria since 2011 including a flux of more than six hundred thousand refugees, adding to its complicated demographic realities.

This notable Jordanian resilience is related to a relatively strong sense of social cohesion, strong support for the Jordanian regime from both Western powers and the Gulf Arab monarchies, and an internal security apparatus that is highly capable of exercising govern-ance, sometimes through authoritarian measures and repression of

Jordan's Muslim Brotherhood (see Sharp, 2018: 1; also Ryan, 2018). Thus, the combination of relatively high levels of institutional strength and governance, as well as the political willingness exhibited by both Israel and Jordan explain the relative absence of illicit transnational flows across their borders. In that sense, the second hypothesis does not seem to be relevant in a direct way, but its inversed logic remains valid.

Hypothesis 3: The Prevalent Socioeconomic Conditions of the Neighboring States

Much of the bordering economic relations, both licit and illicit, between Israel and its neighbors, including Jordan and Egypt, are conditioned upon the same economic rationale that refers to the socio-economic disparity between developed and underdeveloped countries, despite the low levels of economic interaction and integration between the two dyads (see Press-Barnathan, 2009). For instance, Israel and Jordan have a similar population (about nine million in Israel and ten million in Jordan). Yet, Israel is considered a high-income country with a GDP of nearly US$348 billion and a GDP per capita of US$42,115, whereas Jordan is considered a lower-middle-income country, with a GDP of about US$41 billion and a GDP per capita of US$5,677 (see El-Anis, 2018). By contrast, Egypt, with almost ten times the population of Israel (about ninety-five million), has a GDP of less than US$300 billion and a relatively poor GDP per capita of US$2,800. These facts explain the economic rationale for the occurrence and proliferation of illicit transnational flows, particularly regarding drugs, arms, and human trafficking. We can thus corroborate the validity of the third hypothesis, especially with reference to the Israeli-Egyptian border, while being less relevant in the Israeli-Jordanian dyad.

The Egyptian-Israeli Case

Black markets and transnational crime have flourished in the Sinai Peninsula since the late 1990s, as a function of the economic deprivation and political alienation suffered by the Bedouin local population, in relation to the rest of Egypt. Most of the Sinai Bedouin residents believe that they were left out of the relative economic boom of Egypt; hence, such marginalization has been a primary reason for their involvement in illicit activities, both local and transnational (see IDF,

2014: 4). Excluded from the formal economy, Bedouin clans found opportunities for economic survival in cannabis and narcotics production, as well as smuggling of goods, weapons, and people. In that context, the scale of human trafficking and smuggling picked up in 2006 regarding African refugees looking for asylum and economic opportunities in the developed world; that is, Israel (see Laub, 2013; and van Reisen, Estefanos, and Rijken, 2012). Thus, the socioeconomic marginalization of the local Bedouin population in Sinai has been a major cause for the security challenges posed to the Egyptian state, and by extension, to Israel as well. Conversely and similarly, on the Israeli side of the border, Israeli Bedouins have been involved in illicit transnational flows, as related to their poor and marginalized status within the Israeli society (see Gleis, 2007).

According to Watanabe and Nunlist (2015), the Sinai Bedouins developed a parallel economy through drug smuggling, contraband, and human smuggling and trafficking to Israel, as well as illicit trade with Gaza using a network of tunnels. By 2009, these illicit transnational activities were reported to have become the Bedouins' principal source of income, with trading routes extending as far as Libya and Sudan. In 2007, Israel felt comfortable enough to remove troops and equipment from its border police (*Mishmar Hagvul*). In contrast, by 2010 the increasing number of illegal migrants and refugees from African countries led Israel to construct an electrified, computerized border fence along its entire border with Egypt that was completed in 2013, and to re-militarize its border with Egypt (see Dyer and Kessler, 2014: 24).

Conclusions

In this chapter, we have examined two peaceful borders as related to the peaceful resolution of the Arab-Israeli conflict in the Middle East regarding the transition from war to negative peace between Israel and Egypt (in 1979), and the formalization of peaceful relations between Israel and Jordan (in 1994). In both cases, we show that international peace, especially in the case of Israel-Egypt, has been a permissive condition for the occurrence and proliferation of illicit transnational flows, including transnational crime and terrorism. Yet, we explain the variance between the two cases with reference to the three variables assessed throughout the book: the degree of physical and institutional openness of the peaceful borders; the degree of governance and institutional strength of the bordering states; and the prevalent socioeconomic conditions of the neighboring states.

Perusing these two successful examples of peaceful territorial change in the Middle East, we find a complicated and even contradictory logic that links peaceful borders with illicit transnational flows. On the one hand, transnational crime and terrorism threaten the security, and by extension the peace, of the neighboring countries. On the other hand, those non-state security threats might enhance the interstate cooperation of the neighboring countries by increasing their trust and security cooperation. For instance, in the Egyptian-Israeli relations, some analysts suggest that the peace agreement created the space for the proliferation of transnational crime and terrorism; furthermore, the neighboring states have been too slow and vulnerable (especially Egypt) to adapt to the new realities of these new non-state threats. Yet, Israel and Egypt have shown flexibility and pragmatism in adapting the clauses of the Peace Treaty to allow for increased security cooperation in coping with these new threats (see Laub, 2013). Thus, whereas peaceful borders have enabled the occurrence of illicit transnational flows that did not exist between the two countries during their previous state of war, transnational crime and terrorism have a more indirect positive impact. These illicit flows have (unintentionally) promoted the cooperation and improved the security ties between the neighboring countries.

Furthermore, the comparison between the two peace dyads shows that there is an important variation in terms of the occurrence and proliferation of illicit transnational flows, despite the similarities in terms of negative peace, socioeconomic disparities, and the relative effectiveness of fortified borders in neutralizing illicit transnational flows (especially terrorism). The Egyptian-Israeli case has registered significant instances of transnational crime and terrorism, whereas the Israeli-Jordanian dyad is almost a non-case, except for drugs trafficking. What explains this variance? First, in geopolitical terms, the Israeli-Jordanian border is much more important for both countries to control and monitor, in contrast to the backward Israeli-Egyptian border along Sinai, the vast borderland particularly neglected if not rejected by the Egyptian state. Second, in terms of governance, Israel and Jordan have shown high degrees of resilience, determination, political willingness, and strength in regulating their common border since 1967, even before establishing a formal peace in 1994. Third, there are no artificial buffer zones in the bilateral security regime established between Jordan and Israel, so the presence of a foreign peacekeeping force is redundant and unnecessary, if not counterproductive, in facing these new non-state security threats. Fourth, as Tamar Arieli (2012) argues, the overdominance of the security discourse in managing the peaceful Israeli-Jordanian border drastically limits the development of collaborative civilian cross-border endeavors, despite the treaty's formal language arguing for cooperation and economic integration. Thus, the weakness of local civilian expression and the scarcity of transnational civilian contacts across the border enables the continuing dominance of the security discourse. By extension, this high degree of securitization further limits the amount of illicit transnational activities.

In contrast, the roots of the governance deficit in the Sinai Peninsula relates to the relative weakening of the Egyptian state, dealing with acute domestic economic, security, and political problems in the prelude and the aftermath of the Arab Spring. Hence, the capability and willingness of the Egyptian Army and other security services to act decisively against terrorism and crime in Sinai has significantly diminished between 1982 and 2013. More recently, under the current regime of President el-Sisi, the Egyptian regime has become much more determined in its struggle against terrorism and lawlessness in the borderlands, yet, at the expense of human rights and the rule of law (see Dentice, 2018).[6]

---

[6] We thank Yaron Schneider for his comments on this point.

7 | The Southern African Borders in the Postapartheid Era

Introduction

In this chapter, we assess the links between the peaceful borders of the Southern African countries and the occurrence and proliferation of illicit transnational flows. Peace broke out in Southern Africa following the end of the regional and civil wars involving South Africa, Angola, Mozambique, and Namibia, and especially the domestic peaceful change that took place in South Africa in 1994, ending the apartheid regime and leading to the normalization of relations between South Africa and its neighbors (see Buzan and Waever, 2003: 233–238).

We treat *Southern Africa* as a region that includes most of the sixteen members of the Southern African Development Community (SADC), as it excludes two member-states, the Democratic Republic of the Congo (in Central Africa) and Tanzania (in East Africa), since they do not belong to the region in geographic and geopolitical terms. The relevant Southern African countries that have land borders are Angola, Botswana, Eswatini (Swaziland), Lesotho, Malawi, Mozambique, Namibia, South Africa, Zambia, and Zimbabwe.[1]

Since the early 1990s, Southern Africa has evolved from being a zone of conflict into a zone of peace. Namibian independence in 1990, the end of the civil wars in Mozambique in 1992 and Angola in 2002, and particularly the end of apartheid in 1994 embodied a transition from war to peace, leading to the integration of South Africa in its region in economic and political terms (see de Albuquerque, Lins, and Wiklund, 2015: 1; and Söderbaum, 2004: 79–80). With the end of its apartheid regime, South Africa became the leading and legitimate country in the

---

[1] SADC includes also the island states of Comoros, Madagascar, Mauritius, and Seychelles, which do not share land borders.

region, playing a paramount role in promoting regional institutions (see Flemes, 2009).

Over the past two decades, relations among southern African states have been more peaceful than at any other time since their independence. Most of the countries in SADC have also enjoyed domestic peace and relative political stability, with the exceptions of Zimbabwe and Lesotho (see Schoeman and Muller, 2009). Thus, we consider the region as a whole as a zone of stable peace, yet not necessarily a pluralistic security community (see Aeby, 2018: 3; Hammerstad, 2005: 77; Hawkins, 2012: 3; and Söderbaum, 2004).

Although it is arguably the most stable and peaceful region in Africa, Southern Africa is not immune to new threats to peace and security, as it confronts significant challenges to human security. These challenges include domestic armed conflicts short of war and decentralized forms of violence, such as urban riots, organized crime, and small insurgencies in the state peripheries, oftentimes related to high levels of poverty and inequality (see Aeby, 2018; and von Soest and De Juan, 2018). Furthermore, joining the unfolding security landscape, there are political crises deficits, which have become the most acute source of national and regional instability. The reference is primarily to weak state institutions, relatively low levels of governance, and high levels of corruption, all leading to hybrid and complex relations between the political establishments and organized crime (see Aeby, 2018: 3–4; Blum, 2016: 25; de Albuquerque, Lins, and Wiklund, 2015: 1; and von Soest and De Juan, 2018: 1, 4).

Similar to the Latin American region, Southern Africa is peculiar for its socioeconomic contrasts. On the one hand, levels of economic and human development in countries like South Africa, Namibia, and Botswana are relatively higher than in the rest of sub-Saharan Africa. On the other hand, income inequality in the region is among the highest in the world, which explains the overall propensity for criminality, both domestic and transnational. Southern Africa has some of the world's most unequal societies, with enormous socioeconomic cleavages that emerged during the times of colonialism and racial segregation, though they have also persisted after decolonization and its imperfect or incomplete democratization (see Aeby, 2018: 5; de Albuquerque, Lins, and Wiklund, 2015: 1; and von Soest and de Juan, 2018: 1).

South Africa, the most important country in the region in economic and military terms, has become a hub for transnational criminal activity, from drug trafficking to human trafficking (see Blum, 2016: 10; and Shaw, 2015: 174). Due to its preeminent political and economic preponderance, South Africa has become a safe haven for transnational criminal networks in the region, a land of opportunity for foreign criminals, as well as a market for criminal commodities like drugs and stolen goods (see Blum, 2016: 10–11; Martin, 2011; Shaw, 2002: 291, and 2015; and Shaw and Ellis, 2015). South Africa has held the dubious and infamous role of lynchpin for criminal activities in the region, since most of the notable international criminal groups in the region operate from, across, or in relation to South Africa (ENACT, 2019: 39). There is a diverse array of criminal markets in the country, including heroin and synthetic drugs, in addition to environmental-crime markets for fauna and nonrenewable resources, usually facilitated by mafia-style gang actors.

The combination of open borders since the end of apartheid, the institutional weaknesses of many neighboring states (especially Mozambique and Zimbabwe), and the spillover of their problems have turned issues of internal and human security into a main preoccupation for the country. As a major recipient of economic migrants from the rest of Africa, South Africa is mostly concerned about opening its borders even wider to its neighboring countries (see Fabricius, 2018: 4). At the core of Southern Africa, South Africa constitutes a regional hub for two distinctive worlds, one licit and the other illicit, from airlines and finance to the smuggling of people and wildlife.[2] This duality is also reflected in South Africa's relatively high scores, in comparative terms, regarding *both* high levels of criminality and high levels of institutional resilience in the attempts to cope with organized crime (ENACT, 2019: 39).

In addition to its regionalization, globalization also acts as a permissive condition that facilitates the links between peaceful borders and illicit transnational flows in the region. Globalization has had a certain impact on the integration of democratic South Africa into the international economy, after many years of isolation caused by its apartheid regime. South Africa has opened its borders to the world, not only physically, but also economically, including its financial, communication, and transportation systems. This process of economic and technological opening has also softened state control in many areas, including

---

[2] We thank Timothy Shaw for his insights on this point.

the monitoring and prevention of illicit transnational flows across its land borders. The globalizing economy has contributed to an environment where violent non-state actors can benefit from the "dark side of globalization" embodied by transnational crime, whereas markets are deregulated, trade is globalized, and the demand for illicit commodities is growing in the African continent (see Devor, 2013: 32, 71).

The Evolution of the Peaceful Borders in Africa in General, and in Southern Africa in Particular

The African Perspective

In contrast to Europe and the Americas, the African continent is a relative newcomer to the Westphalian concept of international borders separating independent nation-states. After African states gained their independence from European colonial rule in the 1950s and 1960s, their artificial and poorly demarcated borders were among the most potent source of conflict and political stability. Improper border design and the partitioning of ethnic groups by the European colonial powers contributed to the underdevelopment and instability of many postcolonial African countries (see Gashaw, 2017; and Herbst, 1989).

Although intrastate conflicts seem to have replaced interstate ones since the end of the Cold War, the prospects of destabilizing borders in Africa are still very real, especially in light of the continent's ever-expanding population, concomitant to its shrinking economic and natural resources and opportunities, and high levels of migration. African borders have therefore remained mostly porous, lacking proper demarcation and delimitation. This explains the ease with which governance-related national conflicts in individual states have spilled over to others, facilitating the presence of violent non-state actors engaging in illicit transnational flows and operating across international borders (see Crocker, 2019; ENACT, 2019: 85–94; Nguendi Ikome, 2012; and Varin and Abubakar, 2017).

Nowadays, African countries are increasingly facing daunting tasks of managing their borders in ways that secure their sovereignty and territorial integrity while at the same time ensuring that their borders become bridges rather than barriers for transborder cooperation, including migration and mobility, and regional integration. On the one hand, many African states have signed into the African Union's Protocol on the Free Movement of Persons in Addis Ababa in January 2018, followed by the African Continental Free Trade Agreement (AFCTA) signed in March 2018 in Kigali (see African Union, 2018). On the other hand, African states want to prevent illegal entries and exiting of people, goods, and other illicit flows across their borders; thus limiting also the free movement of licit goods and people, so they can better control and regulate their common borders (see Aning and Pokoo, 2017; and Udelsmann Rodrigues, 2012).

The Southern African Borders

As in other African regions, most of the Southern African borders were originally delimited by the colonial powers during the Berlin Conference (1884–5). They have not changed significantly after 1945, since the postcolonial African states adopted the doctrine of *uti possidetis* (recognizing their former colonial borders as their sovereign ones). There have been several border disputes, but the only boundary conflict that threatened to become a war was the one involving Namibia and Botswana in 1997–9. The countries had a long dispute about the ownership of the Kasikili Island in the Chobe River, which forms a substantial part of the border between them. The UNHCR reported that between October 1998 and February 1999, more than 2,400 Namibians crossed the border into Botswana. Ultimately, the International Court of Justice ruled that the island belonged to Botswana. There was also a case of peaceful territorial change, involving the 1995 transfer of Walvis Blay, a South African enclave, to Namibia (see Griggs, 2000: 4, 6, 13).

Compared with other African regions, most SADC states have emerged from colonial domination relatively recently, and many of them are riddled with internal political conflicts and weak governance mechanisms, so that their attempts to cooperate in the security sphere started at a very low level and later than in other regions of the continent. Mozambique, Angola, and Zimbabwe are former colonies that gained independence in the context of decolonization in 1975. Mozambique and Angola were Portuguese colonies that experienced virulent civil wars after declaring independence, between 1975 and 1992 (in the Angolan case, the civil war continued intermittently until 2002) (see Devor, 2013: ii). Rhodesia (later renamed Zimbabwe) gained independence unilaterally in 1965, although shortly after that it descended into chaos from the outbreak of civil war between the white minority and the black majority, until the early 1980s.

There is an important thread linking the current shortcomings in governance to the previous experience of the national liberation movements and the guerrilla groups that left a lingering legacy to the post-decolonization regimes in Southern Africa (see Piccolino, 2016). In some cases, like the Zanu-PF in Zimbabwe, and the Mozambique Liberation Front (FRELIMO) in Mozambique, the parties of liberation replaced the former oppressive colonial regimes, mimicking until today many of their repressive and authoritarian practices (see Aeby, 2018: 4).

South Africa's path has been quite different, insofar as it did not have a long-time colonial legacy. Instead, it achieved formal independence in 1961. It was ruled by a racist white minority, which denied civil and political rights to the majority of the population. The apartheid regime lasted for almost fifty years, and ended in 1994 with a peaceful transition and the election of Nelson Mandela as South Africa's President. As the apartheid regime was ostracized by its fellow African states, it led to what Buzan and Waever (2003: 234) call a "regional security complex" of hostile relations among its members, reinforced by its aggressive foreign policy from the 1960s until the early 1990s. These regional security dynamics were characterized by enmity and open hostilities between South Africa, the regional hegemon, and the rest of the Southern African countries (see Booth and Vale, 1995: 287; and Hammerstad, 2005: 75).

The common regional strategy during those years was militarization, a process by which Southern African states used force in their attempts to resolve their political conflicts. As South Africa gradually established itself as the predominant regional power, it invested heavily in its military, aiming to ensure its military superiority in the region. Thus, during the apartheid years, South Africa militarily confronted all of its regional neighbors, including military interventions in the civil wars in Angola and Mozambique by supporting right-wing guerrillas against the leftish regimes, as well as in Botswana, Lesotho, and Zimbabwe. Furthermore, it carried out a nuclear weapons program in cooperation with Israel, the United States, the German Federal Republic, and France, among others. This program was eventually dismantled with the end of the apartheid regime (see Lacovsky, 2021; and Schofield, 2014: 86–92). South Africa fought also a colonial war against Namibia, which gained independence from it in 1989. In 1979, the so-called "frontline states" (against South Africa) – namely, Angola, Botswana, Lesotho, Mozambique, Swaziland, Tanzania, Zambia, and Zimbabwe – established the Southern African Development Coordination Conference (SADCC), which eventually became SADC in 1992, as a form of economic cooperation and integration to minimize their economic dependence upon South Africa (see Buzan and Waever, 2003: 234–235).

The years marking the end of the Cold War brought about significant changes in the geopolitical landscape of Southern Africa. The end of the civil wars in Mozambique and Angola, together with the peaceful transformation of Rhodesia into Zimbabwe in 1980 and the end of apartheid in South Africa in 1994 ushered in a period of unprecedented peace and stability in Southern Africa. The peaceful transition to a multi-racial democracy in South Africa in 1994 removed a major obstacle to the region's desire for closer political and economic integration, incorporating South Africa into the region.

When apartheid ended in 1994, South Africa's borders were formally opened and prompted integration into regional structures of economic and political cooperation (see Blum, 2016: 10; and Hammestad, 2005: 73–74, 77). In celebration of such developments, the SADC Secretariat marked the New Year (in 1995) calling for the removal of all border controls in Southern Africa, emphasizing a changed mood in the quality of interstate relations as never before there had been a greater propensity for cooperation (Booth and Vale, 1995: 286). Still, many borders had never been effectively monitored and controlled before. The result was a significant increase of both licit and illicit transnational flows, including thousands of legal and illegal migrants from Lesotho, Zimbabwe, and Mozambique into South Africa (see Wotela and Letsiri, 2015).

Since 1994, the Southern African security complex has witnessed an increasing degree of regionalization and regional cooperation and integration, alongside domestic political crises (see Brosig, 2013). The post-1994 regional challenges and problems included crises of governance in Lesotho, Swaziland, Zimbabwe, Madagascar, and Malawi (see Cawthra, 2010; and Khadiagala and Lyons, 2001). In the last two decades, SADC has been, and continues to be, confronted by issues, challenges, and threats related to the new security threats emanating from poverty and inequality, economic underdevelopment, food and energy security, cross-border transnational criminal flows, and more recently, piracy (see van Nieuwkerk, 2014).[3]

Transnational Crime and Illicit Transnational Flows across the Southern African Borders

Beyond the states that formally make up the Southern African region, assessing the realm of peace and security in the region requires us to refer to a whole host of violent non-state actors. Such actors are not only transnational non-state actors in the sense that they are not controlled by the state in which they are based, but also in the sense that they operate across state borders. Some participate directly in violence associated with armed conflict – most notably, rebels, warlords/strongmen, militia, and even gangs or bandits that take advantage of a power vacuum and/or a culture of impunity. Private military corporations (PMCs, or in other words, mercenaries) have also played a role in the security realm of the region, such as the South African PMCs who were active in conflicts in the continent throughout the 1990s, until they were banned by South African legislation introduced in 1998 (see Bosch and Maritz, 2011). Other actors have played a significant role in facilitating conflicts within the region – corporations and individuals dealing with weapons, minerals, "blood diamonds," and other resources implicated in funding conflicts (see Hawkins, 2012: 7–8; Shaw, 2002; Shaw and Gastrow, 2001; and Varin and Abubakar, 2017).

Some of the most significant VNSAs in this context are transnational organized criminal actors. Crimes of various types have escalated within and across Southern African countries in the last two decades, partly propelled by demographic and urbanization trends, and the breakdown of community and family structures, alongside the impact of globalization and regionalization. Moreover, similar to the cases of Central America and Colombia, patterns of domestic and transnational crime relate to the legacy of long armed conflicts (civil wars, international wars, and wars of national liberation). The end of these wars led to inept and insufficient demobilization packages for regime and anti-regime soldiers, as well as a serious deficit in human capital, such

---

[3] Piracy is an important illicit transnational flow and crime, and it is present in the Southern African region. However, in this volume we focus only on transborder land illicit flows such as drug trafficking, human trafficking, and weapons trafficking, without covering the maritime space or the virtual (cyber) space.

as low literacy and skill levels (see Blum, 2016; and Rotberg and Mills, 1998).

Moreover, crime, both domestic and transnational, has been exacerbated by the collapse of authoritarian and racist regimes, as well as by the emergence of liberal market economies; local and international criminals have tended to exploit the concomitant increase in cross-border movements of both licit and illicit flows. Migration and social change have also contributed to the proliferation of international criminal syndicates (see ENACT, 2019: 89–90; and Hübschle, 2010: 75–80).

In line with its escalation in both scope and pace, organized crime has grown to become a paramount security threat throughout the region (see Blum, 2016; Hübschle, 2010; Shaw, 2015; and Shaw and Ellis, 2015). It has manifested itself in a wide range of activities, including smuggling, car hijacking and theft, armed robbery, drug trafficking, counterfeiting, human smuggling and trafficking, illegal logging and fishing, kidnappings for ransom, disappearance and mutilations of albino citizens and trafficking of their organs and limbs, and wildlife crimes (Blum, 2016: 12).

Transnational illicit flows include mostly illegal immigration, human smuggling, and human trafficking; the spread of small weapons; and drugs trafficking, in addition to smuggling of goods, especially the illicit trade in fauna (see ENACT, 2019: 39, 74–75; and Shelley, 2010: 22). Many of these crime activities are carried out by transnational organized criminal groups, which operate across the region's borders and in many cases are internationally linked to Italian, Russian, and Chinese criminal organizations. Conversely, in contrast to other regions of the continent like the Maghreb, West Africa, and the Horn of Africa, Southern Africa has not been a target for transnational terrorism, with the exception of a few incidents in South Africa in the 1990s (see von Soest and De Juan, 2018: 3).

Mark Shaw and Stephen Ellis (2015) explain the evolution of transnational networks of organized crime in Southern Africa by dividing it into several stages, starting in the 1970s and 1980s with a rapid expansion of TOCs in the region, following liberation from colonial rule. According to Gastrow (2012: 8), uneven decolonization also contributed to fostering TOCs in the region. After the Southern African states liberated themselves from colonial rule, European settlers moved to neighboring states not yet liberated, involving themselves in smuggling and trading illegal commodities. Since the new postcolonial states were involved in institutional and political transformations, including building institutional mechanisms, establishing central authority and governance infrastructures, they tended to neglect their borderlands, resulting in less rigid border controls and a weaker monitoring of illicit transnational flows (see Devor, 2013: 42).

The early postcolonial trans-border smuggling was followed by a second period of consolidation of transnational crime, during the transition to regional peace and democratization. Instead of dissolving with the end of apartheid in South Africa, these criminal networks went through several adaptation processes. Criminal operations became more "sophisticated and well-resourced" [and] "an alliance evolved between key individuals and institutions within [the] regional states themselves" after criminals forged long-term relations with the state (Shaw and Ellis, 2015: 10).

In the third stage, in the last decade, the most notorious types of transnational organized crime evolved. Whereas in the 1990s police forces were mainly preoccupied with motor vehicle theft and weapons trafficking following the end of the Mozambican civil war in 1992, these illicit transnational flows have been overtaken by drug trafficking nowadays. During the last decade especially, collusion of corrupt governments with TOCs emerged around cross-border criminal activities, directly linking some of the states in the region to illicit criminal activities, within and across their borders (see Hübschle, 2010: 85–92).

Even in South Africa, with a high score of resilience due to the establishment of effective security institutions under civilian control, there has been troubling deterioration at the local level, when part of the police responsible for the collection of crime intelligence has been "politically compromised" (Blum, 2016: 25). For instance, there are reliable reports that the South African Police Force (SAPF) has been involved not only with crime and petty corruption, but also in a hundred of serious and violent crimes, including armed robbery, house robbery, rape, murder, and serious assaults, in the period between January 2009 and April 2010 only (see Ndebele, Lebone, and Cronje, 2011).

Even though transnational organized crime in the region is by no means a new phenomenon, its current scope, scale, and impact are unprecedented. In the light of the relative peace and stability that characterize present-day Southern Africa and the opening up of international trade and regional cross-border activities, the infiltration and operation of transnational organized crime and illicit flows has expanded concomitantly. The profits of human trafficking in the region are around US$7–12 billion a year. Illegal arms trafficking and drug trafficking are the only other crimes that might exceed these figures in yearly estimated profits (Devor, 2013: 43).

Drug Trafficking

In the last decade, drug trafficking has grown to constitute the greatest transnational organized crime concern in Southern Africa. Even though Southern Africa is not a main world producer of narcotics, it is a major intercontinental route for drug trafficking, linking Latin America, South Asia, and Southeast Asia. According to UNODC statistics, South Africa is one of the top suppliers of marijuana and cocaine. At the same time, domestic consumption of hard drugs (including heroin and cocaine) seems to have increased in the country and the region as well (Blum, 2016: 16; and Hübschle, 2010: 23–34).

Due to their heavy traffic of drugs, Mozambique and South Africa stand out as the two countries most related to drug trafficking in the region. Mozambique occupies a special position, as the "second most active drug transit point in Africa," after Guinea-Bissau (*Guardian*, 2015, quoted in Blum, 2016: 17). Due to its strategic position along the Indian Ocean, its long and porous borders with Malawi, South Africa, Swaziland, Tanzania, Zambia, and Zimbabwe have turned the country into a key transport hub regarding its landlocked neighbors, Malawi, Zambia, Zimbabwe, and Swaziland, both for licit and illicit transnational flows. Hence, Mozambique is the Southern African transit point for South Asian hashish and heroin, as well as South American cocaine destined for European and South African markets (Council of the European Union, 2011: 1–3).

As for South Africa, the end of its international isolation in 1994 and the opening of its borders have resulted in its increased involvement with the drug trade (see Omar, 1997; and Rothberg and Mills, 1998: 14). In the face of the global clampdown on the transnational drug trade, traffickers have sought new countries to transship drugs to their traditional markets in the United States and in Europe, as well as to expand their trade by creating new markets in these transit countries.

Accordingly, South Africa has become a major transshipment center for heroin, hashish, and cocaine, as well as a major cultivator of marijuana in its own right. Within Southern Africa, South Africa is nowadays the center of this expanding drive with its neighboring states, used primarily as secondary points for further transshipment to its own territory (see Hübschle, 2010: 93; and Shaw, 2002).

The rising position of South Africa in the drug trafficking and drug trade realms relates to its relatively sophisticated banking infrastructure and financial institutions (in comparison to its neighbors), which have been attractive instruments for the laundering of drug money on national, regional, and in some cases even international fronts. The country's long, porous borders, comprising some ninety-six points of entry have ensured that drug traffickers have a vast number of options available to smuggle their drugs both in and out of the country. Other Southern African countries, such as Angola, Namibia, Zambia, and Zimbabwe are used as stopover points for cocaine traffickers partly in an effort to alter trafficking routes and thus escape detention. The limited governance capacity of these countries' authorities have also made them attractive destinations for couriers seeking to enter South Africa from the source countries (see Blum, 2016; and Rotberg and Mills, 1998).

To cope with drug trafficking, in 2012 the UNODC and SADC launched the regional program 2013–16, "Making the Southern African Development Community (SADC) Region Safer for Crime and Drugs." This program had three goals: strengthening regional border control and management capacities in order to combat drug trafficking; supporting efforts against corruption and strengthening justice institutions; and improving drug prevention, treatment, and care. Acknowledging the threats posed by the flow of illicit activities across Southern African borders, this program emphasized the need for developing comprehensive regional border-control management capable of preventing human trafficking and facilitating counter-narcotics efforts (see UNODC, 2012b).

Arms Trafficking and Proliferation of Small Weapons

Along with human trafficking and drug trafficking, the uncontrolled spread of small weapons has become a sensitive issue in the Southern African region. This relates to the long legacy of violent conflicts, in both the domestic and international realms, as well as the capacity of

South Africa to manufacture arms and ammunition by itself, in comparison to its neighbors (see Florquin et al., 2019: 27–28). Obvious explanations for the illicit flows of weapons (especially small arms) in the region include rising rates of criminal violence, poor education, lack of social services, the wide displacement of people, and a general decline in economic activity (Stott, 2007: 12). The diffusion of small weapons, and arms trafficking in general, are part of the broader criminal activities that take place on a daily basis in the region. Moreover, as compared to other regions in the continent, Southern Africa has the highest number of civilian-held firearms (9.4 per 100 people), and some of these weapons have been stolen and diverted to criminal organizations (Florquin et al., 2019: 31, 53–54).

As the Southern African region has moved to establish peaceful and normal relations among its member-states and to improve the flow of regional trade, so has the cross-border flow of people, goods, and vehicles intensified, thus facilitating the illicit trafficking in weapons. An examination of the poor regional border-security conditions provides a possible explanation as to why it is possible for weapons to be smuggled with relative impunity, especially out and into South Africa (see Schroeder and Lamb, 2006).

Of all the cross-border crimes, arms smuggling has sparked the most concern for poor border security and controls, especially in South Africa, which sustains one of the highest murder rates in the world (about 35.2 per 100,000 people) (see Snodgrass, 2015). This has become all the more pervasive since the end of the apartheid rule, with the concomitant growing rates of immigrants and refugees. Moreover, the country has a long history of having a militarized police state and a sequel of protracted armed conflicts that prompt domestic violence (see Rotberg and Mills, 1998: 6, 10–11; and Snodgrass, 2015). As with the case of drug trafficking, most of the illicit flows of weapons trafficking takes place across the South African-Mozambican border. In addition, two years ago, Zimbabwe reported the involvement of poaching organizations in the trafficking of weapons (Florquin et al., 2019: 41).

At the regional level, the SADC Committee on Small Arms seeks to control the illicit flow of small arms trade, urging its members to observe and enforce UN arms embargoes and criminalize their violations. In the early 2000s, all of the SADC members ratified a Protocol on the Control of Firearms, Ammunition, and other Related Materials that entered into force on November 8, 2004. The resolutions are out there, though their strict and effective implementation are still pending, as related to the relative lack of capabilities and political willingness of many of the member-states in enforcing these measures.

Human Trafficking and Human Smuggling

Trafficking in human beings, especially of women and children, is not new to the Southern African landscape. It affects mostly women, men and children who are exploited in forced labor, commercial sex, forced begging, and forced criminality. It is a demand-driven global business with a huge market for cheap labor and commercial sex, confronting insufficient policy frameworks and trained personnel aimed at preventing and confronting it. Moreover, while trafficking in persons is a major international and even global issue, poor documentation in the region masks the true extent of this modern-day form of slavery (see Devor, 2013: 12).

Southern Africa provides fertile ground for traffickers who prey on the vulnerability created and nurtured by a number of factors, including lingering violent conflicts, poverty and inequality, limited access to healthcare and education, gender inequalities, high unemployment, and a general lack of opportunities, especially for women. Although human trafficking in Southern Africa has yet to assume the dimensions acquired in other regions of the African continent, as Central Africa and the Horn of Africa, it is an important human security issue (see Ironanya, 2018).

Moreover, the region's human trafficking flows are more diverse and transnational, not only domestic. For instance, victims detected in South Africa come from neighboring countries, as well as from different parts of the continent, including West and East Africa. As in the case of drug trafficking, Mozambique is a typical transit state regarding human trafficking. The route through Maputo, Mozambique's capital, is one of the main ways for trafficking people into South Africa (Devor, 2013: 3). In addition to Mozambique, Swaziland is another source of child-trafficking victims into South Africa (Shelley, 2010: 289).

Furthermore, South Africa and additional Southern African countries also report victims from other regions of the world, including East Asia, South Asia, and to a lesser extent, Eastern Europe. South Africa,

Mozambique, Zambia, and Lesotho are source, transit, and destination countries for human trafficking. In addition, South Africa is an origin and transit country for human trafficking toward Europe and North America (see Bello and Olutola, 2020; and UNODC, 2016b: 116).

South Africa has turned into a main destination for human trafficking, due to its better economic conditions, in comparison to most of the countries in the region, and to other regions in the continent. It provides a stable market for the services of trafficked people from regional and extra-regional locations. Armed conflicts and concomitant dislocations, political and economic upheavals, food insecurity, and lack of economic opportunities, make South Africa an economic magnet that attracts migration from across the continent, despite the high levels of domestic crime and the blight of the AIDS epidemic, with 7.1 million people living with HIV. South Africa is also a transit and source country for the international market in human trafficking. As the most important transportation hub in Southern Africa (and in Africa as a whole), South Africa offers direct flights and shipping to Europe and Asia. The growing scale of human trafficking from Africa to Europe and the Middle East suggests that South Africans are already feeding into this transnational illicit business (see Bello and Olutola, 2020).

Following the democratic elections in 1994, South Africa has reportedly experienced a sharp increase in immigration, both legal and illegal, from neighboring countries, especially Mozambique, Zimbabwe, and Angola. With the dismantling of apartheid and the transition to a multiracial democratic state, South Africa has confronted many of the same immigration-related politics and policy dilemmas faced by other immigrant-receiving countries, such as the United States and many Western European countries. This is reflected in ongoing demands for resettling refugees, an increased burden on the state welfare system, tension between citizens and foreign newcomers over jobs and scarce economic resources, and a growing xenophobia (see Croucher, 1998: 640).

As for human smuggling, many asylum seekers cross the Zimbabwean-South African border as illegal migrants, about one-fourth of them facilitated by non-state actors active in the borderland between Zimbabwe and South Africa (see Araia, 2009; and UNODC, 2018a: 80). According to UNHCR data, in 2016, more than 35,000 people applied for asylum in South Africa (a significant decrease compared to 2009, when more than

200,000 asylum applications were submitted) (see UNODC, 2018a: 80). Some of the reasons for illegal migration include poor borderline control, corruption, fraud and fake documentation, economic conditions in the home countries, opportunities for crime, and fraudulent asylum claims (see Martin, 2011).

Explaining the Reality of Peaceful Borders and Illicit Transnational Flows in Southern Africa

Hypothesis 1: The Degree of Physical and Institutional Openness of the Peaceful Borders

As in the rest of the continent, porous borders in Southern Africa, especially in line with the outbreak of regional peace and the end of apartheid in South Africa, partly explain the occurrence and proliferation of illicit transnational flows. On the one hand, borders have gradually become transit points for smuggling and other illegal crossborder activities and illicit transnational flows, including the illegal movement of people and goods, bringing about instability and conflict. On the other hand, there has been a regionalist discourse of an *African Renaissance*, as reflected in the plans for economic integration, cooperative management of resources, and common infrastructures, embodied by the African Union in general and by SADC in particular (see Griggs, 2000: 1).

Even before the transition to peace in the early 1990s, many of the Southern African countries, perhaps with the exception of South Africa, tended to neglect the control of their borders. Consequently, with the end of military conflicts in the region between South Africa and the Frontline States, the already-porous borders have become more open and demilitarized and, therefore, more susceptible for illicit transnational flows. Thus, there is an important link between the open, soft, often neglected, porous, unregulated, and uncontrolled borders within the Southern African region and the occurrence and proliferation of illicit transnational flows of drugs, weapons, and people (see Nsereko, 1997: 192). For instance, the extensive borders of Mozambique are difficult to control, which makes the activities of transnational organized crime actors less risky as well as more profitable (Devor, 2013: 70).

Cross-border crime has taken advantage of the lack of physical and institutional regulation and control of the borders, thus providing fertile ground for the occurrence of these illicit transnational flows. Illicit transnational flows have been facilitated as well by the common and often long and open borders of the region, in addition to the improved communications systems by road, rail, and sea, and the concomitant flow of people and goods through the common borders (Nsereko, 1997: 192).

The openness of the South African borders since 1994 allowed for massive illegal border crossings and immigration, tax evasion due to smuggling and trafficking, and increased transnational criminal activity in general, exacerbated by widespread corruption of border officials (see Griggs, 2000: 5). Whereas the African Union encourages the African states to sign the Niamey Convention on Cross-Border Cooperation to increase the free cross-border movement of people and goods, South Africa has not done that yet, wary and aware of throwing open its borders even wider (Fabricius, 2018: 4).

Not only are the peaceful borders of Southern Africa open and porous, they are also integrated within the framework of SADC, so that integration has also contributed to the occurrence and proliferation of illicit transnational flows. In this context, the border between Botswana and Zimbabwe might be an exception to the regional rule. In 2003, Botswana, the Southern African country with the lowest score of criminality in the region, built a fence that was supposed to run along 500 out of the 813-kilometer border with Zimbabwe, allegedly to stop the spread of foot-and-mouth disease (FMD) among livestock. The fence became also a formidable barrier to thousands of illegal Zimbabwean migrants flocking into Botswana, as well as other illicit transnational flows (see Kopinski and Polus, 2012: 98–111). Thus, with the exception of the Botswana-Zimbabwe border, we validate the first hypothesis for the Southern African region.

Hypothesis 2: The Degree of Governance, Institutional Strength, and Political Willingness

Turning to the domestic political landscape of Southern Africa, all of the countries in the region, except for Swaziland, which is a monarchy, are at least nominally multiparty parliamentary democracies. Partial or imperfect democratization has thus been the most noticeable political trend in the postapartheid, post–Cold War era. However, democracy has not necessarily brought stability and development, as it remains fragile in many countries, jeopardized by weakened governance frameworks that make effective enforcement difficult (see Blum, 2016: 12–19; and Mutume, 2007: 3). Progress has been uneven and, in some cases, countries are trapped in a particular phase of democratic transition, or even facing democratic reversals, like in Zimbabwe (see Sachikonye, 2017). By contrast, Botswana and South Africa get relative high scores in terms of their institutional and legal resilience in coping with organized crime (see ENACT, 2019: 39, 98).

The Southern African countries constitute a very heterogeneous group with regard to democratic practices, degrees of governance, and institutional strength. According to the *Ibrahim Index of African Governance* (in 2015), the region is home to six of the ten best-governed countries in Africa: Mauritius (rated 1); Botswana (3), South Africa (4); Namibia (5); Seychelles (6); and Lesotho (10). Other countries in the region fare much worst, especially Mozambique and Zimbabwe (de Albuquerque, Lins and Wiklund, 2015: 3).

Most of the Southern African states (perhaps with the partial exceptions of Namibia, Botswana, and to a lesser extent South Africa) are relatively weak, due to their historical and political conditions. Many states in the region have gone from relatively recent decolonization to civil wars for control of the newly independent governments. Consequently, they lack political legitimacy, an established democratic culture, and sufficient resources – both political and economic – to adequately display and perform their governing functions. In many of these countries, the informal economy is intertwined with the formal economy, with high levels of corruption and even criminalization of the state, so many states have symbiotic political relationships with criminal actors along the lines of alliance and enforcement-evasion, if not integration, rather than confronting organized crime (as in the peculiar case of Botswana). Therefore, with weak enforcement capabilities, underpaid officials, and porous national borders, most of the Southern African countries seem to provide the appropriate political environment for violent non-state actors to engage in illicit transnational flows (see Blum, 2016: 8; Devor, 2013: 32; and Mutume, 2007: 3).

State and organized crime are inextricably linked, since in some cases state institutions tolerate and even take advantage of criminal activities for their own economic and/or political purposes, so the state sometimes becomes a facilitator of criminal activity. It is therefore not necessarily (or only) the existence of transnational organized crime in the region that may pose the great security and political challenges to human security, but rather the intrinsic state involvement in these illicit activities (see Shaw, 2015: 184–185, quoted in Blum, 2016: 7).

Many states in the Southern African region suffer from weak law enforcement and high levels of corruption. Moreover, state involvement in organized crime is not confined to weak or failed states only. It might be also noticeable in middle-income states and functioning democracies like South Africa (see ENACT, 2019: 39). This may suggest that the phenomenon is not necessarily linked to general poverty levels, but also, to the postcolonial state structures and the way important links were established among new governments in the postindependence era, neocolonial political and economic interests, as well as an increasing globalized private sector (Blum, 2016: 8). In this context, the politics of many Southern African states has become more privatized, whereas private power-holders have also become increasingly violent and criminalized in their behavior (see Devor, 2013: 31). Moreover, the state plays an active role in enabling criminal activities in the region, thus establishing criminal politics and hybrid linkages with criminal non-state actors (see Blum, 2016: 8). Thus, organized crime is facilitated by corruption and by collusion between public and private actors and criminals (Hübschle, 2010: 85–91).

Zimbabwe is probably the most notorious example of this negative pattern. It broke its colonial dependence unilaterally, followed by a civil war and the long-time personal dictatorship of Robert Mugabe until November 2017. The inability to set up functioning political institutions paved the way for turning the country into a failed state in the early years of the twenty-first century. In comparison, some other countries in the region – Zambia, Mozambique, and Lesotho (in addition to South Africa, Namibia, and Botswana) – have performed better, and they are considered part of a group of "emerging African countries," improving their weak governance functions, alongside their socioeconomic indicators (see Radelet, 2010). Yet, in many of these Southern African countries, the increase of organized crime, both national and transnational, depends to a certain extent upon official institutions and individual state officials (see Blum, 2016: 8; and Devor, 2013: 31).

South Africa remains the regional hegemon with a critical role to play in the region; it is an emerging middle power and a potential regional power. It is able to project military power, it dominates the region economically, and, following its remarkably peaceful transition to democracy, it has a wealth of experience in conflict resolution and democratic transition to draw on. As mentioned above, ENACT scored South Africa very high in its resilience to respond effectively to crime, reflecting "the country's strong legal and institutional framework that are able to effectively respond to the organized-crime threat, despite their erosion in recent years ... The standout feature of South Africa's resilience is the strength of the country's civil society" (ENACT, 2019: 39). At the same time, the country has been plagued by public corruption, high levels of poverty and inequality, widespread criminal activity, and lack of professionalism in its public service, all this showing the limited capacities and the relative lack of political willingness of the South African state. Hence, it is difficult to characterize contemporary South Africa as a state with effective levels of governance, due to its widespread political corruption, especially under former President Jacob Zuma (2009–18) (see *The Economist*, December 9, 2017: 13; 23–28).

By contrast, Botswana stands out in the region and the entire African continent with one of the highest scoring in terms of resilience vis-à-vis organized crime, and one of the lowest scores in terms of criminality. The country shows little evidence of corruption, achieving high scores for international cooperation, political leadership and governance, and the enacting of effective national policies and laws, clearly demonstrating what a strong political will (alongside effective capacities) can do to curb crime, both local and transnational (ENACT, 2019: 98). In sum, we corroborate the relevance of the second hypothesis for the Southern African region.

Hypothesis 3: The Prevailing Socioeconomic Conditions of the Neighboring States

Similar to diverse levels of governance, Southern Africa is characterized by significant socioeconomic stratification. Botswana, South Africa, and Namibia are considered as upper-middle-income countries (with GNI per capita of $7,595, $6,160, and $5,227, respectively; World Bank, 2017). By contrast, Malawi, Mozambique, and Zimbabwe are low-income, very poor countries, with GNI per capita of $338, $415, and $1079, respectively (World Bank, 2017). In between, we find Angola, Lesotho, Swaziland, and Zambia, as lower-middle income countries, with GNI per capita of $4,170, $1,181, $3,224, and

$1,509, respectively (World Bank, 2017). The disparity in the socioeconomic conditions is especially striking along the South African-Mozambican and South African-Zimbabwean borders.

Economics plays a paramount role in explaining the rationale for the illicit transnational flows across the region's borderlands. High unemployment rates in South Africa (about 27 percent) and Mozambique (about 25 percent) have opened the floodgates for human trafficking, both as a domestic and as a transnational phenomenon. Salvation Army's Major Margaret Stafford has emphasized that the "demand for cheap labor and sexual services keep growing" (quoted in Masweneng, 2018). The primary driving force for the supply is poverty, linked to poor education standards and lack of employment opportunities that propel vulnerable people into the hands of traffickers. Therefore, migration patterns from neighboring states into South Africa have turned the country into a trafficking hub.

Overwhelming poverty, marginalization, and inequality both within and between the regional states remains the bedrock of human insecurity in Southern Africa, as elsewhere in Africa. Many Southern African states are plagued with poverty and inequality, with regressive distributions of income (especially in the cases of Namibia and South Africa, which perform very poorly on the Gini index due to their relative wealth and high levels of income inequality). Poverty and inequality in the distribution of income partly explain the incidence of crime, as a major destabilizing factor in Southern African societies (see Hawkins, 2012: 9).

While many economies in Southern Africa are currently experiencing impressive levels of growth (especially Angola, Mozambique, and Botswana), poverty remains a harsh reality for the majority of the population in the region. In this context, the increase in transborder economic links facilitated by the opening of borders has enabled the occurrence of transnational illicit activities, including drug and human trafficking. The obvious consequence for millions of people with no economic horizon and hope is to flee to find better opportunities elsewhere. Migration produces legal and illegal movement of workers, especially to South Africa, and oftentimes drives thriving human trafficking and smuggling business.

South Africa has developed a kind of center–periphery relationship with its neighbors in the region, accounting for more than 50 percent of the Southern African aggregate GDP of SADC (SADC, 2016). Such economic disparity has made South Africa a preferred destination for migrants arriving from poorer neighboring countries, who fled their homes because of deteriorating socioeconomic conditions. The economic asymmetry between South Africa and most of its neighbors creates flows of capital and people, posing a challenge for South Africa to deal with uncontrollable influx of migrants, both legal and illegal (Griggs, 2000: 22). Thus, the more prosperous and developed South Africa becomes, the more it attracts the trafficking of people for sexual exploitation and cheap labor, sustaining a vicious cycle of illicit transnational activities across the Southern African borders. Hence, we fully corroborate the validity of the third hypothesis.

Conclusions

In Southern Africa, like in other regions of the African continent, the main sources of insecurity, both for ordinary people and for states' stability, are located within the countries' borders rather than across them. In today's Southern Africa, insecurity arises more often from the power excesses and failures of inept and corrupt governments, dire socioeconomic conditions, and domestic crime and violence, than from foreign or transnational threats. The recent troubles in Zimbabwe are the clearest examples of instability in Southern Africa nowadays, as they manifest publicly as disputes over how to carry out land reforms and how to organize presidential succession, even after the removal of Robert Mugabe in 2017. In domestic terms, crime and violence are paramount issues and challenges regarding human security, which reverberate and thrive with the occurrence and proliferation of illicit transnational flows.

The threat of interstate warfare and violence in the SADC region has receded in the last twenty years, as the region has experienced a significant transition from war to stable peace, completed with the domestic peaceful change of South Africa in 1994 and the end of the Angolan civil war in 2002.[4] At the formal level of regional integration, the Southern African Development Coordination Conference (SADCC) of the Frontline States transformed itself into the Southern African Development Community (SADC) in 1992. After its transition to democracy, South Africa joined and completed SADC in August 1994 (alongside the DRC, Seychelles,

---

[4] Although it is a formal member of SADC, we do not consider the Democratic Republic of Congo to be a part of Southern Africa.

and Mauritius). In time, SADC grew to play a very positive role in institutionalizing cross-boundary cooperation (see Griggs, 2000: 16). At the same time, in the aftermath of peace and integration, open and porous peaceful borders among the Southern African countries have enabled the occurrence and proliferation of both licit and illicit flows.

Border and boundary problems have significant implications for peace and security. Although border-related interstate conflicts have been displaced by governance-related intrastate conflicts, the poorly demarcated or neglected borders in Southern Africa are still sources of instability, allowing for the occurrence of illicit transnational flows. Transnational factors have become increasingly prominent as a reflection of the decay and failure of state governance, as well as the possibility of domestic and "intermestic" conflicts. For example, by analyzing crisis regions as "bad neighborhoods" (Weiner, 1996), factors such as arms and refugee transnational flows have been identified as potentially destabilizing. Against the background of structural weakness of several Southern African states, cross-border informal and criminal activities that transcend international borders further undermine the possibilities for more effective governance of the borderlands in the region. This is evident in the case of the Zimbabwean and Mozambican borders.

Both SADC and the encompassing African Union (AU) promote a regional policy of open borders and economic if not political integration. The institutional drive for more open borders reveals that many of the Southern African borders are already open, perhaps too widely open, allowing for the occurrence of transnational illicit flows. As Peter Fabricius (2018) cogently suggests, "As the backlog in demarcating borders and the prevalence of crime, terrorism, and other illicit activities in border areas illustrates, [Southern] Africa's primary frontier problem is not that it controls its borders too rigidly, but that it does not control them enough." This has been a chronic problem for many Southern African countries, following the outbreak of regional peace since the end of the Cold War and the demise of the apartheid regime in South Africa.

8 | *ASEAN and the Southeast Asian Borders*

Introduction

In this chapter, we examine the links between peaceful borders among the Southeast Asian countries and the occurrence and proliferation of illicit transnational flows, especially with regard to drug trafficking, human trafficking and smuggling, and arms trafficking. Southeast Asia consists of eleven countries located between Eastern India and China, and is geographically divided into "mainland" and "island" (or maritime) zones. The mainland, Indochina, is actually an extension of the Asian continent, including Burma, Thailand, Laos, Cambodia, and Vietnam. Conversely, maritime Southeast Asia includes Malaysia, Singapore, Indonesia, the Philippines, and the new country of East Timor (see Ellings and Simon, 1996, 1).[1]

Southeast Asia is the most stable and peaceful among the Asian regions, as compared to Northeast Asia, Central Asia, South Asia, and West Asia. Stability-inducing forces in the region include the absence of significant interstate conflicts, the existence of bilateral arrangements for enhancing cooperation, and a culture of cooperation based on mutual interests that has been fostered by the regional organization, the Association of Southeast Asian Nations (ASEAN).

ASEAN was established in August 8, 1967, with the signing of the Bangkok Declaration by Indonesia, Malaysia, Philippines, Singapore, and Thailand. Brunei Darussalam joined on January 8, 1984; Vietnam on July 28, 1995; Laos and Myanmar on July 23, 1997; and finally Cambodia on April 30, 1999 (see Narine, 2018). Except for East Timor, all Southeast Asian countries are members of ASEAN, and they are all formally at peace (see Severino, 2001). There are no

---

[1] For the purpose of this chapter, we focus upon the land borders of Burma, Thailand, Laos, Cambodia, and Vietnam.

major military conflicts or immediate traditional security threats to and within the region, perhaps with the exception of the South Chinese Sea maritime disputes involving China and several ASEAN countries (Stromseth, 2019: 4–5). This peaceful environment has enabled most of the countries in the region to experience substantial and sustained economic growth, taking the opportunity to integrate themselves more fully into economic globalization and to liberalize their investment and trade regimes (see Ellings and Simon, 1996: 2; and Mahbubani and Sing, 2017).

With the end of the Cold War, peace broke out in Southeast Asia following the Vietnamese withdrawal from Laos in 1988, and from Cambodia in 1989, leading to the Paris Peace Agreements of October 1991, which ended the conflict in Cambodia with the assistance of both ASEAN and the United Nations. This paved the way for ASEAN to unite all the countries of the region in a common security regime, based on the Westphalian principles of sovereignty and nonintervention, though not necessarily constituting a military alliance or a full-fledged pluralistic security community (see Buzan and Waever, 2003: 154–155; and Severino, 2001).

With the formal end of the Vietnamese-Cambodian War in 1991, the Southeast Asian region has moved from being a zone of conflict to becoming a zone of peace. Even before that, Southeast Asia had not seen any significant armed conflict among its ASEAN members. Since 1991, the ASEAN countries have moved from negative peace to stable peace. Moreover, the degree of economic, military, political, social, and scientific interaction among the ASEAN countries has grown enormously since the establishment of the regional organization fifty-two years ago.

The prospects for a robust, full-fledged pluralistic security community among the ASEAN member states are still premature (see Jones and Smith, 2007; and Khoo, 2015). There have been some cases of armed border skirmishes between Thailand and Laos in 1984 and 1987. There were incursions of Burmese troops on Thai territory in hot pursuit of ethnic rebels in 2010–12. There was also the Preah Vihear temple incident that escalated into a serious armed skirmish between Thailand and Cambodia in 2011. Yet, the possibility of war has remained very remote since 1991, so we characterize the region as a zone of stable peace. Moreover, Southeast Asia has actually witnessed a general decline in domestic conflicts and insurgencies, with the exceptions of Myanmar, the Philippines, and Thailand (see Tønnesson, 2015: 8).

The turn of the twenty-first century seemed to justify an optimistic outlook for the region. Yet, rapid economic, political, and geopolitical changes both within and outside Southeast Asia have recently increased the level of insecurity in the region in three different dimensions. First, since the end of the Cold War, the potential greatest security threat to Southeast Asia emanates from China, a rising superpower whose insatiable thirst for oil, gas, and other natural resources led it to grab and claim territory in the South China Sea since the 1990s (see Stromseth, 2019).

Second, since 9/11, Islamic terrorism and domestic insurgency have emerged as significant threats to a few countries of the region, mostly at the subnational level, but also with transnational implications and reverberations. Nowadays, several Southeast Asian states confront both inter- and intrastate violence, complicated by the fact that substate actors act across national boundaries. Hence, there are currently several militant, substate nationalist and transnational organizations in Southeast Asia of varying sizes and degrees of overtness and radicalism, in Indonesia, Philippines, and Thailand (see Bertrand, 2019; and Clad et al., 2011).

Third, transnational crime has been growing rapidly in the region, amid widespread corruption and weak governance in several countries, facilitating illicit flows of drugs, wildlife, timber, natural resources, people, and counterfeit goods (see Broadhurst, 2016; Idris, 2019b; and UNODC, 2013). The regional reality is that most countries in Southeast Asia still lack the systems, capabilities, and sometimes the political willingness necessary to address these new transnational threats, as governments are increasingly overwhelmed by the rapid increase in transnational cross-border movements of different kinds, both licit and illicit (see Idris, 2019b: 2).

Among the different regions we have surveyed in this book, Southeast Asia stands out as the ultimate example for the permissive conditions of international peace and globalization in enabling the occurrence of illicit transnational flows across peaceful borders. The insertion of India and China as giant dynamos of the global economy has expanded opportunities for interregional flows both licit and illicit (see Broadhurst, 2016; and Chouvy, 2013: 3). As in other regions of the world, economic globalization offers criminal and terrorist groups both more effective means to operate seamlessly across borders and much greater opportunities to make money. It also provides high volume cross-border flows of people, commodities, and money within which criminals and terrorists can camouflage their transnational transactions. Thus, electronic financial flows and money laundering make it harder for law enforcement agencies to track and control these illicit activities (see Eilstrop Sangiovanni, 2005: 10; and Shelley, 2014a: 10, and 2018: 1–13).

The Evolution of Peace and Integration in Southeast Asia, 1967–2020

Southeast Asia emerged as a region of independent countries following processes of decolonization, both peaceful and violent, that took place in the aftermath of World War II (with the exception of Thailand, which had never been a colony). Philippines obtained independence in 1946, Burma in 1948, Indonesia in 1949, Cambodia in 1953, Laos and Vietnam, which split into North and South Vietnam, in 1954, Malaysia in 1963, and Singapore in 1965.

Following a change of government in Indonesia in 1965, which ended its hostilities with Malaysia, several countries in Southeast Asia – Indonesia, Malaysia, Philippines, Singapore, and Thailand – established the Association of Southeast Asian Nations (ASEAN), on August 8, 1967. In 1971, the ASEAN countries issued the Declaration of a Zone of Peace, Freedom, and Neutrality in Southeast Asia, which created the precedent for the establishment of a nuclear-free zone in December 1995. Furthermore, in 1976, they signed the Treaty of Amity and Cooperation in Southeast Asia (TAC), which effectively established peaceful relations among its members, despite their territorial and maritime disputes (see Severino, 2001).

The absence of war among the members of ASEAN, with the exception of sporadic border skirmishes, stood in sharp contrast to the long Vietnam War from 1955 to 1975, the Vietnamese occupation of Cambodia from 1979 to 1989, and the domestic violence widespread within some of these countries. In the latter case, it is worth mentioning the Indonesian repression of East Timor between 1975 and 1999, the former struggle of the Philippine government against its New People's Army, and the volatile domestic situation in Burma turned Myanmar since 1989 (see IISS, 2014; and Kacowicz, 1998: 24). Nowadays, only three Southeast Asian countries continue to suffer from serious internal armed conflict and domestic insurgency: Myanmar, the Philippines, and Thailand (IISS, 2014: 111–120; and Tønnesson, 2015: 8).

The region as a whole was heavily affected by Cold War military intervention by the superpowers, especially that of the United States in Vietnam from the early 1960s until the reunification of Vietnam in 1975, following the United States' defeat and withdrawal. The Cold War's own dynamics divided the Southeast Asian states into two blocs. One, the so-called Indochina, consisted of Vietnam, Laos, and Cambodia, who all aligned with the Soviet Union; the other consisted of the ASEAN sphere, sustaining an anti-Communist, anti-Soviet, and anti-Chinese stance. Even the ASEAN bloc was divided among Thailand, Singapore, and the Philippines, who favored stronger ties with the United States, and Malaysia and Indonesia, who preferred a more exclusionary, or nonaligned framework (see Acharya, 2009: 176; and Buzan and Waever, 2003: 134).

Under the radical and genocidal Khmer Rouge regime, Cambodia competed and clashed with Communist Vietnam following its reunification in 1975, leading to a war between them and the occupation of Cambodia by Vietnamese armed forces until 1989. By contrast, Southeast Asia has not seen any significant armed conflict among its extant ASEAN members. After the end of the Vietnam War in 1975, ASEAN reached out to reunited Vietnam and to Laos, but conditions were not ripe and that rapprochement had to wait another decade. For much of the 1980s, the tragic Cambodian conflict troubled the ASEAN nations and required their attention. Finding a suitable solution to that conflict had priority over achieving other regional goals (see Alagappa, 1993).

In the early 1990s, both international and regional dynamics sparked a radical change in Southeast Asia's security landscape. More specifically, the end of the Cold War and the end of the Cambodian-Vietnam War came to fruition with the signature of the Paris Peace Accords of October 1991, which ultimately paved the way for the unfolding of a new era in interregional affairs. First, both the Soviet Union and the United States removed their military presence from Southeast Asia. Second, the Paris Peace Accords helped to resolve the main point of discord between the ASEAN and Indochina blocs. The mediation of members of the ASEAN bloc in the Cambodian conflict and their direct contact with Vietnam in the late 1980s eventually produced a substantial change in the latter. In 1991, Vietnam adopted a "new outlook" in its foreign policy, and this reshaped its own priorities. Instead of searching for hegemony in Indochina, Vietnam wished to become a "friend with all countries" (quoted in Emmers, 2005: 657; see also Alagappa, 1993). Moreover, the Paris Accords of 1991 led the United Nations to oversee a peaceful transition and reconstruction of Cambodia after a virulent civil war with foreign intervention, through the election of a democratic transitional government in 1993 (see Doyle, 1995).

In December 1995, a Southeast Asian Nuclear Weapons Free Zone Treaty (SEANWFZ) was concluded (the Bangkok Treaty), and entered into force on March 28, 1997. The parties to the treaty included all ten countries of the region, though Cambodia, Laos, and Myanmar were not yet members of ASEAN. The SEANWFZ marked a major break-through for the region, as it was the first agreement signed by all ten of the Southeast Asian countries, leading to the "One Southeast Asia" concept (see Acharya and Boutin, 1998: 224; and Kin Wah, 1997).

As Michael Leifer states, the history of this region is the history of "a phased state of reconciliation" (Leifer, 1999: 27). One clear example of this phased reconciliation is the ASEAN enlargement itself, which started in 1984 after the newly independent Brunei joined. The recon-ciliation peaked when Vietnam joined the ASEAN family in 1995. Later on, in 1997, Laos and Myanmar became members of ASEAN, and Cambodia followed suit in 1999. Burma (nowadays Myanmar) gained admission, despite its pariah status then (and perhaps still today), recognizing that its isolation would push it into the arms of China (see Buzan and Waever, 2003: 155).

Nowadays, more than six hundred million people living in the region have witnessed remarkable progress and prosperity in the fifty-four years since the formation of ASEAN, which has maintained the regional peace among its members (see Mahbubani and Sing, 2017: 1). As a formidable regional association that promotes economic, political, and security cooperation among its ten members, the group has spurred economic integration, signing six free-trade agreements with other regional econ-omies, including China and India.

The "ASEAN Way": Regional Norms and Economic Integration

One of the normative explanations for the economic achievements of ASEAN is the so-called ASEAN way, referring to relations among its members based on dialogue and consultation, rather than posturing and confrontation (see Severino, 2001). Amitav Acharya (2001: 47) argues that regional institutions may learn their norms from global organizations and other regional groups while assuming, at the same time, the content of their own local social, cultural, and political environment. Accordingly, ASEAN's norms came from a mix of these two sources. Among the norms ASEAN borrowed from the outside, the following are the most relevant: those dealing with the nonuse of force and the peaceful settlement of disputes; those concerning regional autonomy and collective self-reliance; the doctrine of noninterference in the internal affairs of states; and consensus-based collective decision-making (see Acharya, 2004).

The aforementioned norms are closely intertwined with local norms. Within this context, Acharya (1998: 56) pointed out the existence of a specific strategic culture designed for resolving regional problems, known as the "ASEAN way." Acharya highlights four sources for this particular strategic culture: (1) the close and personal ties among ASEAN's leaders, (2) the expression of cultural similarities, (3) the regulatory norms of ASEAN, and (4) the processes of interaction and socialization. In other words, the "ASEAN way" is a way of doing business (in both political and economic terms), following certain shared regional patterns: informality, a nonconfrontational bargaining style, and consensus building.

Regional Economic Interdependence

One of the main ideas that supported the establishment of ASEAN was the shared desire of the member states to create better regional conditions that would allow them to invest resources in their domestic economic development and create cooperation. Cooperation includes deepening economic ties aimed at accelerating economic growth and increasing regional economic interdependence, as originally stated in the Bangkok Declaration of 1967 (see Hernandez, 1998).

In terms of economic integration, the Southeast Asian states have adopted the loose model of open regionalism. This model seems to suit the ASEAN nations as it favors economic ties with extra-regional actors over an economic integration strategy focused exclusively in the region. ASEAN had little choice but to choose such a model as most of the Southeast Asian nations have adopted an outward-looking strategy of economic insertion into economic globalization, especially since the 1970s (see Ariff, 1994).

Moreover, since the 1980s, free-market policies have been adopted almost unanimously throughout the region. Southeast Asian states privatized public assets, carried out financial deregulation, and adopted prudent fiscal policies. Overall, despite the enormous financial crisis and crackdown of 1997 in Thailand and Indonesia, the outward-looking strategy of the ASEAN states has been a resounding success, as most of the nations in the region have enjoyed sustained economic growth.

Regional Integration and Infrastructure Initiatives
In the last decade, there have been substantial efforts to further increase integration and physical connectivity within the region, with a special focus placed upon boosting economic growth. Since 2009, the ASEAN Master Plan for Connectivity has been enhancing the physical infrastructure; developing effective institutions, mechanisms and processes; and empowering people-to-people connectivity (see UNODC, 2016c, 3). China and India, as the giant economic neighbors to ASEAN, have expanded their economic interdependence and investments with and within the region, boosting interregional trade of goods and services, and encouraging their companies to develop production in Vietnam, Cambodia, and Indonesia (UNODC, 2016c, 3). When considered as a single economy, the ASEAN Economic Community (AEC) is the seventh largest economy in the world, with a combined GDP of US $2.4 trillion (UNODC, 2016c: 5).

In this context, we should emphasize ASEAN's efforts at enhancing the physical and economic integration of the Southeast Asian countries that are members of the Greater Mekong subregion (GMS). The Greater Mekong is a transnational region of more than three hundred million people, launched as a development program in 1992 by the Asian Development Bank. It includes the latecomers of ASEAN: Cambodia, Laos, Myanmar, and Vietnam, as well as Thailand and the Yunnan Province and Guangxi Zhuang Autonomous region of China (see UNODC, 2016c: 7–8).

ASEAN four's newest members have suffered immensely from the Cold War proxy wars and its aftermath. Hence, as a post-conflict peace-building effort, ASEAN has been giving a particular attention to the development of this subregion in which all of them are located, including human resources development. In 2003, a cross-border transport agreement (CBTA) was signed with the goal of eliminating non-physical barriers to cross-border movements. It has focused upon sixteen points of entry and exit within the GMS, apparently being effective at reducing time and effort needed to cross the national borders (UNODC, 2016c: 8).

Transnational Crime across the Southeast Asian Borders

For several decades, the borders of mainland Southeast Asia, especially in the GMS, were penetrated by transnational illicit flows, essentially human trafficking and drug trafficking. Human trafficking refers to a broad regional prostitution market, with Thailand as the most notorious core (see Shelley, 2010: 30, 44, 157–166). As for drug trafficking in opium and heroin, it links to the equally infamous "Golden Triangle," the Mekong subregion where Myanmar meets northern Thailand, northern Laos, and southwest China. During the second half of the twentieth century, the Golden Triangle was notoriously known for its role in the global narcotic trade. This was due to the topography of the mountainous terrain and the lingering conditions of civil war that led to the formation of many "narco-armies" such as the former Mong Tai Army of Sino-Shan warlord Khun Sa in Myanmar (see Broadhurst and Farrelly, 2014: 638–640).

The organized criminal groups in the Golden Triangle are linked to local insurgencies and transnational criminal syndicates, as well as corrupt elements of the local and national bureaucracies in the three countries (Laos, Myanmar, and Thailand), establishing political alliances between the governing elites and criminal elements. In the last decade, the area is no longer dependent on the illicit drug trade alone. In addition, the illicit transnational flows include complementary trade in weapons and people, as well as gambling (see Broadhurst, 2016; and Broadhurst and Lee, 2013). The improvement of physical infrastructures in the Mekong area has forged new transport routes in the region; thus, actually benefitting the illicit transnational flows alongside the licit ones (see Chouvy, 2013: 14).

The diversity of the criminal groups in the Golden Triangle reflects the complexity of the Southeast Asian region. At the same time, the nature of the criminal activities undertaken are broadly similar, as they are often grounded in poverty and economic underdevelopment. In addition, among the drivers and enablers of organized crime we should include corruption, weak democratic foundations, and lack of enforcement; lack of alternative (licit) sources of livelihood; the persistent conflict in Myanmar's Shan State; the growth and improvement in regional transport influence; and the Chinese influence (Idris, 2019b: 2–3).

Transnational crime has readily prospered throughout this subregion, sometimes thanks to the absence of strong bilateral and regional law enforcement cooperation among the ASEAN countries. Moreover, in some cases, organized crime interacts with terrorist groups and with ruling elites, both civilian and military. In this case, organized crime and political extremism become symbiotic sources of illicit wealth and lethal violence (see Broadhurst and Le, 2013: 11–12).

Violent non-state actors come from the subregion itself, including subnational actors and insurgent movements, as well as from China and Japan. Transnational crime groups include the Chinese "black societies" or triads, Japanese organized crime (Yakuza), and the military-style ethnic groups controlling drug production in the Golden Triangle, especially in Myanmar (see Broadhurst and Le, 2013: 5). Decades of armed conflicts in Vietnam, Laos, Cambodia, and Myanmar, have spurred the production and traffic of several drugs, including opium, heroin, and methamphetamine. Civil wars and international wars have also created the flow of hundreds of thousands of refugees across the Southeast Asian borders, allowing for the growth of black markets, regional sex trade (especially in Thailand), and weapons trafficking (see Chouvy, 2013: 23).

The UNODC East Asian and Pacific regional threat assessment estimated in 2016 that transnational crime groups earned about $90–100 billion per year from various illicit sources in Southeast Asia. Narcotic production and trafficking in drug precursors have been the most lucrative, followed by illegal wildlife and timber trading. Other illicit activities include illegal disposal of e-waste and the use and disposal of prohibited chemicals; human trafficking and smuggling, including child exploitation materials; maritime crime, with piracy, cargo theft, and illegal fishing; product counterfeiting and intellectual property theft of "high street" goods and products; fake or counterfeit medicines, with ED (erectile dysfunction drugs) and "Tramadol"; and illicit gambling (Broadhurst, 2016: 3).

The effects of these illicit transnational flows have been devastating. In UNODC's own terms,

The illegal trade of people, drugs, wildlife, and counterfeits has a destabilizing effect by generating money for criminal and non-state groups that is laundered into the legitimate economy. It distorts the regional economy, victimizes individuals and hurts the broader community of people and businesses that adhere to the rules and regulations. In addition, illegal trade means lost tax revenues, particularly with counterfeit goods. This reduces the benefits of trade liberalization, because taxes are supposed to offset the loss of tariff revenues. (UNODC, 2016c: 3)

In sum, as Jeremy Douglas, the UNODC Regional representative argued, "These illicit activities are a threat to security, good governance, human rights, and sustainable development" (UNODC, 2016c: 1).

Drug Trafficking

Drug trafficking is a nefarious example of how regional integration and the improvement of physical infrastructures have facilitated illicit transnational flows within the region, as well as exploiting connections with neighboring countries, such as India and China. Heroin and synthetic drugs, of which methamphetamine is the most popular, are produced mainly in Myanmar and trafficked heavily throughout the region. After Afghanistan, Myanmar remains the world's second-largest heroin producer. Heroin and methamphetamine are consumed regionally and they are exported to China, India, and further away to Japan, Australia, and the Americas (Chouvy, 2013: 2; and UNODC, 2016c: 19–20).

According to UNODC estimates, the regional illicit drug market in Southeast Asia is worth over US$30 billion per year. The region hosts the world's largest methamphetamine market, as well as the second-largest heroin market. Almost all the heroin produced in Southeast Asia is consumed in East Asia and the Pacific. Opiate users account for the majority of problem drug users in countries such as Vietnam, Myanmar, Mongolia, Indonesia, Singapore, and Malaysia (UNODC, 2013: vi and 51–53). While the business models of the two drugs are rather different, production of these drugs can take place where states institutions are relatively weak and the chances of interception and arrests are rather low (see East Asian Forum, 2017).

The Golden Triangle has been one of the leading regions producing drugs worldwide. The production of narcotics, already existing since the late 1970s, has rapidly increased in the 1990s due to
the drug trafficking activities of different transnational criminal
groups and the rampant level of corruption among government
officials in the region, especially in Myanmar and Thailand. An
effective distribution network allowed drug traffickers to transport
heroin and methamphetamines from the Golden Triangle into
Thailand, as well as into China's Yunnan Province (see Emmers,
2003: 3–4).

Nowadays, several countries of Southeast Asia have succeeded in
reducing the scope of the drug production; hence, almost all of the
heroin and opium production has been confined in recent years to
politically contested areas of Myanmar. Even in Myanmar, there has
been a downward trend that started in 2014. This is due to the continuing shift in the regional drug market away from opium and heroin
toward synthetic drugs (see Nyein, 2020; and UNODC, 2013: 53). In
the last few years, two parallel trends developed in the heroin market in
Southeast Asia: a decreased demand for heroin occurring simultaneously with decreases in opium poppy cultivation in Myanmar
(UNODC, 2019: 48). Nevertheless, production and trafficking of heroin remains a problem in the Mekong region, with seizures increased in
Myanmar, Thailand, and Vietnam in 2018, and to a lesser extent in
Singapore (UNODC, 2019: 51).

As for the consumption of pill-form methamphetamine, a form of
amphetamine-type stimulant (ATS) (*"yaba," "shabu,"* or "ice-good-to-
know"), it remains a very popular synthetic drug in Southeast Asia,
particularly in Thailand. It is produced in Myanmar's Shan State, as
well as in China, while Cambodia serves as a transit country for drugs
produced in Myanmar, which enter Cambodia from its northeast border
with Laos (see UNODC, 2013: 63). UNODC estimates methamphetamine consumption to be driven by at least 3.43 million but as many as
20.6 million users, including over 10 million users of illicit amphetamines in the region alone. This number is staggering when compared
to the estimates for opiate users, at between 2.83 and 5.06 million, in the
entire East Asia and Pacific region (see UNODC, 2016c).

Initially considered a Southeast Asian regional problem, but now
trafficked far more widely into parts of South and East Asia and to the
West, the pills produced in Golden Triangle laboratories (especially in

Myanmar) have been defined as a new epidemic of narcotics production. Due to high profits, ease of operation, and ever-expanding demand, the production and trade of synthetic drugs is the crime type with the greatest potential for expansion in Southeast Asia (see UNODC, 2016c). This feature alone gives it an unprecedented capacity for the criminalization of societies and economies, crowding out legitimate economic activities.

The recently published UNODC Report on Southeast Asia (UNODC, 2019) shows that countries in the region have failed in their fight against drug trafficking, in particular regarding methamphetamine. This failure is due to the lack of a regional precursor control strategy and weak national capacities to enforce existing laws in a systematic and coherent way (UNODC, 2019: 25). On a more positive note, the seizure of methamphetamine tablets and crystalline methamphetamine have increased, although this was probably a consequence of the higher demand. In 2018, the largest seizure of methamphetamine took place in the region, with around 120 tons seized (UNODC, 2019: 43). Around 53 percent of that amount was seized in Thailand alone, which reflects two trends: an increase in the flows of methamphetamine being trafficked from Myanmar across the border to Thailand, as well as enhanced enforcement capabilities (UNODC, 2019: 42–43).

Arms Trafficking and the Proliferation of Small Weapons

Trade in weapons is one of the criminal enterprises that have survived in the Golden Triangle for a long time. The regional arms market has developed since the Indochina wars of the 1960s and 1970s, and many criminal and rebel groups show that weapons trafficking, including the proliferation of small arms, is relatively easy (see Broadhurst and Le, 2013: 14). Former armed conflicts have spurred international and regional trade in small arms that is still very active and regionally integrated, especially in Cambodia, Myanmar, Thailand, and even among supporters of Acehnese secessionist movements in Indonesia (see Chouvy, 2013: 18).

Human Trafficking and Smuggling

Southeast Asia is one of the most vulnerable regions in the world regarding human trafficking, with estimates of more than 200,000 women and children being moved each year for sex work alone (see Betz, 2009; Emmers, 2003: 18; and Shelley, 2010: 157–166). This is explained by a number of conditions, including natural disasters, the legacy of military conflicts leading to large numbers of displaced people and refugees, the area's huge population, the effects of the economic crisis of the late 1990s, growing urbanization, extensive poverty, loose labor regulations, and unharmonized migration controls (see Caballero-Anthony, 2018: 19; Emmers, 2003: 6; and UNODC, 2019: 70).

The illegal trade in women has become a great source of income for people-traffickers and it remains difficult to apprehend, as it is obscured within the broader phenomenon of undocumented migration. During the years 2012–14, more than sixty percent of the 7,800 identified victims were trafficked for sexual exploitation, whereas about eighty-five percent of the victims were trafficked from within the region, with Thailand as the leading destination for trafficking victims from Cambodia, Laos, and Myanmar. Malaysia has also been a destination for human trafficking from Indonesia, the Philippines, and Vietnam (see UNODC, 2016b). In recent years, following the ethnic cleansing of the Rohingya Muslim ethnic minority in Myanmar, about 5,000 Rohingya were trafficked or smuggled into Bangladesh, sometimes rescued by the local police and brought back to refugee camps (see Caballero-Anthony, 2018: 20).

We should pay particular attention to the trafficking of women and girls for sexual exploitation within the Greater Mekong subregion, due to high levels of sex tourism from the West, especially in Thailand and to some extent in Cambodia, as well as a strong domestic demand. According to UNODC, the number of trafficked victims in Thailand from neighboring countries in 2013 was approximately 3,750 and 272 in Cambodia. The generated income was approximately US$ 45,000 per victim per year, or about US$ 181 million in gross revenues for their traffickers (UNODC, 2013: iv). Most of the trafficking victims who were not Thais came from poorer countries in the region, especially from Cambodia, Laos, and Myanmar (UNODC, 2013: 17). Conversely, the trafficking of sex workers from a relatively rich country to a poorer one also took place, like in the case of trafficked Vietnamese women who make up a small share of sex workers in Cambodia (see UNODC, 2013: 18; and Shabbir et al., 2011).

Some Southeast Asian countries have witnessed a certain increase in the detention of victims of trafficking in persons, such as the case of Thailand "where the number of detected victims increased after legislative or programmatic action have clearly contributed to improving the identification of victims and the effectiveness of criminal justice responses" (UNODC, 2019: 82). However, impunity remains endemic since the low levels of victim detections and criminal convictions demonstrate that the struggle against human trafficking is far from succeeding in Southeast Asia.

As for human smuggling, there is a general trend toward a steady increase in both legal and illicit movement of people across borders in the region. Growing demand among marginalized communities to move toward areas of better economic opportunity has created profit opportunities for a range of criminal actors, from traditional "snakehead" groups of Chinese gangs to smaller ad hoc operators (see UNODC, 2018b: 69–94). There are several drivers behind this rising demand for transnational mobility. Most basic explanations include poverty, high birth rates, and persecution of key rural populations in southern China and across Southeast Asia. Across the region, communities have become increasingly attuned to the benefits of remittances from family members working abroad; many of these financial flows have become so large as to have significant positive benefits for national economies, such as in the case of the Philippines (see Idris, 2019b: 2–3).

Making it easy for people to travel in Southeast Asia by opening borders and enhancing physical infrastructures and connectivity is important for the objectives of promoting business, trade, tourism, and economic growth. At the same time, there has been more room for labor exploitation and for human smuggling of illegal migrants. For instance, unskilled labor migrants who look for employment opportunities in Thailand, Singapore, India, and China come from the less developed countries in the area, including Cambodia, Laos, Myanmar, and Vietnam. They might also come from labor-abundant countries such as Indonesia and the Philippines (see UNODC, 2016c: 21, and 2018b: 74–77). Many irregular migrants cross the borders through the services of criminal smugglers, who make about US$ 192 million for their illicit tasks. Thailand remains the economic magnet for the illegal labor market in the region, benefitting from freer labor regulations and loose migration controls (UNODC, 2016c: 21).

Terrorism: Subnational and Transnational

Terrorism in Southeast Asia has been traditionally confined to national borders, usually on periphery areas within some Southeast Asian countries, such as southern Thailand, the island of Mindanao, and the Cordillera Mountain range in Luzon in the Philippines. These regions, often dominated by ethnic minorities that express themselves in sub-state nationalist movements, have long featured weak state institutions and local people who have lagged behind in most measures of socioeconomic development (see Clad et al., 2011: 89–90; and Bertrand, 2019). As such, low-level insurgencies erupted, but the demands were usually local and parochial. If there was an international or transnational component to them, it was that in some cases they associated themselves with transnational, global communist movements during the Cold War, while trying to dissociate or be ambiguous about potential linkages to Islamic transnational terrorist organizations since the end of the Cold War (Bertrand, 2019: 104).

Conversely, the region has witnessed the presence of explicit transnational terrorists ideologically linked to jihadism and political Islam. In Southeast Asia, jihadists engage in a type of "triangular arbitrage" to exploit the geopolitical differences between Indonesia, Malaysia, and the Philippines, taking advantage of the fragmented archipelagic geography of maritime Southeast Asia (Temby, 2018). The activities of the al-Qaeda-linked Jemaah Islamiyah (JI) has led Southeast Asia to become a major front of international terrorism, targeting the interests of the United States and its allies in the region. JI has deep political and ideological roots in the region, focusing in Indonesia, and having links with groups and individuals in the Philippines (the Moro Islamic Liberation Front, and the Abu Sayyaf Group), Thailand (Gerakan Mujahidin Islam Pattani), and Malaysia (Kumpulan Muyahidin Malaysia) (see Clad et al., 2011; and Singh, 2018).

Transnational terrorism has led to some incipient international and regional cooperation, also in coordination with the United States, by introducing new technologies to scan passports in airports throughout the region to be able to track movement of terrorist suspects. Within the international bodies of ASEAN and the United States dealing with counterterrorism, their joint committees are the same as those that deal with transnational crime (see Press-Barnathan, 2014). As in Latin America, this refers to the economic logic of a market in which a regular payment for illegal and smuggled arms takes place through drug trafficking, and vice versa, so there is an economic symbiosis between terrorists and criminals (see Shelley, 2014a: 10–12).

Explaining the Reality of Peaceful Borders and Illicit Transnational Flows in Southeast Asia

Hypothesis 1: The Degree of Physical and Institutional Openness of Peaceful Borders

The peaceful environment in the region has led to economic integration, enhanced trade, and economic growth. At the same time, improved infrastructure and free trade agreements in Southeast Asia have facilitated the movement of people and commodities; thereby, also creating significant parallel opportunities in the form of illicit transnational flows (see Broadhurst and Le, 2013: 6). As the UN Report of December 26, 2016, warns: "They are building highways across themselves, they are putting new infrastructures in place, and they are having ten to twenty percent increases in trade every year going into or through their territories ... [but] they simply do not have the protection measures in place." The reference is to customs control and policing systems for the monitoring of peaceful borders, to cope effectively with criminal illicit transnational flows (quoted in UNODC, 2016c:1).

The reticence to develop effective regional governance mechanisms to cope with transnational crime and terrorism relates to the very nature of the ASEAN normative framework, which is very sensitive to nonintervention in domestic affairs. Thus, Southeast Asian countries' firm normative commitment to a strict Westphalian understanding of national sovereignty, as epitomized by the "ASEAN values," poses a formidable obstacle for their international and transnational cooperation in facing these new transnational security threats (see Emmers, 2003: 11).

Due to their regional peace and stability, Southeast Asian countries have enjoyed impressive growth in their GDP in recent years. Such progress has been in large part due to regional agreements that promoted freer movement of people, goods, and capital, leading, in turn, to an increase in trade and overall economic growth, with reference to the ASEAN Free Trade Area (AFTA) and to the ASEAN Economic Community (see East Asian Forum, 2017). Moreover, improved infrastructure and rapid physical integration have facilitated the free movement of people and commodities. This has also enabled and enhanced transnational criminal opportunities, making the occurrence of illicit flows – drug trafficking, human smuggling and trafficking, and arms trafficking – more possible. Regional integration has expanded licit economic opportunities, but illicit markets have tended to develop simultaneously.

Even before the transition and consolidation of peace in the early 1990s, many of the Southeast Asian countries, perhaps with the exception of Malaysia and Singapore, tended to neglect – mostly for political reasons and/or lack of institutional capacity – the control and monitoring of their international peaceful borders. The reality in the region is that many countries still lack the will and the capabilities necessary to properly address transnational threats and illicit flows, due to political, institutional, and political economy reasons.

Regional development and integration have led regional states to a political decision, out of an economic rationale, to remove physical and non-physical barriers at their frontiers, in order to ensure more practical and efficient border crossings for people, goods, and money (for instance, with reference to the GMS subregion, see UNODC, 2016c: 7). That has followed a number of infrastructure initiatives that have enhanced connectivity among trading partners, thereby increasing the access to remote borderlands. In this way, the shift from border control to border facilitation transformed the borders into more soft and open in both physical and institutional terms (see UNODC, 2013: 10, and 2016c: 1).

As the region keeps increasing its connectivity by creating and strengthening trade linkages, threats stemming from trafficking and transnational organized criminality are also becoming integrated within the region, as well as beyond it, through interregional links with powerful neighbors such as India and China (see Tagliacozzo, 2001; and UNODC, 2016c: 1, 19). Therefore, open, porous, and integrated borders have been a boon for the occurrence and proliferation of transnational illicit flows across the peaceful borders of mainland Southeast Asia. In this sense, we corroborate the validity of the first hypothesis.

Hypothesis 2: The Degree of Governance, Institutional Strength, and Political Willingness

The Southeast Asian region includes a very heterogeneous group of states with respect to their political regimes. Democracy barely took root in the region; it has not been internalized as a paramount value.

Hence, peace and regional institutional building in Southeast Asia has lacked a commitment to liberal democracy (see Acharya, 2001). Instead, the main goal has been to enhance sovereignty and to maintain regime survival "in the face of domestic and external threats, especially communist subversion" (Acharya, 2001: 379).

Most of the Southeast Asian countries have experienced long periods of authoritarian rule with some attempts at democratization. Hence, democracy does not seem to have played a critical role in explaining the Southeast Asian peace and regional-building projects. According to the Freedom House's report of 2018, Indonesia, Malaysia, the Philippines and Myanmar are "partly free" regimes, whereas Brunei, Laos, Thailand, and Vietnam are "not free" (quoted in Simandjuntak, 2018).

In terms of the degree of governance and institutional strength of the neighboring states, there is an important variation across the countries of the region. Most of the Southeast Asian states (with the exceptions of Singapore and Brunei, and to a lesser extent Malaysia and Vietnam) are relatively weak, due to their historical and political conditions, which caused them to suffer from fragile domestic institutions and significant socioeconomic problems (Emmers, 2003: 10).

The various challenges and difficulties embedded in coping with transnational crime in Southeast Asia relate to a series of domestic, rather than external factors, including internal instability and widespread corruption. Corruption and weak judicial oversight remain serious issues in the Philippines, Indonesia, and Malaysia. Due process remains a significant obstacle in countries like Vietnam, Cambodia, and Laos. Indonesia and the Philippines experience ethnic tensions and cleavages that affect the proper functioning of their political institutions. In the specific context of facing transnational terrorist threats, the domestic legal framework has been rather limited and incomplete. Moreover, in countries like Indonesia that underwent a significant democratization process, the public is extremely sensitive to any harsh state measures against jihadi terrorist suspects, because this runs the risk of undermining hard-won human rights achievements.[2]

The levels of corruption in the region are rather staggering, so that the majority of the Southeast Asian countries are positioned in the bottom half of the Corruption Perceptions Index for 2015. According to Transparency International (2015), most of the Southeast Asian

---

[2] We thank Galia Press-Barnathan for her comments on this point.

countries earned meager and failing scores in terms of perception of corruption: Indonesia, 37/100; Philippines, 35/100; Thailand, 35/100; East Timor, 35/100; Vietnam, 33/100; Laos, 30/100; Myanmar, 28/100; and Cambodia, 21/100. Under these conditions, the "protection" dimension of organized crime for illicit markets becomes paramount, as non-state actors might accommodate parallel governance functions unfulfilled by legal institutions, especially in some multi-border areas like the Golden Triangle, where criminal non-state actors actually control some of the borderlands (see Broadhurst, 2016; Broadhurst and Farrelly, 2014; and Shelley, 2010: 44).

The gap between the legal framework and the enforcement of laws at the national level facilitates the occurrence and proliferation of illicit transnational flows. In the case of Myanmar in the 1990s, the ruling Burmese military government did enter into ceasefire agreements with insurgent groups and organized criminal actors in the Burma-China borderlands, still allowing them to carry out illicit activities, in what it has been known as "ceasefire capitalism" (see Idris, 2019b: 3; and Woods, 2011). Moreover, in a recent report, Caballero-Anthony (2018: 211) depicted the gruesome case of the discovery of mass graves of trafficking victims along the border between Malaysia and Thailand in 2015, which incriminated a Thai general and several police officers among sixty-two people convicted of human trafficking. Thus, political and military elites have engaged for several decades in political cooperative schemes with criminal actors in degrees of alliance or enforcement evasion, rather than confrontation.

In contrast to Myanmar, Cambodia, and Vietnam, Malaysia and Singapore are the two countries with the best regulatory frameworks in the region, in terms of administrative and economic governance. As for political governance, the only countries with high scores regarding low levels of corruption are Singapore (84/100) and Brunei (58/100), whereas Malaysia got a bare 49/100 (see Transparency International, 2015). Accordingly, we should expect the Malaysia-Singapore maritime border to be less vulnerable to illicit transnational flows, such as drug trafficking and human trafficking. In comparative terms that is the case, though it relates to the fact that the two countries share a maritime boundary and that they are physically connected only by two causeways. Although the two countries face a similar set of transnational security challenges, their perceptions differ due to their different law-enforcement capacity. Thus, Singapore is confident of its ability to deal with drug issues and illegal migrant workers (see Sato, 2012: 140). In sum, we corroborate the validity of the second hypothesis in most of the Southeast Asian peaceful borders, with the exception of the Singapore-Malaysian maritime border.

Hypothesis 3: The Prevailing Socioeconomic Conditions of the Bordering States

Similar to its diverse levels of governance, Southeast Asia sustains significant socioeconomic stratification. As the UN Report of February 26, 2016, states, "this region is highly unique … [w]ith countries ranging from some of the richest, such as Singapore, to some of the poorest, like Laos and Myanmar." As Southeast Asia has some of the world's fastest growing economies, it also depicts extremes of inequality and destitution that their governments ineffectively manage. Such inequalities help generate many forms of crime alongside the related problems of poor governance and corruption.

According to the World Bank figures of 2017, Singapore, Malaysia, Brunei, and Thailand are considered as relatively high-income countries (with GNI per capita of $52,600, $28,650, $28,290, and $17,090 respectively). In the second economic tier, we find two upper-middle-income countries, Vietnam and East Timor (with GNI per capita of $6,450 and $6,330 respectively). By contrast, the remaining five Southeast Asian countries are lower-middle-income countries: Indonesia, Philippines, Laos, Myanmar, and Cambodia in descending order of economic wealth (with GNI per capita of $3,847, $3,660, $2,270, $1,455, and $1,230, respectively). In this sense, it is not surprising to identify Thailand as the magnet for regional labor and illicit transnational flows from its poorer neighbors, Myanmar, Laos, and Cambodia. Since the early 1990s, millions of workers have migrated to Thailand, both licitly and illicitly (see Broadhurst, 2016; and UNODC, 2013: 7). Thailand shares borders that extend 1,118 miles with Myanmar, 1,090 miles with Laos, as well as 500 miles with Cambodia. It becomes obvious that the lion's share of transnational flows, both licit and illicit, takes place across the economic divide within the GMS region, from the poorer countries to Thailand.

The only border that reflects a very different socioeconomic situation is the Malaysian-Singaporean maritime border. Indeed, in comparative terms, we trace a lower level of illicit transnational flows across the two countries that enjoy high levels of economic development and proven capabilities and willingness to control their borders. Singapore, for instance, considers terrorism and maritime piracy as more daunting transnational security threats than drug trafficking, human trafficking, and arms trafficking, which are under relative control and suppression (Sato, 2012: 140). To sum up, we corroborate the third hypothesis in most of the Southeast Asian peaceful borders, with the exception of the Malaysia-Singapore maritime border.

Conclusions

Regional peace in the Southeast Asian region, especially after 1991, has contributed to its phenomenal economic growth and development, which, in turn, has led to higher levels of integration of suppliers and consumers, production networks, and infrastructure, creating a dense regional and interregional network of economic interdependence, as well as embedding the ASEAN member-states within economic globalization (see Haftel, 2010). At the same time, expanding economic and infrastructure links around the region have also facilitated the occurrence of illicit transnational flows, including transnational organized crime and terrorism (UNODC, 2016c: 45).

Although ASEAN has sought to follow in the steps of the European model regarding the enacting of a common and effective response to the new transnational security threats of crime and terrorism, it has lagged behind in its institutional efforts and yet expected positive results. We explain this partially by the normative limitations of the so-called ASEAN values in allowing for mechanisms of regional governance that might imply some forms of supra-nationality and voluntary surrender of national sovereignty norms to the benefit of a more supra-national regional body. In this sense, as Jeremy Douglas argued in 2016, "controlling illegal flows of goods, people, and money has increasingly become a challenge that governments cannot address alone" (Foreword in UNODC, 2016c; see also Broadhurst, 2016: 9; Broadhurst and Le, 2013: 15–16; and Emmers, 2003: 11).

The security agenda in Southeast Asia has expanded in the last two decades in new and uncharted directions, coping with the new security threats of the twenty-first century. Yet, despite their regional peace and integration, the ASEAN countries find inherent difficulties and limitations in designing and implementing an effective regional response to cope with these new security threats (see Tagliacozzo, 2001: 254).

Faced with a myriad of destabilizing factors, including economic difficulties, indigenous radical Moslem groups, communal violence, and drugs, human, and arms trafficking, the Southeast Asian states must still find an effective way to manage their common security concerns, especially in relation to these illicit transnational flows (see Caballero-Anthony, 2018: 21). There is a lingering dilemma to be resolved between the need for regional and global governance to cope with transnational criminality, versus the existing practical and normative reality of national jurisdictions and sovereignty.

The issue of transnational crime addresses the question of national sovereignty. On the one hand, illicit transnational flows pose a threat to the national sovereignty and the territorial integrity of independent states, sometimes jeopardizing their legitimacy and governance mechanisms. On the other hand, effective cooperation in combating transnational crime and terrorism requires a political decision by national governments to surrender some parts and pieces of their sovereignty for the benefit of international, regional, and global cooperation. In this sense, the Southeast Asian countries have traditionally been strong defenders of the sanctity of national sovereignty and nonintervention. Therefore, they confront a political dilemma of how to find the proper equilibrium between nonintervention and reaching effective anti-criminal and anti-terrorist cooperation. This dilemma is common to all countries and regions of the world, not just to Southeast Asia. We assess this dilemma in the final chapter of this volume.

9 | Comparisons, Policy Recommendations, and Conclusions

Introduction

In this concluding chapter, we aim to delineate theoretical insights drawn from relevant comparisons among the case studies analyzed and to suggest policy recommendations. Specifically, we examine and reassess the three hypotheses we formulated in Chapter 2, identify and map relevant patterns from the different case studies across several regions of the world, offer several policy recommendations based on these patterns, and draw some general conclusions.

Throughout this book, we have embarked on a novel and systematic effort to empirically test the reality of peaceful borders and illicit transnational flows, usually carried out by violent non-state actors (VNSAs), such as transnational criminal and terrorist groups, engaged in drug trafficking, human trafficking and smuggling, and arms trafficking. These VNSAs tend to exploit the looseness and demilitarization of peaceful borderlands, by taking advantage of the jurisdictional arbitrage created by sovereign borders. Differences between states' jurisdictional authority, regulatory structures, governance mechanisms, and socioeconomic conditions drive the activity of these illicit non-state actors, which much like firms and corporations take advantage of such jurisdictional arbitrage, following a similar economic logic.

The starting point of our research has been the assumption that both international peace and globalization are permissive conditions for the occurrence and proliferation of illicit transnational flows across peaceful borders. International peace can be a preexisting situation for a long time, like in North America, most of South America, and Western Europe. Alternatively, it can break out from a transition from war to peace (negative peace) following international agreements, like those between Israel and Egypt and Israel and Jordan in the Middle East, in

Southern Africa, and Southeast Asia, or following the formal end of civil and "intermestic" wars, like in Central America, Colombia, former Yugoslavia, and Cambodia. Moreover, peace can "upgrade" from extant low to higher levels of peace, like in the Southern Cone of South America; higher levels of peace also entail higher levels of economic and social integration.

A second permissive condition refers to the general effects of economic globalization. We live in a world where globalization has altered the sociopolitical map of nation-states, including new communications and transportation technologies that facilitate the flow of ideas, information, people, capital, and services across national borders. In many respects, globalization has deterritorialized international relations, making international borders less relevant, regardless of the state of peace or war. We can refer here to the "dark side of globalization," in the form of illicit transnational and global networks of crime and terrorism, embedded in the global economy (see Naím, 2005; and Shelley, 2014a). Increased levels of globalization in trade, finance, goods, and the free movement of people have produced an environment prone to transnational VNSAs such as transnational criminal organizations (TCOs) to move illicit profits and illegal goods, to provide illicit services, as well as to smuggle and traffic people across borders.

Yet, international peace and globalization cannot explain the variance in the occurrence and proliferation of illicit transnational flows across peaceful borders. Hence, aiming at unraveling a more complete picture, the main research question we have asked in this book is: "*Under which conditions might peaceful borders enable the occurrence and proliferation of transnational illicit flows across borders, usually carried out by violent non-state actors, including transnational criminal groups and terrorists?*"

To answer this question, we hypothesized that the occurrence and proliferation of illicit transnational flows across peaceful borders is a function of the variance in three different conditions: the degree of physical and institutional openness of the peaceful borders; the degree of governance and political willingness of the neighboring states in controlling their peaceful borders; and the prevalent socioeconomic conditions of the neighboring states. We turn to discuss briefly the main insights drawn from comparing the different case studies analyzed in the book, while assessing the relative relevance of the three hypotheses.

Comparing the Case Studies and Assessing the Hypotheses

Table 9.1 summarizes the empirical findings across the eleven case studies regarding the occurrence and proliferation of illicit transnational flows.

The empirical picture summarized in Table 9.1 is complex. First, the US-Canada and Israel-Jordan cases stand out due to the relative absence of illicit transnational flows, in contrast to the other cases. Second, transnational terrorism in the Western Hemisphere is associated only with some of the Colombian borders and with the TBA area of Argentina-Brazil-Paraguay. In other regions of the world, terrorism is also absent across the Israeli-Jordanian border and in Southern Africa, whereas it takes place mostly across the maritime countries of ASEAN in Southeast Asia and in the European continent. We turn now to a detail analysis of each of the three hypotheses.

Hypothesis 1: The Degree of Physical and Institutional Openness of the Peaceful Borders

H1: The more open, soft, and integrated the peaceful borders between the neighboring states are, *the greater the occurrence and proliferation of illicit transnational flows involving violent non-state actors.*

We base the argument in favor of open, soft, and porous borders on the economic logic of interdependence, deriving from enhanced processes of globalization and regionalization. It stems from Liberal premises about the overall effects of free trade and peace. Moreover, there are instances where borders are softened by the implementation of official state policies, through the deliberate creation of free trade zones aimed at facilitating economic integration and advancing transnational flows. Conversely, in the cases of the Northern Triangle, the Colombian borders, the TBA, the Western Balkans, Southern Africa, and Southeast Asia, porousness is the result of relatively weak states that are unable to effectively control their borders, regardless of the state of peace or war. In any case, the opening of borders for licit transnational flows enables the concomitant proliferation of illicit transnational ones, like in the cases of Southern Africa and Southeast Asia. We summarize the empirical evidence for Hypothesis 1 in Table 9.2, so we can draw several observations from it.

Table 9.1 *Comparing the cases*

Cases	Drug Trafficking	Arms Trafficking	Human Smuggling and Trafficking	Terrorism
US-Canada, 1994–2020	Yes	Yes (minor)	No	No
US-Mexico, 1994–2020	Yes	Yes	Yes	No
Northern Triangle, 1991–2020	Yes	Yes	Yes	No
Colombian borders, 1991–2020	Yes	Yes	Yes	Yes (until 2017)
TBA (Triple Frontier), 1991–2020	Yes	Yes	Yes	Yes
EU/Schengen, 1995–2020	Yes	Yes	Yes	Yes
EU/Western Balkans, 1995–2020	Yes	Yes	Yes	Yes
Western Balkans, 1995–2020	Yes	Yes	Yes	Yes
Israel-Egypt, 1982–2013	Yes	Yes	Yes	Yes
Israel-Egypt, 2013–2020	Yes	No	No	No
Israel-Jordan, 1994–2020	Yes	No	No	No
Southern Africa, 1995–2020	Yes	Yes	Yes	No
Southeast Asia, 1991–2020	Yes	Yes	Yes	Yes (particularly in "maritime" Southeast Asia)

Table 9.2 *The degree of physical and institutional openness of the peaceful borders*

Cases	Type of Border	Integrated Borders?	Hypothesis Validated?
US-Canada, 1994–2020	Open and controlled	Yes	No
US-Mexico, 1994–2020	Hard and fortified	Yes	No
Northern Triangle borders, 1991–2020	Open and porous (except Guatemala-Belize)	Yes	Yes
Colombian borders, 1991–2020	Open and porous (except Colombia-Panama)	No	Yes
TBA borders, 1991–2020	Open and porous	Yes	Yes
EU (Schengen regime, internal borders), 1995–2020	Open and porous	Yes	Yes (regarding terrorism and human smuggling/trafficking)
EU-Western Balkans, 1995–2020	Hard and controlled	No	No
Western Balkans, 1995–2020	Open and porous	To a limited extent	Yes
Israel-Egypt, 1982–2013	Open and porous	No	Yes
Israel-Egypt, 2013–2020	Hard and fortified	No	Yes
Israel-Jordan, 1994–2020	Hard and fortified	No	Yes
Southern Africa, 1995–2020	Open and porous (except Botswana-Zimbabwe)	Yes	Yes
Southeast Asia, 1991–2020	Open and porous (except Singapore-Malaysia)	Yes	Yes

First, the hypothesis holds for seven of the eleven cases analyzed in the book (the borders of the Northern Triangle countries of Central America; most of the Colombian borders except for the Colombia-Panama one; the TBA of Argentina-Brazil-Paraguay; the Schengen "internal" borders in the European Union; the borders among the Western Balkan states; the Southern African borders; and most of the Southeast Asian borders). Second, we disprove the hypothesis in the cases of the dyads involving US-Canada, Argentina-Chile, and Argentina-Uruguay, which sustain open and integrated border regimes while displaying relative low volumes of illicit transnational flows. Third, we demonstrate the reversed logic of the hypothesis in the cases of hard and fortified borders that effectively contain the occurrence of illicit transnational flows; that is, Israel-Egypt since the erection of a barrier in 2013, and Israel-Jordan. We argue that hard and fortified borders can be effective in stopping transnational flows, mostly transnational terrorism, but only in cases when there is no significant economic integration across the peaceful borders (see Avdan and Gelpi, 2017: 14–16, 25). In normative terms, fences, walls, and barriers are criticized in terms of an attempt to stop both legal and illegal flows of immigrants, by violating human rights. Fourth and conversely, in the case of the US-Mexican hard and fortified border, there is an occurrence and proliferation of illicit transnational flows. We register human smuggling, and drug and human trafficking from Mexico to the United States, as well as firearms that are smuggled from the United States to Mexico across their relatively sealed borders. We can explain this in terms of lack of governance and political willingness, as well as by the high level of economic integration and the economic rationale beyond these illicit transnational flows.

Fifth, in the case of the Schengen regime within Europe, porousness is the result of the EU's opening of the borders of and within their member-states by political choice, as the ultimate form of peace and integrated border regimes (but without becoming a federal state). The erasing of internal borders within Europe has facilitated transnational terrorism and illegal migration, whereas drug trafficking and human smuggling have taken place across the external borders of the EU. We postulate that the erasing of jurisdictional arbitrage within Europe has led to a decrease in transnational criminality in the medium and long terms as TCOs cannot take advantage of different legal systems across the European borders. At the same time, the external borders of the

Schengen regime with Southeast Europe, despite being hard and controlled, have been penetrated by illicit transnational flows, due to an economic rationale and lack of governance and political willingness on the part of several Western Balkan countries, as well as geopolitical and geographical conditions, such as topography.

Sixth, in terms of economic integration and the type of border regimes in the borderlands, we find most of the borders interdependent and/or integrated. These are the cases of US-Canada, US-Mexico, the Northern Triangle, the TBA area, Schengen, Southern Africa, Southeast Asia, and, to some extent, among the Western Balkan countries. Since economic integration facilitates the proliferation of both licit and illicit economic transactions, we identify a positive correlation between high levels of integration and illicit transnational flows in most of these cases (with the partial exception in the US-Canadian border, due to strong governance mechanisms in place).

Hypothesis 2: The Degree of Governance, Institutional Strength, and Political Willingness

H2: The less committed and able neighboring states are to control their peaceful borders in terms of governance, the greater the occurrence and proliferation of illicit transnational flows involving violent non-state actors.

The weak state–strong state continuum of governance, expressed by the degree of state autonomy, legitimacy, and institutionalization, is essential to evaluate states' capabilities and readiness to be physically present at the borderlands and control their peaceful borders. Unlike developed countries, we assume that many developing countries, catalogued as relatively weak and fragile, suffer from a governance deficit in the borderlands regarding their ability to regulate and control their national borders.

In contrast to strong states, weak states tend to show low levels of political institutionalization and governance, and high levels of corruption. According to this second hypothesis, gaps in governance across countries are prone to facilitate transnational crime, in accordance with the logic of jurisdictional arbitrage. This may lead VNSAs to take advantage and exploit the asymmetries in the levels of governance and in the exercise of the rule of law across the peaceful borders.

Moreover, the degree of governance is not just a function of capabilities and institutional strength. It also depends upon the political decision, volition, and willingness to address the illicit transnational flows, engaging in policies toward illicit and criminal non-state actors ranging from integration (basically a symbiotic criminal state), through alliance and enforcement-evasion, all the way to violent confrontation, through the militarization of the "war" against organized crime (see Barnes, 2017). For a myriad of reasons, ranging from political corruption, type of leadership, economic interests, interest groups and lobbies, and ideological and normative motivations, states that have the functional capabilities (like the United States), might lack the political willingness to cope with these transnational threats in effective ways. We summarize the empirical evidence for Hypothesis 2 in Table 9.3.

From reading Table 9.3, we can draw the following observations. First, we find that all the dyads involving weak states and/or significant governance gaps between strong and weak neighboring states experience illicit transnational flows, to varying degrees. Second, it seems that the logic of jurisdictional arbitrage is particularly pertinent in cases of significant gaps in governance across neighboring countries, as in the cases of US-Mexico, the Colombian borders, the TBA area, the EU-Western Balkan borders, Southern Africa, and Southeast Asia. Third, low levels of governance in weak states translate into poor regulatory structures that impede the efficient control of borders against the occurrence and proliferation of illicit transnational flows. Moreover, high levels of corruption in the police and other law enforcement agencies might hamper anti-criminal and counterterrorist efforts as well, as in the cases of the Northern Triangle, TBA (with an emphasis upon Paraguay), some of the Southern African borders (except perhaps for the borders of Namibia and Botswana), and the Golden Triangle in Southeast Asia.

Fourth and conversely, according to the reversed logic of this hypothesis, we identify a positive correlation between dyads involving relatively strong and functioning states and the absence of significant illicit transnational flows. These are indeed the cases of US-Canada, Brazil-Argentina, Israel-Jordan, Israel-Egypt after 2013, and Malaysia-Singapore. From the data assembled in Chapter 3, we can add the cases of Argentina-Chile and Argentina-Uruguay to this list as well.

Fifth, the case of the Schengen regime in the EU is a peculiar one. Despite the absence of jurisdictional arbitrage across its internal

Table 9.3 *The degree of governance and institutional strength of the neighboring states*

Cases	Institutional Strength/ Governance Gaps	Hypothesis Validated?
US-Canada, 1994–2020	Strong states, capacity and willingness	Yes
US-Mexico, 1994–2020	Mexico: functioning state, but not strong; USA: lack of willingness (regarding weapons and drugs)	Yes
Northern Triangle, 1991–2020	Weak states	Yes
Colombian borders, 1991–2020	Relatively weak and gaps of governance (Colombia-Venezuela; Colombia-Panama)	Yes
TBA borders, 1991–2020	Paraguay weak; governance gaps: Paraguay-Brazil and Paraguay-Argentina	Yes
EU (Schengen regime), 1995–2020	Mostly strong states	No (regarding terrorism and human smuggling)
EU-Western Balkans, 1995–2020	Governance gaps	Yes
Western Balkans, 1995–2020	Relatively weak; governance gaps	Yes
Israel-Egypt, 1982–2013	Egypt relatively weak; governance gaps	Yes
Israel-Egypt, 2013–2020	Egypt becoming stronger; still governance gaps	No
Israel-Jordan, 1994–2020	Relatively strong	Yes
Southern Africa, 1995–2020	Relatively weak; gaps in governance	Yes
Southeast Asia, 1991–2020	Some countries weak; gaps in governance	Yes

borders, Europe has experienced significant illicit transnational flows, including human smuggling and trafficking, and terrorism. Therefore, as for its external borders with the Western Balkan countries, we validate the hypothesis.

Hypothesis 3: The Prevalent Socioeconomic Conditions of the Bordering States

H3: *The poorer the socioeconomic conditions in the borderlands and/ or the broader the economic disparity across the peaceful borders of the neighboring states, the greater the occurrence and proliferation of illicit transnational flows involving violent non-state actors.*

An alternative explanation for the occurrence and proliferation of illicit transnational flows across peaceful borders underlines the importance of the political economy of the bordering states and their borderlands. According to this hypothesis, poor economic conditions, especially a disparity in the socioeconomic conditions across the borderlands, might facilitate the occurrence and proliferation of both licit and illicit transnational flows, mostly in the form of human smuggling and trafficking, parallel to legal flows of migration across borders. There is a supply-and-demand economic logic in place; in other words, relatively rich countries tend to function as economic magnets for both licit and illicit poorer economies, attracting migrants both legal and illegal. We summarize the empirical evidence for Hypothesis 3 in Table 9.4.

From reading Table 9.4, we can draw the following observations. First, we corroborate the validity of this hypothesis in all the relevant case studies, with the exceptions of the US-Canadian border, and the peculiar case of the Israeli-Jordanian border. In the latter case, despite the economic disparity between the neighboring countries, there has not been significant occurrence and proliferation of illicit transnational flows, due to their capabilities and political willingness in controlling their common border, as well as the lack of economic integration.

Second, we clearly demonstrate the logic of economic supply and demand. Illicit transnational flows travel from poorer countries to richer ones, in parallel to licit transnational flows, such as migration. The examples include flows from Mexico to the United States; from the Northern Triangle countries via Mexico to the United States; from Southeast Europe to Western Europe; from Africa and the Middle

Table 9.4 *The prevalent socioeconomic conditions of the neighboring states*

Cases	Socioeconomic Conditions	Hypothesis Validated
US-Canada, 1994–2020	Rich and developed countries	Yes
US-Mexico, 1994–2020	Huge economic disparity	Yes
Northern Triangle, 1991–2020	Poor countries	Yes
Colombian borders, 1991–2020	Poor and middle income; economic disparity across borders	Yes
TBA borders, 1991–2020	Paraguay poor; large disparity vis-à-vis Argentina and Brazil	Yes
EU/ Schengen, 1995–2020	Rich and developed countries	No
EU-Western Balkans, 1995–2020	Economic disparity between EU and Balkans	Yes
Western Balkans, 1995–2020	Economic disparity among countries in the region	Yes
Israel-Egypt, 1982–2020	Economic disparity between the countries	Yes (until 2013)
Israel-Jordan, 1994–2020	Economic disparity between the countries	No
Southern Africa, 1995–2020	Disparity between South Africa and many of its neighbors	Yes
Southeast Asia, 1991–2020	Disparity among countries in the region; many poor and low-income countries	Yes

East to the European countries; from Africa via Egypt (Sinai) to Israel; from Zimbabwe and Mozambique to South Africa; and from Laos and Myanmar to Thailand.

Conversely, we find positive linkages between high levels of socioeconomic development of the neighboring countries and the relative absence of illicit transnational flows. We assume that peaceful borderlands characterized by high levels of economic development and integration provide an environment less conducive to the occurrence and proliferation of illicit transnational flows, even though the borders might become open, porous, and even irrelevant as in the case of the Schengen regime in the EU. This linkage is relevant only in a few cases, including US-Canada and Argentina-Brazil in the Americas, Malaysia-Singapore in Southeast Asia, Slovenia-Croatia in Southeast Europe, and to a lesser extent across middle-income countries in Southern Africa such as South Africa, Namibia, and Botswana.

Mapping Patterns and Linkages among the Hypotheses

We can now map and delineate the main patterns drawn from the analysis of the different case studies, in line with the three hypotheses in Table 9.5, as follows:

First, the existence of international peace in many regions of the world – especially since the end of the Cold War – is a permissive

Table 9.5 *Validity of the hypotheses regarding the links between peaceful borders and illicit transnational flows*

Cases	Hypothesis 1 – Borders	Hypothesis 2 – Governance	Hypothesis 3 – Political Economy
US-Canada, 1994–2020	No	Yes	Yes
US-Mexico, 1994–2020	No	Yes	Yes
Northern Triangle, 1991–2020	Yes	Yes	Yes
Colombian borders, 1991–2020	Yes	Yes	Yes
TBA borders, 1991–2020	Yes	Yes	Yes
EU/Schengen, 1995–2020	Yes	No	No
EU-Western Balkans, 1995–2020	No	Yes	Yes
Western Balkans, 1995–2020	Yes	Yes	Yes
Israel-Egypt, 1982–2013	Yes	Yes	Yes
Israel-Egypt, 2013–2020	Yes	No	No
Israel-Jordan, 1994–2020	Yes	Yes	No
Southern Africa, 1995–2020	Yes	Yes	Yes
Southeast Asia, 1991–2020	Yes	Yes	Yes

condition, alongside globalization, that enables the occurrence and proliferation of illicit transnational flows across peaceful borders. Yet, neither international peace nor globalization are necessary or sufficient conditions for the occurrence and proliferation of these illicit transnational flows, which, in some cases, even predated the transitions from war to peace. Thus, to explain the variance in the occurrence of these illicit transnational flows we must examine the interactions among the type of borders, the political and institutional context, and the political economy of the borderlands.

Second, the only peaceful and open border that has not experienced a large occurrence of illicit transnational flows, with the exception of drug trafficking and some minor arms trafficking, is the US-Canadian one. Despite the high level of economic integration between the two countries, it seems that the high levels of governance and political willingness to monitor their border, in addition to their favorable economic conditions, have significantly reduced the scope of these illicit transnational flows.

Third, we have recorded four cases of "hard" peaceful borders, three of them hard and fortified – US-Mexico, Israel-Egypt after 2013, and Israel-Jordan – and experiencing contradictory instances of illicit transnational flows. In the Middle Eastern cases, the securitization of the borders and the lack of economic integration explain the effectiveness in their control, reducing (or even eliminating) illicit transnational flows altogether. In contrast, that is not the case for the US-Mexican border, despite the existence of a formidable barrier in about one-third of the borderlands, and the plans of Donald Trump to seal the border. That does not seem to be possible, due to the political economy of the borderlands, and the lack of political willingness of both countries to deal effectively with the threats posed by these illicit transnational flows in terms of domestic politics. Thus, the United States is reluctant to address the demand side regarding drug trafficking and the supply side regarding arms trafficking.

Fourth, weak states and gaps in governance, capabilities, and political willingness across neighboring countries provide a convincing explanation for the occurrence and proliferation of illicit transnational flows, in tandem with open and porous borders, and poor socioeconomic conditions and/or economic disparities across countries. In contrast, strong states enjoying high levels of governance sustain the capacity to deter, contain, and disable illicit transnational flows, but only if they also have the political willingness to do so. For instance, the convoluted example of the Schengen regime demonstrates that political realities are more complicated than our abstract theoretical formulations. In other words, whereas jurisdictional arbitrage within the Schengen regime does not generally operate as an incentive for transnational criminal activities, the EU still remains vulnerable to terrorism, illegal migration flows, and drug and weapons trafficking emanating from its external borders (i.e., Southeast Europe/Western Balkans), which can literally flow freely within and across its internal borders.

Fifth, a political economy argument regarding the logic of supply and demand, relying on poor economic conditions and economic disparity across peaceful borders, is very relevant to make sense of the linkages between peaceful borders and illicit transnational flows, the only exception here being the Israeli-Jordanian case. In contrast, rich and developed economies sustain the means and capabilities to thwart illicit transnational flows. This happens only if similar socioeconomic conditions prevail across the international borders, and the right political conditions are in place, including the political willingness to confront both the supply and the demand of illicit transnational flows, overruling domestic political considerations to ignore (if not openly collaborate with) criminal groups.

Sixth, in addition to these observable patterns as related to type of borders, political and institutional arrangements, and political economy, in the perusal of the eleven case studies we identified two additional elements that further explain the reality of peaceful borders and illicit transnational flows:

- *The geopolitical location of regions and subregions, as hubs for transnational illicit flows*: Notwithstanding the type of borders, political structures, and political economy, some of the countries and regions are prone, in geographic and geopolitical terms, to become areas of transnational crime, even if they are also zones of peace. These areas are what Stuart Brown and Margaret Hermann define as "black spots" (Brown and Hermann, 2020). In the Americas, that is the case of the Northern Triangle in Central America, the TBA in the southern cone of South America, and some of the Colombian borders. Elsewhere, we can recognize the Western Balkans as a gateway to the European Union, South Africa as the Southern African nexus to the world, and the Golden Triangle (the Mekong subregion) in Southeast Asia at the heart of Indochina.

- *The legacy of civil and intermestic wars*: The end of civil and inter-mestic wars usually generate a regional environment favorable for the promotion of peace and integration. That is the case for the end of civil wars in the Northern Triangle of Central America in the late 1980s and early 1990s and Colombia in 2016, the end of the wars in Southern Africa, the end of the Yugoslavian Wars in 1995, and the end of the Cambodian war in 1991. At the same time, we can identify also a legacy of violence and criminality lingering from these wars, which facilitates the proliferation of violence and crime. This takes place both domestically and transnationally in the form of arms trafficking and human smuggling and trafficking negatively affecting the efforts of postwar reconstruction and the building of effective governance mechanisms (see Andreas, 2011a and 2011b; and Shelley, 2018).

Policy Recommendations

Based on the aforementioned findings, we consider now what states and other non-state actors can do to cope effectively with the challen-ging reality of peaceful borders and illicit transnational flows. In this section, we suggest several policy recommendations, as follows:

- Be aware of the normative dilemmas of human security regarding peaceful borders and illicit transnational flows.
- Increase cooperation and develop effective mechanisms of govern-ance at all the possible levels: national, international (bilateral), regional, and global.
- Promote and prefer peace rather than war, but be aware of its potential unintended consequences.

Be Aware of the Normative Dilemmas of Human Security Regarding Peaceful Borders and Transnational Illicit Flows

There is an inherent normative dilemma between enhancing border security and the promotion of human rights. As Beth Simmons cogently argues, "Pressures for border security do not always sit easily alongside other values that have been central to the post [World War II] order," such as the promotion of human rights (Simmons, 2019: 3). Opening, softening, and demilitarizing borders might fit a Liberal and cosmopolitan rationale, though it might also create new security threats in the form of facilitating illicit transnational flows. On the one hand, the physical closure of borders, including the erection of barriers, fences, and walls, is an effective tool in coping with transnational terrorism (see Avdan and Gelpi, 2017). On the other hand, these draconian policy tools infringe upon the freedom of movement, create economic distortions in the borderlands, and utterly violate the human rights of potential migrants and asylum seekers, like in the case of the militarization of the US-Mexican border vis-à-vis migrants and refugees from Central America (see Dunn, 1996; and McKibben, 2015).

In a similar way, many researchers have argued that the militarization of the "War on Drugs" by the United States, Mexico, and Colombia, whether at the local, national, or regional levels, has exacerbated an already terrible record of violation of human rights in Latin America (see Bartilow and Eom, 2009: 97). Hence, the policy and normative dilemmas remain how to find a proper balance between these contending considerations of security versus the protection and promotion of human rights. This is particularly relevant in issues related to migration, both legal and illegal (see Simmons, 2019: 33–36).

Open the borders, but act to discourage transnational criminality. Usually, the call for a hard border regime in response to ever-rising transnational crime draws on incomplete and questionable evidence, if not racial (or even racist) stereotypes. Specialists in cross-border crime acknowledge that the hardening of borders for goods and peoples creates a lucrative market for organized transnational criminals, involved in drug trafficking, human trafficking and smuggling, and arms trafficking (Zielonka, 2001: 521). In our globalized world, there are different ways through which rich countries can help the poor ones: export capital to them; import products from them; or "import" the global poor from the Global South through the opening of borders and the encouragement of migration flows (Gilpin quoted in Doyle, 2000). Our policy recommendation emphasizes the last option in particular. This is the argument suggested also by Martín Arias Duval, the former Argentine official responsible for border control, and well as the famous Peruvian writer Mario Vargas Llosa (see Vargas Llosa, 2017), emphasizing the need for civil control and the demilitarization of peaceful borders.

Draw the distinction between certain illicit transnational flows and the activities of malign violent non-state actors. There is a tendency to bring together illicit transnational flows and the activities perpetrated by malign VNSAs. Yet, it is important to draw a distinction between some of the illicit activities perpetrated by malign transnational VNSAs (like ISIS, Hezbollah, *Maras*, and BACRIM) and illicit transnational flows that are unrelated to them, or even assisted by "benign" non-state actors. For instance, as we described in Chapter 4, there has been a mobilization of civil society groups across the US-Canadian border in 2017–19 to help irregular migrants and residents from the United States to cross illegally into Canada. Similar cases can be traced in the European continent, vis-à-vis the refugees coming from Africa and the Middle East.

In terms of human security, violent non-state actors might at times perform positive governance roles. There seems to be a considerable variation in the functions of governance when we assess the role of VNSAs through a different lens from that of the official statist perspective; for instance, by changing the official narrative to that of the local population(s) at the borderlands. Thus, if we employ a human security rather than a national security analytical lens, we find that some VNSAs, like the Jihadist groups in Sinai (Egypt), the FARC in Colombia, and even some drug cartels in Colombia and Mexico, have provided security and governance for the local population at the borderlands, when the state has been absent. For instance, one of the unintended consequences of the peace in Colombia in 2016 has been the disarmament and dismantling of the FARC as a military force in 2017, which used to provide governance functions at the Colombian border with Ecuador (see Idler, 2016: 3 and 2018). In this context, one of the trickiest policy questions we should address is whether local non-state actors' governance structures can and should be co-opted and incorporated into official structures of governance, at the municipal and national levels.

Address border security through a comprehensive and people-centered framework that addresses the root causes of border security. In some peculiar cases, like the Israeli-Jordanian border, securitization and the scarcity of transnational civilian contacts across the borders might limit the amount of illicit transnational activities. Yet, this is probably the exception to the rule. Instead, in many other cases where there are civilian contacts across the borders, a multiplicity of government and nongovernment stakeholders, including local and civil society groups should be involved in keeping peace and security at the border. This should include a comprehensive effort to enhance capacity building for marginalized communities and cooperation at the borderlands (see Idler, 2016: 3 and 2018). Thus, the argument here is that the state should be able to "occupy" and monitor its borders without exercising violence (see Pearce, 2020).[1]

Nowadays, we have to be aware that criminal, non-conflict armed violence is associated with many more direct fatalities than war in countries like Mexico, Brazil, Guatemala, Honduras, El Salvador, and South Africa. Hence, there is an urgent need to escape the trap of traditional interstate securitization, and to enhance the tenets of human security, being aware that most of the violence occurring in today's world is domestic and "intermestic," rather than international. The obvious policy recommendations refer to the improvement of socioeconomic conditions and governance in the borderlands mostly affected by poverty and inequality, underdevelopment, organized crime, drug trafficking, and gang violence, like the Northern Triangle in Central America and the Golden Triangle in Southeast Asia (see Runde and Schneider, 2019).

Furthermore, political leaders should be aware that their policies, whether they are effective or not (for instance, *mano dura* seems to have been counterproductive in the Northern Triangle and in Mexico), cannot completely eradicate criminal activities. States can reduce the amount and scope of criminal activities, both in the domestic realm and at the borderlands, but they cannot bring these activities to zero. This is due to the logic of arbitrage and the political economy of demand and supply, so we should consider crime from a political-economy rather than institutional perspective (see Finchkenauer and Albanese, 2014: 20; and Galeotti, 2011: 601). Hence, states have to learn how to effectively cope with criminal organizations, in a painful process of political trial and error alongside the continuum of criminal politics as elaborated by Barnes (2017), ranging from integration through alliance and enforcement-evasion, all the way to confrontation when necessary.

---

[1] We thank Marcos Alan Ferreira for his comments on this point.

Increase Cooperation and Effective Governance at All the Possible Levels: National, International, Regional, and Global

Confronting a collective good problem (in this case, a "collective bad," as epitomized by transnational criminal flows and transborder terrorism), requires better cooperation between neighboring states, as well as between them and the international community as a whole. The elements of international assistance and cooperation that are pivotal in achieving an effective response to illicit transnational flows include political and economic development, legal support, military and police assistance, intelligence sharing, and international cooperation against crime and terrorism (see Carlson, 1997).

Since transnational organized crime and terrorism are a byproduct of globalization, states should learn how to find global solutions instead of attempting to tighten the national controls (i.e., borders) to cope with a transnational, global problem. Yet, the inherent problem here, as recently illustrated in the outbreak of the COVID-19 pandemic, is that national leaders are still reluctant to cooperate beyond their national borders and to think in regional and even global terms, due to their national territorial entrapment and national(ist) tunnel vision of "methodological territorialism" (Kacowicz and Mitrani, 2016: 210–211).

To cope effectively with the challenges and threats posed by transnational drug trafficking, human trafficking and/or smuggling, arms trafficking, and terrorism, there is a growing need for international, regional, and even global or supranational cooperation, in line with establishing efficient mechanisms of regional and global governance. Yet, a lingering dilemma has to be resolved, in policy terms, between the need for regional and global governance to cope with transnational criminality, and the existing norms and practices of national jurisdictions and sovereignty that constrain such cooperation (see Gastrow, 2012).

Look for creative solutions regarding cooperation at and beyond the physical borders to cope with illicit transnational flows. Geopolitical scholars like Emmanuel Brunet-Jailly have advanced the intriguing idea that nowadays we witness "a-territorial processes." In his view, borders are embedded in individuals, goods, and/or information detached, perhaps by thousands of kilometers, from the physical international boundary line (Brunet-Jailly, 2017: 7). Hence, perhaps the most effect-ive way of combating illicit transnational flows might not take place at the border proper. For instance, the term "remote policing" illustrates the most efficient way of combating organized transnational criminal activities; this policing is not done at border checkpoints but in a broader zone or even within the entire territory of crime-exporting and crime-importing countries (Zielonka, 2001: 522). For instance, as we mention in Chapter 4, the US-Canadian Action Plan of 2011 estab-lished a Perimeter Security, accelerating the legitimate flow of people, goods, and services, and carrying out border functions physically away from the border itself.

In this context, the policy dilemma remains how to keep the borders open for licit flows, while controlling them in order to mitigate and repel illicit flows. Border security depends mostly upon trust, intelligence, and international cooperation, more than physical control of the border or at the border itself. Thus, most experts agree that improving police and security cooperation between neighboring countries is more efficient than investing in large numbers of border guards or in expensive surveillance tech-nology (Zielonka, 2001: 523).

Bilateral and regional cooperation in fighting transnational crime can consolidate bilateral and regional peace. At the bilateral level, out of the linkages between peaceful borders and the occurrence of illicit transnational flows, there might evolve a vicious–virtuous cycle lead-ing to the possibility of enhancing international cooperation. The logic is as follows: an initial transition from war to international peace has led to the establishment of peaceful borders, and to the subsequent occurrence and proliferation of transnational illicit flows. At the same time, crime and terrorism might lead to another unin-tended consequence of peace – this time positive. It might create the incentive for formerly hostile neighbors to cooperate and to improve their security ties in order to cope with these new transnational security threats, even if their transition to peace has remained at the most basic level of negative peace. This cycle has been clearly illus-trated in the evolving peaceful relations between Israel and Egypt from 1979 to the present.

At the regional level, there has been significant progress in advancing schemes of regional governance like that of the EU. Thus, the particular configuration of Europe as a "pooling of sovereignties" creates better conditions for regional cooperation and collaboration in coping with the challenges of transnational crime and terrorism in Europe and beyond. By contrast, in Southeast Asia, the firm normative commitment of the regional countries to a Westphalian understanding of national sovereignty, as epitomized by the "ASEAN values," poses a formidable obstacle for their international cooperation in facing these transnational and global security threats.

At the global level, many resolutions of the United Nations Security Council have called for international cooperation to fight against corruption, money laundering, and illicit transnational flows such as drug trafficking, human smuggling and trafficking, and arms trafficking. The problems raised by these illicit flows are not only local and binational, or even regional; they are inherently global. Thus, the solutions should be also transnational and global; they should be elaborated at the regional level in the form of existing or enhanced schemes of regional integration. States and other non-state actors should also consider the possible cooperation between schemes of regional governance and those (still very embryonic) of global governance. Yet, the expected results are far from evident or encouraging at this early stage.

While transnational organized crime groups pose a serious problem by themselves, only eliminating some of these groups will not necessarily stop all of the illicit transnational flows. For instance, national efforts have successfully diverted production or trafficking (of drugs and arms) to other countries, but as long as there is an economic logic of supply and demand, national law enforcement alone cannot resolve the problem due to the mechanism of jurisdictional arbitrage. Rather, bilateral, regional and global strategies, involving a wide range of both public and private actors, are required to establish mechanisms of regional and global governance to address the security challenges posed by these illicit transnational flows (see UNODC, 2010: vi). Ultimately, controlling, if not eradicating transnational crime is part of a larger project of global governance. Yet, globalization has progressed faster than our collective ability to regulate it through mechanisms of global governance, so the results remain so far very modest. This also relates to the lingering reluctance of nation-states to give up their sovereign and autonomy in favor of supranational schemes.

Promote and Prefer Peace Rather than War, but Be Aware of Its Potential Unintended Consequences

Are illicit transnational flows, including crime and terrorism, unintended consequences of peace? The basic premise in this book has been the proposition that in our age of globalization, peaceful relations among neighboring countries permit the occurrence and proliferation of illicit transnational flows, as potential *unintended consequences of peace.*[2]

As we showed throughout this book, domestic and international peace might render unintended consequences that must be theoretically and empirically addressed and understood; still, as a normative choice, we prefer peace to its alternative, war. Peace brings, establishes, and institutionalizes peaceful borders. These peaceful borders evolve from a preexisting situation, from a transition from war to negative peace, or from an upgraded movement from negative peace to higher levels of peace and integration. In some cases, international peace relates also to domestic peace, following the end of a civil war or an intermestic conflict.

As we reviewed in this book, there are both positive and negative consequences of peace, both intended and unintended. If we follow a Liberal path, we would expect and wish for the deepening of peace and the transition to a stable peace and a pluralistic security community. If we stick to a Realist path, we might be more skeptical and modest, sticking to the satisfaction with the status quo and the maintenance of a "negative" or precarious peace only, still preferable to violent conflicts and wars.

Among the potential negative unintended consequences of peace, we have to confront a complex reality that links the existence of peaceful borders with the occurrence and proliferation of illicit transnational flows, including criminal and terrorist activities, as new security challenges and threats in our complex and uncertain twenty-first century. These threats, in turn, might have a positive effect in bringing neighbors closer and together, to cooperate against these illicit transnational flows,

---

[2] We can define an *unintended consequence of peace* as an "effect of purposive social action which is different from what was wanted at the moment of carrying out the act, and the want of which was a reason for carrying it out" (Baert, 1992, 1905, quoted in Daase and Fiensendorsf, 2010, 9). Hence, there is a relevant gap between the original intentions and the potential and unexpected outcomes, which might be positive or negative, in normative terms.

thus strengthening their evolving peaceful relations. As for the end of civil wars, they might also lead to both positive and negative unintended consequences. Among the negative implications, we find a lingering legacy of armed conflict, proliferation of weapons, a postwar environment conducive to criminality, and even a governance vacuum left by guerrillas and terrorist groups that demobilized and turned occasionally into inept or inefficient political parties.

Conclusions

Traditional international norms that regulate border disputes and interstate relations are ill-equipped to address the new security threats of the twenty-first century, framed, among other issues, in terms of criminal and terrorist transnational flows. It is precisely the economic and political movements toward regional integration and globalization, as well as the outbreak and subsequent maintenance of international and regional peace across borders, which make the traditional military function of borders as an external boundary delimiting territorial sovereignty, relatively irrelevant. Yet, borders still matter and fulfill important functions in our age of peace and globalization.

In this book, we have developed and empirically examined an analytical framework in an attempt to better explain and understand the reality of peaceful international borders and illicit transnational flows. These peaceful borders reflect the continuation of the preexisting peaceful status quo; as well as the transitions from war to negative peace, and from negative peace to higher forms of peace and integration, including stable peace and the emergence of pluralistic security communities.

While international peace and economic globalization are permissive conditions, there is much more variance in the occurrence and proliferation of these illicit transnational flows across peaceful borders than in the existence of international peace, which is a parameter in many regions and continents of the world, including the Americas, Europe, Southern Africa, and Southeast Asia. The systematic empirical testing of the three hypotheses teaches us about the relevance of variables such as the degree of physical and institutional openness of the peaceful borders; the degree of governance, institutional strength, and political willingness of the neighboring states in controlling their borders; and the prevalent socioeconomic conditions of the bordering states.

In this book, we have examined dyads and regions of peace in the post–Cold War period for the last thirty years or so, although we still do not have a longue durée perspective. Moreover, we did not compare the different case studies to previous historical periods of war and conflict that also witnessed significant illicit transnational flows. After all, the starting point for this research has been a condition of peace, whether preexisting or new, and a temporal domain limited mostly to the last thirty years since the end of the Cold War. A comparison of transnational illicit flows from previous periods of war to our contemporary era of peace constitutes an agenda for further research, but it is well beyond the scope of this intellectual journey that took us across several regions and countries around the world in four different continents.

Assuming that we have not reached yet a stage of positive peace (see Galtung, 1975), then we have to be aware of the relevance of human security and new security threats in this age of prevalent international peace, globalization, and global issues such as climate change and the COVID-19 pandemic. People nowadays largely do not die from international wars, but mostly from civil wars, domestic and transnational crime and violence, and to a lesser extent, from pandemics and from terrorism. True international peace remains the ultimate permissive condition and framework of reference for today's international relations. Still, it is neither a necessary nor a sufficient condition to address the unfolding threats that make up our contemporary security landscape – domestically, regionally, and globally. In normative terms, by the end of the day, we still choose peace, even if it might carry sometimes unintended, even pernicious consequences.

References

Abbott, Philip K. 2004. "Terrorist Threats in the Tri-Border Area: Myth or Reality?," *Military Review*, 51–55.

Acharya, Amitav. 1998. "Culture, Security, Multilateralism: The 'ASEAN Way' and Regional Order," *Contemporary Security Policy* 19 (1): 55–84.

Acharya, Amitav. 2001. *Constructing a Security Community in Southeast Asia: ASEAN and the Problem of Regional Order*. London: Routledge.

Acharya, Amitav. 2004. "How Ideas Spread: Whose Norms Matter? Norm Localization and Institutional Change in Asian Regionalism," *International Organization* 58 (2): 239–275.

Acharya, Amitav. 2009. "The Strong in the World of the Weak: Southeast Asia in Asia's Regional Architecture," in Green, Michael J., and Gill, Bates (eds.), *Asia's New Multilateralism: Cooperation, Competition, and the Search for Community*. New York: Columbia University Press, pp. 172–192.

Acharya, Amitav, and Boutin, Ken. 1998. "The Southeast Asia Nuclear Weapon-Free Zone Treaty," *Security Dialogue* 29 (2): 219–230.

Aeby, Michael. 2018. "Peace and Security Challenges in Southern Africa: Governance Deficit and Lacklustre Regional Conflict Management," *Policy Note* 4: 1–6.

African Union. 2018. "Protocol to the Treaty Establishing the African Economic Community Relating to Free Movement of Persons, Right of Residence and Right of Establishment." Addis Ababa, January 29. au.int/sites/default/files/treaties/36403-treaty-protocol_on_free_movement_of_persons_in_africa_e.pdf.

Aguiar, José Carlos G. 2015. "Making Sense of Borders: Global Circulations and the Rule of Law at the Iguazú Triangle," in Jaskoski, Maiah, Sotomayor, Arturo C., and Trinkunas, Harold A. (eds.), *American Crossings: Border Politics in the Western Hemisphere*. Baltimore: Johns Hopkins University Press, pp. 189–203.

Alagappa, Muthiah. 1993. "Regionalism and the Quest for Security: ASEAN and the Cambodian Conflict," *Journal of International Affairs* 46 (2): 439–467.

Alexandrova-Arbatova, Nadia. 2004. "European Security and International Terrorism: The Balkan Connection," *Southeast European and Black Sea Studies* 4 (3): 361–378.

Amidror, Yaakov, and Lerman, Eran. 2015. "Jordanian Security and Prosperity: An Essential Aspect of Israeli Policy," *BESA Center Perspective Papers* 323, December 27.

Andreas, Peter. 2003. "Redrawing the Line: Borders and Security in the Twenty-First Century," *International Security* 28 (2): 78–111.

Andreas, Peter. 2005. "The Mexicanization of the US-Canada Border: Asymmetric Interdependence in a Changing Security Context," *International Journal* 60 (2): 449-62.

Andreas, Peter. 2009. *Border Games: Policing the U.S.-Mexico Divide*, 2nd ed. Ithaca, NY: Cornell University Press.

Andreas, Peter. 2010. "The Politics of Measuring Illicit Flows and Policy Effectiveness," in Andreas, Peter, and Greenhill, Kelly M., (eds.), *Sex, Drugs, and Body Counts: The Politics of Numbers in Global Crime and Conflict*. Ithaca, NY: Cornell University Press, pp. 23–45.

Andreas, Peter. 2011a. "Symbiosis between Peace Operations and Illicit Business in Bosnia," in Cockayne, James, and Lupel, Adam (eds.), *Peace Operations and Organized Crime*. London: Routledge, pp. 33–46.

Andreas, Peter. 2011b. "Illicit Globalization, Myths, Misconceptions, and Historical Lessons," *Political Science Quarterly* 126 (3): 403–425.

Andreas, Peter. 2015. "Illicit Americas: Historical Dynamics of Smuggling in the United States' Relations with Its Neighbors," in Jaskoski, Maiah, Sotomayor, Arturo C., and Trinkunas, Harold A. (eds.), *American Crossings: Border Politics in the Western Hemisphere*. Baltimore: Johns Hopkins University Press, pp. 153–170.

Andreas, Peter, and Duran Martinez, Angélica. 2015. "The International Politics of Drugs and Illicit Trade in the Americas," in Domínguez, Jorge I., and Covarrubias, Ana (eds.), *Routledge Handbook of Latin America in the World*. London: Routledge, pp. 376–390.

Andreas, Peter, and Greenhill, Kelly M. 2010. "Introduction: The Politics of Numbers," in Andreas, Peter, and Greenhill, Kelly M (eds.), *Sex, Drugs, and Body Counts: The Politics of Numbers in Global Crime and Conflict*. Ithaca, NY: Cornell University Press, pp. 1–22.

Andreev, Svetlozar A. 2004. "The Borders in Southeast Europe: Democratic Legitimacy and Security Issues in an Enlarging European Union," *Southeast European and Black Sea Studies* 4 (3): 379–398.

Aning, Kwesi, and Pokoo, John. 2017. "Between Conflict and Integration: Border Governance in Africa in Times of Migration," *International Reports* 1: 54–65.

Araia, Tesfalem. 2009. "Report on Human Smuggling across the South Africa/Zimbabwe Border," *Migrant Rights Monitoring Project*, Forced Migration Studies Program, www.refugeeresearch.net/node/277.

Arana, Ana. 2005. "How the Street Gangs Took Central America," *Foreign Affairs* 84 (3): 98–110.

Arias, Enrique Desmond. 2010. "Understanding Criminal Networks, Political Order, and Politics in Latin America," in Clunan, Anne L., and Trinkunas, Harold A. (eds.), *Ungoverned Spaces: Alternatives to State Authority in an Era of Softened Sovereignty*. Stanford: Stanford University Press, pp. 115–135.

Arieli, Tamar. 2012. "Borders of Peace in Policy and Practice: An Analysis of the Israel-Jordan Border Management," *Geopolitics* 17 (3): 658–680.

Arieli, Tamar. 2016. "Municipal Cross-Border Cooperation in the Post Conflict Environment: The Gulf of Aqaba," *Territory, Politics, Governance* 4 (3): 319–336.

Arieli, Tamar, and Cohen, Nissim. 2013. "Policy Entrepeneurs and Post-Conflict Cross-Border Cooperation: A Conceptual Framework and the Israeli-Jordanian Case," *Policy Sciences* 46 (3): 237–256.

Ariff, Mohamed. 1994. "Open Regionalism a la ASEAN," *Journal of Asian Economics* 5 (1): 99–117.

Arsovska, Jana, and Kostavos, Panos A. 2008. "Illicit Arms Trafficking and the Limits of Rational Choice Theory: The Case of the Balkans," *Trends in Organized Crime* (11): 352–378.

Ashour, Karim. 2016. "Egypt's North Sinai Post-2011 Revolution: The Nexus between Ungovernability Dimensions and Terrorism," MA Thesis in Global Affairs, Cairo: The American University in Cairo.

Astorga, Luis, and Shirk, David A. 2010. "Drug Trafficking Organizations and Counter-Drug Strategies in the U.S.-Mexican Context," UC San Diego: Center for U/S/-Mexican Studies. https://escholarship.org/uc/item/8j647429.

Atzili, Boaz. 2012. *Good Fences, Bad Neighbors: Border Fixity and International Conflict*. Chicago: University of Chicago Press.

Avdan, Nazli, and Gelpi, Christopher F. 2017. "Do Good Fences Make Good Neighbors? Border Barriers and the Transnational Flows of Terrorist Violence," *International Studies Quarterly* 61 (1): 14–27.

Bacon, Esther A. 2007. "Balkan Trafficking in Historical Perspective," in Thachuk, Kimberley (ed.), *Transnational Threats: Smuggling and Trafficking in Arms, Drugs, and Human Life*. Westport: Praeger Security International.

Baert, Patrick. 1992. *Time, Self, and Social Being: Temporality within a Sociological Context*. Belfast: Avebury Press.

Bagley, Bruce M. 2008. "Globalización y crimen organizado en Latinoamérica y el Caribe," in Solis, Luis G., and Aravena, Francisco R. (eds.), *Crimen*

Organizado en América Latina y el Caribe. Santiago de Chile: FLACSO, pp. 109–138.

Bagley, Bruce M., Rosen, Jonathan D., and Kassab, Hanna S. 2015. *Reconceptualizing Security in the Americas in the Twenty-First Century.* Lanham: Lexington Books.

Baker, Alan. 2012. "Sinai, the New Egypt, and the Egypt-Israel Peace Treaty," *JCPA Report* 12 (19).

Barajas, Ismael A., Sisto, Nicholas P., Ayala Gaytán, Edgardo, Chapa Cantú, Joana and Hidalgo López, Benjamín. 2014. "Trade Flows between the United States and Mexico: NAFTA and the Border Region," *Journal of Urban Research* 10.

Barak, Oren. 2017. *State Expansion and Conflict: In and between Israel/ Palestine and Lebanon.* Cambridge: Cambridge University Press.

Barak, Oren, and Cohen, Chanan. 2013. "The 'Modern Sherwood Forest': Theoretical and Practical Challenges," in Miodownik, Dan, and Barak, Oren (eds.), *NonState Actors in Intrastate Conflicts.* Philadelphia: University of Pennsylvania Press, pp. 12–33.

Bargent, James. 2019. "Ecuador: A Cocaine Superhighway to the United States and Europe," *InSight Crime*, October 30. insightcrime.org/news/a nalysis/Ecuador-a-cocaine-superhighway-to-the-us-and-europe/.

Bar-Joseph, Uri. 1987. *The Best of Enemies: Israel and Transjordan in the War of 1948.* London: Frank, Cass & Co.

Barnes, Nicholas. 2017. "Criminal Politics: An Integrated Approach to the Study of Organized Crime, Politics, and Violence," *Perspectives on Politics* 15 (4): 967–987.

Bar-Siman-Tov, Yaacov. 2000. "Israel-Egypt Peace: Stable Peace?," in Kacowicz, Arie M., Bar-Siman-Tov, Yaacov, Elgström, Ole, and Jerneck Magnus (eds.), *Stable Peace among Nations.* Lanham, MD: Rowman and Littlefield, pp. 220–238.

Bartilow, Horace A., and Eom, Kihong. 2009. "Busting Drugs While Paying with Crime: The Collateral Damage of U.S. Drug Enforcement in Foreign Countries," *Foreign Policy Analysis* 5 (2): 93–116.

Bartolome, Mariano C. 2002. "La Triple Frontera: Principal Foco de Inseguridad en el Cono Sur Americano," *Military Review*: 61–74.

Bar-Tuvia, Shani. 2018. "From Push-Backs to Pull-Backs of Asylum Seekers: The Role of International Norms in Bilateral Migration Control Cooperation," Unpublished Paper. Jerusalem: The Hebrew University of Jerusalem, Department of International Relations.

Bechev, Dimitar. 2006. "Carrots, Sticks, and Norms: The EU and Regional Cooperation in Southeast Europe," *Journal of Southern Europe and the Balkans* 8 (1): 27–43.

Bello, Paul O., and Olutola, Adewale A. 2020. "The Conundrum of Human Trafficking in Africa," *Online First*. www.intechopen.com/online-first/th e-conundrum-of-human-trafficking-in-africa.

Benítez Manaut, Raúl. 2018. "Mexico and Its Role in North America's Security: Between Terrorism and Organized Crime," in Suarez, Marcial A.G., Villa, Rafael D., and Weiffen Brigitte (eds.), *Power Dynamics and Regional Security in Latin America*. New York: Routledge, pp. 319–342.

Bergin, Paul R., Feenstra, Robert C., and Hanson, Gordon H. 2009. "Offshoring and Volatility: Evidence from Mexico's Maquiladora Industry," *The American Economic Review* 99 (4): 1664–1671.

Bergman, Marcelo S. 2006. "Crime and Citizen Security in Latin America: The Challenge for New Scholarship," *Latin American Research Review* 41 (2): 213–227.

Berryman, Philip. 1985. *Inside Central America: The Essential Facts Past and Present on El Salvador, Nicaragua, Honduras, Guatemala, and Costa Rica*. New York: Pantheon Books.

Berthelet, Pierre. 2017. "How the EU Is Making Major Strides Fighting Terrorism," *The Conversation*, August 27.

Bertrand, Jacques. 2019. "Nationalism, Religion, and Sub-State National Identity in Southeast Asia: Regional and Global Relevance," in Press-Barnathan, Galia, Fine, Ruth, and Kacowicz, Arie M. (eds.), *The Relevance of Regions in a Globalized World: Bridging the Social Sciences-Humanities Gap*. London: Routledge, pp.93–106.

Betz, Diana. 2009. "Human Trafficking in Southeast Asia: Causes and Policy Implications," M.A. Thesis. Monterey, CA: Naval Postgraduate School.

Bigo, Didier, and Guild, Elspeth. 2010. "The Transformation of European Border Controls," in Ryan, Bernard, and Valsanis, Mitsilegas (eds.), *Extraterritorial Immigration Control: Legal Challenges*. Leiden: Brill, pp. 252–273.

Birch, Melissa H. 2014. "Paraguay and Mercosur: The Lesser of Two Evils?," *Latin American Business Review* 15 (3–4): 269–290.

Blum, Constanze. 2016. "Transnational Organized Crime in Southern Africa and Mozambique," *FES – Peace and Security Series*. Maputo: Friedrich-Ebert-Stifung Mozambique.

Booth, Ken, and Vale, Peter. 1995. "Security in Southern Africa: After Apartheid, Beyond Realism," *International Affairs* 71 (2): 285–304.

Bosch, Shannon, and Maritz, Marelic. 2011. "South African Private Security Contractors Active in Armed Conflicts: Citizenship, Prosecution, and the Right to Work," *PIR* 14 (7): 71–125.

Bosworth, James. 2010. "Honduras: Organized Crime Gaining amid Political Crisis." Working Paper Series on Organized Crime in Central

America. Washington, DC: Woodrow Wilson International Center for Scholars, December.

Brafman Kittner, Cristina. 2007. "The Role of Safe Havens in Islamic Terrorism," *Terrorism and Political Violence* 19: 307–329.

Brands, Hal. 2010. *Latin America's Cold War*. Cambridge, MA: Harvard University Press.

Briscoe, Ivan Briscoe. 2008. "Trouble on the Borders: Latin America's New Conflict Zones," *FRIDE*, July 2008, pp. 1–9.

Broadhurst, Roderic. 2016. "Asia's Underworld: Transnational and Organized Crime in Asia," Working Paper, 1–14.

Broadhurst, Roderic, and Farrelly, Nicholas. 2014. "Organized Crime 'Control' in Asia: Experiences from India, China, and the Golden Triangle," in Paoli, Letizia (ed.), *The Oxford Handbook of Organized Crime*. Oxford: Oxford University Press, pp. 634–654.

Broadhurst, Roderic, and Le, Vy Kim. 2013. "Transnational Organized Crime in East and Southeast Asia," in Tan, Andrew T. H. (ed.), *East and Southeast Asia: International Relations and Security Perspectives*. London: Routledge.

Brosig, Malte. 2013. "The African Security Complex: Exploring Converging Actors and Policies," *African Security* 6 (3–4): 171–190.

Brown, Stuart S., and Hermann, Margaret G. 2020. *Transnational Crime and Black Spots: Rethinking Sovereignty and the Global Economy*. London: Palgrave Macmillan.

Brunet-Jailly, Emmanuel. 2007. "Introduction: Borders, Borderlands, and Porosity," in Brunet-Jailly, Emmanuel (ed.), *Borderlands: Comparing Border Security in North America and Europe*. Ottawa: University of Ottawa Press, pp. 1–17.

Brunet-Jailly, Emmanuel. 2008. "Cascadia in Comparative Perspective: Canada-U.S. Relations and the Emergence of Cross-Border Regions," *Canadian Political Science Review* 2 (2): 104–124.

Brunet-Jailly, Emmanuel. 2017. "Director's Report," in *Borders in Globalization: Exploring Borders in the 21st Century*. Victoria: Center for Global Studies, University of Victoria, pp. 6–9.

Bruns, Bettina, Happ, Dorit, and Zichner, Helga (eds.). 2016. *European Neighbourhood Policy: Geopolitics between Integration and Security*. London: Palgrave/Macmillan.

Bull, Benedicte. 1999. "'New Regionalism' in Central America," *Third World Quarterly* 20 (5): 957–970.

Buzan, Barry. 1983. *People, States, and Fear: The National Security Problem in International Relations*. Chapel Hill: University of North Carolina Press.

Buzan, Barry, and Waever, Ole. 2003. *Regions and Powers: The Structure of International Security*. Cambridge: Cambridge University Press.

Caballero-Anthony, Mely. 2018. "A Hidden Scourge," *Finance and Development* 55 (3): 18–21.

Cantor, David James. 2014. "The New Wave: Forced Displacement Caused by Organized Crime in Central America and Mexico," *Refugee Survey Quarterly*: 1–35.

Carlson, Thomas S. 1997. "The Threat of Transnational Organized Crime to U.S. National Security: A Policy Analysis Using a Center of Gravity Framework," *CSC*.

Carpenter, Ami. 2012. "Civilian Protection in Mexico and Guatemala: Humanitarian Engagement with Drug Lords and Gangs," *The Homeland Security Review* 6 (2): 109–136.

Cawthra, Gavin. 2010. *The Role of SADC in Managing Political Crisis and Conflict: The Cases of Madagascar and Zimbabwe*. FES – Peace and Security Series, No. 2. Maputo: Friedrich Ebert Foundation.

CBS News. 2018. "Illegal U.S. Northern Border Crossings up 142 Percent from Last Year," August 6, 2018, 7:49 AM. cbsnews.com/news/illegal-northern-border-crossings-on-the-rise/.

Centeno, Miguel A. 2002. *Blood and Debt: War and the Nation-State in Latin America*. University Park: Pennsylvania State University Press.

Cheatham, Amelia. 2019a. "Central America's Turbulent Northern Triangle," *Backgrounder*, Council on Foreign Relations, October 1. www.cfr.org/back grounder/central-americas-turbulent-northern-triangle.

Cheatham, Amelia. 2019b. "Mexico's Drug War," *Backgrounder*, Council on Foreign Relations, October 22. www.cfr.org/backgrounder/mexicos-drug-war.

Child, Jack (ed.). 1986. *Conflict in Central America: Approaches to Peace and Security*. London: C. Hurst and Co.

Chinchilla, Fernando A. 2011. "Open Borders of Latin America," *FOCAL*, July. www.focal.ca/publications/focalpoint/478-july-2011-fernando-a-ch inchilla.

Chipman, John, and Lockhart Smith, James. 2009. "South America: Framing Regional Security," *Survival* 51 (6): 77–104.

Chouvy, Pierre-Arnaud. 2013. "Introduction: Illegal Trades across National Boundaries," in Chouvy, Pierre-Arnaud (ed.), *An Atlas of Trafficking in Southeast Asia: The Illegal Trade in Arms, Drugs, People, Counterfeit Goods, and Natural Resources in Mainland Southeast Asia*. London: I. B. Tauris, pp. 1–28.

Clad, James, McDonald, Sean M., and Vaughn, Bruce (eds.). 2011. *The Borderlands of Southeast Asia: Geopolitics, Terrorism, and Globalization.* Washington, DC: National Defense University Press.

Clavel, Tristan. 2017. "Mexico Cartel Tied to Argentina's Second-Largest Cocaine Sting," *Brief, InSight Crime,* June 21. insightcrime.org/news/brief/mexico-cartel-tied-argentina-second-largest-cocaine-sting/.

Clunan, Anne L. 2010. "Ungoverned Spaces? The Need for Reevaluation," in Clunan, Anne L., and Trinkunas, Harold L. (eds.), *Ungoverned Spaces: Alternatives to State Authority in an Era of Softened Sovereignty.* Stanford: Stanford University Press, pp. 3-13.

Clunan, Anne L., and Trinkunas, Harold A. 2010. "Conceptualizing Ungoverned Spaces: Territorial Statehood, Contested Authority, and Softened Sovereignty," in Clunan, Anne L., and Trinkunas, Harold L. (eds.), *Ungoverned Spaces: Alternatives to State Authority in an Era of Softened Sovereignty.* Stanford: Stanford University Press, pp. 17–33.

Cocco, Emilio. 2017. "Where Is the European Frontier? The Balkan Migration Crisis and its Impact on Relations between the EU and the Western Balkans," *European View* 16: 293–302.

Cockayne, James, and Lupel, Adam. 2011. "Introduction: Rethinking the Relationship between Peace Operations and Organized Crime," in Cockayne, James, and Lupel, Adam (eds.), *Peace Operations and Organized Crime: Enemies or Allies?* London: Routledge, pp. 1–19.

Colburn, Forrest D., and Cruz, Arturo S. 2016. "Latin America's New Turbulence: Trouble in the 'Northern Triangle'," *Journal of Democracy* 27 (2): 79–85.

Colombia Government, Office of the Presidency. 2016. "Final Agreement to End the Armed Conflict and Build a Stable and Lasting Peace," November 24. especiales.presidencia.gov/co/Documents/20170620-dejacion-armas/acuerdos/acuerdo-final-ingles.pdf.

Commission to the European Parliament and the Council. 2017. *Reporting on the Follow-Up to the EU Strategy towards the Eradication of Trafficking in Human Beings and Identifying Further Concrete Actions.* Brussels: European Parliament.

Commission to the European Parliament and the Council. 2018. *Second Report on the Progress made in the Fight against Trafficking in Human Beings, as required under Article 20 of Directive 2011/36 EU on Preventing and Combatting Trafficking in Human Beings and Protecting its Victims.* Brussels: European Parliament.

Congressional Research Service, February 19, 2020. "Mexico: Evolution of the Mérida Initiative, 2007–2020." https://fas.org/sgp/crs/row/IF10578.pdf.

Cook, Philip J., Cukier, Wendy, and Krause, Keith. 2009. "The Illicit Firearms Trade in North America," *Criminology and Criminal Justice* 9 (3): 265–286.

Corrin, Chris. 2005. "Transitional Road for Traffic: Analyzing Trafficking in Women From and Through Central and Eastern Europe," *Europe-Asia Studies*, 47 (4): 543–560.

Council of the European Union. 2011. "Country Report on Mozambique," *Cordrogue* 44, June 20, Document 13591/10. register.consilium.europa. eu/doc/srv?=EN&f=ST%201170%202011%20INIT.

Council of the European Union. 2014. *Cordrogue 101*, December 17, Document 16959/14. data.consilium.europa.eu/doc/documents/ST-16959-2014-INT/en/pdf.

CQ, Chuckwu. 2017. "Transnational Organized Crime in the Former Yugoslav and Post-Soviet Republics: A Desk Review," *Journal of Political Sciences and Public Affairs* 5 (3): 1–7.

Craig, Tim. 2018. "Easing the Journey North," *The Washington Post*, August 3.

Cragin, Kim, and Hoffman, Bruce. 2003. *Arms Trafficking and Colombia*. Washington, DC: Rand.

Crocker, Chester A. 2019. *African Governance: Challenges and Their Implications*, Winter Series, Issue 119. Palo Alto, CA: Hoover Institution.

Croucher, Sheila. 1998. "South Africa's Illegal Aliens: Constructing National Boundaries in a Post-Apartheid State," *Ethnic and Racial Studies* 21 (4): 639–660.

Cruz, José Miguel. 2011. "Criminal Violence and Democratization in Central America: The Survival of the Violent State," *Latin American Politics and Society* 53 (4): 1–33.

Cruz, José Miguel. 2015. "The Root Causes of the Central American Crisis," *Current History* 114 (769): 43–48.

Cubel, Fernando M. 2016. "El Estado de la Seguridad en América Latina 2015," Instituto Español de Estudios Estratégicos, 01/2016.

Cuevas, Facundo, and Demombynes, Gabriel 2009. Drug Trafficking, Civil War, and Drives of Crime in Central America [unpublished].

Daase, Christopher, and Friesendorf, Cornelius. 2010. "Introduction: Security Governance and the Problem of Unintended Consequences," in Daase, Christopher, and Freisendorf, Cornelius (eds.), *Security Governance and the Problem of Unintended Consequences*. New York: Routledge, pp. 1–20.

Davis, Diane E. 2006. "The Age of Insecurity: Violence and Social Disorder in the New Latin America," *Latin American Research Review* 41 (2): 213–227.

DEA (Drug Enforcement Administration), Federal Bureau of Investigation (FBI), and Royal Canadian Mounted Police (RCMP). 2006. *Canada/US Organized Crime Threat Assessment*.

de Albuquerque, Adriana Lins, and Hull Wiklund, Cecilia. 2015. "Challenges to Peace and Security in Southern Africa: The Role of SADC," *Studies in African Security* Memo 5594: 1–4.

Delcour, Laure. 2010. "The European Union: A Security Provider in the Eastern Neighbourhood?," *European Security* 19 (4): 535–549.

Dentice, Giuseppe. 2018. "The Battle for Sinai: The Inside Story of Egypt's Political Violence," *Analysis* 322: 1–10, April.

Deutsch, Karl W., et al. 1957. *Political Community and the North Atlantic Area*. Princeton, NJ: Princeton University Press.

Devor, Camilla P. 2013. "An Analysis of the Continuation and Expansion of Transnational Organized Crime: The Case of Human Trafficking in Mozambique." Stellenbosch University, Faculty of Arts and Social Sciences, MA Thesis in International Studies.

Dienner, Alexander C., and Hagen, Joshua. 2010. "Introduction: Borders, Identity, and Geopolitics," in Diener, Alexander C., and Hagen, Joshua (eds.), *Borderlines and Borderlands: Political Oddities at the Edge of the Nation-State*. Lanham, MD: Rowman and Littlefield, pp. 1–14.

Dingott Alkopher, Tal, and Blanc, Emmanuelle. 2017. "Schengen Area Shaken: The Impact of Immigration-Related Threat Perceptions on the European Security Community," *Journal of International Relations and Development* 20 (3): 511–542.

Domínguez, Jorge, Mares, David, Orozco, Manuel, Scott Palmer, David, Rojas Aravena, Francisco, and Serbin, Andres. 2003. "Boundary Disputes in Latin America," *Peaceworks*, No. 50. Washington, DC: U.S. Institute of Peace.

Domínguez, Roberto. 2018. "Security Governance in Latin America," in Suarez, Marcial A.G., Villa, Rafael D., and Weiffen, Briggite (eds.), *Power Dynamics and Regional Security in Latin America*. New York: Routledge, pp. 53–76.

Dowty, Alan. 2012. *Israel/Palestine*, 3rd ed. Cambridge: Polity Press.

Doyle, Michael W. 1995. *UN Peacekeeping in Cambodia: UNTAC's Civil Mandate*. Boulder, CO: Lynne Rienner.

Doyle, Michael W. 2000. "Global Economic Inequalities: A Growing Moral Gap," in Wapner, Paul, and Riz, Lester Edwin J. (eds.), *Principled World Politics: The Challenge of Normative International Relations*. Lanham, MD: Rowman and Littlefield, pp. 79–97.

Drescher, Cedric. 2017. "Transnational Crime as a Threat to Peace in the 21st Century," Paper presented at the International Closing Conference of the Collaborative Research Center (SFB) 700 Governance in Areas of

Limited Statehood – New Modes of Governance? Berlin, Freie Universität, June 22–24.

Dube, Arindrajit, Dube, Oeindrila, and García-Ponce, Omar. 2013. "Cross-Border Spillover: U.S. Gun Laws and Evidence," *American Political Science Review* 107 (3): 397–417.

Dudley, Steven S. 2010. "Drug Trafficking Organizations in Central America: Transportistas, Mexican Cartels, and Maras," *Working Paper Series on U.S.-Mexico Security Collaboration Joint Project on U.S.-Mexico Security Cooperation*, coordinated by the Mexico Institute at the Woodrow Wilson Center and the Trans-Border Institute at the University of San Diego.

Dugas, John C. 2001. "Drugs, Lies, and Audiotape: The Samper Crisis in Colombia," *Latin American Research Review* 36 (2): 157–174.

Dunn, Timothy. 1996. *The Militarization of the U.S.-Mexico Border, 1978–1992*. Austin: Center for Mexican American Studies, University of Texas.

Duquet, Nils (ed.). 2018. *Illicit Gun Markets and Firearms Acquisition of Terrorist Networks in Europe*. Brussels: Flemish Peace Institute.

Duquet, Nils, and Goris, Kevin. 2018. *Firearms Acquisition by Terrorists in Europe: Research Findings and Policy Recommendations*. Brussels: Project SAFTE.

Dyer, Emily and Kessler, Oren. 2014. *Terror in the Sinai*. London: The Henry Jackson Society. henryjacksonsociety.org/wp-content/uploads/201 4/05/HJS-Terror-in-the-Sinai-Report-Colour-Web.pdf.

East Asia Forum. 2017. "Organized Crime Threatening the Development of Southeast Asia," August 25.

Eilstrup Sangiovanni, Mette. 2005. "Transnational Networks and New Security Threats 1," *Cambridge Review of International Affairs* 18 (1): 7–13.

Eisenberg, Laura Zittrain, and Caplan, Neil. 2010. *Negotiating Arab-Israeli Peace*, 2nd ed. Bloomington: Indiana University Press.

El-Anis, Imad. 2018. "Jordan in 2018: Too Stable to Fail, Too Small to Flourish," *Geographical Overview: Middle East and Africa*: 220–223.

Ellings, Richard J., and Simon, Sheldon W. (eds.). 1996. *Southeast Asian Security in the New Millennium*. London and New York: M.E. Sharpe.

Ellis, R. Evan, and Ortiz, Roman D. 2017. "Why the U.S. Can't Ignore Latin America's Security Challenges," *World Politics Review*, March 28, pp. 1–13. www.worldpoliticsreview.com/articles/21672/why-the-u-s-can-t-ig nore-latin-america-s-security-challenges.

Emmers, Ralf. 2003. "The Threat of Transnational Crime in Southeast Asia: Drug Trafficking, Human Smuggling and Trafficking and Sea Piracy," *UNISCI Discussion Papers* (May): 1–11.

Emmers, Ralf. 2005. "Regional Hegemonies and the Exercise of Power in Southeast Asia: A Study of Indonesia and Vietnam," *Asian Survey* 45 (4): 645–665.

ENACT. 2019. *Organized Crime Index Africa, 2019*. Pretoria: Institute for Security Studies.

Espach, Ralph, and Haering, Daniel. 2012. "Border Insecurity in Central America's Northern Triangle," *Report of the Regional Migration Study Group*, convened by the Migration Policy Institute (MPI) and the Latin American Program of the Woodrow Wilson Center. Washington, DC: Wilson Center.

European Commission. 2010. *Final Report: Cross-Border Cooperation in Latin America: Contribution to the Regional Integration Process, October.* Gronau, Germany: Association of European Border Regions. ec.europa.eu/regional_policy/sources/international/pdf/final_report_cbc_la.en.pdf.

European Commission. 2014. "The EU Explained: Borders and Security," November.

European Commission. 2018a. "Organized Crime and Human Trafficking." https://ec.europa.eu/home-affairs/what-we-do/policies/organized-crime-and-human-trafficking_en.

European Commission. 2018b. "EU-Counter Terrorism Strategy," *Consilium*, October 25. consilium.europa.eu/en/policies/fight-against-terrorism/eu-strategy/.

European Commission. 2018c. *Data Collection on Trafficking in Human Beings in the EU*. Lancaster: Lancaster University.

European Commission. 2019. "Report from the Commission to the European Parliament and the Council: Evolution of the 2015–2019 Action Plan on Firearms Trafficking between the EU and the South-East Europe Region." https://ec.europa.eu/home-affairs/sites/homeaffairs/faile s/what-we-do/policies/european-agenda-secretary/20190627_com-2019-293-commission-report_en.pdf.

European Monitoring Center for Drugs and Drug Addiction EMCDDA. 2017. "Cannabis Policy: Status and Recent Developments," February. Luxembourg: Publications Office of the European Union.

European Monitoring Centre for Drugs and Drug Addiction EMCDDA. 2018. *European Drugs Report 2018: Trends and Development*. Luxembourg: Publications Office of the European Union.

European Monitoring Center for Drugs and Drug Addiction EMCDDA. 2019. *European Drug Report 2019: Trends and Development*. Luxembourg: Publications Office of the European Union.

Europol. 2018. *TESAT: European Union Terrorism Situation and Trend Report*. Brussels: European Union Agency for Law Enforcement and Cooperation.

Eurostat Working Group on Crime Statistics. 2015. "Trafficking of Human Beings." *Statistics Working Paper.* https://ec.europa.eu/anti-trafficking/si tes/antitrafficking/files/eurostat_report_on_trafficking_in_human_ben gins_-2015_edition.pdf.

Fabricius, Peter. 2018. "Can Africa's Borders Really Become Bridges?," Institute for Security Studies, June 7.

Farah, Douglas. 2012. "Transnational Organized Crime, Terrorism and Criminalized States in Latin America: An Emerging Tier – One National Security Priority," Strategic Studies Institute, US Army War College, Carlisle Barracks, PA. www.strategicstudiesinstitute.army.mil.

Farrah, Raoul, and Muggah, Robert. 2018. "Europe Faces a 'Welcoming Crisis' When It Comes to Migration and Refugees. It is Not Fair," *Open Democracy*, December 20. opendemocracy.net/can-europe-make-it/Euro pe-faces-welcoming-crisis-when-it-comes-to-migrant/.

Felbab-Brown, Vanda. 2017a. "The Hellish Road to Good Intentions: How to Break Political-Criminal Alliances in Contexts of Transition," *Crime-Conflict Nexus Series* 7, April 2017.

Felbab-Brown, Vanda. 2017b. "The Wall: The Real Cost of a Barrier between the United States and Mexico," *Brookings Report*, August. brookings.edu/ essay/the-wall-the-real-costs-of-a-barrier-between-the-united-states-and-mex ico/.

Felbab-Brown, Vanda. 2017c. "Hooked: Mexico's Violence and U.S. Demand for Drugs," *Brookings Report*, May 30. www.brookings.edu/bl og/order-from-chaos/2017/05/30/hooked-mexicos-violence-and-u-s-de mand-for-drugs/.

Ferreira, Marcos Alan S. V. 2016. *Combate ao terrorismo na América do Soul: Uma análise comparada das políticas do Brasil e dos Estados U\nidos para a Tríplice Fronteira*. Curitiba: Editora Prismas.

Ferreira, Marcos Alan S.V., and Framento, Rodrigo de S. 2019. "Degradação da Paz no Norte do Brasil: O Conflito entre Primeiro Comando da Capital (PCC) e Família do Norte (FDN)," *Revista Brasileira de Políticas Públicas e Internacionais* 4 (2): 91–114.

FIDH, International Federation for Human Rights. 2019. "Guatemala: Recent Measures by Jimmy Morales' Government Are a Blow to the Institution of Democracy," *Statement, International Federation for Human Rights*, January 9. fidh.org/en/region/Americas/Guatemala/Gu atemala-recent-measures-by-jimmy-morales-government-are-a-blow-to.

Finckenauer, James, and Albanese, Jay. 2014. "Transnational Organized Crime in North America," in Albanese, Jay, and Reichel, Philip (eds.), *Transnational Organized Crime: An Overview from Six Continents* (Thousand Oaks, California: Sage), pp. 29–56.

Flemes, Daniel. 2009. "Regional Power South Africa: Co-operative Hegemony Constrained by Historical Legacy," *Journal of Contemporary African Studies* 27 (2): 135–157.

Flint, Colin. 2005. "Introduction: Geography of War and Peace," in Flint, Colin (ed.), *The Geography of War and Peace: From Death Camps to Diplomats*. Oxford: Oxford University Press, pp. 3–15.

Flores, Esteban. 2017. "Walls of Separation: An Analysis of Three 'Successful' Border Walls," *Harvard International Review* 38 (3): 10–12.

Florquin, Nicolas, Lipott, Sigrid, and Wairagu, Francis. 2019. *Weapons Compass: Mapping Illicit Small Arms Flows in Africa, January*. Geneva: Small Arms Survey, Graduate Institute of International and Development Studies.

Folch, Christine. 2012. "Trouble on the Triple Frontier," *Foreign Affairs* 91.

Fosson, Gabriel. 2011. "The Serbian Government's Response to European Human Trafficking," *European Journal of Crime, Criminal Law, and Criminal Justice* 19: 183–198.

Fuentes, Juan Alberto, and Pellandra, Andrea. 2011. "El estado actual de la integración en Centroamérica," *CEPAL Series Estudios y Perspectivas*, No. 129. Mexico DF.

Fund for Peace. 2015. "The Fragile States Index." Fragilestatesindex.org.

Gaddis, John L. 2005. *The Cold War: A New History*. New York: Penguin.

Gagne, David. 2015. "Latin America's Top Five Most Dangerous Border Regions," *InSight Crime*, January 29.

Galeotti, Mark. 2004. "Introduction: Global Crime Today," *Global Crime* 6 (1): 1–7.

Galeotti, Mark. 2011. "Global Crime: Political Challenges and Responses," *Perspective on Politics* 9 (2): 497–601.

Galicki, Zdzislaw. 2005. "International Law and Terrorism," *American Behavioral Scientist* 48 (6): 743–757.

Galtung, Johan. 1975. *Essays in Peace Research*. Vol. 1. Copenhagen: Christian Ejlers.

García, Mercedes. 2016. "Alliance for Prosperity Plan in the Northern Triangle: Not Likely a Final Solution for the Central American Migration Crisis," *Council on Hemispheric Affairs*, March 3.

Gardini, Gian Luca. 2006. "Making Sense of Rapprochement between Argentina and Brazil, 1979–1982," *European Review of Latin America and Caribbean Studies* 80 (2): 57–71.

Garzón, Juan Carlos, and Olson, Eric L. (eds.). 2013. *La Diáspora criminal: La difusión transnacional del Crimen Organizado y cómo contener su expansión*. Washington, DC: Wilson Center.

Gashaw, Tasew. 2017. "Colonial Borders in Africa: Improper Design and Its Impact on African Borderland Communities," in *Africa Up Close.* Washington, DC: Wilson Center, November 17.

Gastrow, Peter. 2012. "Catching Up with Transnational Criminal Organizations: Time for New Thinking," *IPI-Global Observatory.*

George, Alexander L., and Bennet, Andrew. 2005. *Case Studies and Theory Development in the Social Sciences.* Cambridge, MA: MIT Press.

Giatzidis, Emil. 2007. "The Challenge of Organized Crime in the Balkans and the Political and Economic Implications," *Journal of Communist Studies and Transition Politics* 23 (3): 327–351.

Gibas-Krzak, Danuta. 2013. "Contemporary Terrorism in the Balkans: A Real Threat to Security in Europe," *The Journal of Slavic Military Studies* 26 (2): 203–218.

Gibler, Douglas M. 2007. "Bordering on Peace: Democracy, Territorial Issues, and Conflict," *International Studies Quarterly* 51: 509–532.

Gibler, Douglas M. 2012. *The Territorial Peace: Borders, State Development, and International Conflict.* Cambridge: Cambridge University Press.

Gimenez Beliveau, Verónica, and Montenegro, Silvia (eds.), *La Triple Frontera: Dinámicas culturales y procesos transnacionales.* Buenos Aires: Espacio Editorial.

Giraldo, Jeanne, and Trinkunas, Harold A. 2015. "Transnational Crime," in Collins, Alan (ed.), *Contemporary Security Studies*, 4th ed. Oxford: Oxford University Press, pp. 384–399.

Gleis, Joshua L. 2007. "Trafficking and the Role of the Sinai Bedouin," *Terrorism Monitor* 5 (12).

Gleis, Joshua L., and Berti, Benedetta. 2012. *Hezbollah and Hamas: A Comparative Study.* Baltimore: Johns Hopkins University.

Goertz, Gary, Diehl, Paul F., and Balas, Alexandru. 2016. *The Puzzle of Peace: The Evolution of Peace in the International System.* Oxford: Oxford University Press.

Gold, Zach. 2014. "Security in the Sinai: Present and Future," *ICCT Research Paper*, March. www.occt.nl/download/file/ICCT-Gold-Security-In-The-Sinai-March2014.pdf.

Gold, Zach. 2015. "Sinai Militancy and the Threat to International Forces," *Strategic Assessment* 18 (2): 35–45.

Golding, Heather. 2002. "Terrorism and the Triple Frontier," *Woodrow Wilson Update on the Americas*, April, No. 4: 1–4.

Goldman, Ogen. 2011. "The Globalization of Terror Attacks," *Terrorism and Political Violence* 23 (1): 31–59.

Grabbe, Heather. 2000. "The Sharp Edges of Europe: Security Implications of Extending EU Border Policies Eastwards," *Occasional Papers* 13, The Institute for Security Studies, Western European Union, Paris.

Greenfield, Victoria A., Nuñez-Neto, Blas, Mitch Ian, Chang, Joseph C., and Rosas, Etienne. 2019. "Human Smuggling and Associated Revenues: What Do or Can We Know About Routes from Central America to the United States?," *Homeland Security Operational Analysis Center/Rand*, pp. 1–78. www.rand.org/pubs/research-reports/RR2852.html

Griggs, Richard A. 2000. "Boundaries, Borders and Peace-Building in Southern Africa: The Spatial Implications of the 'African Renaissance'," *Boundary and Territory Briefing* 3 (2): 1–30.

Gruszczak, Artur. 2017. "European Borders in Turbulent Times: The Case of the Central Mediterranean 'Extended Borderland'," *Politeja* 5 (50): 23–45.

Guerrero, Ramiro A. 2006. *Triple Frontera: Terrorismo o criminalidad?* Buenos Aires: Seguridad y Defensa, Gráfica Sur Editora.

Haftel, Yoram Z. 2010. "Conflict, Regional Cooperation, and Foreign Capital: Indonesian Foreign Policy and the Formation of ASEAN," *Foreign Policy* 6 (2): 87–106.

Hall, Tim. 2013. "Geographies of the Illicit: Globalization and Organized Crime," *Progress in Human Geography* 37 (3): 366–385.

Hammerstad, Anne. 2005. "Domestic Threats, Regional Solutions? The Challenge of Security Integration in Southern Africa," *Review of International Studies* 31 (1): 69–87.

Harkabi, Yeoshafat. 1972. *Arab Attitudes to Israel.* Jerusalem: Keter Publishers.

Harkabi, Yeoshafat. 1977. *Arab Strategies and Israel's Response.* New York: Free Press.

Hassanein, Haisam. 2018. "Beyond Security: Steps toward Warmer Egypt-Israel Relations," *Policy Notes*, PN 49, The Washington Institute for Near East Policy, pp. 1–49.

Hassner, Ron E., and Wittenberg, Jason. 2015. "Barriers to Entry: Who Builds Fortified Boundaries and Why?," *International Security* 40 (1): 157–190.

Hataley, Todd, and Leuprecht, Christian. 2013. "Organized Crime Beyond the Border," National Security Strategy for Canada Series, MacDonald-Laurier Institute, Canada, pp. 1–22.

Hawkins, Virgil. 2012. "An Overview of Peace and Security in Southern Africa," *Southern African Peace and Security Studies* 1 (1): 1–84.

Herbst, Jeffrey. 1989. "The Creation and Maintenance of National Boundaries in Africa," *International Organization* 43 (4): 673–692.

Hernandez, Carolina G. 1998. "Southeast Asia: The Treaty of Bangkok," in Thakur, Ramesh (ed.), *Nuclear Weapons-Free Zones*. London: Macmillan, pp. 81–92.

Hiemstra, Nancy. 2019. "Pushing the U.S.-Mexico Border South: United States' Immigration Policing throughout the Americas," *International Journal of Migration and Border Studies* 5 (1–2): 44–63.

Higonnet, Etelle (ed.). 2009. *Quiet Genocide: Guatemala, 1981–1983.* New York: Routledge.

Hokovský, Radko. 2016. "The Concept of Border Security in the Schengen Area," *Central European Journal of International and Security Studies* 10 (2): 72–93.

Holm, Hans-Henrik, and Sorensen, Georg. 1995. "Introduction," in Holm, Hans-Henrik, and Sorensen, Georg (eds.), *Whose World Order? Uneven Globalization and the End of the Cold War.* Boulder, CO: Westview Press, pp. 1–17.

Holmes, Jennifer S. 2002. "Terrorism, Drugs, and Violence in Latin America," *Latin American Research Review* 37 (3): 217–230.

Holmes, Leslie. 2009. "Crime, Organized Crime and Corruption in Post-Communist Europe and the CIS," *Communist and Post-Communist Studies* 42 (2): 265–287.

Holsti, Kalevi. 1996. *The State, War, and the State of War.* Cambridge: Cambridge University Press.

Hristov, Jasmin. 2014. *Paramilitarism and Neoliberalism: Violent Systems of Capital Accumulation in Colombia and Beyond.* London: Pluto Press.

Hübschle, Annette. 2010. *Organized Crime in Southern Africa: First Annual Review.* Pretoria: Institute for Security Studies.

Hudson, Rex. 2003. *Terrorist and Organized Crime Groups in the Tri-Border Area (TBA) of South America.* Washington, DC: Library of Congress.

Huntington, Samuel P. 1968. *Political Order in Changing Societies.* New Haven: Yale University Press.

Hurrell, Andrew. 1998. "Security in Latin America." *International Affairs* 74 (3): 529–546.

Idler, Annette I. 2014. "Arrangements of Convenience: Violent Non-State Actor Relationships and Citizen Security in the Shared Borderlands of Colombia, Ecuador, and Venezuela." Ph.D. Thesis, Oxford University.

Idler, Annette I. 2016. "Securing Peace in the Borderlands: A Post-Agreement Strategy for Colombia," Department of Politics and International Relations, Oxford University, pp. 1–7.

Idler, Annette I. 2018. "Preventing Conflict Upstream: Impunity and Illicit Governance across Colombia's Borders," *Defence Studies* 18 (1): 58–75.

Idris, Iffat. 2019a. "Serious and Organized Crime in Jordan," K4D: Knowledge, Evidence, and Learning for Development – Helpdesk Report, UK Department for International Development, pp. 1–13.

Idris, Iffat. 2019b. "Drivers and Enablers of Serious Organized Crime in Southeast Asia," K4D: Knowledge, Evidence, and Learning for Development – Helpdesk Report, UK Department for International Development, pp. 1–15.

InSight Crime's 2015. 2016. "Latin America Homicide Round-up." Thursday, 14 January 2016. www.insightcrime.org/news-analysis/insight-crime-homicide-round-up-2015-latin-america-caribbean.

International Crisis Group. 2008. "Guerrilla Groups in Colombia."

International Crisis Group. 2014. "Corridor of Violence: The Guatemala-Honduras Border," Latin American Report 52. Brussels: International Crisis Group.

International Crisis Group. 2018. "Mexico's Southern Border: Security, Violence, and Migration in the Trump Era," *Report No. 66, Latin America and the Caribbean*, May 9.

International Institute for Strategic Studies [IISS]. 2014. *Regional Security Assessment 2014: Key Developments and Trends in Asia-Pacific Security*. London: IISS.

International Labor Organization. 2014. *Thematic Labor Overview: Transition to Formality in Latin America and the Caribbean*. Lima: ILO, Regional Office for Latin America and the Caribbean.

Iroanya, Richard Obinna. 2018. *Human Trafficking and Security in Southern Africa: The South African and Mozambican Experience*. London: Palgrave/Macmillan.

Isacson, Adam. 2015. "Northbound 'Threats' at the United States-Mexico Border: What Is Crossing Today, and Why?," in Jaskoski, Maiah, Sotomayor, Arturo C. and Trinkunas Harold A. (eds.), *American Crossings: Border Politics in the Western Hemisphere* (Baltimore: Johns Hopkins University Press), pp. 130–150.

Israeli Anti-Drug Authority. 2011. www.antidrugs.org.il/english/pages/131 5.aspx.

Israeli Defense Forces [IDF]. 2014. "The Sinai Peninsula: The Weapons Transfer Threshold," *MSIS Information Report*, March.

Jácome, Francine. 2014. "Security Perceptions in Latin America," *Think Piece* 4: 1–5.

Jaskoski, Maiah. 2015. "The Colombian FARC in Northern Ecuador: Borderline and Borderland Dynamics," in Jaskoski, Maiah, Sotomayor, Arturo C., and Trinkunas, Harold A. (eds.), *American Crossings: Border Politics in the Western Hemisphere*. Baltimore: Johns Hopkins University Press, pp. 171–188.

Jaskoski, Maiah, Sotomayor, Arturo C., and Trinkunas, Harold A. 2015a. "Borders in the Americas: Theories and Realities," in Jaskoski, Maiah, Sotomayor, Arturo C., and Trinkunas, Harold A. (eds.), *American Crossings: Border Politics in the Western Hemisphere*. Baltimore: Johns Hopkins University Press, pp. 1–15.

Jaskoski, Maiah, Sotomayor, Arturo C., and Trinkunas, Harold A. 2015b. "Conclusions," in Jaskoski, Maiah, Sotomayor, Arturo C., and Trinkunas, Harold A. (eds.), *American Crossings: Border Politics in the Western Hemisphere*. Baltimore: Johns Hopkins University Press, pp. 205–225.

Jimenez Aguilar, Carlos M., and Thoene, Ulf. 2019. "Frontier Development Policy and Local Governance in South America," *Territory, Politics, Governance*, http://doi.org/10.1080/2162267.2019.1612271.

Johnson, Tim. 2011. "Violent Mexican Drug Gang, Zetas, Taking Control of Migrant Smuggling," *Miami Herald*, August 11.

Joll, James. 1976. *Europe since 1870*. Harmondsworth, Middlessex: Penguin Books.

Jones, David M., and Smith, Michael L. R. 2007. "Making Process, Not Progress: ASEAN and the Evolving East Asian Regional Order," *International Security* 32 (1): 148–184.

The Jordan Times. 2018. "Drug Trafficking: A Regional Menace," May 12. jordantimes.com/opinion/editorial/drug-trafficking-regional-menace.

Judt, Tony. 2005. *Postwar: A History of Europe since 1945*. London: Penguin Press.

Kacowicz, Arie M. 1994. *Peaceful Territorial Change*. Columbus: University of South Carolina Press.

Kacowicz, Arie M. 1996. "The Process of Reaching Peaceful Territorial Change: The Arab-Israeli Conflict in Comparative Perspective," *The Journal of Interdisciplinary History* 27 (2): 215–245.

Kacowicz, Arie M. 1998. *Zones of Peace in the Third World: South America and West Africa in Comparative Perspective*. Albany: SUNY Press.

Kacowicz, Arie M. 2000. "Stable Peace in South America: The ABC Triangle, 1979–1999," in Kacowicz, Arie M., Bar-Siman-Tov, Yaacov, Elgstrom, Ole, and Jerneck. Magnus (eds.), *Stable Peace among Nations*. Lanham, MD: Rowman and Littlefield, pp. 200–219.

Kacowicz, Arie M. 2005. *The Impact of Norms in International Society: The Latin American Experience, 1881–2001*. Notre Dame, IN: University of Notre Dame Press.

Kacowicz, Arie M. 2013. *Globalization and the Distribution of Wealth: The Latin American Experience, 1982–2008*. Cambridge: Cambridge University Press.

Kacowicz, Arie M. 2015. "Regional Peace and Unintended Consequences: The Peculiar Case of the Tri-Border Area of Argentina, Brazil, and Paraguay," in

Jaskoski, Maiah, Sotomayor, Arturo C., and Trinkunas, Harold A. (eds.), *American Crossings: Border Politics in the Western Hemisphere*. Baltimore: Johns Hopkins University Press, pp. 89–108.

Kacowicz, Arie M., and Bar-Siman-Tov, Yaacov. 2000. "Stable Peace: A Conceptual Framework," in Kacowicz, Arie M., Bar-Siman-Tov, Yaacov, Elgstrom, Ole, and Jerneck. Magnus (eds.), *Stable Peace among Nations*. Lanham, MD: Rowman and Littlefield, pp. 11–35.

Kacowicz, Arie M., Lacovsky, Exequiel, and Wajner, Daniel F. 2020. "Peaceful Borders and Illicit Transnational Flows in the Americas," *Latin American Research Review* 55 (4): 727–741.

Kacowicz, Arie M., and Mares, David R. 2016. "Security Studies and Security in Latin America: The First 200 Years," in Mares, David R., and Kacowicz, Arie M. (eds.), *Routledge Handbook of Latin American Security* (London: Routledge), pp. 11–29.

Kacowicz, Arie M., and Mitrani, Mor. 2016. "Why Don't We Have Coherent Theories of International Relations and Globalization?," *Global Governance* 22 (2): 189–208.

Kahler, Miles. 2006. "Territoriality and Conflict in an Era of Globalization," in Kahler, Miles, and Walter, Barbara D. (eds.), *Territoriality and Conflict in an Era of Globalization*. Cambridge: Cambridge University Press, pp. 1–21.

Karawan, Ibrahim A. 2002. "Identity and Foreign Policy: The Case of Egypt," in Telhami, Shibley, and Barnett, Michael (eds.), *Identity and Foreign Policy in the Middle East*. Ithaca, NY: Cornell University Press, pp. 155–168.

Kashgari, Tamim K. 2011. "Transjordan and Israel: Examining the Foundations of a Special Relationship," *Inquiries* 3 (3): 1/1. inquiriesjournal.com/articles/411/Transjordan-and-israel-examining-the-foundations-of-a-special-relationship.

Kessler, Gabriel. 2011. "Crimen organizado en América Latina y el Caribe: Ejes de debate sobre narcotráfico, tráfico de arms y de personas," *Cuadernos de seguridad* 14.

Khadiagala, Gilbert M., and Lyons, Terrence. 2001. "Foreign Policy Making in Africa: An Introduction," in Khadiagala, Gilbert M., and Lyons, Terrence (eds.), *African Foreign Policies: Power and Process*. Boulder, CO: Lynne Rienner, pp. 41–65.

Khoo, Nicholas. 2015. "The ASEAN Security Community: A Misplaced Consensus," *Journal of Asian Security and International Affairs* 2 (2): 180–199.

Killias, Martin. 1993. "Will Open Borders Result in More Crime?," *European Journal on Criminal Policy and Research* 1 (3): 7–9.

Kin Wah, Chin. 1997. "ASEAN: The Long Road to 'One Southeast Asia,'" *Asian Journal of Political Science* 5 (1): 1–19.

Kligman, Gail, and Limoncelli, Stephanie. 2005. "Trafficking Women after Socialism: From, To, and Through Eastern Europe," *Social Politics: International Studies in Gender, State, and Society* 12 (1): 118–140.

Kliot, Nurit. 1995. "The Evolution of the Egypt-Israel Boundary: From Colonial Foundations to Peaceful Borders," *Boundary and Territory Briefing* 1 (8): 1–21.

Kmezić, Marko. 2020. "Recalibrating the EU's Approach to the Western Balkans," *European View* 19 (1): 1–8.

Kopinski, Dominik, and Polus, Andrzej. 2012. "Is Botswana Creating a New Gaza Strip? An Analysis of the 'Fence Discourse,'" in Udelsmann Rodrigues, Cristina, and Tomàs, Jordi (eds.), *Crossing African Borders: Migration and Mobility*. Lisbon: Centro de Estudos Internacionais, pp. 98–111.

Krasner, Stephen D. 1999. *Sovereignty: Organized Hypocrisy*. Princeton, NJ: Princeton University Press.

Krasniki, Kole. 2016. "Organized Crime in the Balkans," *European Scientific Journal* 12 (19): 204–220.

Labrador, Rocio C., and Renwick, Danielle. 2018. "Central America's Violent Northern Triangle," *Backgrounder*, Council on Foreign Relations, June 26.

Lacovsky, Exequiel. 2019. "Assessing the Emergence of Nuclear Weapons Free Zones: The Latin American Non-Proliferation Experience in Comparative Perspective," Ph.D. Thesis, Jerusalem: Hebrew University of Jerusalem, Department of International Relations.

Lacovsky, Exequiel. 2021. *Nuclear Weapons Free Zones: A Comparative Perspective*. London: Routledge.

Lakhani, Nina, and Tirado, Erubiel. 2016. "Mexico's War on Drugs: What Has It Achieved and How Is the US Involved?," *The Guardian*, December 8.

Laqueur, Walter, and Rubin, Barry (eds.), *The Israel-Arab Reader: A Documentary History of the Middle East Conflict*. New York: Penguin, pp. 338–341.

Latin American Commission on Drugs and Democracy. 2009. *Drug and Democracy: Toward a Paradigm Shift*.

Laub, Zachary. 2013. "Egypt's Sinai Peninsula and Security," *Council on Foreign Relations Backgrounder*.

Leifer, Michael. 1999. "The ASEAN Peace Process: A Category Mistake," *The Pacific Review* 12 (1): 25–38.

Leiken, Robert S., and Rubin, Barry (eds.). 1987. *The Central American Crisis Reader: The Essential Guide to the Most Controversial Foreign Policy Issue Today*. New York: Summit Books.

Lesser, Gabriel, and Batalova, Jeanne. 2017. "Central American Immigrants in the United States," *Migration Information Source*, April 5. www.migrationpolicy.org/article/central-american-immigrants-united-states.

Levitz, Stephanie. 2020. "More than 16,000 People Nabbed by RCMP between Border Crossings inn 2019," *CTVNews*, January 16. ctvnews.ca/Canada/more-than-16000-people-nabbed-by-rcmp-between-border-crossings-in-2019-1.4770504.

Lewis, Martin W. 2011. "International Land Borders: Hard and Soft," *Geocurrents, May* 11, pp. 1–9.

Lindstrom, Nicole. 2004. "Regional Sex Trafficking in the Balkans," *Problems of Post-Communism* 51 (3): 45–52.

Lodge, Juliet. 1993. "Preface: The Challenge of the Future," in Lodge, Juliet (ed.), *The European Community and the Challenge of the Future*. New York: St. Martin's Press, pp. xiii–xxvi.

London, Yaron. 2019. "It's the Drugs, Stupid?," *Opinion*, YNET, February 26. www.ynetnews.com/articles/0,7340,L-5469687,00.html

Looft, Christopher. 2012. "Are Salvadoran 'Maras' Infiltrating Belize?," *InSight Crime Brief*, July 19. insightcrime/org/news/brief/are-salvadoran-maras-infiltrating-belize/.

López-Dóriga, Elena. 2018. "Refugee Crisis: The Divergence between the European Union and the Visegrad Group," Essay, December 6. Navarra: Universidad de Navarra, Global Affairs-Strategic Studies. unav.edu/web/global-affairs-detalle/-/blogs/refugee-crisis-the-divergence-between-the-european-union-and-the-visegrad-group.

Lozano, Daniel. 2018. "Frontera caliente: El drama del éxodo venezolano tiene en vilo a la región," *La Nación*, February 12.

Mahbubani, Kishore, and Sng, Jeffery. 2017. *The ASEAN Miracle: A Catalyst for Peace*. Singapore: Ridge Books and NUS Press.

Makarenko, Tamara. 2004. "The Crime-Terror Continuum: Tracing the Interplay between Transnational Organized Crime and Terrorism," *Global Crime* 6 (1): 129–145.

Mann, Mindy. 2013. "The Materialization of Human Trafficking in the Middle East and Impediments to its Eradication," *Human Rights and Human Welfare*: 84–98. www.du.edu/korbel/hrhw/researchdigest/mena/Trafficking.pdf

Manwaring, Max G. 2005. *Street Gangs: The New Urban Insurgency*. Carlisle, PA: Institute of Strategic Studies, Army War College.

Manwaring, Max G. 2007. *A Contemporary Challenge to State Sovereignty: Gangs and Other Illicit Transnational Criminal Organizations in Central America, El Salvador, Mexico, Jamaica, and Brazil*. Carlisle, PA: Institute of Strategic Studies, U.S. Army War College.

Manz, Beatriz. 2008. "Central America (Guatemala, El Salvador, Honduras, Nicaragua): Patterns of Human Rights Violations," *Writenet/Refworld*, August. refworld.org/pdfid/48ad1eb72.pdf.

Marcella, Gabriel. 2008. *War without Borders: The Colombia-Ecuador Crisis of 2008*. Carlisle, PA: Institute of Strategic Studies, US Army War College.

Marcella, Gabriel. 2013. "The Transformation of Security in Latin America: A Cause for Common Action," *Journal of International Affairs* 66 (2): 67–82.

Mares, David R. 2016. "The United States' Impact on Latin American Security Environment: The Complexities of Power Disparity," in Mares, David R., and Kacowicz, Arie M. (eds.), *Routledge Handbook of Latin American Security*. London: Routledge, pp. 302–312.

Mares, David R. 2019. "Violence, Markets, and Drugs: Explaining the Variation in Levels of Drug-Related Violence," unpublished manuscript.

Mares, David R., and Arie M. Kacowicz. 2016. "Introduction," in Mares, David R., and Kacowicz, Arie M. (eds.), *Routledge Handbook of Latin American Security*. London: Routledge, pp. 1–7.

Marinova, Nadedja K., and James, Patrick. 2012. "The Tragedy of Human Trafficking: Competing Theories and European Evidence," *Foreign Policy Analysis* 8 (3): 231–253.

Marteu, Elisabeth. 2018. "Israel and the Jihadi Threat," *Survival* 60 (1): 85–106.

Martin, Guy. 2011. "Illegal Migration and the Impact of Cross Border Crime," *Defence Web*. March 9. www.defenceweb.co.za/security/border-security/feature-illegal-migration-and-the-impact-of-cross-border-crime/

Martínez, Oscar J. 1994. "The Dynamics of Border Interaction: New Approaches to Border Analysis," in Schofield, Clive H. (ed.), *Global Boundaries: World Boundaries*, Vol. 1. New York: Routledge, pp. 1–15.

Martínez, Oscar J. 2012. "Men Who Sold Women: Human Trafficking Networks in Central America," in Dudley, Steven (ed.), The Mafia's Shadow: Slavery in Latin America, *InSight Crime, Investigation and Analysis of Organized Crime*, pp. 8–35. insightcrime.org/images/PDFs/2 016/The_Mafias_Shadow_Slavery.pdf.

Massey, Douglas S., Durand, Jorge, and Pren, Karen A, 2016. "Why Border Enforcement Backfired," *American Journal of Sociology* 121 (5): 1557–1600.

Masweneng, Kgaugelo. 2018. "Human Trafficking is Silently Tearing South Africa Apart, Experts Say," *Times Live*, May 30.

McCullough, J. J. 2018. "When It Comes to the Border, Trump Won't Make Canada Great Again," *The Washington Post*, May 31.

McDermott, Jeremy. 2014. "The Urabeños – The Criminal Hybrid," *InSight Crime – Investigations*, May 2. insightcrime.org/investigations/the-urabenos-the-criminal-hybrid/.

McDougal, Topher L., Shrink, David A., Muggah, Robert, and Patterson, John H. 2015. "The Way of the Gun: Estimating Firearms Trafficking across the U.S.-Mexico Border," *Journal of Economic Geography* 15 (2): 297–327.

McKibben, Cameron. 2015. "NAFTA and Drug Trafficking: Perpetuating Violence and the Illicit Supply Chain," *Council on Hemispheric Affairs*, March 20, pp. 1–13.

Medeiros Filho, Oscar. 2017. "A South American Defense Structure: Problems and Prospects," *Contexto Internacional* 39 (3): 673–689.

Mejía, Sonia A. 2014. "Estado y crimen organizado en América Latina: Posibles relaciones y complicidades," *Revista Política y Estrategia* 124 (2): 73–107.

MEMO [Middle East Monitor]. 2019. "Israel to Start Exporting Gas to Jordan, Egypt within Weeks," December 4. middleeastmonitor/com/201 91204-israel-to-start-exporting-gas-to-jordan-egypt-within-weeks/.

MFO. 2019. "MFO Troop Contributions." mfo.org/en/contingents.

Mesa, Manuela, and Moorhouse, Emmy. 2008. *Claves para entender la violencia de carácter transnacional en Centroamérica*, Documentos de Trabajo # 6, CEIPAZ, Madrid, December.

Migdal, Joel S. 1988. *Strong Societies and Weak States: State-Society Relations and State Capabilities in the Third World*. Princeton, NJ: Princeton University Press.

Milian, Jairo Hernandez. 2008. "El crimen organizado en América Latina y el Caribe: Mapeo del caso centroamericano." Paper presented in the Mexico DF: Seminario Internacional. Mexico, DF: Friedrich Ebert.

Miller, Benjamin. 2007. *States, Nations, and the Great Powers: The Sources of Regional War and Peace*. Cambridge: Cambridge University Press.

Millet, Richard. 2007. "Weak States and Porous Borders: Smuggling along the Andean Ridge in Transnational Threats," in Thachuk, Kimberley L. (ed.), *Transnational Threats: Smuggling and Trafficking in Arms, Drugs, and Human Life*. Westport, CT: Greenwood Publishing Group.

Moloney, Anastasia. 2017. "Venezuela Crisis Forces Women to Sell Sex in Colombia, Fuels Slavery Risk," *Reuters*, June 6.

Montes, Juan. 2020. "Tensions Rise at Mexico's Southern Border with Guatemala," *The Wall Street Journal*, January 20. wsk/com/articles/ten sions-rise-at-mexicos-southern-border-with-guatemala-115795633320.

Moravcsik, Andrew. 1998. *The Choice for Europe: Social Purpose and State Power from Messina to Maastricht*. Ithaca, NY: Cornell University Press.

Moustakis, Fotios. 2004. "Soft Security Threats in the New Europe: The Case of the Balkan Region," *European Security* 13 (1): 139–156.

Muggah, Robert, and Diniz, Gustavo. 2013. "Securing the Borders: Brazil's 'South America First' Approach to Transnational Organized Crime," *Strategic Papers* 5, Igarapé Institute, pp. 1–28.

Mundt, Marcia D. 2019. "El Salvador's New President Must Tackle Crime, Unemployment, and Migration – but Nation Is Hopeful," *The Conversation*, February 25. theconversation.com/el-salvadors-new-president-must-tackle-crime-unemployment-and-migration-but-nation-is-hopeful-111499

Mutume, Gumisai. 2007. "Organized Crime Targets Weak African States," *Africa Renewal* 21 (2): 3.

Naím, Moises. 2005. *Illicit: How Smugglers, Traffickers, and Copycats are Hijacking the Global Economy*. New York: Anchor Books.

Nanda, Ved P. 1990. "The Validity of United States Intervention in Panama under International Law," *American Journal of International Law* 84 (2): 494–503.

Narine, Shaun. 2018. *The New ASEAN in Asia Pacific and Beyond*. Boulder, CO: Lynne Rienner.

National Security Council (US Government). 2013. "Transnational Organized Crime: A Growing Threat to National and International Security." www.whitehouse.gov/administration/eop/nsc/transnational-crime/threat; accessed on August 26, 2013.

Ndebele, Thuthukani, Lebone, Kerwin, and Cronje, Frans. 2011. "Broken Blue Line: The Involvement of the South African Police Force in Serious and Violent Crime in South Africa," *Unit for Risk Analysis*, South African Institute of Race Relations, February, pp. 1–32.

Newman, David. 2005. "Conflict at the Interface: The Impact of Boundaries and Borders on Contemporary Ethnonational Conflict," in Flint, Colin (ed.), *The Geography of War and Peace: From Death Camps to Diplomats*. Oxford: Oxford University Press, pp. 32–344.

Newman, David. 2006. "The Lines that Continue to Separate Us: Borders in Our 'Borderless World,'" *Progress in Human Geography* 30 (2): 143–161.

Nguendi Ikome, Francis. 2012. "Africa's International Borders as Potential Sources of Conflict and Future Threats to Peace and Security," *Institute for Security Studies Paper*, No. 233.

Nordlinger, Eric. 1981. *On the Autonomy of the Democratic State*. Cambridge: Cambridge University Press.

Novakoff, Renee. 2015. "Transnational Organized Crime: An Insidious Threat to U.S. National Security Interests," *Prism* 5 (4): 135–149.

Nsereko, Daniel D. Ntanda. 1997. "When Crime Crosses Borders: A Southern African Perspective," *Journal of African Law* 41 (2): 192–200.

Nyein, Nyein. 2020. "Myanmar Opium Cultivation in Decline: UN Report," *The Irrawaddy*, February 4. https://irrawaddy.com/news/burma/myan mar-opium-cultivation-decline-un-report.html.

Oelsner, Andrea. 2005. *International Relations in Latin America: Peace and Security in the Southern Cone.* London: Routledge.

Oelsner, Andrea. 2009. "Consensus and Governance in Mercosur: The Evolution of the South American Security Agenda," *Security Dialogue* 40 (2): 191–212.

Olson, Eric L. 2016. "Migrant Smuggling and Trafficking at the Rio Grande Valley: Ten Observations and Questions." Washington, DC: The Wilson Center.

Olson, Eric L. 2017. *The Evolving Mérida Initiative and the Policy of Shared Responsibility in U.S.-Mexico Security Relations.* Washington, DC: The Wilson Center.

Omar, Dr. AM. 1997. "The Drug Trade in Southern Africa," *South African Journal of International Affairs* 5 (1): 141–155.

Pallini, Thomas. 2020. "Photos Show The Emergency Makeshift Borders European Countries Have Erected in an Attempt to Stop the Spread of COVID-19," *Business Insider*, April 4. businessinsider.com/coronavirus-european-borders-closed-in-response-to-covid-19-2020-4.

Parkinson, Charles. 2013. "Report Reveals Extent of Human Trafficking in Colombia," *InSight Crime*, November 15.

Passas, Nikkos. 2003. "Cross-Border Crime and the Interface between Legal and Illegal Actors," *Security Journal* 16 (1): 19–37.

Patrick, J. Michael. 2007. "The Economic Cost of Border Security: The Case of the Texas-Mexico Border and the US VISIT Program," in Brunet-Jailly, Emmanuel (ed.), *Borderlands: Comparing Border Security in North America and Europe.* Ottawa: University of Ottawa Press, pp.

Patrick, Stewart. 2011. *Weak Links: Fragile States, Global Threats, and International Security.* Oxford: Oxford University Press.

Payan, Tony. 2014. "Theory-Building in Border States: The View from North America," *Eurasia Border Review* 5 (1): 1–18.

Payan, Tony, and Vasquez, Amanda. 2007. "The Costs of Homeland Security," in Brunet-Jailly, Emmanuel (ed.), *Borderlands: Comparing Border Security in North America and Europe.* Ottawa: University of Ottawa Press, pp. 231–258.

Paz, Yonathan. 2011. "Ordered Disorder: African Asylum Seekers in Israel and Discursive Challenges to an Emerging Refugee Regime," *New Issues in*

Refugee Research, Research Paper No. 205, March, Geneva: UNHCR, pp. 1–21.

Pearce, Jenny. 2020. *Politics without Violence? Towards a Post-Weberian Enlightenment*. London: Palgrave/Macmillan.

Penski, Victoria Dittmar. 2018. "Why Are Violent Non-State Actors Able to Persist in the Context of the Modern State?," *Journal of Intelligence, Conflict, and Warfare* 1 (1): 1–23.

Piccolino, Giulia. 2016. "Conference Report: The Legacy of Armed Conflicts: Southern Africa and Comparative Perspectives," *Africa Spectrum* 51 (3): 123–134.

Piccone, Ted. 2019. *Peace with Justice: The Colombian Experience with Transitional Justice*. Washington, DC: The Brookings Institute, July. brookings.edu/wp-content/uploads/2019/06/FP_20190708_colombia.pdf.

Pion-Berlin, David. 2005. "Sub-Regional Cooperation, Hemispheric Threat: Security in the Southern Cone," in Fawcett, Louise, and Serrano, Monica (eds.), *Regionalism and Governance in the Americas: Continental Drift*. New York: Palgrave-Macmillan, pp. 211–227.

Pion-Berlin, David 2017. "The Military and Internal Security Operations in Latin America," *Política y Estrategia* 130: 101–123.

Podeh, Elie. 2015. *Chances for Peace: Missed Opportunities in the Arab-Israeli Conflict*. Austin: University of Texas Press.

Popescu, Gabriel. 2012. *Bordering and Ordering the 21st Century: Understanding Borders*. Lanham, MD: Rowman and Littlefield.

Prassad, Eswar S., Rogoff, Kenneth, Wei, Shang-Jin, and Kose, M. Ayhan. 2007. "Financial Globalization, Growth, and Volatility in Developing Countries," in Harrison, Ann (ed.), *Globalization and Poverty*. Chicago: University of Chicago Press, pp. 457–516.

Presidencia de México. 2019. "Plan Nacional de Desarrollo, 2019–2024." https://lopezobrador.org.mx/wp-content/uploads/2019/05/PLAN-NACIONAL-DE-DESARROLLO-2019-2024.pdf

Press-Barnathan, Galia. 2006. "The Neglected Dimension of Commercial Liberalism: Economic Cooperation and Transition to Peace," *Journal of Peace Research* 43 (3): 261–278.

Press-Barnathan, Galia. 2009. *The Political Economy of Transitions to Peace*. Pittsburgh, PA: University of Pittsburgh Press.

Press-Barnathan, Galia. 2014. "Between the Global and the Local: US-ASEAN Counter-Terrorism Cooperation from an Interactional Perspective," manuscript. Jerusalem: The Hebrew University of Jerusalem, Department of International Relations.

Rabinovich, Itamar. 2004. *Waging Peace: Israel and the Arabs, 1948–2003*. Princeton, NJ: Princeton University Press.

Radelet, Steven. 2010. *Emerging Africa: How 17 Countries are Leading the Way*. Washington, DC: Center for Global Development.

Ramos, José M. 2007. "Managing US-Mexico Transborder Cooperation on Local Security Issues and the Canadian Relationship," in Brunet-Jailly, Emmanuel (ed.), *Borderlands: Comparing Border Security in North America and Europe*. Ottawa: University of Ottawa Press, pp. 259–275.

Ranstorp, Magnus. 2010. "Introduction," in Ranstorp, Magnus (ed.), *Understanding Violent Radicalization: Terrorist and Jihadist Movements in Europe*. London: Routledge, pp. 1–18.

Ribando Seelke, Clare. 2011. "Mérida Initiative for Mexico and Central America: Funding and Policy Issues," *Current Politics and Economics of the United States* 13 (4): 59–86.

Rigirozzi, Pía, and Tussie, Diana (eds.). 2012. *The Rise of Post-Hegemonic Regionalism: The Case of Latin America*. Berlin: Springer.

Risse, Thomas. 2011. "Governance in Areas of Limited Statehood: Introduction and Overview," in Risse, Thomas (ed.), *Governance without a State? Policies and Politics in Areas of Limited Statehood*. New York, NY: Columbia University Press, pp. 1–35.

Rodgers, Dennis, and Baird, A. 2015. "Understanding Gangs in Contemporary Latin America," in Decker, Scott H., and Pyrooz, David C. (eds.), *Handbook of Gangs and Gang Responses*. New York: Wiley, pp. 478–502.

Rodgers, Dennis, and Muggah, Robert. 2009. "Gangs and Non-State Armed Groups: The Central American Case," *Contemporary Security Policy* 30 (2): 301–317.

Ronen, Yitzhak. 2017. "From Cooperation to Normalization? Jordan-Israel Relations since 1967," *British Journal of Middle Eastern Studies* 44 (4): 559–575.

Rotberg, Robert I., and Mils, Greg (eds.). 1998. *War and Peace in Southern Africa: Crime, Drugs, Arms, and Trade*. Washington, DC: Brookings Institution.

Rubio Grundell, Lucrecia. 2015. "EU Anti-Trafficking Policies: From Migration and Crime Control to Prevention and Protection," *Policy Brief* 2015/09, European University Institute, pp. 1–12.

Runde, Daniel F., and Schneider, Mar I. 2019. "A New Social Contract for the Northern Triangle," May, *Report – CSIS, Center for Strategic and International Studies*.

Russell, Roberto, and Calle, Fabián. 2009. "La 'periferia turbulenta' como factor de la expansión de los intereses de seguridad de Estados Unidos en América Latina," in Hirst, Monica (ed.), *Crisis de estado e intervención internacional: Una Mirada desde el Sur*. Buenos Aires: Edhasa, pp. 29–72.

Ryan, Curtis R. 2012. "The Armed Forces and the Arab Uprisings: The Case of Jordan," *Middle East and Governance* 4 (2012): 153–167.

Ryan, Curtis R. 2015. "Jordan in the Crossfire of Middle East Conflicts," *Orient: German Journal for Politics, Economics, and Culture of the Middle East* 56 (4): 32–49.

Ryan, Curtis R. 2018. "Hashemite Kingdom of Jordan," in Gasiorowski, Mark, and Yom Sean L. (eds.), *The Government and Politics of the Middle East and North Africa*. London: Routledge, pp. 111–136.

Saab, Bilal Y., and Taylor, Alexandra W. 2008. "Criminality and Armed Groups: A Comparative Study of FARC and Paramilitary Groups in Colombia," *Studies in Conflict and Terrorism* 32 (6): 455–475.

Sachikonye, Llyod. 2017. "The Protracted Democratic Transition in Zimbabwe," *Taiwan Journal of Democracy* 13 (1): 117–136.

Salcedo-Albarán, Eduardo, and Santos, Diana. 2017. "Firearms Trafficking: Central America," *The Global Observatory of Transnational Criminal Networks – Research Paper* No. 17, VORTEX Working Papers No. 31, pp. 1–20.

Salter, Mark B., and Piché, Geneviève. 2001. "The Securitization of the US-Canada Border in American Political Discourse," *Canadian Journal of Political Science* 44 (4): 929–951.

Sampó, Carolina. 2018. "Vivir entre Maras y grupos de exterminio: Una aproximación a los más graves problemas de seguridad pública en El Salvador," in Correa Vera, Loreto (ed.), *Sociedad, seguridad y conflicto en América Latina*. Panama City: SIEC, pp. 95–108.

Sampó, Carolina, and Troncoso, Valeska (eds.). 2017. *El crimen organizado en América Latina: Manifestaciones, facilitadores y reacciones*. Madrid: Instituto Universitario General Gutiérrez Mellado – UNED.

Sánchez Piñeiro, Oscar M. 2012. "Border Dynamics and the Conflict in Colombia: A Case-Study of Arauca-Apure and Nariño-Esmeraldas," *Peace and Conflict Monitor*, April 1.www.monitor.upeace.org/printer .cfm?idarticle=891

Sandin, Linnea, and McCormick, Gladys. 2019. "'Abrazos No Balazos' Evaluating AMLO's Security Initiatives," *CSIS Commentary*, December 19. csis.org/analysis/abrazos-no-balazos-evaluating-amlos-security-initiatives.

Sato, Yoichiro. 2012. "Perceptions of Transnational Security Threats in Malaysia and Singapore: Windows of Cooperative Opportunities for the United States," *Issues for Engagement: Asian Perspectives on Transnational Security Issues*: 140–153.

Savenije, Wim, and van der Borgh, Chris. 2014. "Anti-Gang Policies and Gang Responses in the Northern Triangle: The Evolution of the Gang Phenomenon in Central America," *The Broker*, July 3.

Savona, Ernesto U., and Mancuso, Marina (eds.). 2017. *Fighting Illicit Firearms Trafficking Routes and Actors at European Level*. Milano: Transcrime – Università Catolica del Sacro Cuore.

Schneider, Yaron. 2020. "Explaining Security Governance in the Borderlands: The Triangle of States, Peacekeeping Operations, and Non-State Actors." Ph.D. Thesis. Jerusalem: Hebrew University of Jerusalem, Department of International Relations.

Schoeman, Maxi, and Muller, Marie. 2009. "Southern African Development Community as Regional Peacekeeper: Myth or Reality?," *African Security* 2 (2–3): 175–192.

Schofield, Julian. 2014. *Strategic Nuclear Sharing*. London: Palgrave/Macmillan.

Scholte, Jaan A. 2004. "Global Trade and Finance," in Baylis, John, Smith Steve, and Owens, Patrica (eds.), *The Globalization of World Politics: An Introduction to International Relations*, 4th ed. Oxford: Oxford University Press, pp. 519–539.

Schwell, Alexandra. 2009. "De/Securitizing the 2007 Schengen Enlargement: Austria and 'the East'," *Journal of Contemporary European Research* 5 (2): 243–258.

Schroeder, Maa, and Lamb, Guy. 2006. "The Illicit Arms Trade in Africa: A Global Enterprise," *African Analist* 1 (3): 69–78.

Sela, Avraham. 1998. *The Decline of the Arab-Israeli Conflict: Middle East Politics and the Quest for Regional Order*. Albany, NY: SUNY Press.

Severino, Rodolfo C. 2001. "ASEAN: Building the Peace in Southeast Asia." Paper presented at the Fourth High Level Meeting between the United Nations and Regional Organizations on Cooperation for Peace-Building, United Nations, New York, 6–7 February.

Sharp, Jeremy M. 2018. "Jordan: Background and U.S. Relations," *Congressional Research Service 7-5700*, February 16.

Shay, Shaul. 2014. "Egypt and the Threat of Islamic Terror," *BESA Center Perspectives Paper* 230, January 1.

Shaw, Mark. 2002. "West Africa Criminal Network in South and Southern Africa," *African Affairs* 101: 291–316.

Shaw, Mark. 2015. "New Networks of Power: Why Organized Crime Is the Greatest Long-Term Threat to Security in the SADC Region," in van Nieuwkerk, Anthoni, and Moat, Catherine (eds.), *Southern African Security Review*. Johannesburg: University of Witwatersrand and Friedrich-Ebert-Foundation, pp. 169–188.

Shaw, Mark, and Gastrow, Peter. 2001. "Stealing the Show? Crime and Its Impact in Post-Apartheid South Africa," *Daedalus* 130 (1): 235–258.

Shaw, Mark, and Ellis, Stephen. 2015. "Does Organized Crime Exist in Africa?," *African Affairs* 114 (457): 505–528.

Shelley, Louise I. 2010. *Human Trafficking: A Global Perspective.* Cambridge: Cambridge University Press.

Shelley, Louise I. 2014a. *Dirty Entanglements: Corruption, Crime, and Terrorism.* Cambridge: Cambridge University Press.

Shelley, Louise I. 2014b. *Human Smuggling and Trafficking to Europe: A Comparative Perspective.* Washington, DC: Migration Policy Institute.

Shelley, Louise I. 2018. *Dark Commerce: How a New Illicit Economy Is Threatening Our Future.* Princeton, NJ: Princeton University Press.

Shelley, Louise I., and Picarelli, John. 2005. "Methods and Motives: Exploring Links between Transnational Organized Crime and International Terrorism," *Trends in Organized Crime* 9 (2): 52–67.

Shifter, Michael. 2012. "Countering Criminal Violence in Central America," *Council Special Report No. 64*, Council on Foreign Relations, April.

Shirk, David A. 2011. *The Drug War in Mexico: Confronting a Shared Threat* (New York: Council on Foreign Relations).

Shlaim, Avi. 1988. *The Politics of Partition: King Abdullah, the Zionists, and Palestine 1921–1951.* Oxford: Oxford University Press.

Siboni, Gabi, and Ben-Barak, Ram. 2014. "The Sinai Peninsula Threat Development and Respond Concept," *Analysis Paper*, No. 31, INSS, January.

Simmons, Beth A. 2006. "Trade and Territorial Conflict in Latin America: International Borders and Institutions," in Kahler, Miles, and Walter, Barbara D. (eds.), *Territoriality and Conflict in an Era of Globalization.* Cambridge: Cambridge University Press, pp. 251–287.

Simmons, Beth A. 2019. "Borders Rules," *Faculty Scholarship at Penn Law*, 2045. https://scholarship.law.upenn.edu/faculty/_scholarship/2045

Simmons, Beth A., Lloyd, Paulette, and Stewart, Brandon M. 2018. "The Global Diffusion of Law: Transnational Crime and the Case of Human Trafficking," *International Organization* 72 (3): 249–281.

Simandjuntak, Deasy. 2018. "The State of Democracy in Southeast Asia," Southeast Asia, Heinrich Böll Stiftung.

Singh, Bilveer. 2018. "Jemaah Islamiyah: Still Southeast Asia's Greatest Terrorist Threat," *The Diplomat*, October 7.

Smith, Karen S. 2005. "The Outsiders: The European Neighborhood Policy," *International Affairs* 81 (4): 757–773.

Snodgrass, Lynn. 2015. "Illegal Guns Fuel Violent Crime, Wreak Deadly Havoc in South Africa," *The Conversation*, October 14. theconversation.com/illegal/guns-fuel-violent-crime-wreak-deadly-havoc-in-south-africa-49006.

Söderbaum, Fredrik. 2004. *The Political Economy of Regionalism: The Case of Southern Africa.* New York: Palgrave.

Sotomayor, Arturo C. 2014. *The Myth of the Democratic Peacekeeper: Civil-Military Relations and the United Nations*. Baltimore, MD: Johns Hopkins University Press.

Sotomayor, Arturo C. 2015. "Legalizing and Judicializing Territorial and Maritime Border Disputes in Latin America: Causes and Unintended Consequences," in Jaskoski, Maiah, Sotomayor, Arturo C., and Trinkunas, Harold A. (eds.), *American Crossings: Border Politics in the Western Hemisphere*. Baltimore, MD: Johns Hopkins University Press, pp. 38–65.

Southern African Development Community [SADC]. 2016. "SADC Selected Economic and Social Indicators, 2016."

Souza, Marillia C. 2016. "Armed Conflict and Drug-Trafficking: The Overflow of Colombian Issues in the border space with Venezuela," Paper presented at the ISA Annual Conference, Atlanta, GE, March 16.

Sparke, Matthew. 2002. "Not a State, but More than a State of Mind: Cascading Cascadias and the Geoeconomics of Cross-Border Regionalism," in Perkmann, Markus, and Ngai-Ling, Sum (eds.), *Globalization, Regionalization, and Cross-Border Regions*. New York: Palgrave, pp. 212–238.

Stephen, Lynn. 2009. "Expanding the Borderlands: Recent Studies on the U.S.-Mexico Border," *Latin American Research Review* 44 (1): 266–277.

Stohl, Rachel, and Tuttle, Doug. 2008. "The Small Arms Trade in Latin America," *NACLA: Report on the Americas* 41 (2): 14–20.

Stone, Hanna. 2011. "Colombia, Panama Sign Border Security Pact," *Insight Crime*, February 12. www.insightcrime.org/news-analysis-colombia-panama-sign-border-security-pact.

Stone, Hanna. 2016. "Organized Crime and Elites in Colombia: An InSight Crime Report," *Open Democracy*, August 18. www.opendemocracy.net /en/democraciaabierta/organized-crime-and-elites-in-colombia-insight-crime-report/.

Stott, Noel. 2007. "Small Arms Proliferation in Southern Africa: Reducing the Impact of 'Real Weapons of Mass Destruction'" *Africa Files* 5 (2): 11–33.

Stromseth, Jonathan. 2019. "The Testing Ground: China's Rising Influence in Southeast Asia and Regional Responses," *Brookings Report*, Washington, DC: The Brookings Institution, November, pp. 1–12. https://brookings.edu /wp-content/uploads/2019/FP-20191119-china_se_asia_stromseth.pdf.

Sullivan, Mark P., and Beittel, June S. 2016. "Latin America: Terrorism Issues," *Congressional Research Service Reports*, # 21049, December 15. fas.org/sgp/crs/terror/RS21049.pdf

Surtees, Rebecca. 2008. "Traffickers and Trafficking in Southern and Eastern Europe: Considering the Other Side of Human Trafficking," *European Journal of Criminology* 5 (1): 39–68.

Susser, Asher. 1999. "The Jordanian-Israeli Peace Negotiations: The Geopolitical Rationale of a Bilateral Relationship," *Davis Occasional Papers* 73, August.

Sverdlick, Ana R. 2005. "Terrorists and Organized Crime Entrepeneurs in the 'Triple Frontier' among Argentina, Brazil, and Paraguay," *Trends in Organized Crime* 9 (2): 84–93.

Tagliacozzo, Eric. 2001. "Border Permeability and the State in Southeast Asia: Contraband and Regional Security," *Contemporary Southeast Asia* 23 (2): 254–274.

Tal, Lawrence. 1993. "Is Jordan Doomed?," *Foreign Affairs* 72(5): 45–58.

Tamminen, Tanja. 2004. "Cross-Border Cooperation in the Southern Balkans: Local, National or European Identity Politics?," *Southeast European and Black Sea Studies* 4 (3): 399–418.

Temby, Quinton. 2018. "Terrorist Arbitrage in Southeast Asia," *New Mandala*, January 19.

Thaler, Kai M. 2017. "Nicaragua: A Return to Caudillismo," *Journal of Democracy* 28 (2): 157–169.

The Economist, December 9, 2017: 23–28.

The Global Initiative against Transnational Organized Crime. 2019. *Hotspots of Organized Crime in the Western Balkans: Local Vulnerabilities in a Regional Context*. Geneva: The Global Initiative against Transnational Organized Crime, May. globalinitiative.net/wp-content/uploads/2019/05/Hotspots-Report-English-13Jun1110-Web.pdf.

The Times of Israel. 2018. "Suspected Drug Ring Nabbed by Security Forces at Egypt Border," May 16.

Thomson, David. 1966. *Europe since Napoleon*. Harmondsworth, Middlesex: Penguin Books.

Tønnesson, Stein. 2015. "The East Asian Peace: How Did It Happen? How Deep Is It? Introduction," *Global Asia* 10 (4): 8–9.

Transparency International. 2015. "Corruption Perception Index." www.transparency.org/cpi.

Traverso, Enzo. 2016. *Fire and Blood: The European Civil War, 1914–1945*. London: Verso.

Traynor, Ian. 2016. "Is the Schengen Dream of Europe without Borders Becoming a Thing of the Past?," *The Guardian*, January 5.

Trejo, Guillermo, and Ley, Sandra. 2020. *Votes, Drugs, and Violence: The Political Logic of Criminal Wars in Mexico*. Cambridge: Cambridge University Press.

Trejos Rosero, Luis Fernando. 2015. "El lado colombiano de la frontera Colombo-brasilera: Una aproximación desde la categoría de area sin ley," *Estudios Fronterizos* 16 (31): 39–64.

Trinkunas, Harold A. 2013. "Reordering Regional Security in Latin America," *Journal of International Affairs* 66 (2): 83–99.

Trinkunas, Harold A., and Clunan, Anne. 2016. "Alternative Governance in Latin America," in Mares, David R., and Kacowicz, Arie M. (eds.), *Routledge Handbook of Latin American Security*. London: Routledge, pp. 99–109.

Tziampiris, Aristotle. 2009. "Assessing Islamic Terrorism in the Western Balkans: The State of the Debate," *Journal of Balkan and Near Eastern Studies* 11 (2): 209–219.

Udelsmann Rodrigues, Cristina. 2012. "Introduction: Crossing African Borders: Migration and Mobility," in Udelsmann Rodrigues, Cristina, and Tomàs, Jordi (eds.), *Crossing African Borders*. Lisbon: Centro de Estudios Internacionais, pp. 4–14.

Umaña, Felipe. 2012. *Threat Convergence: Revisiting the Crime-Terrorism Nexus in the Tri-Border Area*. Washington, DC: The Fund for Peace.

United Nations. 1995. "9th United Nations Congress on the Prevention of Crime and the Treatment of Offenders." A/Conf.169/15/Add.1, April 29-May 8, Cairo.

UNODC (United Nations Office on Drugs and Crime). 2008. *Crime and Its Impact on the Balkans and Affected Countries*. New York: UNODC.

UNODC (United Nations Office on Drugs and Crime). 2010. *The Globalization of Crime: A Transnational Organized Crime Threat Assessment*. New York: UNODC.

UNODC (United Nations Office on Drugs and Crime). 2012a. *Transnational Organized Crime in Central America and the Caribbean: A Threat Assessment*. New York: UNODC.

UNODC (United Nations Office on Drugs and Crime). 2012b. *Making the Southern African Development Community (SADC) Region Safer from Crime and Drugs. Regional Programme, 2013–2016*. New York: UNODC.

UNODC (United Nations Office on Drugs and Crime). 2013. *Transnational Organized Crime in East Asia and the Pacific: A Threat Assessment*. Bangkok: UNODC, Regional Office for Southeast Asia and the Pacific.

UNODC (United Nations Office on Drugs and Crime). 2014. *Global Report on Trafficking in Persons*. New York: UNODC.

UNODC (United Nations Office on Drugs and Crime). 2015. *Study on Firearms*. New York: UNODC.

UNODC (United Nations Office on Drugs and Crime). 2016a. *World Drug Report*. New York: UNODC.

UNODC (United Nations Office on Drugs and Crime). 2016b. *Global Report on Trafficking in Persons*. New York: UNODC.

UNODC (United Nations Office on Drugs and Crime). 2016c. *Protecting Peace and Prosperity in Southeast Asia: Synchronizing Economic and Security Agendas.* Bangkok: UNODC, Regional Office for Southeast Asia and the Pacific.

UNODC (United Nations Office on Drugs and Crime). 2018a. *Global Report on Trafficking in Persons.* New York: UNODC.

UNODC (United Nations Office on Drugs and Crime). 2018b. *Migrant Smuggling in Asia and the Pacific: Current Trends and Challenges,* Vol. 2. Bangkok: UNODC.

UNODC (United Nations Office on Drugs and Crime). 2019. *Transnational Organized Crime in Southeast Asia: Evolution, Growth, and Impact.* Bangkok: UNODC.

UNHCR (United Nations Refugee Agency). 2019. "Refugees and Migrants from Venezuela Top 4 Million: UNHCR and IOM," June 7. unhcr.org/n ews/press/2019/6/5cfa2a4a4/refugees-migrants-venezuela-top-4-million-unhcr-iom.html.

UNHCR (United Nations Refugee Agency). 2020. "UNHCR Welcomes Colombia's Decision to Regularize Stay of Venezuelans in the Country," February 4. unhcr.org/news/briefing/2020/2/5e3930db4/unhcr-welcomes-colombias-decision-regularize-stay-venezuelans-country.html.

United Nations Security Council. 2012. "Security Council, concerned at Threat Posed by Illicit Cross-Border Trafficking, Asks for Assessment of UN Efforts in Helping States Counter Challenges." SC/10624, 6760th Meeting, 25 April.

United Nations Security Council. 2014. Resolution 2195, "Security Council, Adopting Resolution 2195 (2014), Urges International Action to Break Links between Terrorists, Transnational Organized Crime." SC/11717, 7351st Meeting, December 19.

United States Congress. 2016. "Northern Border Security Review Act." www .congress.gov/114/plaws/publ267/PLAW-114publ257.pdf

US Department of Homeland Security. 2011. "United States-Canada Beyond the Border: A Shared Vision for Perimeter Security and Economic Competitiveness." www.dhs.gov/sites/default/files/publications/us-canada-btb-action-plan.pdf.

US Department of Homeland Security. 2015. "U.S. Customs and Border Relations, Fiscal Years 2009–2014 Strategic Plan."

US Department of Homeland Security. 2018. "Northern Border Strategy."

United States Office of National Drug Control Policy, Executive Office of the President of the United States. 2020. "National Drug Control Strategy: Northern Border Counter-narcotics Strategy."

US State Department. 2010–2016. *Country Reports on Terrorism,* Series 2010–2016. Washington, DC: US Government.

US State Department. 2019. *Trafficking in Persons Report.* Washington, DC: U.S. Government. state.gov/wp-content/uploads/2019/06/2019-Trafficking-in-Persons-Report.pdf.

Van der Laan, Franca. 2017. *Strategic Monitor 2017 – Transnational Organized Crime.* The Hague: The Clingendael Institute (February 27). Clingedael.org/publication/strategic-monitor-2017-transnational-organised-crime.

Van Nieuwkerk, Anthoni. 2014. "The Strategic Culture of Foreign and Security Policymaking: Examining the Southern African Development Community," *African Security* 7 (1): 45–69.

Van Reisen, Mirjam, Estefanos, Meron, and Rijken, Conny. 2012. *Human Trafficking in the Sinai: Refugees between Life and Death.* Brussels: Tilburg University, September 26.

Van Schendel, Willem. 2005. "Spaces of Engagement: How Borderlands, Illegal Flows, and Territorial States Interlock," in van Schendel, Wilem, and Abraham, Itty (eds.), *Illicit Flows and Criminal Things: States, Borders, and the Other Side of Globalization.* Bloomington, IN: Indiana University Press, pp. 38–67.

Varela, Carlos Alberto. 2018. "Security Crisis in the Colombo-Ecuadorian Border: The Other Side of the Colombian Peace Process," *LSE – International Development,* July 9. https://blogs.lse.ac.uk/internationaldevelopment/2018/07/09/security-crisis-in-the-colombo-ecuadorian-border-the-other-side-of-the-colombian-epace-process/

Vargas, Eugenio Weigend, and Bhatia, Rukman. 2019. "Beyond Our Borders but Within Our Control," *Center for American Progress,* November 1. www.americanprogress.org/issues/guns-crime/news/2019/11/01/476576/beyond-borders-within-control/.

Vargas Llosa, Mario. 2017. "Abrir las fronteras para acabar con el negocio de las mafias," *La Nación,* May 22.

Varin, Caroline, and Abubakar, Dauda (eds.). 2017. *Violent Non-State Actors in Africa: Terrorists, Rebels, and Warlords.* London: Palgrave/Macmillan.

Venezuela Investigative Unit. 2018. *Venezuela: A Mafia State?, InSight Crime: Investigation and Analysis of Organized Crime.* insightcrime.org/wp-content/uploads/2018/05/Venezuela-a-Mafia-State-InSight-Crime-2018.pdf.

Villafuerte Solis, Daniel. 2007. "The Southern Border of Mexico in the Age of Globalization," in Brunet-Jailly, Emmanuel (ed.), *Borderlands: Comparing Border Security in North America and Europe.* Ottawa: University of Ottawa Press, pp. 311–350.

Vogeler, Ingolf. 2010. "Types of International Borders along the U.S.-Mexico Border," *Geography Online* 10 (1): 1–6.

Von Lampe, Klaus. 2014. "Transnational Organized Crime in Europe," in Albanese, Jay, and Reichel, Philip (eds.), *Transnational Organized Crime: An Overview from Six Continents*. Thousand Oaks, CA: Sage, pp. 75–92.

Von Soest, Christian, and De Juan, Alexander. 2018. "Dealing with New Security Threats in Africa," *GIGA Focus/Africa* 2 (May).

Voortman, Aude. 2015. "Terrorism in Europe: Explaining the Disparity in the Number of Jihadist Foreign Fighters between European Countries," *Student Paper Series* 20, Institut Barcelona Estudis Internacionals, pp. 1–38.

Wajner, Daniel F. 2020. "International Legitimacy and Conflict Resolution: Analyzing Legitimation Dynamics during Peace Negotiations in Intractable Conflicts," Ph.D. Thesis. Jerusalem: Hebrew University of Jerusalem, Department of International Relations.

Wajner, Daniel, F., and Roniger, Luis. 2019. "Transnational Identity Politics in the Americas: Reshaping 'Nuestraamerica' as Chavismo's Regional 'Legitimation Strategy'" *Latin American Research Review* 54 (2): 468-75.

Walser, Ray. 2010. "State Sponsors of Terrorism: Time to Add Venezuela to the List," *Backgrounder* 2362, January.

Walsh, John, and Ramsey, Geoff. 2016. "Uruguay's Drug Policy: Major Innovations, Major Challenges," *Improving Global Drug Policy: Comparative Perspectives and UNGASS*, Washington, DC: Brookings Institution, pp. 1–19. Brookings.edu/wp-content/uploads/2016/07/Walsh-Uruguay-final.pdf.

Watanabe, Lisa, and Nünlist, Christian. 2015. "Sinai Peninsula: From Buffer Zone to Battlefield," *CSS Analyses in Security Policy* 168 (February): 1–4.

Wayne, Earl A. 2017. "The War on Drugs: The Narco States of North America." https://nationalinterest.org/feature/the-war-drugs-the-narco-states-north-america-22967.

Wayne, Earl A., and Olson, Eric L. 2017. "Mexico and the U.S. Agree on a Vision for Fighting Drugs," May 23. www.wilsoncenter.org/article/mexico-and-the-us-agree-vision-for-fighting-drugs.

Weiffen, Brigitte. 2012. "Persistence and Change in Regional Security Institutions: Does the OAS Still Have a Project?," *Contemporary Security Policy* 33 (2): 360–383.

Weiner, Myron. 1996. "Bad Neighbors, Bad Neighborhoods: An Inquiry into the Causes of Refugee Flows," *International Security* 21 (1): 5–42.

Wells, Miriam. 2013. "UN Warns of Rise in Human Trafficking Within Colombia," *InSight Crime Analysis*, April 16. www.insightcrime.org/news/brief/un-warns-growing-human-trafficking-colombia/.

Wienand, Sandra, and Tremaria, Stiven. 2017. "Paramilitarism in a Post-Demobilization Context? Insights from the Department of Antioquia in Colombia," *European Review of Latin American and Caribbean Studies* 103: 25–50.

Williams, Phil. 2010. "Here Be Dragons: Dangerous Spaces and International Security," in Clunan, Anne L., and Trinkunas, Harold A. (eds.), *Ungoverned Spaces: Alternatives to State Authority in an Era of Softened Sovereignty*. Stanford: Stanford University Press, pp. 34–54.

Williams, Phil. 2016. "Illicit Threats: Organized Crime, Drugs, and Small Arms," in Mares, David R., and Kacowicz, Arie M. (eds.), *Routledge Handbook of Latin American Security*. London: Routledge, pp. 266–276.

Wong, Diana. 2005. "The Rumor of Trafficking: Border Controls, Illegal Migration, and the Sovereignty of the Nation-State," in van Schendel, Willem, and Abraham, Itty (eds.), *Illicit Flows and Criminal Things: States, Borders, and the Other Side of Globalization*. Bloomington: Indiana University Press, pp. 69–99.

Woods, Kevin. 2011. "Ceasefire Capitalism: Military-Private Partnerships, Resource Concessions, and Military-State Building in the Burma-China Borderlands," *The Journal of Peasant Studies* 38 (4): 747–770.

Woody, Christopher. 2019. "The Architect of Mexico's War on Cartels Was Just Arrested in Texas and Accused of Drug Trafficking and Taking Bribes," *Business Insider*, December 10. businessinsider.com/Genaro-garcia-luna-arrested-in-texas-on-drug-trafficking-charges-2019-12.

World Bank. 2017. "GDP Ranking," and "GNI (Current US$)."

Wotela, Kambidima, and Letsiri, Cleophas. 2015. "International Movements, Post-Apartheid Dispensations, and Illegal Immigration into South Africa," *The Journal for Transdisciplinary Research in Southern Africa* 11 (4): 99–117.

Yagoub, Mimi. 2014. "Panama Police Clash with Colombia's FARC in Cross Border Drug Corridor," *InSight Crime Brief*, July 15. insightcrime.org/news/brief/panama-police-clash-with-colombias-farc-in-cross-border-drug-corridor/.

Zacher, Mark W. 2001. "The Territorial Integrity Norm: International Boundaries and the Use of Force," *International Organization* 55 (2): 215–250.

Zartman, William I. 2010. "Introduction: Identity, Movement, and Response," in Zartman, William I. (ed.), *Understanding Life in the Borderlands: Boundaries in Depth and in Motion*. Athens: University of Georgia Press, pp. 1–18.

Ziegler, Ruvi. 2015. "No Asylum for 'Infiltrators': The Legal Predicament of Eritrean and Sudanese Nationals in Israel," *Immigration, Asylum and Nationality Law* 29 (2): 172–191.

Zielonka, Jan. 2001. "How New Enlarged Borders Will Reshape the European Union," *Journal of Common Market Studies* 39 (3): 507–536.

Zohar, Eran. 2015. "The Arming of Non-State Actors in the Gaza Strip and the Sinai Peninsula," *Australian Journal of International Affairs* 69 (4): 438–461.

Index